D0221965

Rethinking World Politics

Series Editor: Professor Michael Cox, *London School of Economics*

In an age of increased academic specialization where more and more books about smaller and smaller topics are becoming the norm, this major series is designed to provide a forum and stimulus for leading scholars to address big issues in world politics in an accessible but original manner. A key aim is to transcend the intellectual and disciplinary boundaries which have so often served to limit rather than enhance our understanding of the modern world. In the best tradition of engaged scholarship, it aims to provide clear new perspectives to help make sense of a world in flux.

Each book addresses a major issue or event that has had a formative influence on the twentieth-century or the twenty-first-century world which is now emerging. Each makes its own distinctive contribution as well as providing an original but accessible guide to competing lines of interpretation.

Taken as a whole, the series will rethink contemporary international politics in ways that are lively, informed and – above all – provocative.

Also by Ray Kiely

Sociology and Development: The Impasse and Beyond
The Politics of Labour and Development in Trinidad
Globalisation and the Third World (co-edited)
Industrialization and Development: A Comparative Analysis
The Clash of Globalisations
Globalization and After (co-edited)
Empire in the Age of Globalisation
The New Political Economy of Development

Rethinking Imperialism

Ray Kiely

palgrave
macmillan

First published 2010 by
PALGRAVE MACMILLAN

Palgrave Macmillan in the UK is an imprint of Macmillan Publishers Limited,
registered in England, company number 785998, of Houndmills,
Basingstoke, Hampshire RG21 6XS.

Palgrave Macmillan in the US is a division of St Martin's Press LLC,
175 Fifth Avenue, New York, NY 10010.

Palgrave Macmillan is the global academic imprint of the above companies
and has companies and representatives throughout the world.

Palgrave® and Macmillan® are registered trademarks in the United States,
the United Kingdom, Europe and other countries

ISBN 978–0–230–20105–7 hardback
ISBN 978–0–230–20106–4 paperback

This book is printed on paper suitable for recycling and made from fully
managed and sustained forest sources. Logging, pulping and manufacturing
processes are expected to conform to the environmental regulations of the
country of origin.

A catalogue record for this book is available from the British Library.

A catalog record for this book is available from the Library of Congress.

10   9   8   7   6   5   4   3   2   1
19 18 17 16 15 14 13 12 11 10

Printed and bound in China

Contents

List of Tables

Foreword

There is probably no idea in world politics that has proven more controversial than 'imperialism'. Arising in the late nineteenth century in a lengthy debate that culminated in Lenin's extraordinarily influential pamphlet of the same name, the notion thereafter increasingly came to be used rather indiscriminately, either to characterize anything great white powers happened to do abroad in their various colonies, or, after 1945, as a slogan with which to attack the United States. No doubt its continued association with Marxism, and the more general collapse of European colonial rule after 1945, did little to enhance the popularity of the idea. Indeed, during the Cold War, the notion began to acquire something of a dubious reputation in the West; and in spite of a brief surge of writing on the topic during the Vietnam War, imperialism as an organizing concept began to fade once again from the intellectual scene. Certainly, amongst most Western academics, imperialism as a construct came to be viewed with almost antiquarian irony: something that may have once usefully described the world when it was being carved up by the Europeans but of little use in analysing the modern world in all its complexity.

All this remained true until the George W. Bush administration decided to invade Iraq in 2003. Almost at a stroke the debate about imperialism was given a whole new lease of life. Who now could not think of US foreign policy in anything other than imperial terms? Even some of the Bush people themselves, not to mention their neo-conservative allies, gave credence to the notion. The key issue, they argued, was not whether the United States was (or was not) an Empire – it most obviously was – but why Americans kept denying the fact. Indeed, they continued in a quite un-American fashion, 'What precisely was wrong with Empires?' They delivered peace. They advanced the cause of civilization. And they were preferable to the alternative. Look what happened to Europe after all following the fall of the Roman Empire. And look what might happen to the world today – they warned – if the United States were to go the same way.

If nothing else the debate about the modern American Empire has created a space where ideas that once dared not speak their name can now be discussed without the usual riposte that this is just another attempt by fading radicals to maintain their intellectual credibility in the academic market-place. Certainly, there is nothing faded about Ray Kiely's wonderfully wide-ranging study! His *tour d'horizon* does several things: provide an incisive history of imperialism as an idea; show how complex the serious debate about imperialism has actually been; and perhaps most important of all for understanding American foreign policy in the twenty-first century, point to a very clear connection between modern liberalism and contemporary US imperialism as a political project. Here he makes the strongest and boldest claim of all, one that I hope will take the debate about the world and its disorders – to which liberalism in his view is adding – on to a higher intellectual plain than where it has been situated for many years. In every sense, Professor Kiely has rethought an idea and opened up a discussion that should now move from the margins to centre stage.

MICHAEL COX
Professor and Co-Director IDEAS and
Department of International Relations
London School of Economics and
Political Science, UK

Acknowledgements

Thanks to Steven Kennedy and Stephen Wenham at Palgrave Macmillan, and to the series editor Michael Cox. Thanks also to those who read or commented on draft papers related to this book, particularly Liam Campling, Bryan Mabee, Alfredo Saad-Filho and Rick Saull, as well as the anonymous reviewers. Special thanks to various other people, including Mum and Dad, Jenny, Lynn, Shani, Henry, Bob, Jeff, and to Claire, Kim, Amy, Katy, Anna and Luke (but not geek). Above all, thanks to Emma, Will and Ella, for Low, Will Oldham (alas unshared), *The Wire*, cricket, Fireman Sam, and love and support.

RAY KIELY

1

Introduction – Imperialism: What's in a Name?

Talk of imperialism and empire came back into fashion in a big way in the first decade of the twenty-first century, to some extent displacing globalization as the keynote term of social and political analysis. In large part this was the result of the belligerent foreign policy of the Bush administration from 2001–8 in the US which some saw as a revival of more overt power relations at the expense of a more liberal and ethical multilateral international agenda (Held 2004; Habermas 2006). I will take issue with both sides of this equation in the course of this book, but its central purpose is to stand back from the specifics of the Bush presidency to provide a much broader 'rethink' of the meaning and nature of imperialism both in its earlier evolution and, more particularly, during and since the Cold War.

Imperialism is a term that has been used in many ways. Its revival in recent years is often associated with one or more of the following: rivalries and conflicts between advanced capitalist states; efforts by western powers to 'liberalize' or 'democratize' the 'failed states' that make up the 'axis of evil'; the necessity for capitalist expansion into the under-developed world; the related thirst of the major powers to secure access to, or control of, certain strategic resources in the developing world; the domination of some states over others; the exploitation by the core states of the rest of the world; the Americanization of the world; the domination of corporations and private profit over public need. These definitions capture something of what is meant by the term imperialism. Most are critical of imperialism and embrace a political stance that claims to be 'anti-imperialist'. But on the other hand, as we will see, some positions in the imperialism debate are

1

clearly supportive of imperialism and the need for US hegemony, or empire.

The rest of this introduction will provide a preliminary definition of the term imperialism, and a summary of the structure of the book.

Empire and Imperialism: Histories and Definitions

Imperialism is a term closely linked to, but distinguishable from, empire and colonialism. Empire is derived from the Latin term *imperium*, and was originally used to refer to the capacity to make laws within a territory. As the size of such a territory grew in the Roman empire, imperium became *Imperium*, which 'came to mean rule over extensive, far-flung territories, far beyond the original "homeland" of the rulers' (Howe 2002: 13). This definition of empire relates to that of colonialism, a term used in the nineteenth century to refer to 'systems of rule, by one group over another, where the first claims a right (a "right" again usually established by conquest) to exercise exclusive sovereignty over the second and to shape its destiny' (Howe 2002: 30–1).

Imperialism is often used to refer to the processes whereby empire is maintained and expanded. It was a term that came into common use in the second half of the nineteenth century, which first referred to the failed expansionist policies of Napoleon III in France in the 1860s. It was then applied to imperialist politicians in Britain, such as Disraeli and Salisbury, whose 'imperialist persuasion' meant that they were enthusiastic for foreign conquest and overseas expansion. But it became more firmly established in the late nineteenth century, as a number of critics – Marxist and liberal – challenged the new wave of colonial expansion from the 1880s onwards, condemning the new 'age of imperialism' (Howe 2002; 23–30; Young 2001: 25–30, 109–12). As the term developed, imperialism essentially came to be defined as 'the exercise of power either through direct conquest or (latterly) through political and economic influence that effectively amounts to a similar form of domination' (Young 2001: 27). Doyle (1986: 30) similarly defines empire and imperialism as 'effective control, whether formal or informal, of a subordinated society by an imperial society'. More specifically, he suggests that 'Empire is a relationship, formal or informal, in which one state controls the effective political sovereignty of another political society. It can be achieved by force, by political collaboration, by economic, social or cultural dependence. Imperialism is simply the process or policy of establishing or maintaining an empire' (Doyle 1986: 11). In this way, imperialism describes the mechanisms by which one country or region came to dominate another. This, in a nutshell, is the standard definition of imperialism, centred on the notion of territorial domination.

Marxists were very influential in developing a critical account of imperialism, which classical accounts (discussed in Chapter 4) linked to a specific period of capitalist development in the late nineteenth and early twentieth century. Much of the Marxist debate in that period was concerned with the relationship between economic competition between capitals and geo-political rivalries between capitalist states. However, many accounts of imperialism have also focused on the domination of some territories by others, either directly through colonialism, or indirectly through 'non-territorial empire' (Strange 1989). This approach came to dominate radical theories of imperialism after 1945, in the context of the end of formal empire and increased cooperation between former rival capitalist states. These later debates thus focused less on the *causes*, and rather more on the *consequences* and effects of imperialism, above all in the peripheries of global capitalism. Many accounts of imperialism therefore examine the inter-relationship between capital accumulation on a world scale, the relationship between capitalist states, and how these factors give rise to processes of domination and subordination in the international order. These three factors constitute the main focus of theories of imperialism, and are central to the discussion that follows.

But there is also another approach to imperialism, which is central to any attempt to rethink the relevance of the idea to the early twenty-first century. This refers to those accounts which actually support imperialism, and the case made for progressive, liberal imperialism. This has a long history that stretches back to the likes of James Mill and John Stuart Mill, right through to current cases for integrating rogue and failed states in the early twentyfirst century. These include neo-conservative arguments for US primacy, but also more multilateral and even cosmopolitan cases for US hegemony in a neo-liberal economic order. This apology for imperialism is also examined in depth in the chapters that follow.

Rethinking Imperialism: a Brief Summary of the Argument and Structure of the Book

The rethink presented in this book presents a critical account of imperialism, but one that takes the liberal apology for imperialism very seriously, above all because it provides crucial raw material for understanding why imperialism retains its relevance as a critical concept in the current international order. What this book essentially argues is this: in order to provide a critical account of contemporary imperialism, we must take seriously the case for liberal imperialism, less as an analysis, and more as a *political project*. This involves an account of both the political economy and geo-politics of contemporary (liberal) imperialism, and the relationship between them. Current apologists for US military power regard it as one means among others for integrating otherwise 'non-integrating economies'. Many critics, including many theorists of globalization and cosmopolitanism may disagree on the (military) means, preferring economic reform and institutional restructuring as better ways of promoting integration. This book will argue that *all* these means are flawed, in that they believe that greater economic openness will integrate poorer economies. I will suggest instead that these neo-liberal means, military or economic, will not lead to integration but further reinforce marginalization. And this argument will be made by reviving the theory of *free trade imperialism*, that was once associated with nineteenth-century British imperialism. In providing such a critique of liberal imperialism, the book will analyse and point to the limitations of classical Marxist accounts of imperialism, though the arguments that follow will critically draw on the work of Trotsky and Kautsky.

Table 1.1 below provides a brief periodization of imperialism since the late eighteenth century, examining its key features and where it is discussed in the rest of the book.

While some chapters emphasize some issues more than others, taken together, the chapters that follow examine in detail the relationship between global capital accumulation, the international state system, and the changing hierarchies in the international order. Chapter 2 examines the origins of capitalism, through an examination of core-periphery, or 'imperialist' relations in the mercantilist era. The origins of the division of the world into core and periphery are examined, as well as the mechanisms that sustained this division up until the nineteenth century. The relationship between early colonial

Table 1.1   A brief history of imperialism

Period	Main features of imperialism
Pre-1830s	Mercantile imperialism. Associated with the rise of early capitalist social relations in Britain, but also non-capitalist relations in other core territories. Core-periphery linkages contributed to, but did not cause, capitalist development. **Chapter 2**
1840s to 1870s	Free trade imperialism. Associated with trade liberalization in Europe and British hegemony, and de-industrialization in the periphery. **Chapter 3 (also Chapters 4 and 7)**
1880s to 1945	'Classical imperialism'. Associated with new geo-political rivalries among core countries, culminating in two world wars. Also sees the consolidation of the subordinate role of the periphery in the international capitalist order, including a new era of colonial annexation. **Chapter 4**
1945 to 1989/91	Cold War imperialism between the superpowers based on divergent socio-economic orders. In the capitalist world, increased cooperation between advanced capitalist countries under US leadership. In the periphery, the end of colonialism and extension of state sovereignty, but continued military intervention and continued economic subordination, even as the Third World (unevenly) industrializes. **Chapter 5**
1989/91	End of the Cold War and intensification of (neo)liberal international order (from 1979 onwards). US hegemony reconfigured after crisis of 1970s. Cooperation between core states continues in the context of the globalization of production. This globalization does not however erode global uneven development. For some this context is used to highlight continued geo-political competition, while critics argue that cooperation between states remains more significant, and that uneven and combined development can only explain inequalities that arise out of global capital accumulation. In particular, the globalization of production does not erode core-periphery distinctions. The end of the Cold War also gives rise to cases for humanitarian military intervention on the cosmopolitan grounds that the rights of individuals are more important than the sovereignty of (rogue or failed) states. **Chapters 6 and 7**
2001– onwards	Further intensification of liberal humanitarianism after September 2001. Possible challenges to US hegemony in face of Iraq war, possible hegemonic challengers and global recession from 2007 onwards. **Chapters 8 and 9**

plunder, capitalist accumulation, and the industrial revolution is therefore a central theme of this chapter. Chapter 3 then examines the relationship between early capitalist development in Britain and the promotion of free trade policies in much of the rest of the world, establishing the argument that the mid-nineteenth century was an era of free trade imperialism. It also examines early cases made for liberal imperialism on humanitarian grounds, an issue taken up in later chapters. Chapter 4 develops further these themes through an examination of the period from the late nineteenth century to 1914, and indeed beyond up to 1945. The focus here is on classical, mainly Marxist, theories of imperialism, but also the (neo-liberal) argument that the period up to 1914 was one of progressive capitalist expansion, followed by a system of protectionism after 1914. The argument of both classical Marxists and neo-liberals will be challenged, and indeed I will suggest that their contentions are not as far removed from each other as is sometimes suggested. Chapters 2–4 will also attempt to distinguish between non-capitalist and capitalist forms of imperialism, and will do so in part through an examination of arguments about English 'exceptionalism'. I will challenge the idea that 'backward' England – and its imperialism – was somehow never properly capitalist.

The second half of the book moves on to examine the post-war period of capitalist expansion under US hegemony. It will examine the nature of US imperialism after 1945, and contrast this with its Soviet rival. It will also examine the liberal nature of this imperialism, different from the European imperialisms of the period from 1880 to 1945, though having some continuities as well as differences with British imperialism, particularly from 1846 to around 1932. Chapter 5 focuses on the specificity of the US state, the end of empire and development, and the internationalization of capital after 1945. Central to the argument will be that a new kind of non-territorial empire emerged in the capitalist world after 1945, based on the extension of state sovereignty alongside the, long-term, commitment to the removal of barriers in terms of trade, investment and financial mobility. This 'imperialism without frontiers' essentially meant the expansion of 'America' beyond American borders, reflected in the internationalization of capital, the restructuring of western Europe and Japan and uneven expansion of Fordism, selective free trade, and commitment to independence in the Third World.

Chapter 6 examines the rise of neo-liberalism in the context of the end of the post-war boom. The central role of the US state will be examined through the role of financial stability through high interest rates in the late 1970s and early 1980s, and the geo-political impact of the end of the Cold War. The focus of this chapter is on the reconfiguring of US hegemony under neo-liberalism, and how the end of the Cold War actually consolidated cooperation between the advanced capitalist powers, rather than giving rise to a new era of intensified conflict between them. Central to this claim will be an examination of how enhanced liberalization encouraged cooperation, but Chapter 7 will show how this very same liberalization led to a new era of neo-liberal imperialism, whose effects were most acute in the global South. The main argument of Chapter 7 is that the recent globalization of manufacturing production has not eroded global uneven development and marginalization, and that in fact the free trade imperialism associated with neo-liberalism has actually intensified it. The global economic crisis that broke out in 2007 has not altered this, but actually further strengthened neo-liberal domination.

Chapter 8 examines the second central feature of contemporary liberal imperialism, that of 'humanitarian intervention'. Focusing on the revival of empire talk after 2001, the chapter re-examines liberal cases for empire. This will involve some consideration of neo-conservative views that influenced the decision to go to war with Iraq in 2003, but also wider liberal cosmopolitan cases for humanitarian military intervention. These arguments are then challenged through an examination of the relationship between politics and violence, and how this manifests itself in liberal discourses of humanitarian wars, and the problematic concept of collateral damage. The chapter will also draw out the contradictions between the geo-politics and the political economy of neo-liberalism, and how the integrating rationale of the former is undermined by the marginalizing effects of the latter.

The focus of Chapters 7 and 8 is therefore on the reality of contemporary imperialism. Chapter 9 examines the future of imperialism through an assessment of whether or not US hegemony is in decline. This is done through an assessment of potential challengers, such as the European Union and especially China, both generally and more specifically through an assessment of the global economic crisis that developed from 2007.

Finally, Chapter 10 concludes the book by summarizing and further developing the argument about the nature of contemporary liberal imperialism, and assessing anti-imperialist alternatives. The focus in this concluding chapter is an examination of 'America' and 'empire', not as political realities, but rather as political projects, and of alternative political projects. It will be argued that the debate between those advocating a progressive liberal imperialism and those rejecting it is part of a wider crisis of politics, and particularly the question of what constitutes progressive politics today. The chapter and book conclude by advocating a position that rejects both liberal imperialism and a crude anti-imperialism.

2
Early Capitalism and Mercantile Imperialism

This chapter examines imperialism in the context of the early development of capitalism, up to the period of the mid-nineteenth century. This is done by focusing on a number of closely related theoretical approaches – under-development and world systems theory, and the 'new global history' – which suggest that British take off in the early nineteenth century was closely linked to, or even caused by, the contribution of the colonies, particularly in the New World and India. Although these theories are concerned with a long history of relations between the developed core and under-developed periphery, and we will return to their claims in later chapters, they deserve some initial treatment as they have a particular conception of capitalism and its origins. Their argument is that imperialism largely caused the take off of capitalist development in what came to be the advanced countries, and Britain in particular. This chapter therefore focuses on the claims made by this theory in the period of mercantilism.

The chapter starts by assessing the contribution of the periphery to the development of capitalism in the centre. This is done in the first section, which outlines dependency and world systems theories and the claims made by those who contend that they have a new, genuinely global approach to the study of history. The second section subjects these to arguments to critical scrutiny. My argument is that the peripheral contribution to the development of the core was not insignificant, but that this contribution alone was not sufficient to develop the latter along capitalist lines. The conclusion then brings the argument together, and examines the relationship between imperialism and early capitalist development – or put differently, the relationship between capitalism and mercantile imperialism.

The Origins Debate: Core, Periphery and Global History

One of the main arguments made concerning the origins of capitalist development in the core countries is that the colonies and the periphery, through colonialism, slavery, and plunder, were central to the industrialization of the core countries. This is associated with, among others, Williams' (1987) thesis concerning the link between capitalism and slavery, Frank's (1969a and b) arguments on the links between development and under-development, Wallerstein's (1974a and b) world systems theory, Blaut's (1993) rejection of Eurocentric diffusionism, Frank's later (1998) arguments concerning the centrality of Asia to world history, Pomeranz's (2000) arguments that East and West were at similar levels of development until around 1800, and Hobson's (2004) thesis concerning the 'Eastern Origins of Western Civilisation'. These arguments require further elaboration before subjecting them to critical scrutiny. This is done by examining the relationship between capitalism and slavery, the claims of under-development and world systems theory, and the contentions of the 'new global history'.

Capitalism and Slavery

The argument that there was a close causal connection between New World slavery and the emergence of industrial capitalism is mainly associated with the work of Eric Williams (1987). His basic argument is that slavery was an economic phenomenon, and it played a major causal role in the early development of the industrial revolution in Britain (Williams 1987: 52). Once the US won its independence, slavery ceased to be so profitable and the New World declined in importance for Britain. The move to abolition – of the slave trade in 1807 and of slavery in 1834 (followed by emancipation in 1838) – was therefore less the product of humanitarian concerns and was mainly driven by economic motives. In particular, it was intimately tied to the movement away from monopoly towards the advocacy of free trade, and reflected the growing importance of the domestic market in Britain (Williams 1987: 135; also Hobson 2004: 266–73). Williams argues that the profits from slavery provided an important source for capital investment, and that the New World provided an important market for British-made goods.

Williams thus played an important part in the development of historical work that attempted to specify the links between peripheries and cores in the world economy, and which suggested that such links worked against the interests of the former. This was not necessarily novel, and Marx himself had reflected on the links between capitalism and slavery, arguing that:

> The discovery of gold and silver in America, the extirpation, enslavement and entombment in mines of the indigenous population of that continent, the beginnings of the conquest and plunder of India, and the conversion of Africa into a preserve for the commercial hunting of blackskins, are all things which characterise the dawn of the era of capitalist production. These idyllic proceedings are the chief moments of primitive accumulation. (1976: 915)

Nevertheless, Williams' contentions concerning the close links between the New World and industrialization in the core countries are important, and the claims were developed further by Andre Gunder Frank and Immanuel Wallerstein.

Under-Development and World Systems Theory

These two theories are well known, and have been extensively criticized (Brenner 1977; Limqueco and MacFarlane 1983; Kiely 1995; Teschke 2003). Nonetheless, the ideas associated with these theories remain influential, both in terms of analyses of contemporary imperialism, and in the work of new global historians. The essential argument is that core or metropolitan countries developed by under-developing the periphery. Therefore, development and under-development are two sides of the same coin – the poor world is poor because it has been under-developed by the developed world, and the rich world is rich because it has under-developed the poor world (Frank 1969a). This approach can be dated back at least as far as the nineteenth century (Cowen and Shenton 1996: ch.2). However, in the post-war era, it was initially associated with the work of Paul Baran (1957: 22–4), who argued that while competitive capitalism progressively developed the productive forces, the rich world also exploited the poor world via a process of surplus extraction, in which wealth was transferred from the latter to the former. Unlike Baran, who (albeit ambiguously – see Chapter 5) continued to focus on capitalist social relations, Frank argued that the world had been capitalist since the sixteenth century, and that the main defining feature of capitalism was the exploitation of satellites by metropolitan countries. Like Baran, Frank argued that this exploitation took place through a process of surplus transfer, which meant that the satellites 'remain under-developed for the lack of access to their own surplus..' (Frank 1969a: 9). Therefore, some nations develop at the expense of others in a zero-sum game. Capitalism therefore needs to be conceptualized as a world system, divided between exploiting metropoles and exploited satellites.

Immanuel Wallerstein's world systems theory similarly rejected the idea that 'national societies' are appropriate units of analysis, and also argued that capitalism should be theorized as a single world economy. Capitalism emerged in the sixteenth century, based on the 'full development of market trade' (Wallerstein 1974a: 391). The increased spread of market relations gave rise to a global division of labour and specialization, in which different components of the world system sold goods on the international market. Through specialization came differentiation, with some parts of the world having a monopoly over other parts, and therefore gaining a greater share of global wealth. Wallerstein characterizes this division as a three-tiered one: a core, periphery and semi-periphery. A pattern of labour control arises in response to different forms of economic activity, with the core using wage labour, the semi-periphery using share-cropping and the periphery using coerced cash crop labour. This division is reinforced by the development of varying state structures, with strong states developing in the core, and weak states in the periphery. The differences in 'state strength' facilitate monopoly power and unequal exchange between the three regions, with the core winning most of the benefits (Wallerstein 1974b: 355).

The New Global History

Frank's later work (1998) constitutes a (partial) break from his earlier 'development of under-development' thesis. In one respect, *Re-Orient* radically departs from his earlier contentions, to the point of even suggesting that the latter remained part of the Eurocentric framework that he was trying to avoid. He also makes the same criticism of those with whom he otherwise has some sympathy, including Wallerstein, Arrighi and Blaut (Frank 1998: 26–34, 46). On the other hand, his later argument repeats the contention that the contribution of the periphery to the development of the core was central.

The starting point of *Re-Orient* is the claim that the world system has historically been centred on Asia, and that Europe only became the dominant power in the nineteenth century. He is therefore sympathetic to Abu-Lughold's argument that there was an Asian dominated world economy from 1250 to 1350, but he challenges her claim that this went into decline after this period. He also challenges the orthodoxy in world systems theory, namely that the world economy was one dominated by Europe from the sixteenth century onwards. Frank (1998: 75) instead argues that the period from 1400 to 1800 was one characterized by an Asian-dominated world economy, and that Europe remained a marginal player in this order. Europe had a long-standing trade deficit with Asia, and financed this by plundering gold from the Americas, which in turn paid for the import of goods from Asia. Drawing on a range of secondary sources, Frank (1998: 172–4) goes on to suggest that in 1750, Asia was responsible for about 80 per cent of total world production, and that in 1800, China's per capita income stood at $210, compared to the $198 of what became the developed world. Crucially then, for Frank, Asia was a more efficient region, which long enjoyed higher productivity than Europe.

Frank then moves on to suggest the reasons why an industrial revolution occurred first in backward Europe. Drawing on earlier work which attempted to theorize expanding and contracting long waves of economic growth (Frank and Gills 1993), he argues that Asia led the expansions from 1000/1050 to 1250/1300, and from 1450 onwards. However, a new period of contraction from 1750 onwards gave Europe the opportunity to overcome its marginal position. In particular, there were opportunities presented by natural resources (coal and other raw materials), cheap food imported from the colonies, and beneficial world prices in the form of higher wages and cheap sources of capital. Although he accepts that it was not the only source, Frank holds on to his earlier argument that the extraction of surplus from the periphery was the crucial factor in financing the development of the (new, European) core (Frank 1998: 294–7).

His third argument however, attempts to move beyond some of the problems associated with his earlier thesis. These problems are considered in detail below, but briefly, while the extraction of resources from one area to another amounts to a regional redistribution of wealth, it does not on its own expand total wealth. What, then, caused Europe to innovate and therefore by implication, what hindered innovation in China? Frank's argument is that higher wages in Europe stimulated innovation, while lower wages in China made it rational for innovation not to take place. Cheaper labour existed in China because a more efficient agrarian system allowed wages to stay low (Frank 1998: 307), which was further reinforced by a higher demographic/land resource ratio, which in 1770 was 3.6 to 3.8 per hectare, compared to 1.5 in England (Frank 1998: 308). This, rather odd, argument seems to amount to the contention that higher wages and low productivity made innovation rational in Europe, while low wages and higher productivity made it irrational in China.

These arguments will be challenged below. For the moment, we need to draw out the basic contentions. Frank argues that Asia has historically been dominant in the world order, and that European dominance only arrived as late as the nineteenth century. European dominance was achieved partly through the availability of certain raw materials, but above all because of the colonial plunder of the New World and the stimulus to innovation given by high wages in Europe.

The work of Kenneth Pomeranz (2000; 2002) can also be located within this tradition of global history. Like Frank, his colleague Bin Wong (1997) and Hobson (2004: 207–10), Pomeranz is concerned with highlighting the similarity between levels of development in Europe and in Asia. More precisely, he suggests that parts of China were as productive as the most advanced parts of Europe, up until as late as the end of the eighteenth century (see also Arrighi 2007). This is especially true of the Yangzi delta, the most developed region in China at the time. His starting point is that an increase in population and the development of a specialized division of labour and market exchange can, for a period of time, promote economic growth. This favourable context for growth existed in the Yangzi delta as much as the most productive parts of Europe, especially England, until the great divergence in about 1800. What explains this divergence is the limits of population growth in rela-tion to land supply, and thus the limits in the supply of food and raw materials. Both England and the Yangzi delta faced this problem, but it was dealt with by the former in such a way that accumulation was sustained. English (and European) mercantile expansion made possible the establishment of raw material and food producing peripheries using slave labour, thus allowing them to overcome the land/population crisis, and relieving 'the strain on Europe's supply of what was truly scarce: land and energy' (Pomeranz 2000: 20). In other words, expansion into the New World provided 'ecological relief' to the Malthusian land/ population crisis, in the process creating a new periphery, 'which enabled Europe to exchange an ever growing volume of manufactured exports for an ever growing volume of land-intensive products' (Pomeranz 2000: 20). Ecological relief was further reinforced by the use of Britain's coal reserves, which was 'crucial to its nineteenth century breakthrough, and (unlike textiles) not dependent for its full flowering on European access to overseas resources' (Pomeranz 2000: 61).

Coal and the New World therefore 'appear at the right time to explain a crucial divergence' which Pomeranz (2000: 280) dates as late as 1800. Together these two factors relieved the constraint of the finite amount of land, which parts of Europe successfully overcame, in contrast to China. Central to Pomeranz's arguments are three controversial contentions: (i) that in 1800, agricultural productivity and output was not markedly different in the most advanced regions of Europe and China; (ii) that coal played a central role in the (British) industrial revolution, and this is a major factor in explaining the great divergence; (iii) that the expansion of merchant capital into the New World was the other crucial factor that explained Europe's leap over China, and that therefore, by implication, the colonial encounter was central to European industrial development.

The ideas of these historians are put together in an impressive synthesis by John Hobson (2004). He challenges what he calls the 'Eurocentric myth of the pristine West' (Hobson 2004: 1) and argues that a global economy developed around the year 500, which was dominated by Eastern technology and communications (Hobson 2004: ch.2). It was only after 1492 that Europe became increasingly involved in these networks, and only as late as the nineteenth century that Europe leapt ahead of the rest of the world. Moreover, it did so only by appropriating the already developed technologies of the East, particularly China (Hobson 2004: ch.9) and through colonial plunder (Hobson 2004: chs10 and 11). Although there are disagreements over specifics, these arguments are broadly accepted by the new global historians. These now need some further consideration.

The New Global History: a Critique

Although the focus of the 'new global history' is slightly different from earlier theories of under-development, there is also considerable continuity. The former particularly focuses on the similarities in patterns of development between different parts of the world until relatively recently, and like post-colonial theory, emphasizes the ways in which Eurocentric historians have re-written this history (Said 1978). But unlike much post-colonial theory, the new global history does not confine itself solely to questions of how 'the East' has been represented by historians, novelists and social scientists. Rather it goes to great lengths to provide a more accurate account of history, and move from a position of deconstruction to reconstruction. And it is here that the continuity with older approaches is most clear.

Both approaches rightly suggest that capitalism is an international phenomenon, not confined to the nation-states of the 'core' countries. They also both suggest that the division of the world into centres and peripheries has occurred because the former has in some sense exploited the latter. They reject the argument that capitalism exists in one country, and the related notion that the expansion of capitalism constitutes a progressive development for the peripheral countries (Blaut 2000; Pomeranz 2000: 14–15; Hobson 2004: 12–14). Ultimately then, the argument is that imperialist relations were central to the development of European capitalism.

We will return to the question of Eurocentrism and Marxism in later chapters, so we can be brief on this question at this point. The quotation from Marx above on the close links between slavery, colonialism and primitive accumulation, and similar statements linked 'the veiled slavery of the wage earners in Europe' and the 'unqualified slavery' of the New World (Marx 1977: 925), suggest a position more subtle than one that saw a simple diffusion of capitalism throughout the globe. Marx (in Marx and Engels 1974: 298) also suggested that 'commerce in countries which export principally raw produce increased the misery of the masses', and even recognized that while free trade was in some respects progressive, it remained true that countries could develop at the expense of other countries (Marx 1984: 269–70; and see next chapter).

But textual authority is less important than a theoretically informed historical analysis of the origins of capitalism. This section thus focuses on this debate, linking historical and empirical material with the different theoretical starting points of the two approaches. My argument is that a Marxist approach is more useful, and that this can also provide the basis for a theory of 'the international', and by implication, of imperialism. Moreover, it is one that does not uphold a theory of international capitalist diffusion, but rather one that suggests the operation of uneven – and unequal – capitalist development.

This section first develops some specific criticisms of the theories outlined above, and in pointing to common problems, suggests that these derive from their shared starting point, which is a trade-based determinism and a reified, ahistorical account of the market. I then move on to discuss the most important issue, which is the socio-economic relationship between periphery and core, and the degree of necessity of the former for the development of the latter.

Rather than take each of the contentions individually, my critique will be thematic. First, I will examine the claim that Europe was not more advanced than Asia until 1800. Second, I will then examine the evidence concerning the links between the New World – and the periphery more generally – and the development of Europe. And third, I will use this critique to draw out the theoretical weaknesses of the arguments of world systems theories and new global histories, and by implication briefly suggest an alternative understanding of the origins (and indeed, definition) of capitalism.

Europe and Asia

The first argument made by a number of the writers discussed above is that in 1800, parts of China and/or Asia were at similar, or more advanced, levels of development than the most advanced parts of Europe. This suggests that Europe faced similar Malthusian constraints to China, as population outstripped the supply of land and agricultural output. But in fact, the weight of the historical evidence suggests that labour and land productivity had already undergone substantial improvements in parts of Europe (and specifically England or Britain) before 1800. Pomeranz (2000: 216) draws on Clark (1991) and Ambrosoli (1997) to argue that 'English agricultural productivity had not changed much between 1750 and 1850' and that 'per acre and total yields from arable land remained flat and the threat of decline constant, until Britain began mining, importing and later synthesizing fertilizer, mostly after 1850'. In fact Clark's (1991: 458) account does recognise increased growth in wheat yields from 1600 to 1800, and only suggests that this growth slowed down – but did not stagnate – after this period. Others have gone further, estimating that English output per acre increased by 70 per cent from 1705 to 1775, and by a further 58 per cent from 1775 to 1845 (Brunt 1999). Overton

(1998: 82) argues that increases in land productivity were also accompanied by increases in labour productivity, and this more or less doubled from 1700 to 1851. Estimates for the earlier period of 1500 to 1750 suggest that labour productivity increased by a minimum of 52 per cent and a maximum of 67 per cent (Allen 2000: 20). Over this period, land ownership became increasingly concentrated, and capitalist farms of 100 acres or more increased from 14 per cent of all farms in the 1600s to 52 per cent of all farms by 1800. These farms made up 66 per cent of all farmland by the latter date (O' Brien 1996: 237). This concentration reflected the increased capitalist nature of English farming, which meant that the context of competition encouraged investment in new, productivity enhancing methods, which was further facilitated by the concentration of farmland which arose out of the competitive process. The increase in productivity and output allowed for a movement away from the countryside and into the towns, which could be sustained by increased agricultural output. This labour force was also a necessary, but not sufficient, factor in providing supplies of labour for the industrial revolution (see below). Thus, from 1550 to 1800, Britain's population tripled while the proportion of the labour force engaged in agriculture declined from 80 per cent (1500) to 20 per cent in 1850 (Overton 1998: 8).

These figures undermine the arguments that Britain and parts of Europe faced a Malthusian crisis by 1800. What then of the claims made for Asia? Pomeranz argues that the Yangzi delta was facing a Malthusian crisis by 1800, while Frank argues that Asian agriculture was actually more efficient than its European counterpart. Critics have suggested that in fact, the Yangzi delta was characterized by increasingly sub-divided land, which occurred in the context of population growth expanding more rapidly than increases in output (Allen 1992: 73–4). This does not necessarily mean that China was characterized by stagnation, and indeed output through increases in land productivity did occur. This was partly a product of the 'resource blessing' of rice, a particularly productive grain, partly through increasing the amount of land under cultivation, and partly through improvements in the efficiency and intensity of production, including the use of increasing amounts of labour in production (Elvin 1973). All these factors served to increase the productivity *of land* in parts of China. But they did not increase the productivity *of labour*. In other words, technological progress was labour-using rather than labour-saving (Kang Chao 1986: 21–3).

Maddison (1998: 25) suggests that per capita income in China remained unchanged from 1280 to 1700. Clearly growth did occur, but not as quickly as in parts of Europe, and crucially, this growth would eventually reach definite Malthusian limits. Thus, Brenner and Isett (2002: 625) suggest that output was falling in both China as a whole, and in the Yangzi delta, from 1700 onwards. Duchesne (2001/2: 456) goes further, arguing that by the early nineteenth century, 'there seems to have been little room or leeway for additional expansion', and that China was approaching an 'ultimate constraint'. This point is not necessarily incompatible with Pomeranz's thesis as applied to China, but the argument of comparability up to 1800 cannot be sustained.

These points are reinforced by further consideration of Pomeranz's argument concerning coal. As we have seen, he argues that the use of coal was central to overcoming the Malthusian limits faced by the British economy in 1800. But this argument is flawed for two reasons. First, coal was already widely used in the British economy by 1800, which *reflected* the reality of industrial growth, rather than *caused* it. Thus, the Newcomen steam engine was already in use in most large mines by the early eighteenth century (Landes 1969: 101), and there was growing demand for coal as industrial output expanded at a rate of 2.1 per cent a year from 1780 to 1801 (Crafts 1989: 66). Second, coal was not the only major source of power and even by 1800, many steam engines continued to use water power, which was also the main source of power in the textiles industry. Thus, the industrial revolution was already well under way by 1800, and was not put into place by the sudden use of coal as a source of power. Furthermore, industrialization continued into the nineteenth century and was a major reason why Britain increasingly chose to import wheat from abroad. Contrary to Pomeranz's arguments then, this increase in food imports was not a product of a Malthusian crisis, but a product of industrial specialization. Moreover, almost all of the wheat was imported from Russia, Prussia and Ireland, and not from the New World (Brenner and Isett 2002: 644).

There are good reasons then, for questioning Pomeranz's thesis. Frank makes the stronger argument that in fact Chinese production was more efficient than Europe's. The data above undermines this argument, but this still leaves the fact that Europe did run trade deficits with Asia for much of the period from 1400 to 1800, something that is central to Frank's overall argument. The problem however is that Frank ignores the concentration of world shares of trade and the relative unimportance of Asian trade to Europe. In 1720, as Frank himself at one point suggests, Europe's share of world trade was 69 per cent, while Asia's share stood at only 11 per cent. By 1750 Europe's share had increased to 72 per cent. In dismissing these figures, Frank (1998: 183) asserts that 'this unabashedly Eurocentric claim is disconfirmed by the evidence discussed in the present book'. But as Duchesne (2001/2) points out, the claim that these figures are somehow Eurocentric represents a too easy dismissal of evidence that does not conform to a preconceived – and highly politicized – theory. Indeed, in 1700 Europe accounted for 75 per cent of the imports and 89 per cent of France's exports, and 61 per cent of England's imports and 81 per cent of its exports (Goodman and Honeyman 1988: 57–9). These latter figures on their own do not necessarily disprove Frank's contentions concerning Europe's marginal role in world trade, but when combined with the figures on the concentration of global shares in Europe, they suggest that trade deficits notwithstanding, Asia was, relatively, marginal in an increasingly European dominated world economy (Duchesne 2001/2).

But there is an even greater problem with Frank's analysis. This relates to his argument that Europe was characterized by high wages and low productivity, while China had low wages and high productivity. If this was the case, then it is not clear why China did not develop and leave Europe (further) behind. Frank's (1998: 301) argument at this point is that the period of post-1400 prosperity in China 'polarized the distribution of income and thereby constrained effective demand of mass consumer goods'. But even in the context of polarized income, expansion would actually increase demand. Frank then suggests that population increases would lead to scarcity of resources which would lead to income polarization. As Duchesne (2001/2) points out, the clear implication is that the peasantry were poorer in Asia than in Europe, where wages were higher, and/or that growth in Asia was achieved through increased exploitation of the peasantry in the context of diminishing returns to agriculture. Following Elvin (1973), Frank (1998: 302) agrees that there was capital available to invest in new technology, but there was no incentive to do so due to the plentiful supply of cheap labour, and that this reflected a high population/land resource ratio. But at the same time, Frank also wants to hold on to the claim that China enjoyed higher per capita income and lower wages due to a more efficient agrarian sector. Elvin on the other hand, argues that low demand and low wages reflected the *inefficiency* of, and diminishing returns to, Chinese agriculture. Perhaps in response to Eurocentric representations of Asian stagnation, Frank constantly accentuates the positives in Chinese agriculture, but he does so at the cost of presenting an internally consistent argument. A similar but wider point applies to Hobson's account of the strength of China up to 1840, for if this is the case, then it begs the question asked by John Hall (2007: 150), namely 'why were they more or less incapable of responding to western incursions?' Indeed, the recognition that the non-European world was not stagnant, but also was not as dynamic as Europe by the 1700s, is not an 'Orientalist clause' a disclaimer that allows Eurocentrism in through the back door, as Hobson (2004: 22–3; 2006: 580–1) claims. It is based on a simple recognition, and not necessarily approval, of historical fact.

There remains one possible objection to the argument that Europe forged ahead of the rest of the world. Pomeranz (2000: 218) asks if this is the case, why did living standards in Europe not rise substantially in the early nineteenth century? This is true, and certainly Brenner and Isett (2002) at times come close to presenting British advances as 'trickling down' so that the whole population benefited. The most recent contributions to the 'living standards' debate suggest that wages remained constant from 1790 to 1820, and improved only slowly afterwards (Feinstein 1998; Clark 2001). However, this does not reflect Malthusian limits, but rather the unequal distribution of the benefits of enhanced growth (Williamson 1985), something that simply reflects the *capitalist* nature of British growth.

Core and Periphery: the Colonial Contribution to European Capitalism

The debate over the colonial contribution to the development of Europe is clearly central to debates over the links between imperialism and early capitalism, and the nature of international uneven development. As we have seen, Wallerstein, Williams, Frank, and Pomeranz all contend, in slightly different ways, that the colonial contribution was central to the development of the core countries. Williams thus saw a close connection between slavery and the industrial revolution, even if he was not always clear on its precise nature. However, there is little evidence to suggest that slavery *caused* the industrial revolution, as the profits from slavery were quite low, and there was no great surge of investment at the start of the industrial revolution (Solow and Engerman 1987; Kiely 1996: ch.2). Certainly, as Inikori (1987) contends, the New World was a major market for industrial goods produced in Britain, but this alone does not constitute the basis for a close causal connection, not least because other countries drew on slavery but did not industrialize. Indeed, the industrial revolution eventually became a European phenomenon, which in part can be explained by geo-political competition between states (see Chapter 4), but one where at least some of those most centrally involved in the slave trade – Spain and Portugal – were left behind.

Having said that, the fact that the New World was a significant market for British goods had important implications for deepening the industrial revolution. From around 1699 to 1774, the value of British manufactured exports more than doubled. Over the same period, the destination of these exports changed substantially, with Europe's share declining from 82 to 42 per cent and America and Africa's share increasing from 12 to 43 per cent (Solow and Engerman 1987a: 10). By 1796–8, New World markets – including the US and Canada – accounted for perhaps as much as two-thirds of all British exports (Blackburn 1997: 516). These markets were therefore crucial, and provided a stimulus to further industrial expansion in Britain. Africa and the Americas were thus hardly irrelevant to British industrial development, as Williams rightly contended. Having said that, export markets alone do not constitute a prime causal mechanism accounting for the industrial revolution, and we need to better understand the precise nature of the linkages between the New World and the industrial revolution.

Like Williams, Pomeranz suggests that contact with the New World was crucial, not least for effectively expanding land supplies which were unavailable in Europe. He argues that sugar, cotton and timber were particularly important, as they extended available acreage that Europeans effectively utilized by as much as 25 to 30 million – more than the total farmland of Britain (Pomeranz 2000: 274–8). Drawing on the work of Sidney Mintz (1986), Pomeranz (2000: 274–5) argues that sugar constituted just 4 per cent of caloric intake in the average British diet in 1800, but that by 1900 this had reached 14 per cent. Indeed, he goes further, suggesting that the real figure for 1901 may be as high as 18 per cent. Even if this contention is true, it does not establish the case that New World sugar was central to British or European growth in the nineteenth century. European beet sugar gradually displaced New World sugar throughout the nineteenth century. In 1840, European beet accounted for just 8 per cent of total world production, but by 1900 this had increased to 64 per cent (Goodman and Honeyman 1988: 42). In 1831, 76 per cent of sugar imports into Britain came from the main New World supplier, the British Caribbean, but by 1901 this had fallen to just 4 per cent, while 80 per cent of British supplies came from Europe (Duchesne 2004: 64). Moreover, sugar from the Caribbean was sold to Britain at prices above the world average (Solow and Engerman 1987).

Timber imports from the New World were more significant, although Pomeranz (2000: 273) recognizes that before then, they were insignificant. But this does not mean that timber imports were necessary to resolve a Malthusian crisis in Britain. In fact, timber imports from the New World occurred in the context of the industrial revolution and rising productivity and therefore rising demand in Britain for these products. Pomeranz (2000: 221) himself recognizes that Eastern Europe, Scandinavia and Russia were major suppliers, but later argues that these sources were limited. He bases this assertion on the argument that these were subsistence oriented economies (Pomeranz 2000: 258), which is not consistent with his own recognition that these regions did supply Britain. He therefore provides an additional argument, which is that producers in Europe had limited buying power and so could not buy British goods in return for their timber. In contrast, although Pomeranz recognizes that slave production was cheap, he simultaneously argues that their purchasing power was 'a significant market for imports' (Pomeranz 2000: 265–6).

It is true that the New World did become an increasingly important supplier of timber to Britain after 1800, but this was because of geopolitical decisions made by the British state at the time. The turn to the New World was a response to Napoleon's attempt to block British trade in continental Europe after 1806, and so Britain subsidized the high cost timber trade with British North America and raised tariffs on European timber. In a changed geo-political context, tariffs were reduced and the shift to free trade led to a decline in imports from the New World. British timber imports from the New World (including the United States) fell from 63 per cent of total imports in 1850, to 31 per cent in 1875 to 28 per cent in 1900, while Europe's share increased from 36 per cent in 1850, to 69 per cent in 1875 and 72 per cent in 1900 (Duchesne 2004: 69–70).

Given Britain's total dependence on the import of the necessary raw materials, and its close connection to the Atlantic trade, the case of cotton is perhaps stronger. Cotton goods were particularly export dependent in the early development of the industry, accounting for as much as 50 per cent of total production in 1760, most of which went to Africa and the Caribbean (Blackburn 1997: 522). Even after US independence, export growth soared. Between 1784/6 and 1805/6, export growth as a proportion of output growth was as high as 87 per cent, with most of this going to the New World. The price of raw cotton bought by British manufacturers was also very low, in part because of the cheap costs of slave labour (Blackburn 1997: 555–6). On the other hand, while these figures demonstrate a link between slavery and cotton-based industrialization, so that the former contributed to the development of the latter, they do not do not establish a strong causal link. Even as late as 1841, cotton accounted for only 7 per cent of British GNP (O' Brien 1991: 302). Moreover, Britain's demand for cotton reflected the growing strength of its economy, and particularly the ability of the textile industry to decrease costs and increase output through technological innovation. In terms of the market for British finished products, it was Europe, not the New World, which remained the most significant source of British exports.

On the other hand, Britain did lead the industrial revolution and trade more with the periphery than other nascent developed countries did, and capital formation was important in Britain in the period from 1760 to 1850. But trade with the periphery was not as significant as world systems theorists and new global historians suggest. The savings rate for the British economy from 1781 to 1860 was around 12–14 per cent. For those involved in international commerce, O' Brien (1982: 7) suggests that even if they reinvested 30 per cent of their profits (a figure that it is probably too high), this would mean that trade with the periphery generated a flow of funds that could finance only 15 per cent of gross investment spending in the industrial revolution. If we take these figures at face value then, the colonial contribution to British capitalism was marginal. These specific points led O'Brien (1982: 3) to initially conclude that 'commerce between core and periphery for three centuries after 1450 proceeded on a small scale, was not a uniquely profitable field of enterprise, and while it generated some externalities, they could in no way be classified as decisive to the economic growth of Britain' (O'Brien 1982: 3).

However, as O'Brien recognizes, expressing the value of any sector of the economy as a percentage of national income 'seems almost calculated to create an impression of insignificance' (O'Brien and Engerman 1991: 178). Moreover, the colonial contribution is likely to be low when measured in value terms, if we accept that the process of integration into the world economy was one based on both unequal integration and marginalization. This is because the specialization that was encouraged by integration tended to be in lower-value production, and so the proportionate contribution to the national income of the colonial power would by definition be low (an argument to which we return in later chapters). Partly in response to this problem, O'Brien and Engerman have attempted to examine the contribution of exports to growth cycles in the British economy in the eighteenth century. They found that 95 per cent of the increment to the volume of total British exports from 1700 to 1772–3 was sold in colonial markets, and that while the vast proportion of national output was consumed by the home market, over one-fifth of the increment to total national output was sold abroad. Moreover, the three most dynamic industries in 1801 (cotton, wool, metallurgy) sold 62, 35 and 24 per cent of their gross output abroad. Furthermore, contact with the New World led to all kinds of favourable spin-offs that benefited British capitalism in general, including the development of new ports, roads, canals, and other infrastructure, new sources of credit for potential investors, as well as new networks of merchant activity, and new supplies of food and raw materials. But perhaps more important than this was the way in which the colonial encounter helped to forge the development of British hegemony, not least through the further development of a fiscal-military state and dominant naval and sea power (O'Brien 1999). British military adventures were very costly, and increased the burden on British taxpayers, but this was felt mainly by the general population, and not wealthy merchant or industrial capitalists (Blackburn 1997: 565) – though of course this burden did have the effect of limiting the expansion of the British market for consumer goods.

Nevertheless, these historical developments are still not sufficiently great to confirm the contentions of the strong causal linkages suggested by world systems and under-development theory and the new global historians. Even when these closer connections are recognized, O'Brien (1991: 305; also Engerman 1994) argues that in 1700, Britain exported 8.4 per cent of its national product, 14.6 per cent in 1760, 9.4 per cent in 1780, and 15.7 per cent in 1801. Moreover, trade with the colonies remained only a small proportion of total trade, and accounted for only a small proportion of economic activity. According to Bairoch (1993: 82), from 1720 to 1780–90, foreign trade provided Britain with between 4 to 8 per cent of its total demand, and trade with non-European countries accounted for up to 39 per cent of total British trade, so the periphery absorbed only around 3 per cent of total demand. These figures are even more striking when we shift our analysis from Britain to Europe. In the years 1780 to 90, only around 4 per cent of Europe's GNP was exported, and only around 1 per cent went to the periphery. While imports were higher, they still constituted a small proportion of economic activity, and as we have seen, the periphery's share was a minority of total European imports (O' Brien 1982: 4; Bairoch 1993: 82–4). In the 1790s, 76 per cent of commodity exports originating from Europe went to other European countries, 10 per cent to North America, 8 per cent to the Caribbean and Latin America, 5 per cent to Asia, and 1 per cent to Africa. In other words, the periphery accounted for 14 per cent of European exports. Even if we expand the concept of the periphery so that it includes the southern slave states of the US, the figure is still only 20 per cent. For European imports from the periphery (including the US South), the figure was around 25 per cent of the European total (O' Brien 1982: 4). As we have seen, these figures ignore the specific contribution of the periphery in specific sectors, but overall trade ratios would have to be much higher for the strong causal link that under-development theory and the new global history claims.

Frank (1978: 44) suggests that the main contribution of the periphery to the development of the core was the plunder of precious metals from the Americas. The expansion of the money supply was crucial in the context of expanding trade, and 'the resulting inflation led directly and indirectly to the concentration of capital, the divorce from the means of production and in the increase in exploitation of more and less well paid labour' (Frank 1978: 245). There was certainly an increase in the movement of precious metals to Europe after 1492, but Braudel and Spooner (1967: 446) estimate that by 1650 this added at most 25 per cent to the gold and silver stock of Europe. From 1460 to 1530, European mine output increased five fold, and this was accompanied by an increase in the velocity of circulation, reduction in the weight of coins, and the increased use of paper money (O' Brien 1982: 14) Moreover, it is unclear how the extraction of precious metals from the Americas laid the basis for increased capital accumulation in the way that Frank envisages – in the cases of Spain and Portugal it clearly did not. Indeed, until the 1780s Spain and Portugal dominated international trade, accounting for an amount somewhere between five and seven times as much as that of the British colonies (Bairoch 1993: 81–2).

For all these reasons, the idea that mercantile imperialism *caused* capitalist development in the core is unconvincing. While there certainly was a colonial contribution to capitalist development, this was insufficient on its own to bring about a capitalist social transformation in Europe. Indeed, it could be argued that the notion that capitalist development comes about simply through an increase in the quantity of goods traded in the international economy rests on a theoretically weak basis. This point is addressed in the next sub-section.

Theoretical Objections

The theories discussed so far all usefully point to the emergence of a world economy, and suggest that this was characterized by hierarchies which undermine any idea of imperialism being associated with the progressive diffusion of capitalism. Instead, they suggest that early European capitalism was associated with imperialist relations *from the outset*. On the other hand, the discussion above has also suggested that these theories are all seriously flawed in their analysis of the origins and mechanisms under which 'core-periphery' relations emerged and were maintained. This sub-section will suggest that this is because these theories do not have a convincing theory of capitalism and capitalist development (Wood 2002).

These theories all usefully show that non-European societies were far from static before contact with Europe, and for some periods in history Europe was the backward continent. There were clearly quite highly developed systems of international trade before the eighteenth century for example (Abu Lughold 1989; Hobson 2004: chs2–4). However, as Callinicos (2007b: 65) suggests, '[i]t is … one thing to resist Eurocentrism, another to assert the existence of pre-modern world economies whose linkages were as powerful as those of the modern capitalist system'. By focusing on the undoubted significance of international trade, and not on social relations of production, the theories discussed above effectively dehistoricize what is socially specific about capitalist development (Brenner 1977; also Hilton 1976). For as Dore and Weeks (1979: 65) suggest, '[t]he plunder of one geographic area for the enrichment of a class (or classes) of expropriators has been a characteristic of virtually all historical epochs. If such plunder and appropriation is used to explain the inequality in the level of development among countries, there is no need to introduce capitalism into the analysis.'

This begs the question of why capitalism should be such a central feature of the analysis, and here it is the historically specific dynamism of the capitalist mode of production that is so important. If we focus on production prior to a focus on trade (a theme that runs throughout this book), then we begin to gain a much clearer understanding of the historical significance of capitalism, and by extension, capitalist imperialism. While it may be true that pre-capitalist societies had some kind of dynamism, and so growth and trade did develop, these become far more rapid and cumulative once capitalist social relations of production emerge. This is because it is only under capitalist social relations that an imperative emerges, which forces owners of the means of production to invest and innovate in order to survive. Brenner puts the point clearly:

> unless they are devoid of their full means of subsistence … and the ability to secure their subsistence by force from the direct producers, economic agents will not be *required* to buy necessary inputs on the market. Unless they are required to buy necessary inputs on the market, they will not be obliged to sell on the market in order to survive. Unless they are required to sell on the market in order to survive, they will not be subject to the competitive constraint, their very survival dependent upon their producing competitively. Unless, finally, they are subject to the competitive constraint, they cannot be expected to try to maximize their profits by seeking the gains from trade, so they cannot be counted on to specialize, accumulate, innovate, and move from line to line in response to demand. (2007: 60–1)

The key point then is that it is only with the development of capitalist social relations that the market becomes an imperative, forcing economic agents to innovate in a new environment of disciplinary competition. Exploitation continues under capitalist social relations, as workers are paid a wage lower than the value of the commodities produced, and this is the source of profit in capitalist society (though this may be redistributed among individual capitals). This is in contrast to feudal or other non-capitalist social relations, where wealth was extracted from direct producers through extra-economic coercion, rather than through more directly economic means under capitalism. This means that while there may be some innovation – as in China – there is not the same compulsion to innovate and so the development of the productive forces is nowhere near as rapid as in capitalist societies (Wickham 2005).

Thus, to return to an example discussed above, while New World slavery did provide some benefits to Europeans, it was only (initially) in Britain, where capitalist social relations and thus the competitive accumulation of capital had emerged most fully, that it coincided with an industrial revolution. Slavery may have made some quantitative expansion to British industrialization then, but it did not cause the qualitative change in social relations which ultimately led to the industrial revolution. Focusing solely on trade relations, or even inventions outside of their social context (Hobson 2004), is to confuse the emergence of capital with the development of capitalism. It is not Eurocentric to point out that capitalism did indeed emerge first in Europe. Hobson (2004: 19) suggests that to ask such a question leads inextricably to 'a subtle but erroneous slippage ... [in which] "revealing" the various blockages that held the East back ... ends up ... imputing to the East a permanent "iron law of non-development"'. However, it does not necessarily do such a thing at all, and it is perfectly possible to recognize the reality of innovation outside of Europe without denying that Europe did indeed forge ahead. This does not entail an 'approving Eurocentrism' so much as recognition of historical fact, despite some objections from 'anti-Eurocentric historians' (for instance, Blaut 1993: 5). Hobson (2004: 25, chs10 and 11) does recognize the need for some account of European exceptionalism, albeit by recourse to an over-estimation of the significance of colonial plunder and a rather romantic account of commercial (and social) relations in the East before European primacy (Duchesne 2006).

It should be stressed once again that this argument does not endorse a Eurocentric position or the idea that capitalism can be analysed on a purely 'national' basis. British capitalism benefited from the colonies, and once it emerged, it did not develop these colonies 'in its own image'. Rather, as we will see in later chapters, a more mature capitalism subordinated other parts of the world in ways which held back the latter's development, but which further facilitated development in the core. Indeed, this subordination may have occurred in Europe as well, but for successful resistance there (and in the US), which allowed for state policies that challenged British free trade imperialism. In other words, as later chapters demonstrate, capitalist cores and peripheries did emerge, but these were not a product of a timeless process of surplus extraction, in which cores under-developed peripheries in a zero sum game, as the theories discussed in this chapter contend.

Conclusion: Imperialism and Early Capitalist Development

This chapter has suggested that earlier theories of under-development, and newer accounts of 'global history', are problematic in that they over-estimate the colonial contribution to European capitalism. Capital flows and trade between core and periphery were limited, and many colonial *and colonizing* powers failed to develop along capitalist lines until much later. However, contrary to the claims of Blaut, recognizing these historical facts does not mean that one is forced to adopt the view that European capitalism was historically progressive, as it gradually promoted development elsewhere. Later chapters will challenge the view that imperialism was the pioneer of a progressive capitalism in the periphery. We can also recognize that while the colonial contribution did not cause capitalist development in the core, it was still a factor of some importance. Zero sum games of surplus extraction may exist, and may have existed throughout history, but it was only under capitalism that there was a massive expansion in the amount of wealth produced, and this was because of the emergence of capitalist social relations, and with them, a competitive market imperative.

The question that we now need to turn to is the impact of this competitive market imperative on other parts of the world. We therefore need to move our attention away from analysis of the colonial contribution to early capitalist development, and move to an analysis of the relationship between a more developed capitalism, and how this interacted with less developed parts of the world. This involves an analysis of both the unevenness of capital accumulation, and of the geo-politics of a developing international capitalism. It also involves an engagement with some of the most influential classical political economists, and with different theorists of late nineteenth century imperialism. These issues are addressed in the next two chapters.

3
Liberal Imperialism and Capitalist Expansion

The previous chapter examined the relationship between early capitalist development and empire with particular reference to mercantilism. By the late eighteenth century onwards, a number of important and influential figures began to make a strong case against empire, and the burdens that were said to be placed on Britain. As part of a wider campaign against colonialism, slavery and mercantilism, many classical political economists made the liberal case for free trade, which culminated in the 'cosmopolitan' thinking of Richard Cobden, and the abolition of the Corn Laws in 1846. This suggests that liberalism is incompatible with colonialism and empire, and early imperialism came to an end with the eventual defeat of mercantilism, although it was revived in the late nineteenth century (see next chapter).

Certainly it is true that classical political economy and economic liberalism challenged a particular kind of mercantile empire. But this chapter will also show that there was a considerable degree of ambivalence in attitudes towards empire within classical political economy, culminating in Wakefield's Colonial Reform Movement of the 1830s and 1840s. Perhaps more important, much of the case made against empire was based on mercantilist principles, and the ways in which different economic circumstances, and British economic hegemony, meant that the national interest demanded a different kind of colonial policy, best captured by the phrase 'free trade imperialism'. Furthermore, this was often combined with an ethical case for empire, in which liberals regarded themselves as the teachers of barbaric peoples, moving towards civilization under the tutelage of the morally superior colonizer. The chapter will also tentatively suggest that this

31

type of imperialism – based on free trade and liberal ethical principles – retains considerable relevance for understanding not only Britain's short-lived hegemony in the mid-nineteenth century, but also in understanding imperialism in the twenty-first.

First then, the chapter outlines the critique of mercantile empire made by many classical political economists, such as Smith and Ricardo, and how this influenced wider political debate. Second, the chapter examines the ambiguities towards empire within this tradition, both economic and ethical, through brief consideration of the economic differences between Smith and Ricardo, and wider debates associated with, among others, Burke, John Stuart Mill and Wakefield. Third, the chapter then shows how much of the case against mercantilism was based on an understanding of the utility of free trade to British economic dominance, examining an eighteenth century debate between Josiah Tucker and David Hume, and how this influenced wider thinking in the run up to the end of colonial protectionism. This section also briefly draws on nineteenth-century debates, as well as the important work of historians such as Gallagher, Robinson and Semmel, who are well known to historians but less commonly drawn on by people working in the fields of international relations and international political economy. Their work is important for the development of the notion of free trade imperialism, an approach that will be used in this and later chapters. Finally, the chapter concludes by suggesting – in contrast to some accounts of the nature of British imperialism in the nineteenth century – that free trade imperialism under British hegemony was the first developed capitalist imperialism, and this has implications for understanding and rethinking the classical imperialism of the late nineteenth century.

Classical Political Economy and the Critique of Empire

From around 1776 to 1830, classical political economy largely put forward a case against colonialism. This was linked to the promotion of free trade and a critique of mercantilism. In the section *Of Colonies* from his 1776 classic *An Inquiry into the Nature and Causes of the Wealth of Nations* (1981: 556–641), Adam Smith argued that mercantilism, based on a monopoly of trade between trading partners, benefited only the selfish merchants who engaged in the practice. Based on the principle that countries should not produce what they can buy more cheaply from overseas, Smith upheld the benefits of free trade and open competition, which would lead to specialization, a consequent full employment of resources, and increasing productivity and output as a result.

For Smith (1981: 607–13), colonialism was good insofar as it led to the increasing incorporation of different territories into an international trading order, but it was bad because it was distorted by the monopolistic trading practices associated with mercantilism. This led to the buying of expensive goods and the failure to utilize resources at full capacity, which could only be ensured via the specialization that would arise out of open competition. Smith also argued that wars in protection of empire were expensive and led to an undue burden being placed on the colonial power. This could be resolved either by giving up on empire altogether, or through economic and political union with Britain, whereby each province could have representatives at Westminster, and there could be a programme of tax harmonization across the 'provinces' of the empire. Although Smith recognized that the latter was probably an exercise in speculation, the proposal did envisage a free trade union between Britain and its colonies, something that would later come into effect, albeit without parliamentary representation and tax harmonization (Smith 1981: 620).

Jeremy Bentham was also critical of colonial practices and is often, rightly, regarded as one of the most explicit critics of empire (Pitts 2003). In 1792–3 he produced a small pamphlet called *Emancipate Your Colonies!* (Bentham n.d.), which was privately circulated at the time (but was not actually published until 1830). Bentham saw emancipation as part of a process that could reduce great power conflicts and promote international law, while at the same time fostering limitations on government intervention throughout the world. These two issues were closely connected, as colonialism led to bad government both at home and abroad, part of which were the monopolistic trading practices criticized by Smith. As a good liberal, Bentham regarded government intervention with suspicion, because it threatened individual liberty and economic efficiency. Excessive intervention applied not only at home, but also abroad, and colonialism was indicative of this wider problem of too much government. Bentham was therefore more explicit than Smith in openly calling for the end of colonialism, instructing colonial powers to 'give up your colonies – because you have no right to govern them, because they had rather not be governed by you, because you get nothing by governing them, because you can't keep them, because the experience of trying to keep them would be ruinous, because your constitution would suffer by your keeping them, because your principles forbid you keeping them, and because you would do good to all the world by parting with them' (Bentham n.d.: 47–8). Clearly then, Bentham was a passionate advocate of anti-colonial sentiments, though we will see in the next section that there was some backtracking from this view towards the end of his life.

David Ricardo's anti-colonial case was closely related to perhaps the most sophisticated case for free trade. In his 1819 work, *The Principles of Political Economy and Taxation* (1973), he argued that free trade would benefit Britain, for instance through importing cheaper goods such as cotton from the United States rather than the colonial West Indies. He therefore shared with Smith the view that 'by permitting every country freely to exchange the produce of its industry when and where it pleases, the best distribution of the labour of the world will be effected, and the greatest abundance of the necessaries and enjoyments will be secured' (Ricardo 1973: 227). Where Ricardo developed Smith's approach further was in his argument that free trade was mutually beneficial, even in cases where one country had an initial advantage in both goods being traded. This was the doctrine of comparative advantage, which suggested that specialization was still the best way to ensure efficient outcomes, both for individual countries and the international economy as a whole. Based on a two-sector, two-country model, Ricardo (1973: 82–7) argued that an individual country (A) can still end up with more of both goods by focusing on that good it produces most efficiently and importing the other good from the other country (B). B will export that good in which it has the lowest opportunity cost, and stop producing that good where it has a higher opportunity cost (it will import from A). The result will be an increase in output in both countries, and therefore an increase in world output. Comparative advantage – under certain conditions – envisages a 'win win' situation, in which all countries stop producing goods that they can import more cheaply, and therefore only specialize in producing (and exporting) those goods they can produce relatively most cheaply. For Ricardo then, foreign trade ensured an optimal allocation of resources through specialization, which would lead to mutual benefit through increased collective output, full employment, and low prices. Ricardo assumed that capital could be quickly re-allocated within a national territory, to take advantage of the optimal allocation of resources through specialization. At the same time, capital mobility was desirable at a national level, but not at an international level, as this would undermine the potential for specialization. Specialization through free trade and the exercise of comparative advantage was desirable then, but not the export of capital.

For Ricardo (1973: 213, 260–2), the latter would not occur so long as the former was allowed to take place, and this was because he accepted the principle of Say's Law. Associated with his contemporary, Jean-Baptiste Say (1997: 76), this 'law' suggested that savings are identical to investments, and that investment automatically created its own outlets, and thus 'each surplus product ... provides the means for purchasing another'. If this was the case, then there was no need for capital to be exported as it could always find an outlet for profitable investment at home. Acceptance – or otherwise – of this law was central to cases made for and against empire and imperialism, both in this era and later periods of capitalist imperialism. Indeed, there was some degree of difference between Smith and Ricardo on these issues, as we will see. For the moment, it is enough to emphasize that Ricardo suggested that the exercise of comparative advantage was sufficient to eradicate any incentive to export capital. This could, however, only occur so long as free trade policies were carried out, and therefore Ricardo (1973: 291) argued for the import of food from its cheapest source, which at the time led to his support for the repeal of the Corn Laws.

Though there were important differences, classical political economists were essentially critical of mercantilism and the forms of empire associated with monopoly trading practices. Colonialism and trade with the colonies was either distorted by restrictive trading practices, or constituted a burden on the colonial power, as it meant there was a need for military protection, and/or trade with the products of relatively expensive colonies. Colonialism thus had to be radically altered, or even abolished. On the face of it then, this was a relatively straightforward critique of empire. However, from the early nineteenth century, there developed a new liberal case for empire, and this is considered in the next section.

Liberalism and the Case for Empire

As we saw in the previous section, Bentham was perhaps the most explicit of advocates of colonial emancipation. He saw it as indicative of the problem of too much intervention. Related to this argument, he also accepted the argument that the colonies had no economic contribution to make to the colonial power and were, therefore, a burden on the latter (Winch 1965: 29). As we saw above, the rationale for this argument was that supply automatically created new demand, could thus be re-invested at home, and therefore there was no need to export capital. Bentham gradually began to shift his position however, and came to accept that savings and investment may not be identical, and that the former may be hoarded, and that changes in the quantity of money may influence production and investment levels. It therefore followed that if capital accumulation ran ahead of profitable investment opportunities, then the export of capital may be necessary. If this was the case, then colonies may be useful sources of surplus capital, and so colonialism may be economically beneficial to the colonial power. This association of imperialism with the export of surplus capital was to become a massive influence on later theories of imperialism, both non-Marxist (Hobson) and Marxist (Lenin), including in the post-1945 period (Kidron 1968; Baran and Sweezy 1966).

Bentham's anti-colonialism was thus compromised by a change in his understanding of capital accumulation, and the potential that colonies provided as absorbers of surplus capital. In a postscript to a later version of *Emancipate Your Colonies!*, Bentham reiterated his opposition to excessive government intervention, but also suggested that this could be accommodated within a pro-colonial context (Winch 1965: 38), and he even gave his support to Wakefield's project for colonizing South Australia near the end of his life in 1831.

In terms of the economics of empire, Winch (1965: 84) makes a convincing case that the source of dissent can be traced back to some subtle, but important, differences between Smith and Ricardo. The former is rightly regarded as a major influence on the latter, but still there was an important distinction in their respective interpretations of the accumulation of capital. Smith argued that profit was ultimately determined by the laws of supply and demand, and so as capital increases in a country, profits decline. In other words, the competition between capitals raised wages and undermined profits. Ricardo argued that this may apply in any single sector, but 'this could not happen to the economy as a whole; a fall in the price of all goods merely raises the value of money, leaving prices and costs unchanged in real terms' (Winch 1965: 84). Who was right is of less concern for the moment. What is important was that Smith may have theorized the possibility of extended accumulation through his account of savings and investment, thus paving the way for Say's Law, but his work also implies the possibility of the limits of profitable accumulation, as excess supply cannot be met by demand. Smith argued that this decline in profits could be overcome by the destruction of (excess/surplus) capital, and/or the creation of new markets, including in the colonies. In contrast, Ricardo argued that comparative advantage ensured full allocation of resources and thus supply and demand would balance.

Wakefield's Colonial Reform Movement essentially took Smith's view and developed a liberal – economic – case for empire. He argued that there was a strong economic case for empire, based on the shortage of profitable opportunities that existed in Britain. Colonialism provided a vent for surplus capital, based on the domestic tendency towards limited profitable opportunities and an oversupply of capital. In other words, it opened up new fields for profitable investment. Wakefield argued that free trade was in Britain's national interest, and that while a rigid colonialism was not an absolute necessity, it was certainly economically useful. His argument was that 'although it was not necessary to govern colonies in order to trade with them, it was necessary for the colonies to be brought into existence' (Winch 1965: 88). Canada, Australia and New Zealand should be awarded self-governing status, but as part of a free trade empire under British hegemony.

John Stuart Mill was influenced by Wakefield's economic case for empire, although he claimed to still uphold Say's Law. But perhaps as important, Mill developed a more explicitly cultural case for empire, derived in part from his father's writings on India. Like Wakefield, Mill supported the development of white settler colonies in what came to be known as the dominions, which should, eventually, be granted home rule on account of their civilized status. These colonies could provide an important source for new investment, and alleviate pressures on profitability at home. These pressures were said to be a result of an over-supply of capital (see above) or population pressures which led to wage increases and/or the use of less productive land to grow more food, which in the long run would also put pressure on profits. Colonization should therefore be financed in order to provide relief for domestic population pressures and open up new areas of high productivity. At the same time, Mill paid some attention to the colonies inhabited by 'barbarians', and argued that these could serve Britain's economic needs as well, both as markets for British products and as suppliers of agricultural goods. Crucially, he argued that this would not only benefit Britain, but also these territories, as they could grow through specialization and benefit from security, education and better governance. Liberty could only apply to mature adults or mature societies, and not to backward societies. Therefore, membership of the international society of states was conditional, and based on the idea that only some nations or cultures were capable of exercising reciprocity, conforming to international law, or exercising tolerance (Pitts 2007: 71–6; Sullivan 1983). A precursor to early twenty-first century advocacy of a 'cosmopolitan imperialism' (Cooper 2002; and see Chapter 8), Mill (1984: 121) suggested that '(t)o suppose that the same international customs, and the same rules of international morality, can obtain between one civilized nation and another, and between civilized nations and barbarians, is a grave error, and one which no statesman can fall into'. This was because 'the rules of ordinary international morality imply reciprocity. But barbarians will not reciprocate'. Moreover, 'nations which are still barbarous have not got beyond the period during which it is likely to be for their benefit that they should be conquered and held in subjection by foreigners' (Mill 1984: 121).

Mill therefore suggested that colonialism was for the good of backward peoples, as it potentially lifted them into a more developed stage on the path to civilization. He recognized that some colonies were 'of similar civilization to the ruling country', such as Australia and (in the past) America, and therefore capable of self government. But he also argued that others 'are still a great distance from that state' (Mill 1890: 131), and therefore not fit for representative government. Indeed, India required despotic rule as its people were not, yet, capable of being free. This included colonial rule which would educate the population so that they would be, in time, ready for representative government. This constituted a stark break from the views of Edmund Burke, who tended towards a conservative and romantic view of 'ancient India', and who therefore argued that Britain should be bound by universal moral obligations (Mantena 2007: 115).[1] In this shift, Mill followed the beliefs of his father, whose 1817 opus *History of British India* (1976) was nothing less than 'a full scale assault upon every claim made on behalf of the achievements of Indian arts, science, philosophy and government' (Mantena 2007: 116; also Makdisi

1998). James Mill had argued that the colonies were a drain on British resources, but also that:

> If we wish for the prolongation of an English government in India, which we do most sincerely, it is for the sake of the natives, not of England. India has never been anything but a burden; and any thing but a burden, we are afraid, it cannot be rendered. But this English government in India, with all its vices, is a blessing of unspeakable magnitude to the population of Hindustan. Even the utmost abuse of European power is better, we are persuaded, than the most temperate exercise of Oriental despotism. (Mill 1810: 371)

While both Mills were critical of colonial abuses of power, and believed that all human beings had rights, they also argued that only some individuals and civilizations had reached a stage of development where reason could be properly exercised and rights enjoyed (Mehta 1999; Pitts 2005; 2007). Mill linked this argument to the degree in which individuals in society operate according to utilitarian principles (Mill 1984: 121). Though far from a utilitarian thinker, John Locke had made an earlier case for the colonization of the Americas on the similar grounds that there was no ownership of property, and the exercise of reason had not yet developed in a backward society (Arneil 1994). Even where there was some private ownership of property, native Americans were not sufficiently industrious to make the best use of the land, and so a commercial colonization of improvement was justified (Locke 1980: ch.16; see also Wood 2002: 152–6; 2003: ch. 4). Justification for authoritarian blueprints would be rejected by later liberals, but the 'higher principles' associated with liberal thought would be put to new ends, not least those associated with humanitarian interventions designed to eliminate rogue states and promote liberal democracies, based on the notion that ethical considerations and ideal type liberal models should counteract political realities. We return to this theme in Chapter 8.

Finally, though he was the greatest critic of classical political economy and liberalism, Marx's views on colonialism and early imperialism were also ambiguous. Indeed, given that he was such a powerful critic, his views were perhaps even more ambiguous. We briefly saw in the previous chapter that he was acutely aware of the connections between New World slavery and British industrialization, even if he correctly rejected the view that the former simply caused the latter.

But on the other hand, there is a strong case to be made that Marx was guilty of promoting a diffusionist account of the spread of capitalism, in which capital progressively expanded its influence throughout the world and promoted the development of poorer territories in the process. The case can be made on three grounds. First, he exaggerated the stagnation of non-capitalist modes of production, and essentially made derogatory – and racist – remarks about peoples in these places. Marx and Engels dismissed 'non-historic' nations and gave their support to the annexation of these backward areas by the developed countries that were said to represent progress (Marx and Engels 1974: 81); for example, Engels supported the French conquest of Algeria and the US invasion of Mexico (cited in Larrain 1989: 57). Second, he upheld the idea that the transition to capitalism in England represents a model for other 'societies' to follow, so that 'the country that is more developed industrially only shows, to the less developed, the image of its own future' (Marx 1976: 91). Third, that in doing so, he supported the historic mission of colonialism to promote capitalist development in non-capitalist areas. Thus, Marx and Engels (1974: 82) argued that 'England has to fulfil a double mission in India: one destructive, the other regenerating – the annihilation of old Asiatic society, and the laying of the material foundations of Western society in Asia'.

On the other hand, while Marx consistently recognized that capitalism was a dynamic mode of production that developed the productive forces in historically progressive ways, its ('imperialist') expansion did not necessarily lead to progressive diffusion throughout the rest of the world. Indeed, the 'image of its own future' quote, above, was deleted from later editions of *Capital* (see Wada 1984), and Marx (1984: 124) explicitly argued that his account of the development of capitalism was 'expressly restricted to the countries of Western Europe'. He also backtracked on his support for British colonialism in India, arguing that it was an act of English vandalism that 'pushed the indigenous people not forward but backward' (cited in Larrain 1989: 49). Thus, in contrast to one recent argument that Marx moved away from a diffusionist account of global capitalism towards a romantic account of pre-capitalist societies (Stedman Jones 2008), a more compelling case can be made that Marx broke with his linear approach to social change because he correctly distinguished between the dynamism of capitalist production and the more uneven effects of the extension of the world market (Gulalp 1986; Kiely 1995).

Perhaps the best sense of the ambiguities in Marx's views can be seen by examining his famous 1848 speech on free trade. In this speech, Marx (1977: 269–70) argued that:

> If the free traders cannot understand how one nation can grow rich at the expense of another, we need not wonder, since these same gentlemen also refuse to understand how within one country one class can enrich itself at the expense of another.
>
> Do not imagine, gentlemen, that in criticizing freedom of trade we have the least intention of defending the system of protection.
>
> One may declare oneself an enemy of the constitutional regime without declaring oneself a friend of the ancient regime …
>
> [I]n general, the protective system of our day is conservative, while the free trade system is destructive. It breaks up old nationalities and pushes the antagonism of the proletariat and the bourgeoisie to the extreme point. In a word the free trade system hastens the social revolution. It is in this revolutionary sense alone, gentlemen, that I vote in favour of free trade.

On the face of it, this quote is consistent with the linear reading of Marx. As capitalism is progressive because it develops the productive forces, and creates a class that will lead the transition to socialism in the future, so too is free trade progressive because it is also part of the new capitalist order. Just as colonialism creates capitalism, so too does free trade. This may involve exploitation, but this is necessary at this particular stage in history. On the other hand, the quotation is not simply advocating free trade as a necessary part of the tragic unfolding of 'history'. Marx suggests that it is not only classes but countries that exploit each other, which opens up the possibility that an international division of labour is being created, which does not lead to the progressive diffusion of capitalism throughout the globe. Hence we arrive at a position closer to the outright pessimism concerning the effects of British imperialism in India, and the specificity of earlier transitions to capitalism. Indeed, the 1848 speech makes some highly suggestive comments concerning protectionism, which are very different from Marx's contention that protectionism represents an older, pre-capitalist order. He argues that:

> the protectionist system is nothing but a means of establishing large-scale industry in any given country, that is to say, of making it dependent on the world market, and from the moment that

dependence on the world market is established, there is already more or less dependence upon free trade. Besides this, the protective system helps to develop free competition within a country. Hence we see in countries where the bourgeoisie is beginning to make itself felt as a class, in Germany for example, it makes great efforts to obtain protective duties. They serve the bourgeoisie as weapons against feudalism and absolute government, as a means for the concentration of its own powers and for the realization of free trade within the same country. (Marx 1977: 269–70)

What is interesting about this part of the speech is that it suggests that protectionism may constitute a path to the development of capitalism in Germany, in contrast to the embrace of free trade which may lead to powerful countries effectively dominating developing capitalist countries like Germany.

As we have seen, the ambiguities in Marx's views are shared by liberals, who tended to see free trade as representing the universal interest, as against the specific interests of mercantilist empires. But at the same time, many liberals made the case for empire, on economic or cultural grounds, and they regarded such advocacy as consistent with their support for free trade. For free trade was regarded as being an intrinsic part of the policies promoted by civilized societies. We need to examine these supposed inconsistencies in more depth, and so move on to a closer examination of the relationship between liberalism and free trade on the one hand, and imperialism on the other.

Free Trade Imperialism

The economic case for empire among liberals tended to depend on whether or not a particular theorist believed that there was a tendency for a surplus or glut of capital to develop through the accumulation of capital. Those, like Wakefield, who believed there was a potential for the supply of capital to outstrip demand, believed that colonialism was a useful outlet for such capital surplus. Those, like Ricardo, who believed that free trade ensured specialization and the full utilization of resources, suggested that there was no need for the export of capital, and therefore no need for colonies that could be used to dispose of surplus capital.

But there was a further argument made concerning free trade, which simultaneously supported the seemingly incompatible contentions that colonies were an unnecessary expense on the one hand, and that colonization was necessary to overcome a surplus of capital at home on the other. Colonies could be useful as a vent for surplus, but could also be prohibitively expensive, and this would depend on specific circumstances. What was more important was the way in which free trade represented Britain's national interest. Although this argument reached its peak in the debates over the repeal of the Corn Laws in the 1840s, the debate stretched back at least a hundred years. In 1752, David Hume established a case for free trade which suggested that it would lead to a transfer of wealth from rich to poor countries. He argued that money was a mere facilitator of exchange, which moves from one place to another based on the demand for gold. A fall in the money supply in one location would lead to cheaper prices for the goods produced there. This in turn would lead to an increase in exports, as consumers would demand these cheap goods. The payments for these goods would flood back into the country which had previously experienced a fall in the money supply, which would eventually lead to the restoration of former wage and price levels.

This theory was in many respects an early precursor of Ricardo's theory of comparative advantage and an internationalized version of Say's Law, as well as later twentieth-century theories which suggested a tendency towards equilibrium in international trade. Like these later theories, it was intended to challenge mercantilist theories, specifically related to the movement of gold. This view was challenged however, by a contemporary of Hume's, the Dean of Gloucester, Josiah Tucker. He made the challenge from a perspective which was essentially compatible with free trade critiques of mercantilism, but which drew very different implications from other classical political economists. According to Semmel (1970: 15), Tucker was 'both free trade and economic nationalist, a prophetic combination'. Tucker rejected Hume's arguments that equilibrium would eventually emerge in a situation of free trade, and argued that this ignored very different levels and stages of production between trading nations. Free trade therefore served the interests of already powerful nations, 'as the richer Country hath acquired its superior Wealth by a general Application, and long Habits of Industry, it is therefore in actual Possession of an established Trade and Credit ... a great Variety of the best Tools and Implements in the various kinds of Manufactures ...

good Roads, Canals, and other artificial communications; good Pilots and trained sailors ... whereas the poor Country has, for the most part, all these Things to seek after and procure' (quoted in Semmel 1970: 16). The argument here is extraordinarily prophetic, for Tucker is basically alluding to certain competitive advantages enjoyed by early developers, based on what later came to be called agglomeration tendencies, economies of scale, technological spin-offs, technological know how, and more developed infrastructure. Tucker even envisaged a case to be made for 'technical assistance' to backward territories and nations, in part to ensure a market for the products of the goods produced by the more developed nations, an argument which predates the debates on aid, the new international economic order, and the Brandt reports by two hundred years, as well as adding a further dimension to the debate on surplus capital. Within this system then, free trade favoured the powerful, and although some gains could be made for the poorer countries, these would be slower and at a lower level than the gains made for the former.

The implications of this argument were clear. The restrictive practices of mercantile colonialism constituted an unnecessary expense in terms of military protection for, and high prices from, the colonies. This was close to Smith, Ricardo and Bentham, but Tucker was more explicit as to why this favoured Britain's national interest. In contrast to the arguments of Edmund Burke in the 1770s, Tucker argued that trade restraints were of no use to Britain and that Britain should buy cheap, from a position of productive superiority. In this way, 'Tucker's mercantilist objectives led to his denunciation of the colonial system of mercantilism' (Semmel 1970: 19).

While Tucker saw that free trade represented Britain's interests more effectively than the restrictions of mercantilism, he also recognized that poorer countries 'have it in their power to load the manufactures of the rich country entering their territories, with such high duties as shall turn the scale in favour of their won manufactures, or of the manufactures of some other nation, whose progress in trade they have less cause to fear or envy' (cited in Semmel 1970: 18).

The recognition of this possibility was shared by some of the anti-colonial intellectuals involved in the American war of independence, particularly Alexander Hamilton, who argued in his 1791 *Report on the Subject of Manufactures* (2007) that manufacturing should be fostered through protectionist policies, so that a more advanced division of labour, more specialist machinery and technical spin-offs, and export dependence on agriculture could be avoided. Certainly, under British rule, the US was not allowed to promote tariffs aimed at protecting domestic industry, and could not export goods which may compete with Britain. At the same time raw material production of goods essential to British industries were subsidized. While Thomas Jefferson accepted this division of labour in the post-independence period, it was Hamilton's proposal that gradually became accepted policy, even if official rhetoric suggested otherwise. In the 1812 war with Britain, Congress immediately doubled average tariffs from 12.5 to 25 per cent, and by 1820 they had risen to 40 per cent (Chang 2007: 51). They remained high throughout the nineteenth century, and were a major factor in the civil war, as southern states supported free trade against the protectionist North. Following the example of influential Whig Senator Henry Clay, Abraham Lincoln played a crucial role in forging an alliance between the industrial North and the new West, successfully combining the ideas of modernization through industrialization and westward expansion (Chang 2007: 52–3). Indeed, contrary to the arguments of contemporary advocates of neo-liberal globalization (Bhagwati 2004), the US remained a highly protectionist economy right up until the post-1945 period (Chang 2007: ch.2).

Hamilton's arguments were further developed by Frederick List (1966), particularly in his 1844 work, *The National System of Political Economy*. It was in this work that List made perhaps the most powerful case for protection from foreign competition, in order to develop a manufacturing base and the advantages that this would bring. Like Hamilton, he argued that these were associated with increasing returns, based on technological development, scale economies, and increases in labour productivity. Protectionism was therefore required so that these economic advantages could be developed; in a situation of free trade, industry had no chance of developing as it would be eroded by competition from cheaper imports produced by established overseas (British) producers. List (1966: 79) thus argued that:

A country like England which is far in advance of all its competitors cannot better maintain and extend its manufacturing and commercial industry that by trade as free as possible from all restrictions. For such a country, the cosmopolitan and the national principal are one and the same thing. This explains the fervour with which the most enlightened economists of England regard free trade, and the reluctance of the wise and prudent of other countries to adopt this principle in the actual state of the world.

The 'wise and prudent' included the US President from 1868–76, Ulysses Grant, who similarly argued that:

For centuries England has relied on protection, has carried it to extremes and has obtained satisfactory results from it. There is no doubt that it is to this system that it owes its present strength. After two centuries, England has found it convenient to adopt free trade because it thinks that protection can no longer offer it anything. Very well then, Gentleman, my knowledge of our country leads me to believe that within two hundred years, when America has gotten out of protection all that it can offer, it to will adopt free trade. (Cited in Chang 2006: 287)

List and the work of national political economists were largely dismissed in Britain. By the 1840s, Richard Cobden had emerged as the most articulate advocate of free trade. His advocacy was based on a commitment to cosmopolitanism, whereby commerce between nations would replace conflict, and so stimulate peace between nations. Cobden's case was often presented in quasi-religious terms, which suggested that free trade means 'that you take the article which you have the greatest in abundance, and with it obtain from others the means of enjoying the fullest abundance of earth's goods, and doing so carrying out to the fullest extent the Christian doctrine of "Do ye to all men as ye would they should do unto you"' (quoted in Semmel 1970: 162). Cobden's advocacy in the 1840s was based on the idea that free trade, and liberalism in general, was in the interests of every nation. Specialization would provide wealth and prosperity for all, and would undermine the rationale for both war and empire (Cobden 1903).

However, in the context of the political realities of Britain in 1845–6, and particularly the repeal of the Corn Laws, the case for free trade was made on much more pragmatic grounds. Indeed, following on from the argument already made, the case was essentially made on the neo-mercantilist grounds that this was the best way of promoting Britain's national interest – a position with which List would ironically agree, but which of course led him to make the case for protection for those trading with the workshop of the world. The Anti-Corn

Law League aimed to win support from the working class, but their case was undermined by the organization's opposition to factory reform. It was also sometimes undermined by the argument that the import of cheap corn could facilitate wage cuts as the price of basic food declined and so workers required less purchasing power. The League gradually offered an alternative perspective to this pessimistic scenario, arguing that British industry needs foreign markets, and the best way to guarantee such markets was through free trade. If foreign territories producing agricultural goods did not have access to British markets, then they would have to switch to industrial production, which could threaten British industrial competitiveness and therefore jobs. The Northern free trade newspaper *Struggle* argued that 'While *Whigs* and *Tories* are contending for power, *Foreigners* are stealing our trade – the *hearts* and *vitals* of our country' (quoted in Semmel 1970: 166). The paper even envisaged the relocation of manufacturing capital from Britain to foreign territories, an argument that has become far more prominent in the context of the 'globalization of production' in the late twentieth century, as we will see in Chapter 7. In other words, '[i]t was not to be the vision of a cosmopolitan world economy of Cobden's dream, but rather that of preserving an industrial predominance … which helped to move Peel to action in 1845 and 1846' (Semmel 1970: 149). In the debate over the repeal of the Corn Laws in 1846, it was argued that free trade was the method through which 'foreign nations would become valuable Colonies to us, without imposing on us the responsibility of governing them' (cited in Semmel 1970: 8).

Britain briefly convinced other European countries that free trade represented their interests. Between 1861 and 1866, almost all European countries entered into what became known as the network of 'Cobden treaties', named after Britain's foremost advocate of free trade (Bairoch 1993: 22–4). In the decade of the 1860s, almost sixty treaties were negotiated, 'embracing most of Western Europe, and creating the nearest Europe got to a single market before the 1950s, possibly the 1990s' (Howe 2007: 34). Indeed, it is not an exaggeration to say that intellectual discussion in that decade, with its focus on 'the international', repeated almost every argument made in the decade of globalization in the 1990s (Howe 2007).

However, again in contrast to Cobden's vision, by the late 1870s and early 1880s (and earlier in the US), there was a marked shift back towards protectionism. Indeed, as the next chapter will show, it was the 1860s and not the period from 1880 to 1913, that was really the first era of 'globalization' (Howe 2007). However, like the 1990s, the reality of the 1840s to 1860s was not one that conformed to the wishful thinking of its proponents. The policy of promoting free trade is most infamously associated with the unequal treaties of the nineteenth century. Facing a trade deficit with China due to its increased tea consumption, Britain attempted to export opium produced in India to a potentially large Chinese market. This was illegal to sell in China, and when an illicit cargo of opium was seized in 1841, Britain declared war on China. China's defeat and the signing of the Treaty of Nanking which followed meant that China could no longer set its own tariffs and had to promote free trade policies, including in narcotics imports. Hong Kong was also leased to Britain through this treaty. Thus, 'the practitioners of free trade during this period were mostly weaker countries that had been forced into, rather than had voluntarily adopted, it as a result of colonial rule, or 'unequal treaties' (like the Nanking Treaty), which, among other things, deprived them of the right to set tariffs and imposed externally determined low, flat rate tariffs (3–5%) on them' (Chang 2007: 24). As we will see in Chapter 7, tariff reduction usually takes place today through more subtle means, such as WTO regulation (although some military adventures have also tried to impose rapid trade liberalization), but its effects in terms of subordinating some economies is quite similar.

The argument being made here then, is that free trade represented the interests of already powerful states, and often the case for free trade was made in a blatantly instrumental fashion. However, we should not reduce the idea that free trade was good for all to the vested interests of a few powerful capitalists, no matter how true that happened to be. Liberal ideology did not only reflect the interests of capital, but was also important in attempting to *construct* liberal individuals and nations beyond Britain. As we have already seen, for the Mills this could be achieved through illiberal means, and this reflects a broader tension in liberal thought which we will re-visit in Chapter 8. Parekh suggests that:

> Liberals do believe in equal respect for all human beings, but they find it difficult to accord equal respect to those who do not value autonomy, individuality, self-determination, choice, secularism, ambition, competition and the pursuit of wealth. In the liberal

view, such men and women are 'failing' to use their 'truly' human capacities, to live up to the 'norms' of their human 'dignity' or 'status', and are thus not 'earning' their right to liberal respect. (1995: 97)

As we will see in Chapters 8 and 10, this tension in liberal thought has been particularly visible in the early twenty-first century, and can lead to a form of disciplinary power embodied in the idea that – rational – liberal democracies do not go to war with each other. James Mill (1810: 372) and John Stuart Mill (above) both argued that rational states should not normally intervene in each others affairs, but also that such states could intervene in backward societies for the good of the latter. This is not to say, contrary to some post-colonial critiques of liberal imperialism (Mehta 1999), that empire and imperialism can simply be 'read off' from liberal ideology. Liberalism is too diverse to be castigated in this way. However, what is true is that liberal ideas came to be compatible with a particular account of empire, and these were first apparent in the period from the 1840s to the 1870s (Howe 1999; 2007; Bell 2006).

More generally, the discussion in this section suggests a very different interpretation of the mid-nineteenth century than that usually associated with debates over the question of imperialism. Ironically, the orthodox reading is one generally shared by liberals and Marxists alike, and it is one that suggests that the end of mercantilist empires paved the way for an anti-imperialist era, which was only then eroded by the imperialism associated with monopoly capitalism from the 1880s. This chapter has suggested that in fact the whole of the nineteenth century was an era of imperialism, albeit one which changed after the end of the mercantilist era. The British Empire was a liberal empire and indeed I will suggest that this remained true into the twentieth century. However, unlike apologies for empire, my argument is that this liberal empire was one that was based on the exercise of domination, both economic and cultural.

This has enormous implications for understanding the nature of US imperialism after 1945, as we will see, but first we need to develop the argument further. To do this, we need to briefly examine the influential arguments of Gallagher and Robinson (1953), concerning the imperialism of free trade. They start their argument by pointing out that in the so-called anti-colonial mid-century, there was considerable territorial expansion:

Between 1841 and 1851 Great Britain occupied or annexed New Zealand, the Gold Coast, Labuan, Natal, the Punjab, Sind and Hong Kong. In the next twenty years British control was asserted over Berar, Oudh, Lower Burma and Kowloon, over Lagos and the neighbourhood of Sierra Leone, over Basutoland, Griqualand and the Transvaal: and new colonies were established in Queensland and British Colombia. (Gallagher and Robinson 1953: 2–3)

Their point is not simply that colonial annexation continued, important as this was. It was that Britain employed a number of strategies designed to uphold its dominance. Most common were the establishment of free trade and friendly treaties, in (among others) Persia (1836, 1837), Turkey (1838, 1861) and Japan (1858), as well as China. Gallagher and Robinson (1953: 11) therefore rightly conclude that '(f)ar from being an era of "indifference", the mid-Victorian years were the decisive stage in the history of British expansion overseas, in that the combination of commercial penetration and political influence allowed the United Kingdom to command those economies which could be made to fit best into her own'. Ultimately this made an imperialism of free trade based on 'trade with informal control if possible, trade with rule when necessary' (Gallagher and Robinson 1953: 13). In effect, this theory argues that British imperialism in the nineteenth century 'was not so much a consciously planned operation as a spontaneous process resulting from the exuberance of Britain's economic strength' (Mommsen 1981: 90). This view parallels the argument that the early development of capitalism in England, and then Britain, was less consciously directed than later European capitalisms, the latter of which developed at least partly in response to the geo-political and economic threat from the by then already established British capitalism (Wood 1991). This is not an argument that suggests that the British state did not play an interventionist role – there were high degrees of intervention designed to foster industry, markets, credit and so on (Corrigan and Sayer 1985). In other words, the state promoted a formal separation of 'economy' and 'polity', and this was less clear cut in cases of later European capitalisms, which drew on the legacy of highly centralized absolutist states in order to develop more corporate forms of capitalism (Wood 2003: 119–20; and, see next chapter). These more statist forms of capitalism were accompanied by more formal and more protectionist colonial policies in the late nineteenth century, in contrast to the more openly free trade policies of British imperialism. Free trade imperialism thus reflected Britain's early capitalist development; it was less a matter of British capitalism's backwardness, but rather reflected its *maturity*.

A number of objections have been made to what has come to be known as the 'Robinson–Gallagher' thesis. McDonagh (1962) questions the view that the commitment to free trade can be imperialist, particularly given Richard Cobden's strong anti-imperialist beliefs, while Platt (1968) argues that state officials in Britain were often reluctant imperialists, especially in Latin America. These criticisms certainly have some validity but how relevant they are is another matter. What is very useful about the concept of free trade imperialism is that it demonstrates how more developed capitalist countries can exercise power over less developed ones, largely through 'economic relations' (although these are always backed by state regulation). This is important for understanding late nineteenth-century imperialism and the rise of inter-imperialist rivalries, as well as the emergence of an international division of labour that most benefited 'developed countries'. As we will see, it is also important in understanding informal imperialism in the context of US 'open door' hegemony in the twentieth and twenty first centuries (Williams 1972: LaFeber 1963).

Where the idea of free trade imperialism is less useful is that 'it does not answer the question of where to draw the line between imperialism properly so called and market relationships between countries of different economic potential' (Mommsen 1981: 92–3). The theory is couched at such a level of generality that it cannot account for specific forms of intervention such as colonial annexation or military intervention in the twenty-first century. Many theories of imperialism are guilty of 'reading off' specific military imperialist acts from a general, usually economic theory. As we have seen above, also important are the ideas associated with imperialism, and these should not be reduced to crude ideological justifications for economic and/or political interests. Moreover, the theory of free trade imperialism remains a vital resource for understanding economic imperialism, or what Colas (2007) calls 'empire as market', and particularly imperialism in terms of its effects on the peripheries and semi-peripheries of global capitalism. This theory cannot however explain specific instances of say, military imperialism, though it may still form part of an overall explanation, one we return to in Chapter 8 in the context of the invasion of Iraq in 2003.

Conclusion: Advanced or Backward British Imperialism?

This chapter has examined classical political economy and liberal thought in relation to their conflicting attitudes to colonialism and empire. While the chapter has acknowledged that much of this thought was anti-colonial, it has also suggested that this was not necessarily incompatible with a liberal imperialism of free trade. Indeed, it was shown that much of the case for free trade was made on the grounds that it promoted Britain's national interest.

Although the term imperialism was not commonly used at the time, the argument made in this chapter has been that the first major capitalist nation was imperialist from the outset. This has implications for understanding later theories of imperialism addressed in the next chapter. It also undermines the idea that British capitalism – and imperialism – was somehow backward when compared to its European rivals. The next chapter will also address this issue, and indeed will argue that the European imperialisms of the late nineteenth century were a product of attempts to overcome their backwardness, and Britain's was the more developed form of capitalist imperialism. A few further comments would however be useful at this stage. A very influential counter-argument to what is being suggested here is that both the premature birth and incomplete development of British capitalism eventually led to British decline. British culture came to be dominated by commercial and financial, but not industrial, capitalism, and this reflected the aristocratic origins of English capitalism. Perry Anderson (1992) and Tom Nairn (1964) argue that the development of modern capitalism was hindered by the continuity of older aristocratic practices, including a pre-modern state and archaic culture. Britain was thus ill-equipped to deal with the rise of competitors once capitalism took hold in Europe. For Anderson and Nairn – and as we will see in the next chapter, Cain and Hopkins (1993) – British imperialism reflected the incomplete nature of British capitalism.

The full implications of this thesis are not fully drawn out by Anderson or Nairn. At times the argument appears to be that the 'peculiarities of the English' (Thompson 1965) are unique in that they do not conform to a fully realized capitalist model. But Anderson (1992: 190–2) has also suggested that the British decline of the nineteenth century may be repeated with US decline in the late twentieth century. Chapter 9 examines the question of alleged US hegemonic decline, but as regards Britain, Wood (1991: 15) has convincingly suggested that 'English peculiarities' can be seen in a different light, so that 'the critical factor is not the persistence of the ancient regime so much as the absence of obstacles to the development of this early and unchallenged capitalism'. This approach rejects ahistorical models of capitalist development, and suggests that the defects that eventually undermined British hegemony were the very same factors that promoted capitalist development in England in the first place. As was argued in the last section above, free trade imperialism should be seen in this context. It reflected the fact that British capitalism – and its imperialism – was more *advanced* than its rivals. This led to a brief period of British hegemony, but this was short-lived and it came to be challenged in the late nineteenth century, as European states responded in new ways to British primacy, both at home and abroad. This is discussed in the context of the classical theories of imperialism in the next chapter.

4

Classical Imperialism, 1882–1945

This chapter focuses on the period that is usually described as the era of classical imperialism, from the 1880s to 1945. It is often described as the classical period because it was associated with imperialist world war, and a new wave of colonial annexation, as the European powers, Japan and the US formally colonized territories. Between 1876 and 1915, about a quarter of the globe was distributed or redistributed as colonies, mainly by Britain, France, Germany, Italy, the US, Japan and the Netherlands, and to a lesser extent Portugal (Hobsbawm 1987: 57–9). The chapter focuses on those theories and theorists – usually, but not always Marxist – which attempted to link these new developments to a new phase of capitalist expansion. The, sometimes conflicting, claims of Hobson, Lenin, Bukharin, Hilferding, Luxemburg, Trotsky and Kautsky will first be outlined. The chapter will then move on to re-examine the case for liberal imperialism, with specific reference to British imperialism, which, it will be suggested again, was different from other imperialisms at the time. The third section of the chapter will examine the claims of both the liberal advocates, and classical Marxist critics, of imperialism. Some specific arguments will be made concerning the two conflicting approaches, and it will be suggested that classical Marxist theories are more convincing than liberal apologies for imperialism. But, despite the utility of classical Marxist theories, the chapter will suggest that there are also some common fallacies that unite the liberal and Marxist positions. The third section thus provides not only a critique, but an alternative formulation of imperialism in the period between the 1880s and 1945, based on a more comprehensive understanding of the different kinds of imperialism in place at this time, and how European imperialisms were part of a process of early capitalist development that was in part a response to the more developed capitalist imperialism of Britain. This argument again rejects the idea that British imperialism was commercial rather than capitalist, and based on 'gentlemanly capitalism'. But it equally challenges the view that imperialism in this era was the highest stage of capitalism.

Classical Theories of Imperialism

As we saw in the previous chapter, Marx and Engels' statements concerning imperialism were ambiguous, and tended to fall between an apology based on the idea that imperialism was the pioneer of capitalism, and a more sophisticated critique based on the idea of an unequal international division of labour in which the already developed capitalist countries dominated, and the unlikelihood that the 'European' transition could be repeated elsewhere. In the early twentieth century, a number of Marxist writers developed a theory that they considered appropriate to a new period of capitalism, sometimes called monopoly or finance capitalism.

Before providing a brief exposition of the ideas of the leading theorists, some comments need to be made concerning the specificity of what was being theorized. Classical Marxists at the time were fully aware that imperialism pre-dated this era, and indeed pre-dated capitalism. This was not their main concern. Instead, the focus was on how a new era of imperialism, a general phenomenon, was linked to a new, specific period of capitalism (Kemp 1967). As Brewer (1990: 88–9) suggests, '[i]t is easy to misunderstand the classical Marxist theories of imperialism, since the very word has expanded and altered its meaning. Today, the word "imperialism" generally refers to the dominance of more developed over less developed countries. For the classical Marxists it meant, primarily, rivalry between major capitalist countries, rivalry expressed in conflict over territory, taking political and military as well as economic forms, and tending ultimately, to inter-imperialist war' Thus, to return to the discussion in Chapter 1, the main focus of classical Marxism was more on the causes and consequences of imperialism between the 'great powers', and less on the effects in the so-called periphery, though this was still considered.

Hobson

Hobson's famous work *Imperialism: A Study* (1988), first published in 1902, developed a hugely influential economic theory of imperialism. Although Hobson was not a Marxist, his analysis of 'the economic taproot of imperialism' (Hobson 1988: 71–93) was a major influence on Lenin. Hobson's basic argument was that monopoly meant the concentration of capital in fewer hands, and an increase in the amount of profit that is saved. As savings increased, so domestic investment opportunities become limited as excess savings produce deficient demand unless new investment outlets can be found (1988: 81). For Hobson (1988: 79), one such outlet is the export of capital to new territories: 'Imperialism was the natural product of the economic pressure of a sudden advance of capitalism which could not find occupation at home and needed foreign markets for goods and for investments' This in turn leads to pressure to annex territory in order to safeguard investment. Thus, as Mommsen (1981: 12) explains, for Hobson, 'the tremendous increase in British foreign investment, and the breakneck pace at which African and Asian colonies were acquired or enlarged after 1880, were directly linked to the relative economic stagnation and low standard of living of the working class in Britain itself'.

This close link between capital export and territorial acquisition was central to most of the Marxist theories of imperialism that followed Hobson. It was particularly central to an understanding of imperialism as a necessity for continued capital accumulation. Hobson on the other hand argued that imperialism was not a necessity, and was in fact bad for the dominant and dominated countries. It was not a necessity because the lack of investment opportunities due to demand deficiency at home could be overcome by social reform, and particularly income redistribution, which would remove excess saving and stop the need for capital export. Indeed, he argued that Britain's newly acquired colonies after 1870 were of little value to Britain as a whole (Hobson 1988: 34–40). It was also bad for colonizing countries as it encouraged ill-informed nationalism and imperialist rivalries (Hobson 1988: 113–39). Things were even worse for the colonies, and Hobson (1988: 327) argued that '[f]or Europe to rule Asia by force for purposes of gain, and to justify that rule by the pretence that she is civilizing Asia and raising her to a higher level of spiritual life, will be adjudged by history, perhaps, to be the crowning wrong and folly of imperialism'. The reason that imperialism occurred was because of specific vested interests in the metropolitan countries, such as the arms trade, armed forces and the export and shipping trade (Hobson 1988: 46–61). These specific interests did not represent anything like the national interest, however.

Hilferding

Hilferding's classic work *Finance Capital* (1981), was first published in 1910, though it was not published in English until 1981. It is probably the most sophisticated of all the classical Marxist works on imperialism, and most clearly – but also problematically – sees imperialism as a new period of capitalist development. He argued that imperialism in this era was linked to the growing concentration and centralization of capital, which in turn were closely related to the rise of limited liability, joint stock companies, and the merger of industrial and financial capital into what he called finance capital. Greater concentration and centralization meant that there was a greater need for increasing money for investment. For Hilferding (1981: 225):

> [a]n ever-increasing part of the capital of industry does not belong to the industrialists who use it. They are able to dispose over capital only through the banks, which represent the owners. On the other side, the banks have to invest an ever-increasing part of their capital in industry, and in this way they become to a greater and greater extent industrial capitalists. I call bank capital, that is, capital in money form which is actually transformed in this way into industrial capital, finance capital.

Hilferding suggested that this increased socialization of capital eroded domestic competition and could even lead to the end of economic crisis. But at the same time, it also gave rise to an expansion of capitalism beyond national borders, as the centralization and concentration of capital led to the need for more export markets, investment outlets and areas to extract raw materials (Hilferding 1981: 324). This in turn gave rise to a new era of intensified international competition (Hilferding 1981: 311–36). As Barone (1985: 23) states, '[c]ompetition among domestic rival firms becomes transformed in the international arena into competition between nation-states, each trying to preserve and extend the reaches of its own financial capital, its own bourgeoisie'.

This competition coincided with a new era of tariffs among the developed capitalist countries, as each of them tried to protect at home (through tariffs) and abroad (through colonialism) in order to avoid competition with the most advanced capitalist power, which was still Britain. For Hilferding (1981: 326), '[t]he policy of finance capital has three objectives: (1) to establish the largest possible economic territory; (2) to close this territory to foreign competition by a wall of protective tariffs, and consequently (3) to reserve it as an area of exploitation for the national monopolistic combinations'. In other words, Hilferding (1981: 310) clearly linked protectionism at home and colonialism abroad, suggesting that '[w]hat was once a defensive weapon of the weak has become an offensive weapon in the hands of the powerful'.

This is perhaps Hilferding's most telling insight, though it does come at the cost of the applicability of his view of finance capital to all capitalist powers, especially Britain, as we will see. This will be discussed further in the third section below, but what should be clear is the way in which Hilferding (1981: 325) associated territorial acquisition with a new era of monopoly, or finance, capital. He had little to say about the effects of this expansion in the colonies, but suggested that while this may give rise to the conditions for capitalist industrialization, it was also characterized by forcible expropriation of peasant landholders, forced labour, and racism (Hilferding 1981: 316–19). These observations were not fully developed, but as we have already seen, this was not the main focus of (most) Marxist theories of imperialism at the time.

Bukharin

Bukharin's *Imperialism and World Economy* (2003), was written around 1914–15. It was influenced by Hilferding and developed some of the themes in his work. Bukharin's main focus was on the dual processes of nationalization and internationalization of capital. With the growing centralization of capital, competition within nation-states was reduced, but at the same time intensified at an international level through the formation of 'state capitalist trusts' in the world market. For Bukharin (2003: 126):

> combines in industry and banking syndicates unite the entire 'national' production, which assumes the form of a company of

companies, thus becoming a state capitalist trust. Competition reaches the highest, the last conceivable state of development. It is now the competition of state capitalist trusts in the world market. Competition is reduced to a minimum within the boundaries of 'national' economies, only to flare up in colossal proportions, such as would not have been possible in any of the preceding historic epochs.

These state capitalist trusts were the product of the merger of industry and banking and the emergence of finance capital. Bukharin (2003: 109–10) argued that 'the development of world capitalism leads, on the one hand, to an internationalisation of the economic life and, on the other, to the levelling of economic differences – and to an infinitely greater degree, the same process of economic development intensifies the tendency to "nationalise" capitalist interests, to form narrow "national" groups armed to the teeth and ready to hurl themselves at one another any moment'. Following Hilferding, he argued that finance capital has an interest in territorial expansion, and this is the basis for a new era of imperialism.

Imperialism is thus the outcome of the emergence of finance capital. Again like Hilferding, Bukharin (2003: 127) relates this to the search for profitable outlets for capital, the search for raw materials for expanding industry, and the search for markets for the products of increasingly large industries: '(i)mperialist annexation is only a case of the general capitalist tendency towards centralisation of capital, a case of its centralisation at that maximum scale which corresponds to the competition of state capitalist trusts'. Central to these theories was the idea that inter-imperialist rivalries played an important part in colonial annexation and war (Bukharin 2003: 155–6), an argument also made forcefully by Lenin.

Lenin

Lenin's *Imperialism*, first published in 1916, was written during the First World War, and was scathing of those Marxists like Kautsky who argued that there was the possibility that capitalist powers could combine in an era of cooperation. For Lenin, like Bukharin, inter-imperialist competition was inevitable, and was central to explaining the outbreak of war. This new, and highest stage of capitalism, had given rise to a close linkage between economic, political and military competition, which had intensified at an international level and led to major conflict between imperialist powers, and ultimately war. This formed the basis of classical Marxist interpretations of imperialism: inevitable conflict between imperialist powers.

More specifically, imperialism had five features for Lenin (1977: 177–231): (i) the concentration of production and capital culminating in monopoly; (ii) the merging of bank and industrial capital leading to a new era of finance capital; (iii) the centrality of the significance of capital export; (iv) the formation of international monopolies which divided the world among themselves; (v) the completion of the territorial division of the world among the large capitalist powers.

Most of these features have been discussed above in relation to Bukharin and Hilferding, but more needs to be said concerning the third feature, the export of capital. Lenin (1977: 213) argued that capital in the developed countries had become 'over-ripe' for investment at home, with the result that 'capital cannot find a field for "profitable" investment'. What this meant is not altogether clear: Barratt-Brown (1970: 96) suggests that it meant that there was a falling rate of profit at home, while Brewer (1990: 119) suggests that Lenin is simply accepting Hobson's view that accumulation was slowing down because of low demand and under-consumption. This latter interpretation is probably the more convincing, not least because Lenin then adds his own 'revolutionary' interpretation to attack Hobson's 'reformist' solution to the problem. As we saw above, Hobson argued that the problem of under-consumption could be resolved through redistribution of income to increase the purchasing power of consumers at home. Lenin on the other hand argued that redistribution would not happen, as this would rely on capital behaving in a 'non-capitalist' way (Lenin 1977: 212). Therefore, contrary to Hobson's argument, capital export was inevitable.

For Lenin (1977: 212–13), this push factor was reinforced by the pull factors of high profits, low wages, scarce capital and low land prices. He also argued that capital export was associated with parasitism and decay among the capital exporting countries (Lenin 1977: 240–7), though he simultaneously suggested that colonial profits could lead to the buying off of some workers in the metropolitan countries, through the promotion of a labour aristocracy (Lenin 1977: 245–6). The argument concerning stagnation was close to Hobson who linked imperialism abroad to low living standards at home, but the latter concerning a labour aristocracy was in marked contrast to

Hobson's position. At the same time, Lenin also argued that capital export to new territories could promote capitalist development there (Lenin 1977: 214), though this was not the main concern of his theory. We will see however, in the next chapter that this did become a major focus of later theories of imperialism.

Luxemburg

Luxemburg's main work on imperialism, *The Accumulation of Capital* (1951) was first published in 1913, and had a slightly different focus from the other Marxist theories at the time. Luxemburg was principally concerned with the need for capital to realize surplus value; that is, to find buyers for the goods produced in capitalist society. Capitalism is characterized by expanded reproduction and so, while purchase of means of production and of consumption goods accounts for a proportion of goods consumed, there must be a third source as well. Otherwise, Luxemburg argues, expanded reproduction cannot take place. For Luxemburg this 'third buyer' is the continued existence of a market in the non-capitalist sphere, and this is connected to 'the most outstanding fact of our time: imperialism' (Luxemburg 1972: 60). In other words, capitalism requires non-capitalist social relations in order to sustain expanded reproduction and thus capital accumulation. Luxemburg thus has a theory of imperialism 'that explains the necessity of foreign expansion as a need for external markets within which to realize surplus value' (Barone 1985: 32).

However, capitalist expansion transforms non-capitalist societies into capitalist ones. This undermines the third market and for Luxemburg (1972: 60), 'the point where humanity only consists of capitalist and proletarians, further accumulation will become impossible'. This problematic argument is supplemented by some far more interesting discussion of the processes whereby non-capitalist modes are assimilated and eventually destroyed by the capitalist mode. In particular she outlines the process whereby political, military and economic imperialism lead to the establishment of petty commodity production in the periphery, which eventually culminates in the development of capitalist social relations, paving the way for the transition to capitalist industrialization. This focus on social relations within the periphery was an influence on later Marxist theories of imperialism, such as those associated with modes of production theory (Chapter 5) and Harvey's concept of accumulation by dispossession (Chapter 6).

Luxemburg's analysis of social relations in the periphery is an advance on other classical theories (with the exception of Trotsky), but her main argument is unconvincing. In particular, her theoretical 'proof' that expanded reproduction is impossible if capitalist social relations exist everywhere is incorrect. As Barone (1985: 32; also Brewer 1990: 63) suggests, Luxemburg 'treated the accumulation process as an instant in time rather than a process that unfolds through time'. The increased demand for capital and wage goods in a second phase of accumulation can absorb the excess product from the first phase, and so on in later rounds of accumulation. Capitalist production therefore expands its own market through the accumulation process (Tarbuck 1972: 30). It should be stressed that this point is not made to uphold Say's Law, as discussed in the last chapter, which argues that supply will always create its own demand. Rather, it is to argue that '(u)nderconsumption can exist, but as a periodic phenomenon rather than a permanent affliction of capitalism. By turning it into a permanent affliction … Luxemburg "proved" the impossibility of capitalism itself' (Barone 1985: 33). *Contra* Say's Law, supply does not always and everywhere automatically create its own demand, but *contra* Luxemburg, it is wrong to argue that it never does so.

Kautsky

Karl Kautsky's theory of imperialism has been much neglected, but in many respects it is a hugely impressive achievement. Like other classical theorists, he argued that the era of free trade had given way to a new stage of capitalism, which he also called imperialism. Implicit in this distinction though was some notion of free trade imperialism, which, he argued, was in the interests of industrial nations. He suggested that a 'state which remains agrarian decays politically and usually economically, too, and loses its autonomy in both respects' (Kautsky 1970: 42). Both western Europe and the eastern United States responded to British industrial dominance and support for free trade, and 'imposed protective tariffs against English free trade; and instead of the world division of labour between the English industrial workshop and the agricultural production of all other zones which was England's aim, they proposed that the great industrial states divide those zones of the world that still remained free, as long as the latter could not resist them. England reacted to this. This was the beginning of imperialism' (Kautsky 1970: 43). Kautsky also mentioned in passing that the colonies and semi-colonies were forced (or chose) to continue to produce agrarian goods, which meant that they would remain in the subordinate position that western Europe and the US were escaping from.

This account of imperialism is not so far removed from the classics. Indeed, it may even be an advance on those in that it implies a theory of free trade imperialism, the continued subordination of the periphery, and rivalry in the context of attempts to catch up with Britain. However, Kautsky went further, and this was where there was disagreement with Lenin and Bukharin. He questioned the view that imperialism was the highest stage of capitalism, and above all questioned the view that war was an inevitable outcome of relations between developed capitalist states (Patomaki 2008: 48–9). This argument is sometimes misunderstood – for instance Rees (2005: 5) conflates this view with the liberal peace thesis, which suggests that peace between liberal democratic states is *inevitable*. Kautsky, on the other hand, was arguing against 'inevitablist' positions, either that economic competition between states gave rise to military competition and war, or that relations between liberal states automatically gave rise to peace. Indeed, he could hardly argue that peace was inevitable given that war broke out in 1914, and he developed some of his theoretical positions after it had started (Kautsky 1970: 46).[1]

What Kautsky (1970: 44–5) argued was that '[t]here is no *economic* necessity for continuing the arms race after the World War, even from the standpoint of the capitalist class itself, with the exception of at most certain armaments interests. On the contrary, the capitalist economy is seriously threatened precisely by the contradictions between its states.' At some point in the future, there was a distinct possibility that capital and capitalist states would have to unite, not only because of the destructiveness of war, but because of the growth of national liberation movements in the periphery, and the working class in the core. Kautsky (1970: 46) therefore envisaged a next stage for capitalism, based on 'the translation of cartellization into foreign policy: a phase of *ultra-imperialism*'. This would be based on growing cooperation rather than conflict between capitalist states, 'a holy alliance of the imperialists' (Kautsky 1970: 46), who would agree on how the world should be divided.

Kautsky's views were treated with great hostility by Lenin (1977: 253–7), who tended to argue that such a holy alliance was impossible in the context of the tensions that arose out of the uneven development of international capitalism (Callinicos 2009a: 95; 2009b: 64–5). He also argued that there were only two choices, war or socialism. But it is interesting that Lenin also suggested that

> [t]here is no doubt that the development is going in the direction of a single world trust that will swallow up all enterprises and all states without exception. But the development in this direction is proceeding under such stress, with such a tempo, with such contradictions, conflicts and convulsions … that before a single world trust will be reached, before the respective national finance capitals will have formed a world union of 'ultra-imperialism', imperialism will inevitably explode, and capitalism will turn into its opposite. (2003: 13)

Lenin thus regarded ultra-imperialism as a possibility, but one that was irrelevant to the political tasks of the day, namely that of preparing for imminent world revolution. Given that world revolution is not on the agenda in the early twenty-first century, perhaps the broad claims made by Kautsky require more sympathetic treatment, not least by those claiming continued adherence to Lenin. While it is true that Lenin still saw such cooperation as unlikely in the context of the uneven development of global capitalism (Callinicos 2009b: 64–5), the question of whether such uneven development can be used to explain the existence of a multiple nation-state system based on rivalry and conflict is problematic, as we will see in Chapter 6.

In this light, it should again be stressed that Kautsky was *not* suggesting either inevitable war or inevitable peace, but merely the possibility of increased cooperation between developed capitalist powers. This did not occur in any sustained way until after 1945, and this will be considered in later chapters. The point of relevance here however is that any proper critique of Kautsky can only be made if his theory is regarded as one that talks about possibilities rather than inevitabilities. In this respect Bukharin's (2003: 144–53) critique is interesting and important. As Brewer (1990: 132) suggests, Bukharin's arguments rests on 'the assumption that national blocs of capital, each exploiting exclusive possession of a national economic territory, must remain the basic units between which any ultra-imperialist peace would be made'. At the same time however, Bukharin also identified a further tendency, in which 'an important motive for capital export is the desire to penetrate the protected markets of other nation states from within. Over a long period of time, this can lead to interpenetration of national capitals, with the same group of firms operating within each national economic territory. In this case, a struggle to enlarge one nation's territory at the expense of others becomes economically pointless' (Brewer 1990: 132). This is not an argument that inter-dependence (or even 'globalization') *will* give rise to peace between nation-states. Rather, it is an argument that, in an era where the interpenetration of capitals has replaced national blocs of capital, interaction between states is bound to change.

Kautsky's theory of ultra-imperialism is therefore one that allows more room for contingency than, say, Lenin's theory which identified certain tendencies as *inevitable necessities* (Halliday 2002: 82). The theory of ultra-imperialism is not useful as a historical explanation from the period from the late nineteenth century up until 1945, though Kautsky's account of imperialism is useful. It is also probably the case that Kautsky played insufficient attention to uneven development and the continued existence of competition, between both capitals and states. But the argument that such competition must be more significant than cooperation (between states at least), or that war is an inevitability, is unconvincing, and Kautsky suggests good reasons why this is the case. We return to consider his theory of ultra-imperialism in later chapters.

Trotsky

Trotsky's theory of uneven and combined development was initially an attempt to explain the 'peculiarities' of Russian development prior to the Bolshevik revolution. It was also an essential part of debates among Marxists over revolutionary strategy, and specifically why Russia could not have a bourgeois revolution in the way that stagist Marxists believed that it should. Instead Trotsky suggested that Russia was characterized by neither convergence with the more developed capitalist states, nor continued stagnation, but rather something that combined elements of both. This reflected Russia's integration into the world economy in such a way that some degree of capitalist industrialization occurred, but coincided with backward forms that were not destroyed by capitalist penetration. The result was an influx of foreign capital that, combined with a highly interventionist state, led to the development of a strong – if numerically small –

working class. This led Trotsky to argue that only the working class could lead revolution and therefore it was bound to take on a socialist character (see Lowy 1981).

Trotsky's theory therefore can be regarded as one that focuses on the effects of imperialism, and how this gave rise to neither diffusion nor stagnation, but rather a combination of the two. He argued that:

> From the universal law of unevenness thus derives another law which for want of a better name, we may call the law of combined development – by which we mean a drawing together of the different stages of the journey, a combining of separate steps, an amalgam of archaic with more contemporary forms. (Trotsky 1977: 27–8)

Trotsky increasingly, if sketchily, further developed this theory, both to an analysis of world history and of the ways in which capitalism intensified these processes. There was some degree of capitalist diffusion:

> In contrast to the economic systems that preceded it, capitalism inherently and constantly aims at economic expansion, at the penetration of new territories, the surmounting of economic differences, the conversion of self-sufficient provincial and national economies into a system of financial interrelationships. Thereby it brings about their *rapprochement* and equalizes the economic and cultural levels of the most progressive and the most backward countries. (Trotsky 1970: 18)

But there were also tendencies that hindered diffusion in any straightforward way:

> By drawing the countries economically closer to one another and levelling out their stages of development, capitalism, however, operates by methods of its own, that is to say, by anarchistic methods which constantly undermine its own work, set one country against another, and one branch of industry against another, developing some parts of world economy while hampering and throwing back the development of others. (Trotsky 1970: 19)

While much of this is merely suggestive, we will see that it is a theory that has been revived in recent years. It has been used to explain the coexistence of different modes of production within social formations (Chapter 5). But more specifically, it has been fruitfully used to focus on the setting of 'one branch of industry against another', and explain the continued existence of spatial domination and subordination arising from capital accumulation (Chapter 7). It has also been used, less convincingly, to explain the setting of 'one country against another' and thus the plurality of the international state system and persistence of geo-political conflict (Chapter 6).

Liberal Imperialism Revisited

One prominent argument made by many neo-liberal writers, but also by some maverick radicals who see globalization as a progressive force, suggests that the late nineteenth century was one in which greater global integration led to a tendency towards global convergence between countries. This progressive era of globalization was interrupted in the years 1914–45, as nation-states went to war and carried out disastrous policies that restricted integration, above all through international trade. The post-1945 era opened up new possibilities, although these were limited by continued protectionist policies such as import substitution industrialization in the developing world, and communism in the former second world. Since the 1970s and 1980s, and accompanied by appropriate institutional changes in the 1990s, we are now witnessing a return to the progressive possibilities of the late nineteenth and early twentieth centuries (Sachs and Warner 1997; Lindert and Williamson 2001; World Bank 2002; Desai 2002).

Thus, describing the period from 1870 to 1913, Lindert and Williamson (2001: 1) argue that 'globalization probably mitigated the steep rise in income gaps between nations. The nations that gained most from globalization are those poor ones that changed their policies to exploit it'. In fairness to Lindert and Williamson (2001: 17), they qualify their argument somewhat, and even suggest that the fact that capital tended to flow between rich countries, rather than from rich to poor countries, acted as an 'anti-convergence force', but their general conclusions are upbeat, suggesting that pre-1914 globalization 'looks like a force equalizing average incomes between participating countries' (Lindert and Williamson 2001: 18). These very general arguments are largely backed up by the specific – and somewhat more convincing – claim that there was some convergence between wages and per capita income in western Europe and the north Atlantic from around 1850 to 1914 (Lindert and Williamson 2001: 13).

These arguments have recently been supplemented by attempts to revive the idea of benevolent, liberal empire, and the idea that the US liberalism of the present represents a natural successor to the British liberalism of the past. Niall Ferguson has argued that from around 1850, Britain became an empire that championed the liberal idea of progress. Importantly, his case for empire is essentially based on the correct argument that Britain was different from the other empires in that it was committed to the liberal principle of free trade. Ferguson recognizes that before the Victorian empire, the mercantilist empire was essentially a self-interested 'empire of pirates', but argues that from around 1850 it became an empire that championed liberal idea of progress. He argues that from 1850 to the 1930s

[f]ree trade, free capital movements and free migration were fostered. Colonial governments balanced their budgets, kept tariffs low and maintained stable currencies. The rule of law was institutionalized. Administration was relatively free of corruption, especially at the top. Power was granted to representative assemblies only gradually once economic and social development had reached a level judged to be propitious. This policy 'mix' encouraged British investors to put a substantial portion of their capital in poor countries and to demand relatively low-risk premiums in return. (Ferguson 2003: 11)

Ferguson is certainly not unaware of the failings of liberal empire, but he essentially argues that it was (and is) a force for good, particularly for the poorest countries. It represents the best means of promoting political stability through liberal democracy and economic growth through free markets, albeit under the tutelage of a benevolent empire. Indeed, under 'Anglobalization', capital was more evenly dispersed across the globe than it is under contemporary globalization (Ferguson 2004: 186–93).

Ferguson's case for Empire is echoed by Deepak Lal (2004: 205–07), who argues that progressive empires – including nineteenth century British and twenty-first century American – provide the 'public good' of civil order, which is hugely beneficial to the world, particularly the poorest, as they benefit from an increasingly integrated global market. Lal (2004: 147) suggests that the liberal international order first developed under the British Empire 'was hugely beneficial for the world, particularly its poorest. It saw the integration for the first time of many countries in the Third World into a global economy and the first stirring of modern intensive growth.'

The liberal view of imperialism thus suggests that, in the hands of the British at least, it was a progressive force as it promoted open markets, free trade, and thus economic growth, not only for the colonizer but also the colonized.

Assessing Classical and Liberal Theories of Imperialism

This section provides an assessment of the theories discussed in the first two sections, and this is used to develop an alternative understanding of imperialism in this era. It should be clear that in many respects, the theories are diametrically opposed to each other. Most of the Marxist theories identified in the first section regarded imperialism as being the product of a new era of monopoly, finance capital, which was very different from the era of free trade, liberal capitalism. For Lenin, this was an era of a parasitic capitalism which reflected an era of decay and decline. It was also an era of intensified conflict between the imperialist powers, which had completed the task of dividing the world between them, but this very fact of completion meant that conflict gave rise to war.

On the other hand, liberal cases for imperialism, currently in vogue among a number of economists and historians, argued that the era of liberal capitalism, in Britain at least, had not been transcended. Instead, the British Empire, from around the 1850s onwards, promoted the principles of free trade, and this was good for its own development, and the development of backward regions, including colonies. This was less an era of a decaying, parasitic capitalism, and more one of substantial growth and progressive diffusion. Ironically of course, this analysis has echoes of Marx's support for free trade in the 1840s.

What are we to make of these two approaches to understanding imperialism? The rest of this chapter provides a critical analysis of both, first focusing on the liberal case for empire and the problems with this approach. It then moves on to the classical Marxist approach, particularly focusing on the export of capital, and the problems this provided for classical theories. It will be suggested that the direction of capital flows undermines classical theories, but also liberal cases for imperialism. Finally, an alternative understanding of capitalist imperialism is proposed, which suggests (along with liberals) that there were two different kinds of capitalist imperialism at this time, one associated with developing capitalist powers such as Germany, and one associated with the most developed capitalist power of the time, Britain. This interpretation is then used to challenge the liberal argument that British imperialism at least was a modernizing force. The argument that Britain was a backward capitalism, in this case characterized by commercial rather than capitalist imperialism, will also, once again, be challenged.

Liberal Imperialism

The liberal case for imperialism is based on the expansion of trade in this period and the fact that Britain remained committed to free trade policies. From 1870 to 1913, world trade grew at an annual average of 3.5 per cent (Mitchie and Kitson 1995: table 1.1; Bairoch and Kozul-Wright 1996). But the evidence for an open economy in the nineteenth century is unconvincing. It is true that Britain remained committed to free trade, and this fact does partially undermine the over-generalizations made by classical Marxists who identified imperialism as a new era of monopoly and protectionist capitalism, and strengthen the liberal argument concerning British specificity. On the other hand, the fact that other countries were protectionist in this era is significant in undermining the liberal case for empire, for the newly developing capitalist powers deliberately carried out protectionist policies, as they realized that free trade could not advance their aspiration to catch up with Britain – something that was not allowed to happen in the colonies. In 1913, average tariff rates were high in all the advanced capitalist countries except Britain, which had a free trade policy of open access and therefore zero tariff rates. In contrast, average tariffs on manufactured goods in Austria-Hungary were 18–20 per cent, France 20 per cent, Germany 13 per cent, Sweden 20–25 per cent, and the United States 44 per cent (Bairoch and Kozul-Wright 1996: 8). This last figure was reduced in October 1913 to 25 per cent, with the passing of the Underwood Tariff, and it is probably through this act that the United States acquired a reputation for having a liberal trade regime. However, average tariffs remained high and they increased once again in the 1920s, and by 1925 they averaged 37 per cent (Bairoch 1993: 40).

Given these levels of protection, the argument that the pre-1914 period was an early period of globalization – at least in the ways characterized by neo-liberals – is seriously mistaken. While it is true that there was some convergence among developed countries in the late nineteenth and early twentieth centuries, this only occurred among a few north-west European countries and the US, not the world as a whole. Indeed, this point is accepted by at least one of the most prominent advocates of the benefits of globalization, John Williamson (2002). Moreover, much of this convergence can be explained by migration from land-scarce Europe to land-abundant North America, rather than being the product of any simple causal link between openness and factor price convergence, as assumed by orthodox trade theory, and particularly the Heckscher-Ohlin interpretation of the theory of comparative advantage.[2]

Furthermore, in any case, as we have seen, the period from 1880 to 1913 was hardly one of increased openness, as northern Europe and the US protected their economies from import competition from established producers in Britain. Central to (European and US) capitalist development in this period then were protectionist policies designed to develop high productivity industries, with dynamic spin-offs within the domestic economy, and which can eventually compete against established producers in overseas markets (Chang 2002). These policies were not carried out in the colonies, and the increase in exports to the periphery, particularly after the onset of the industrial revolution, led to widespread de-industrialization. While Europe and the US protected themselves through imposing high tariffs on British imports, India was not allowed to pursue such a policy. When the colonial government in India imposed very low tariffs in 1859, Britain reciprocated. African countries, although starting from lower levels of industrialization, suffered a similar fate, as did the Middle East. Disraeli even commented that '[t]here has been free trade in Turkey and what has been produced? It has destroyed some of the finest manufactures of the world' (quoted in Bairoch 1993: 90). Thus, if we take levels of industrialization for Britain alone to be 100 by 1900, we can get some sense of the levels of de-industrialization in the periphery as a whole. In 1830, the comparable figure was for the periphery was 112; by 1860, it had declined to 83, which declined further to 60 by 1900. Though there was a small increase to 70 by 1913, this still represented a massive decline over the previous fifty years. At the same time, the figure for developed countries as a whole increased from 73 in 1830, to 143 in 1860, to 481 in 1900 and 863 by 1913 (Bairoch 1993: 91). From 1860 to 1914, this represented a decline in the developing world's share of world manufacturing production from over one-third to under a tenth (Kozul-Wright 2006: 116). It could be argued that while this view may help to explain the lack of industrialization in the colonies, it fails to do so in independent countries, such as those in Latin America. However, dominant classes in Latin America in the nineteenth century were not interested in promoting industrialization, but rather were happy to extract surplus produce and labour from dominated classes and import manufactured products from the industrialized capitalist countries. The lack of industrialization thus reflected the entrenched power of landowning classes, which was only partially challenged in the twentieth century, and remains an issue to this day (Cardoso 1972; Larrain 1989: 159–73). This may have meant that such countries were, as Lenin (1977: 230) argued, semi-peripheries, but this was not an issue of concern for those dominant classes in the region.

These points concerning limited industrial development and economic growth in the colonies and semi-colonies can further be expanded to the question of social development. Ferguson (2003: 216) accepts that the 'average Indian had not got much richer under British rule', and cites evidence that per capita income in India increased by just 14 per cent between 1757 and 1947, compared to 347 per cent for Britain. He also accepts that famines occurred in India under British rule, but argues that these were caused by environmental and not political factors (Ferguson 2004: 195).

The problem with this argument is that environment and politics cannot be separated in this way, as effective public action can reduce the effects of drought, and thus prevent famine (Sen 1981). The record of the British is far worse than the record in pre-colonial India (Davis 2001: ch.10), with estimated deaths from famines ranging from 6–8 million (1876–8) to 17–20 million (1899–2000). The British made things worse, first by implementing a system of colonial taxation of fixed rates, rather than the flexible rates of the pre-colonial system, which increased peasant vulnerability in times of drought. And second, once drought had occurred, the colonial administration rejected demands for famine relief in the form of lower taxes or lower food prices, in the belief that (in the words of Viceroy Lytton) such 'humanitarian hysterics' would discourage self-reliance (Davis 2001: 31). Lord Salisbury similarly denounced as a 'species of international communism' the idea 'that a rich Britain should consent to penalize her trade for the sake of a poor India' (Davis 2001: 33). These views ensured a policy in which tax rates remained the same and food surpluses were exported to Britain, rather than to areas of drought in India. The first British Famine Commission Report of 1880 contrasted the British approach to famine relief with that of Mughal India:

> The Emperor opened his treasury and granted money without stint. He gave every encouragement to the importation of corn and either sold it at reduced prices, or distributed it gratuitously amongst those who were too poor to pay. He also promptly acknowledged the necessity of remitting the rents of the cultivators and relieved them for the time being of other taxes. The vernacular chronicles of the period attribute the salvation of millions of lives and the preservation of many provinces to his strenuous exertions. (Cited in Davis 2001: 286)

In similar ways, nineteenth-century China was integrated into 'free trade' relations with Britain which served to increase the vulnerability of the poorer peasants, but without recourse to the coping mechanisms which characterized China before such contact (Davis 2001: 282–3). Of course, given the argument on diminishing returns discussed in Chapter 2, it could be argued that such famines were likely to happen anyway as the public action available in earlier centuries, when output continued to increase, was not available in the nineteenth century, when output was stagnant. But the justification for British colonialism was that development would save India and the colonies from famine, and it is clear that this was not only untrue, but also that Britain actually made things worse. Per capita incomes in the developing world grew very slowly in the colonial era, with an estimated increase from $174 in 1860 to $214 in 1950 (and only $192 in 1913), compared to an increase from $324 in 1860 to $662 in 1913 and $1,180 in 1950 in the metropolis (Bairoch 1993: 95). There was a sharp improvement in per capita income in the developing world in the post-colonial era, and we return to this in the next chapter. These figures clearly paint a very different picture from that of a progressive, modernizing imperialism.

More broadly, Ferguson explains away the dark side of British colonialism by recourse to the so-called sins of omission of colonialism (Ferguson 2004: 193–7). What this means is that the underperformance of some of the colonies 'lies not in British exploitation but rather in the insufficient scale of British interference' in those colonies (Ferguson 2004: 196) In other words, the poorer colonies suffered from insufficient colonialism, and not too much of it, an argument that has resonance in contemporary debates over globalization and American Empire.[3] But this is a tautology, which credits liberal imperialism with all the advances of the colonies and debits anti-colonialism with all that is bad in these same colonies. Liberal empire cannot lose in this argument – it is always liberal, except when it is insufficiently interventionist, so non-liberal outcomes must be explained by insufficient intervention. What this account cannot do is record the concrete history of the liberal *and* authoritarian nature of British colonialism, including the ways in which it hindered the diffusion of 'advanced' capitalism to the peripheries. The punitive taxation of the peasantry and forced labour regimes which characterized production in the colonies, was not only brutal, but also served to hinder a capitalist transition along European lines, and thus served to subordinate these territories in the emerging international division of labour (Nzula *et al.* 1979; Phillips 1987; Hochschild 2006; Marchal 2008; Bagchi 2009).

In practice then, colonial rule was highly ambiguous. In some territories, capitalist development was deliberately hindered and rural tribal rule was championed as a bulwark against what many colonial officials regarded as the dark side of modernity (Kiernan 1972; Mamdani 1996). In these cases, traditions were invented and tribal classifications became fixed in the minds of colonial officials who essentially championed those in the rural areas whom they considered to be noble savages, the last bastions against a selfish, urban modernity. This romanticism was not simply an accommodation to cultural differences, however. These constructed differences became fixed by colonial administration, and were often tied to racist ideas which became more prominent at the time. For instance, Lord Lugard (1965: 79), perhaps the most prominent of all colonial administrators in Africa, was contemptuous of what he called 'Europeanized Africans' in the towns, who differ in mental outlook and physique, and had lost their rural authenticity and developed ideas above the natural order of things. On the other hand, Lord Cromer in the Middle East believed more strongly that western rationalism was needed to improve the 'oriental mind' (see Said 1978), as part of a long-term process of modernization. However, even in this case, modernization was perceived as a process that could occur through integration into world markets alongside the development of small-scale agriculture where 'western rationalist' ideas could be promoted. Any notion that capitalist modernization could only occur through the promotion of protectionist industrial policies – as in Europe – was simply not considered. In both cases then, imperialist rule hindered capitalist development.

In terms of ideology, the nineteenth century saw the development of various theories of racial superiority, which facilitated and served to justify imperialist politics. Though by no means all imperialists accepted the argument, various racist theories emerged which argued that some 'races' were more advanced in terms of biological evolution than others, and that therefore some 'lower races' deserved to be subject to severe discipline. These kinds of arguments developed as the British empire became more coercive in response to resistance in places like India (1857) and Jamaica (1865), which was repelled by imperial repression (Brendon 2007: 146–9; Mantena 2007: 114, 121). By the 1880s, similar arguments were used in the context of new imperialist practices such as the scramble for Africa. This ideology of race and the division of the world into racial 'camps', had devastating consequences, not only for the colonies, but within Europe in the twentieth century. The Nazis' emphasis on race and empire was applied not only beyond, but within Europe, and this idea could be traced back to the thinking on race that became so influential in the nineteenth century (Cesaire 1955; Gilroy 2000; Mazower 2008).

Thus, it is true that, contrary to the claims of some post-colonial theorists (Mehta 1999), the British Empire did not simply flatten out pre-colonial social formations. As Sartori states, recognizing this:

> allows us to show how the empire served to deepen the social forms of 'backwardness' it simultaneously sought to reform; to show how liberalism's linkage to the global economic order of modern capitalism was fraught with perilous contradiction; to show how empire could be an institutional obstacle to the realization of liberal values as easily as (surely, on balance, more easily than) their vehicle; and ultimately to show how the liberal practices of exchange cannot be prophylatically disembedded from the larger, and contradictory, social processes within which they have

operated and continue to operate in the era of globalization. (2006: 642)

However, what Ferguson's argument implies is that these illiberal outcomes can never be the fault of liberal imperialism, because this is not what liberal imperialists *intended* to happen. Instead, the fault must lie with pre-colonial traditionalists who simply fail to recognize what is good for them.

This is an argument that we will re-visit in Chapters 8 and 10, specifically in the context of the Iraq war in 2003, and more generally through examination of liberal imperialism in the current global order. Briefly though, what is at issue here is that liberal imperialism in effect finds rationalization for its actions by simply talking about intentions, and if it comes up against political realities that lead to illiberal political actions (and ideologies), these can be justified on the grounds of good intentions. It is not liberal imperialism that is at fault but the political reality that it must confront. In this way liberal imperialism cannot lose and never has to say it is sorry (Runciman 2006). In effect, this is an argument we have already met, particularly in relation to John Stuart Mill. Imperialism is a civilizing mission, in which liberal colonial powers represent progress and the universal good. The British (and American) empires represent civilization, and therefore they must recognize their global responsibilities. At the same time, non-civilized people must recognize their cultural inferiority, and acquiesce to the superior powers, as part of a learning process in which they will eventually gain the potential for self-development in an unspecified future. If 'liberated' peoples cannot see that it is in their interests, then authoritarian actions and ideas on the part of imperialist powers become 'unfortunate necessities'. In this way, Ferguson's history of the nineteenth century becomes inextricably linked to his political project of liberal imperialism for the twenty first (see further Chapter 10).

Capital Export and the Causes of Imperialism

How then, does the classical Marxist approach fare? Its emphasis on protectionism at home and capital export and territorial acquisition abroad is more useful than the liberal case, although it does not apply to Britain, which remained committed to free trade. But the theories of Hobson, Bukharin and Lenin are found wanting in a number of respects, particularly concerning the issue of capital export. Both Lenin and Bukharin regarded imperialism – including the export of capital to the colonies and semi-colonies – as necessary for capital accumulation to continue, suggesting that it opened up new fields for surplus capital in search of new profits. Bukharin (2003: 45–6) was quite explicit that the direction of capital flows would increasingly be from the developed to the developing capitalist countries. He argued that the location of capital exports 'is, of course, indicated by the difference in the rate of profit (or the rate of interest): the more developed the country, the lower is the rate of profit, the greater is the "overproduction" of capital, and consequently the lower is the demand for capital and the stronger the expulsion process. Conversely, the higher the rate of profit, the lower the organic composition of capital, the greater is the demand for it and the stronger is the attraction.'

However, the relationship between capital export and the colonial and semi-colonial world was much more complex than this. In the case of Britain, the proportion of investment in the empire increased from 36 per cent from 1860–70 to 47 per cent by 1901–10 and then slightly declined to 46 per cent from 1911–13. However, the dominions and India (existing colonies) accounted for most of this investment. The proportion of total investment in Africa (excluding South Africa) stood at only 2.5 per cent in 1913. From 1900 to 1913, the US accounted for 20 per cent, Latin America around 22 per cent, and Europe 6 per cent of foreign investment. In terms of British exports, the empire accounted for 34 per cent from 1881 to 1990, 34 per cent (1901–10) and 36 per cent (1911–13), but again the dominions (18 per cent in 1911–13) and India (11.5 per cent in 1911–13) were far more important than Africa (2 per cent). On the eve of war, Europe (36 per cent), South America (12 per cent) and the US (9 per cent), were also more important (Barratt-Brown 1970: 110).

In the case of other imperialist powers, trade *between* these countries was more important than trade with the colonies. In 1913, 68 per cent of France's trade was with other 'northern' countries, while the figure for Germany was 53 per cent, the US 74 per cent, and other western European countries 70 per cent. As a whole, in the period from 1880 to 1938, only 17 per cent of total developed world exports went to the periphery, and of these, only half went to the colonies (Bairoch 1993: 72–3). Thus, only 9 per cent of total European exports went to the colonies. Given that at this time exports represented only

8–9 per cent of the GNP of developed world countries, exports to the periphery represented only 1.3 to 1.7 per cent and exports to the colonies only 0.6 to 0.9 per cent of the total volume of production of developed countries as a whole (Bairoch 1993: 72–3). This figure was higher for European developed countries, and higher still in the 'exceptional case' of Britain, but even then the figures remain quite low. For Britain, from 1800 to 1938, exports to the colonial and semi-colonial world represented about 40 per cent of its total exports, and its share of exports to GNP was around 12–13 per cent. Thus, even in the case of Britain, exports to the periphery represented only around 4–6 per cent of Britain's total production (Bairoch 1993: 73).

In terms of investment, Lenin (1977: 212–14) accepted that most French and German capital was invested in Europe and the US and not in their colonies, but he wrongly argued that the 'principle spheres of investment of British capital are its colonial possessions'. Moreover, his recognition of the realities of French and German investment undermined the theoretical claims Lenin made for over-ripe surplus capital in the metropolitan countries (Barratt-Brown 1974: ch.8). Indeed, most European foreign investment from 1880 to 1914 hardly fits the clichés of either surplus capital export or modernizing colonialism; rather, investors, often through financial intermediaries, tended to focus on low risk securities backed by real property, located mainly in the developed countries, the dominions, and a few richer Latin America economies (O'Brien 2006).

A related argument concerning the necessity of imperialism is the question of the relationship between raw material provision and industrialization in the core countries. A classic argument made by dependency and under-development theorists is that one form of surplus extraction from periphery to core was through the South providing cheap raw materials that were essential to the development of the core capitalist countries. Applied to the nineteenth and early twentieth centuries, this argument is unconvincing. The main source of energy in this period was coal, and in 1913, in the most industrialized European countries (Belgium, Germany, France, Switzerland, Sweden, Britain), their combined surplus of coal exceeded their consumption by 12 per cent. This was despite the fact that Sweden, Switzerland and France were net coal importers. Britain on the other hand accounted for 6 per cent of total global production, and 27 per cent of its national production was exported (Bairoch 1993: 59). The developed European countries were dependent on the import of oil, but in 1913 oil was a minor source of energy, its share of total energy supply in Europe accounting for less than 1 per cent of its consumption (Bairoch 1993: 61). Moreover, at this time the United States was the main oil producer. The switch to rapid dependence on oil, and reliance on exports from Third World exporters, only took place after the Second World War. In terms of minerals, iron ore was by far the most important metal produced before First World War. Expressed in weight, in 1913, it represented about 95 per cent of the total of metals produced. Most of this was produced by Europe, although there were small amounts exported from North Africa to Europe and Cuba to the US. Japan was much more dependent on iron imports, mainly from Australasian countries. Europe was more dependent on tin imports, 86 per cent of its consumption in 1913 coming from the developing world (Bairoch 1993: 64). But because iron was so central, only around 2 per cent of developed European countries' mineral consumption came from the Third World. There was some dependence on the import of certain textile fibres, such as jute and cotton, although in the latter case, most still came from the US.

Thus, on the eve of the First World War, and therefore at the height of classical imperialism, the developed world produced around 98 per cent of its metal ores, 80 per cent of its textile fibres, and over 100 per cent of its energy supplies (Bairoch 1993: 67–8). In value terms the figure was slightly lower (as the value of ores and textiles was higher than energy products), but it was still around 94–6 per cent (Bairoch 1993: 67–8). It is of course true that certain capitalists did benefit from the colonial encounter, and equally it is true that this encounter has a devastating impact on the colonies. Indeed, under-development occurred in the Third World precisely *because* Third World exports were (on the whole) not necessary for the developed world. While the consumption of Third World imports was not particularly high when measured against total consumption by the developed world, the dependence on these exports was crucial for the poorer countries, where primary goods accounted for 90 per cent of their exports, and in most countries almost 100 per cent of the raw materials produced were exported to the developed world (Bairoch 1993: 70). Similarly, the extraction of colonial tribute from India represented only a small addition to Britain's national wealth in the 1930s (around 3 per cent), but it also represented as much as one-tenth of India's national income (Barratt-Brown 1970: 175). However, these arguments are not the same thing as the contention of classical imperialist theories that colonial expansion was functionally necessary to continued capital accumulation, and that capital tended to move from capital rich to capital poor areas (Barratt-Brown 1972: 63).

Having said that, there is some question as to the extent to which classical Marxist theories of imperialism did argue along these lines. For example, the classics only briefly mentioned the scramble for Africa, and Etherington (1984: 135) contends that Lenin was less concerned with explaining how the world had been divided, and more 'to show the disastrous effects of competition between various blocs of capital upon a world *already divided up*'. This distinction is thus close to that outlined in Chapter 1, namely that of distinguishing between imperialism's effects, rather than its causes. In particular, Lenin was interested in the consequences of expansion for imperialist powers when there were so many already established colonies. Bukharin (2003: 89) also drew out the contradiction between the practice of state protection through tariffs and colonization, while simultaneously demanding the right to sell freely in other territories. It was this conflict that, for Lenin (1977: 254–7) and Bukharin (2003: 110), made war necessary. Although the argument that war was a necessity is unconvincing, Lenin and Bukharin's focus on inter-imperialist rivalries in this era retains considerable utility.

On the other hand, their argument concerning the close link between capital accumulation and capital export is far less convincing. Bukharin (2003: 174–5) argued that the colonies yielded 'a colossal income' which raised the incomes of 'European and American workers', and Lenin (1977: 213–14) argued that super-profits extracted from the periphery led to the development of a labour aristocracy in the core countries. Thus, whatever the status of the argument linking formal colonialism and capitalist expansion, both Lenin and Bukharin regarded the opening up of new fields for surplus capital, and the super-profits that were derived from them, as central to the continued accumulation of capital. It was this argument that influenced later Soviet Marxist theories of imperialism, as well as theories of under-development and dependency (discussed in Chapter 5). However, it was unconvincing, not least because Lenin himself demonstrated that most income derived from foreign investment came from other core capitalist countries.

The argument that capital export to the periphery was necessary to preserve a decaying capitalism in the developed economies is therefore wrong (Callinicos 2009b: 48–50). Most capital was invested in and most trade took place between developed countries, though this investment was generally not yet in manufacturing enterprises associated with multinational companies. The direction of trade and investment undermined the notion of surplus or over-ripe capital, and equally undermined the expectation that this surplus capital would develop the productive forces in the colonies and semi-colonies. It is this fallacy of capital export to the developing world that also lies at the heart of the liberal apology for empire, namely that capital was dispersing throughout the globe, and thereby developing the poorer countries.

Rather than capital failing to find profitable investment fields at home, and leaving the masses at 'semi starvation levels' as Lenin (1977: 212) contended, capital continued to accumulate at home as well as spreading abroad. This involved considerable levels of domestic accumulation, which undermines in part the central focus placed on capital export by classical theories of imperialism. It is therefore incorrect to suggest that this was an era based on 'production principally for export to foreign ruling groups or areas of new settlement abroad' (Halperin 2007: 552–3; also Halperin 1997; 2004). As we have seen, while there was capital export and (after 1893) a considerable expansion of world trade, this complimented, and was not at the expense of, accumulation in the imperialist countries. The implication that follows is that '[f]ar from being the highest stage of capitalism, what these early theorists were observing was (as is now obvious) a relatively early phase of capitalism' (Panitch and Gindin 2003: 6).

In fact, as Panitch and Gindin (2003: 7) imply, the picture was actually more complicated than that, and this is where we return to Gallagher and Robinson's thesis concerning free trade imperialism. What occurred in the late nineteenth century was a European imperialism based on protectionism at home and monopoly trading practices abroad, which coincided with a more established and developed capitalist imperialism, as practised by Britain from the mid-nineteenth century.[4] The former was a reaction to the latter, an attempt – indeed, one that was successful – to resist the dominance of Britain. Bernard Semmel puts the point nicely:

> What was actually happening was that the neo-Mercantilist imperialism of certain continental nations, marked by a revival of protection, development of techniques of dumping, etc., was challenging a 'cosmopolitan' British imperialism. A policy that sought

commercial monopoly was battling a policy whose objective was the securing of free and safe access to markets. In a word, an imperialism of annexation and war was opposing the old imperialism of economic penetration and establishment of informal political controls ... The cosmopolitan imperialism of the mid-nineteenth century was more appropriate to the time of British industrial hegemony, the neo-Mercantilist to the time of keen international competition, competition not only for political control of strategically placed lands in Africa or Asia but for potential markets and sites for investment. (1965: 220)

This distinction between two kinds of imperialism – of a mature capitalist British imperialism and a 'catching up' capitalist imperialism in Europe (and the US and Japan) – is discussed further below. First however, we need to further unpack how this distinction relates, if at all, to the idea that imperialism in this era had economic causes. Clearly much of the data cited above, which shows the limited utility of new colonies for capital accumulation in Europe, shows a high degree of scepticism concerning a causal role for the economy. This is where a number of non-Marxist theories of imperialism, stretching back to Schumpeter (and in some respects Hobson) need further consideration.

Schumpeter (1951: 83–130) argued that imperialism had no place under developed capitalism, and that it therefore had to be explained as a product of *atavism*, which he defined as the survival of political and social structures from a pre-modern age. War and aggressive foreign policies reflected the preservation of feudal structures. Schumpeter (1951: 118) contrasted these pre-modern structures to the internationalism of developed capitalism, which did not need imperialism. This was not so far removed from Hobson's critique of imperialism as being caused by specific vested interests, and indeed archaic political and social structures, rather than being (as in Lenin) a necessity of capitalist accumulation. At the same time, Schumpeter (1951: 118–28) also suggestively argued that a capitalism characterized by what he called monopoly – tariffs, cartels, monopoly prices and so on – could be associated with an aggressive capitalism, and could indeed lead to imperialist wars. This lesser known part of Schumpeter's work is not so far removed from that of Hilferding. Where Schumpeter differs is in seeing 'monopoly' capitalism as archaic, and could be replaced by a more pacific, free trade capitalism. This could be regarded as an early formulation of the liberal or democratic peace thesis, discussed in later chapters.

What is immediately problematic in terms of the economics of the argument is Schumpeter's discounting of the notion that imperialism could be associated with free trade. On the other hand, Schumpeter is using the concept of imperialism in a very specific way. He is essentially arguing that imperialism is associated with territorial acquisition, and this is not a necessity for capitalist expansion, unlike feudalism. Schumpeter's argument then is a challenging one, not least because of the limited economic interest that colonial powers had in their newly acquired territories after the 1880s. One Marxist response to this position, derived from Hilferding (and Kautsky) and already implied in the argument above, is that territorial acquisition by the new European powers was part of a protectionist strategy aimed largely against the established capitalist power, Britain, which responded with territorial acquisition designed to keep markets open. This is a useful argument but it does beg the question of why acquire new territories when they were of such limited economic value, an argument powerfully made in the writings of Fieldhouse (1973) and Cohen (1973)?

In the case of European colonial powers, the economic utility of the colonies may have been regarded as a long term goal, as indeed were the protectionist policies at home, which did not necessarily generate immediate benefits. Moreover, while it is true that capital export was not an imperative, it does not follow that there was no economic benefit at all from imperialism. Arguments that suggest a simple cost-benefit analysis of territorial acquisition miss the point that the 'ultimate economic logic of conquering worthless colonial real estate was to lock up unknown resources to protect world commodity prices and *guarantee returns on existing far flung colonial investments*' (Nowell 2002/3: 319). Each additional unit of investment effectively needed protection from potential competition generated by the rapid development of a new undiscovered zone by a rival imperialism.

This is a useful counter-argument, and one can accept it without suggesting that economic causes were the only important factors. But why should they be? Certainly the idea that inter-imperialist rivalries gave rise to intensified conflicts does not necessarily have to be linked to the functionality of capital export to accumulation, but rather the strategic interests of competing states. These of course were often tied to economic interests, such as Britain's determination to maintain routes to India, but they need not be. This suggests that the state needs to be given a far more central role in understanding 'classical imperialism', one that like imperialism itself needs to break with functionalism, even if there is recognition that the state performs certain functions that sustain accumulation. This issue is addressed further in Chapter 6.

These general points open the way for a greater degree of openness to understanding the specific causes of territorial acquisition in the nineteenth century. Important in this respect may have been the motives of specific imperialists, missionaries, or 'men on the spot', who often used their own initiative to expand, often in the name of restoring law and order and often in the face of suspicion at home. This argument suggests that there were 'peripheral causes' of imperialism/territorial expansion (Fieldhouse 1973: 460–3), and these tended to be contingent on particular circumstances and have quite specific outcomes. For Robinson and Gallagher (1961), these were linked to the possibility of nationalist revolt in Egypt, and the importance of Suez to the empire. This led the British to adopt a strategy of formal colonialism based on 'reconstructing collaboration from the inside' (Robinson 1986: 278). Whether or not this started or accelerated the scramble for Africa has been heavily debated by historians (Sanderson 1974), but it is certainly the case that it was part of a wider crisis of European relations, which included new strategies, forms of rule and annexation in the colonies (Fieldhouse 1961–2).

Where then does this leave more 'systemic' accounts of imperialism, such as those associated with classical Marxism? Undoubtedly, if imperialism is defined as territorial annexation, then there is no functional necessity for this to occur for capitalist accumulation to continue. This opens up a more flexible understanding of the causes of such annexation in the late nineteenth century, but it also opens up a more interesting accounting of the relationship between capitalism and imperialism. In the late nineteenth century, imperialism was indeed associated with inter-imperialist rivalries and deliberate state strategies designed to promote a process of catching up with Britain. Formal (territorial) colonialism at this time was a strategic choice by such states, but it was not a necessity for continued capital accumulation. In terms of the economic *effects* of imperialism in the periphery, as we have seen, it actually hindered capital accumulation there, precisely because it did not allow those policies that European powers employed in order to catch up and ultimately challenge Britain. This essentially brings us back to the theory of free trade imperialism, and the idea that Britain was the most developed capitalist power at the time.

Gentlemanly Capitalism Revisited

As the previous chapter briefly showed, the view that British capitalism was the most fully developed in the nineteenth century is not shared by all commentators. Albeit from somewhat different perspectives, Anderson (1992) Rubinstein (1987) and Ingham (1984) all hold the view that there was no real capitalist revolution in Britain, and instead identify the coexistence of 'pre-modern' institutions such as the Privy Council, monarchy and House of Lords, alongside commercial expansion. This view of the 'incompleteness' of British capitalism is more or less compatible with an interpretation of British imperialism, which regards it as one led by commercial transactions and not the needs of industrial capitalism. This is the basic argument of Cain and Hopkins' (1993) thesis that British imperialism was associated with 'gentlemanly capitalism', based on the dominance of commerce and finance, which had weak links with industry, and was said to derive from roots among the old pre-capitalist aristocracy. For Cain and Hopkins (1987: 10–11), the new imperialism arose 'neither in the "inner logic" of the development of industrial capitalism nor in the simple facts of mere acquisition of new possessions', but was 'an overseas manifestation of a reconstructed form of gentlemanly capitalism centred upon the City of London and the service economy of the home counties'. Similar views can be found in Hobson's focus on the specific interests involved in imperialism, and indeed Engels observation in 1889 concerning 'the political decline and abdication of the bourgeoisie' (cited in Anderson 1992: 138).

This theory usefully attempts to grasp what was specific about British, as opposed to European imperialisms. As we have seen, in terms of the colonies, it was undoubtedly the case that British imperialism was hardly modernizing. Part of the reason for this was the important role of merchant capital impacting and reinforcing pre-capitalist social relations, such as in West Africa (Kay 1975; Phillips 1987). It was also the case that unlike German capitalism for instance, British capitalism was characterized by far fewer direct links between industry and finance, as the discussion of Hilferding above makes clear. The question that arises from these observations though is whether these demonstrate the 'backwardness' of British imperialism, in which imperialist policy was dominated by 'the ethos of aristocracy' (Stokes 1960: 12).

The first point is that while it is true that British imperialism did not 'modernize' the colonies, at least in ways that would have promoted convergence with the metropoles, this was true of *all* imperialisms at the time. What is crucial here is to make the distinction between capitalism and imperialism. The former is based on the exploitation of wage labour as commodity production is generalized, thus giving rise to the competitive accumulation of capital and high rates of economic growth. Following the discussion in Chapter 1, imperialism can be described as a process 'whereby an international division of labour is created through the extension of the conditions of capitalist accumulation on a world scale' (Gulalp 1986: 139). The clear implication is that while capitalism is a progressive mode of production this 'does not necessarily exclude the possibility of imperialism causing underdevelopment' (Gulalp 1986: 139). The failure of imperialism to modernize the periphery did not reflect the existence of a retarded capitalism in Britain, then, so much as a deliberate strategy on the part of *all* colonizing powers to integrate colonies into the world market without promoting capitalist development (Cowen and Shenton 1996: ch.6). As we saw above, this took a variety of forms from the maintenance of rural social structures to integration into world markets (or both), but in none of these cases was capitalist accumulation developed to match European levels.

The second argument suggests that the new imperialism of the late nineteenth century did not make sense from the viewpoint of the imperialist powers, and in the case of Britain at least, was a major factor in British decline (O' Brien 1988; Gamble 1994). We have already discussed this view above, and emphasized the importance of rivalries between capitalist powers, which occurred in the context of different accumulation strategies, but were certainly not reducible to them. While the view that protectionism at home *necessarily* coincided with colonialism abroad is problematic, as Fieldhouse (1973: ch.2) has correctly argued, the fact remains that the two did coincide and were regarded as part of a catch-up strategy by those states wishing to emulate Britain. Under Bismarck, Germany clearly industrialized in response to geo-political pressures, and so the state played a more openly directive role. This was not, *contra* Mayer (1981; see also Halperin 2004), a scenario based on the survival of *ancien*

regimes in Europe, but rather one which saw their capitalist modernization. With the exception of Britain, this took place under the leadership of autocratic states, but these states were also modernizing
states, committed to the expansion of capitalism, in part as a reaction
to British (economic and geo-political) power. This meant European
protectionism at home and territorial expansion abroad, while the
established capitalist power used territorial expansion as a means,
ultimately unsuccessful, to extend its free trade imperialism.

The third point concerns the links between industry, commerce and
finance. Certainly these were greater in Europe than in Britain, but
they were certainly not completely separate in the latter (Daunton
1989). Central to this argument is the view that Britain was not so
much the workshop, as it was the clearing house, of the world. In this
scenario, the British state was more concerned with protecting sterling than it was in promoting industry. Financial and industrial interests can come into conflict, when for example an over-valued
currency can undermine the competitiveness of manufacturing
exports. However, to then suggest that the actions of the British state
in the nineteenth century can be explained by a gentlemanly 'City-
Bank-Treasury' nexus (Ingham 1984: 127–34) is to stretch things too
far. We will come across a similar argument when examining the links
between US imperialism and the 'Wall Street-dollar' regime in the
current period (Gowan 1999), which can hardly be described as a
backward imperialism. But what is clear is that such a radical separation of financial and industrial interests makes no sense, for '(w)ithout
British industry and its exports and its overseas investments, demand
for the pound sterling, for insurance, trade credit, and all the other city
services would have been negligible' (Barratt-Brown 2000: 56).
Indeed, in 1900, the value of the export of goods was three times that
of the value of financial services (Barratt-Brown 1988: 26).
Moreover, 'much of the banking, the shipping and the insurance
which formed a substantial part of Britain's so-called "invisible"
earnings existed to facilitate international trade in British manufacturing goods, and in the raw materials which were imported to make their
production possible' (Cannadine 1995: 190; also Daunton 1989: 136).
In addition, the argument that banking had aristocratic origins is problematic: Lloyds emerged out of forge-master interests, Barclays from
clothing and brewing, JP Morgan from copper smelting and Barings
from cloth (Barratt-Brown 2000: 52) The links may still have been
closer in Europe but this may reflect less their comparative advance,

and rather a deliberate attempt by the state to catch up with Britain (Daunton 1989). The Cain and Hopkins thesis concerning gentlemanly capitalism bears some resemblance to that of Gallagher and Robinson's concerning free trade imperialism, particularly concerning the informal links that characterized the British Empire (Darwin 2002). But what is being suggested here is that more important is what divides the two perspectives. For Cain and Hopkins, gentlemanly capitalism reflected British capitalism's backwardness, but I am suggesting that free trade imperialism actually reflected the advanced state of British capitalism.

Nonetheless, it is true that Britain's early advance became a problem once it encountered competition from others. For Wood:

> Britain's early and unrivalled evolution as a capitalist power left it bereft of the means to reverse the decline set in train, while other European capitalisms were, at least for a time, better equipped. Early English capitalism never faced the need to establish institutions and practices to enhance or accelerate development – for example, certain kinds of state intervention or administrative skills; and its slow and 'natural' industrial revolution, unlike, say, the later German process of industrialization, generated no need for 'the "bureaucratic" creation of a widespread, efficient, system of technical allocation'. (1991: 15; see also Ashman 2009)

The broader point though is that the argument that British imperialism was simply commercial is unconvincing. As Barratt-Brown argues:

> To believe that British capital had basically a banking and merchanting role in the Empire would require us to suppose that there had been in the empire no sugar and cotton plantations, no tea and rubber estates, no gold, silver, copper and tin mines, no Lever Brothers, no oil companies, no Chartered Company, no Dalgety, no British-owned railways and other utilities or mills and factories overseas. (1988: 31)

But this still begs the question of why British finance did engage in significant speculative and/or overseas investments from the late nineteenth century. Answering this question brings us to the heart of the question concerning a supposedly archaic or gentlemanly capitalism. As we have seen, this thesis essentially suggests that financial and industrial interests diverged in Britain and that the latter was sacrificed at the expense of the former. While Anderson (1992) sees this as a reflection of the incompleteness of capitalist development in England, Gerschenkron (1962) more usefully regards it as a reflection of the early development of capitalism in England. As industrial development was more or less self-financing, finance had no option but to move into speculative and overseas ventures. Meanwhile, later European capitalisms developed through much closer ties between industry and finance, an argument supported by both Gerschenkron and Anderson. In Gerschenkron's case at least, this argument is not necessarily wrong, and it is clear that the close ties that developed between industry and finance were indispensable components in the emergence of 'developmentalist states' in Europe, promoting protectionist and pro-industrialization policies, in the late nineteenth century (Ashman 2009). However, we have already suggested that, for some time at least, the ties between industry and finance were closer in England (and Britain) than this argument suggests. Indeed, the English state played a crucial role in constraining the exchange of currencies in the late Middle Ages, and speculation was far more common in European banking systems up until the seventeenth century. Modern English banking emerged in England with the growth of domestic trade, *alongside* the development of industries in the late eighteenth century. Between 1784 and 1793, the growth of new country banks grew three-fold, and these banks were a crucial source of liquidity for industrialists whose assets may have been tied up in long-term investments, but who needed to pay for wages and raw materials (Knafo 2008: 183). However, with the further development of modern banking, this close relationship between industry and finance changed. As money was increasingly issued through banks, there needed to be controls on the money supply in order to control inflationary pressures. The gold standard was introduced by the state in order to control inflation (Knafo 2006). It met with considerable initial opposition from bankers as it imposed tight constraints on them. At the same time, the state also encouraged the development of new, joint stock banks, through the provision of incentives such as limited liability (Davies 1994: 315–22). This led to a shift in the relationship between banking and industry, as it undermined the informal relationships that existed between country banks and industry. Joint stock banks required deposits and so had an incentive to expand in order to increase the potential size of such deposits. It was therefore the state, rather than finance *per se*, and the pursuit of a national system of monetary governance, which served to undermine the informal credit arrangements that had existed between provincial banks and industry. But crucially, this was less an archaic state imprisoned by the never changing interests of English finance, but rather a capitalist state determined to institutionalize the rule of the market (Wood 1991; Knafo 2008). In other words, it was a state that promoted the most developed form of capitalism – and imperialism – that existed at that time.

Conclusion

This chapter has provided a detailed outline and critique of both classical Marxist theories, and liberal apologies for, imperialism from around 1882–1914 and beyond. It has rejected the argument that the liberal British Empire was a progressive, modernizing force, and partially rejected classical Marxist views which suggested that the new imperialism was the highest stage of capitalism. Inter-imperialist rivalries certainly existed, but these reflected the interaction between an established capitalist power, and newly developing capitalist powers that caught up with Britain, using protectionist policies at home and colonial policies abroad. Neither British nor European colonialism were modernizing forces in the colonies and semi-colonies, and indeed both served to intensify subordination in the peripheries of global capitalism. US attempts to implement an open door policy and reconstruct European capitalism were hindered by the Great Depression and renewed conflict between capitalist states. Inter-imperialist rivalries thus continued in an even more brutal form from 1919 to 1945, reflecting the instability of the peace process in 1918–19, and the rise of fascist states in the capitalist world, and the first (highly authoritarian) post-capitalist state in the Soviet Union. It was only after 1945 that imperialism began to take a radically different form in terms of relations between the core states, and in some respects between the core and peripheral states. This is the subject of the next chapter.

5
The Cold War, Post-War Boom and New Theories of Imperialism

This chapter examines post-war capitalism in the context of the end of empires and the Cold War. The focus is on the question of imperialism in the context of the universalization of the nation-state system, and what Rosenberg (1994; see also Stedman Jones 1970) has called the 'empire of civil society'. The chapter argues that the post-1945 international order was very different from that which existed from 1882 to 1945, and that this was not only because of the Cold War, important though this was. As important, or maybe even more important, was the role of the United States in promoting a genuinely global capitalism. This was not one that transcended the nation-state, but rather one that was promoted through sovereign states, including in the colonial world. This coincided with a commitment to an open door policy, which championed the cause of the free movement of capital across national borders. In practice however, this commitment was compromised by both geo-political and economic realities – the existence of the Cold War and fear of communist expansion, the need for reconstruction in Europe, and the promotion of development, with some degree of protectionism, in the former colonies. At the same time, the restrictions on the movement of capital occurred in the context of a deepening internationalization, which was supported by the US state. It was in this context that the post-war boom occurred in the capitalist world. The extension of state sovereignty and the extent of the post-war boom, alongside increased cooperation between the developed capitalist powers, served to undermine earlier theories of imperialism.

91

Nevertheless, new theories developed that attempted to account for this changed international context. The relationship between these developments and the Cold War are all major themes of this chapter.

The chapter starts by examining the nature of US primacy, and its role in constructing a post-war liberal international order. This includes examination of increasing cooperation between the 'advanced' capitalist countries, and the 'invention' of the development discourse after 1945, and how this was influenced by the Cold War. The focus here is therefore on relations between the developed capitalist states in the international order, and the ways in which inter-imperialist rivalries were radically altered and even transcended. The chapter then moves on to examine how the US' commitment to a liberal order was compromised in a number of ways, but perhaps above all in terms of the extent of interventionist policies in supposedly sovereign states in the Third World. This section therefore examines the influence of the Cold War in this process. Finally, the chapter then moves on to examine theories of imperialism in this new context, briefly examining Soviet theories from the 1920s onwards, and then post-war theories associated with neo-colonialism, under-development, dependency and world systems theory.

The US State and the Post-War Liberal International Order

One of the main arguments of this book is that with the rise of US hegemony after 1945, the character of (capitalist) imperialism underwent a significant change. These changes were so great that they call into question Marxist accounts of imperialism which highlight inter-imperialist rivalries, but also, I will argue, undermine some more mainstream, realist accounts of international relations. On the other hand, I will suggest in later chapters that there are also some continuities with nineteenth-century British imperialism, but not with the European imperialisms of the late nineteenth century. This section focuses on the nature of the post-war international order, the leading role of the US in this order, and how this differed from the pre-1945 period.

Crucially, the post-war (capitalist) order was in many respects a liberal order. There was a strong commitment to international cooperation between advanced capitalist states, the promotion of international organizations and multilateral agreements, a long-term commitment to 'open door' policies of free trade, and a commitment to the end of colonial empires and their replacement by newly created sovereign states. The British had attempted to implement all of these except anti-colonialism, as we saw in Chapter 3. However, the US transformation was far more effective and successful. US-led liberal internationalism was in practice compromised, but even then, there were significant differences from the pre-war order of intense competition between advanced capitalist powers, the effective breakdown of international cooperation, competitive devaluations and heightened protectionism in the context of the depression of the 1930s[1] as well as the continued existence of empires. It is also clear that US hegemony after 1945 was used to re-fashion the international capitalist order, and to place the emphasis on cooperation and multilateral relations between the developed capitalist powers.

In order to understand the nature of US hegemony and the 'new American century' from 1941 onwards, we first need to examine, albeit quite cursorily, US imperialism before the Second World War. As we have seen in earlier chapters, the US carried out highly protectionist policies from its birth, right up until the post-1945 period (Bairoch 1993: 32–8, 52–3). But at the same time, the US also expanded its domestic borders (Kiernan 1980; Stephanson 1995). As Cox (2003: 15–16) argues, 'the nation-state we now refer to as the United States of America only became this impressive continental entity because it managed to annex a great deal of territory during the nineteenth century'. This included the purchase of Louisiana from France in 1803, and westward expansion after war with Britain in 1812, which culminated in the seizure of New Mexico, Texas and California, after the defeat of Mexico in 1846.

For the Founding Fathers, Empire, based on the 'expansion of liberty', was a political mission from the (anti-colonial) outset. As the historian Frederick Jackson Turner argued in 1893, freedom was intimately linked to an expanding frontier, which reflected the US' exceptional yet universal nature (see Foner 1999: 137). US national identity was regarded as exceptional in that it was not characterized by the conflicts and colonial practices of old Europe (although the US briefly succumbed in the late nineteenth century), and it was precisely this exceptionalism that made the US a universal nation, something to which others could aspire and learn. Tocqueville (1988: 47) had earlier argued that Anglo-American civilization was 'the product ... of two perfectly distinct elements which elsewhere have often been at war with one another but which in America it was somehow possible to incorporate into each other, forming a marvellous combination. I mean the spirit of religion and spirit of freedom'. In 1845, John O' Sullivan declared that it was the 'Manifest Destiny' of the US to 'occupy and posses the whole of the continent which providence has given to us' (cited in Foner 1999: 50; see also Stephanson 1995: 28–65. This doctrine ignored some unpalatable truths, such as the intimidation, fraud, and violence associated with displacement and slaughter of native Americans, as well as the enslavement of African-Americans (Kiernan 1980: ch.2; Marable 1983). But, in line with Locke's pronouncements in the seventeenth century (see Chapter 3), Manifest Destiny tended to ignore those not considered to be true American citizens, and expansion continued at a rapid pace.

In the 1890s, Secretary of State John Hay promoted an open-door policy which demanded equal access for US goods to the Chinese market. In the late nineteenth century, the US did follow the lead of old Europe and became a formal colonizer, particularly in the Philippines. But in most respects this was an aberration. The US preferred occupations of formally sovereign territories to direct colonialism, designed to ensure the compliance of friendly powers and ensure open access for US companies, particularly in Latin America and the Caribbean. Williams (1972; see also Kolko 1968; 1969; 1985) links this expansion to the specific nature of US imperialism, which essentially adopted an open-door policy based on the need for expanding markets for the products of US corporations, something that had increasingly occurred as industrial interests in the North, supporting protectionism at home and increased exports abroad, defeated the slave-owners in the South (LaFeber 1993). Williams (1972: 29, 45) argues that the period from the 1890s was particularly significant, and suggests that the Spanish-American war over Cuban independence should be seen in this light. The outcome of this war was to ensure independence for Cuba, but one which was compromised by US economic domination of the territory. Earlier, the Monroe Doctrine of 1823 had asserted that European powers had no right to colonize territories in the western hemisphere in which the US had an interest (Kiernan 1980: 8, 92). This idea was 'built on the good old-fashioned ideology – much beloved by European colonials – which assumed that certain areas should, of right, fall within the sphere of influence of one of the great powers' (Cox 2006: 119). These developments hardly fit the myth of an isolationist United

States. From 1801 to 1904, the US used force outside its own (expanding) borders no less than 101 times (Cox 2003: 9). Thus, while this expansion was rationalized in terms of the exceptional but universal character of the US, this was not incompatible with an imperialism based on what Jefferson had called 'the empire of liberty' (Foner 1999: 50). As Westad (2007: 12) states, '[t]he image that made possession of the continent America's "manifest destiny", a term first used in 1845, expressed as myth what in reality was a rather concrete imperialist program'.

After the end of the First World War, the US attempted to promote a more interventionist policy beyond its own backyard. In 1918, President Woodrow Wilson presented his fourteen points to Congress, which essentially promoted a liberal international order throughout the world. This included the right of nations to self-determination but, as became clear once this principle was eventually adopted after 1945, this commitment to sovereignty was conditional (Hoff 2008: ch.2). Wilson sanctioned military intervention in the global South ten times during his presidency, as well as in revolutionary Russia in 1918 (Gardner 1984). His promotion of a liberal international order was also undermined by European opposition overseas and Congressional opposition at home.

The period from 1919 to 1941 saw a struggle between interventionist and isolationist forces, and between multilateral and unilateral forces (Ruggie 1998: 207–10). The divisions were not always straightforward – for example, much of the debate over intervention was about the terms on which the US would become involved in affairs beyond its own immediate sphere of influence, and so interventionism did not necessarily mean multilateralism. Much of this debate was couched in terms of how the US national interest and a liberal international order were compatible. This was because it was believed that a liberal international order would help to prevent conflict between European powers, as liberal inter-dependence would result in 'peaceful' rather than 'aggressive' competition between them. In the words of Cordell Hull, who was US Secretary of State from 1933–44, 'I reasoned that if we could get a freer flow of trade ... so that one country would not be deadly jealous of another and the living standards of all countries might rise, thereby eliminating the economic dissatisfaction that breeds war, we might have a reasonable chance of lasting peace' (cited in Gardner 1956: 9). At the same time however, it was also reasoned that as the most productive power, the

US would benefit most from free trade and states that were open to foreign investment, and liberal expansion would help to contain the communist threat that emerged from 1917. Anti-communism was indeed a central component of Wilson's internationalism. However, before 1941, the hopes for a more internationalist policy were shattered by the failure of the US to join the League of Nations, and by inaction in the face of the rise and expansion of Nazi Germany, Italy's invasion of Abyssinia, and Japan's invasion of Manchuria.

However, the attack on Pearl Harbor in 1941, and the US' consequent engagement in the Second World War, ensured that the US would emerge after 1945 as a different kind of capitalist power (albeit one to which Britain had some aspirations in the nineteenth century). It was not to be one power among many, but the undisputed leader of the capitalist world. Panitch and Gindin (2003: 10) suggest that '[t]he dynamism of American capitalism and its worldwide appeal combined with the universal language of American liberal democratic ideology to underpin a capacity for informal empire far beyond that of nineteenth century Britain's'. The period from 1941 onwards was the beginning of a new American century. A new hegemonic strategy for the US was promoted by the editor of *Life* magazine, Henry Luce, in an article entitled 'The American Century'. Alongside concerns about Roosevelt's New Deal and US isolationism, Luce argued that there should be US involvement in the war and the expansion of US ideals beyond its national borders (Cumings 1999: 278–9; Hoff 2008: 92–3). Luce was particularly keen for western expansion into Pacific Asia, but two years earlier former Roosevelt administration official Dean Acheson had promoted a far more global sense of 'Americanization'. In his 'An American Attitude Towards Foreign Affairs', Acheson rejected isolationism and neutrality in the war, and argued that the US must take a leading role in finding new ways to promote peace, including a commitment to free trade, a stable international monetary system, and the creation of 'a navy and air force adequate to secure us in both oceans simultaneously and with striking power sufficient to reach the outer side of each of them' (cited in Cumings 1999: 281).

Such views were isolated prior to Pearl Harbor, but the period from 1941 to 1950 saw the development of the Bretton Woods agreement, the Marshall Plan and Truman Doctrine, alongside a massive military build-up. Acheson himself returned to government in 1940, and played a prominent role at Bretton Woods and later under Truman, as Secretary of State, influenced the George Kennan strategy of containment, and led the US formation of NATO in 1949. NSC-68[2], the National Security Council document which formulated Cold War strategy, was agreed in 1950, under the Chair of Paul Nitze, but was clearly influenced by Acheson. In 1939, the US had a military personnel numbering just 185,000 and an annual budget of $500 million. A few years after Pearl Harbor, the numbers in the army stood at 1 million, with an air force and navy almost as large, a defence budget (at comparable prices) of over $100 *billion* and a military presence in 119 countries (Cumings 1999: 284).

The doctrine of US hegemony was sold to an 'isolationist' Congress and electorate as one of containment rather than liberal expansion. One result was that in the context of the heightening of a Cold War that was visible before 1945, but was relatively muted in the context of continued inter-imperialist rivalries between capitalist powers (Saull 2007: chs. 1 and 2), realism continued to flourish particularly in the United States.[3] Bi-polar conflict between two mutually incompatible socio-economic orders thus effectively served to obscure the specificity of US power within the capitalist core (Gowan 2002). In the context of the post-Cold War world, this became more apparent, especially 'when American strategic planners scotched any talk of returning to the Western hemisphere after their victory over the last great contender for European hegemony' (Balakrishnan 2006: 9–10). It was therefore only after 1989 that the expansionist nature of US hegemony became completely transparent – notwithstanding considerable military interventions in the Cold War era – and one which has been the source of considerable debate since then. What is clear is that the post-1989 order saw the realization of the Acheson dream, based on the 'unfolding of an internationalist telos yielding the liberal hegemony that the internationalists envisioned' (Cumings 1999: 297; see also Bacevich 2002). This was not a return to the pre-1945 conflicts that characterized European powers, but neither was it the conflict free world conjured up by many theorists of globalization, as we will see in later chapters.

First though, we need to examine in more depth the post-1945 period, for the changes that took place then reflected a considerable shift in US foreign policy. As Saull argues:

The war had transformed US perceptions of itself, and had also produced political and economic circumstances that provided an opportunity for the US to reshape the world in its own image. The presence of US troops on three continents, the weakness of the other major capitalist states and the huge economic imbalance that had emerged by the end of the war almost necessitated US leadership. (2007: 61–2)

Perhaps most interesting in this respect was the successful way in which the US promoted hegemony among other advanced capitalist powers. The Marshall Plan from 1947 promoted European reconstruction, but was itself part of a wider strategy of drawing Europe into an Atlanticist framework (van der Pijl 1984). Crucially, European integration was not regarded as a threat to European hegemony, but was actually part of this strategy (Lundestad 1998). Lundestad suggests that:

> to a remarkable extent the US was able to secure its most important overall objectives in Western Europe; the Soviet Union was contained; West Germany was integrated into Western Europe; an Atlantic military alliance was established under America's firm leadership and with a comprehensive system of US bases; communists; leftist socialists, and fascists were kept out of European governments; the European economies were integrated into an Atlantic framework; Europe was opened to America's mass culture. (2003: 2)

The promotion of European integration within an Atlantic framework was a policy consistently championed by all US administrations up to Nixon's in the late 1960s, and even then, the shift in policy was one towards greater ambivalence rather than outright hostility.

After some initial scepticism, Truman supported the proposal for a European Coal and Steel Community in 1950. Secretary of State John Foster Dulles supported the proposed European Defence Community in 1953, even suggesting that a failure to achieve this goal would lead to 'an agonizing reappraisal of basic United States policy' (cited in Lundestad 1998: 7), a position backed up by his President, Eisenhower. Kennedy's later assertion that '[w]e do not regard a strong and united Europe as a rival but a partner' (cited in Lundestad 1998: 7) was thus perfectly consistent with this approach. As the US economy began to suffer at the hands of its competitors, and the postwar boom came to an end, the US did re-evaluate its stance towards Europe, particularly under Nixon. This was part of the context in which the Bretton Woods agreement effectively came to an end, as the dollar was devalued in an attempt to restore US competitiveness in 1971 (see further below). But as will become clear, this re-evaluation did not lead to open hostility, or (to return to classical theories) a resurgence of inter-imperialist conflict, either in the context of serious world recessions in 1974–5, 1980–2, or 1990–2, or once the Cold War (an obvious factor uniting capitalist powers) came to an end.

Some of these issues will be discussed in this and later chapters, but what needs to be immediately addressed is why the US supported European integration in the first place. Certainly containment of the Soviet Union was one reason, but it was not the only one. Possibly more important was the attempt to manage older European nationalist rivalries, which were contrasted to the forward looking nationalism of the United States, a theme which has constantly re-emerged in US thinking, perhaps most recently in neo-conservative rhetoric in the run up to the Iraq war of 2003. The US saw integration as a way of countering these older nationalisms, and particularly of controlling a revived Germany, whom it had (eventually) fought in two world wars. The US also regarded integration as a bulwark against economic protectionism which it regarded as an accompaniment to archaic nationalisms. This may have been ironic given the US' own history of protectionism, but as we have seen this took place in the context of expanding frontiers, and in any case the US no longer needed protectionism – it was the biggest supporter of free trade in the world, now that it had become the most powerful economy. US capital stood to benefit from integration, through exports to the European market, but perhaps most importantly, through direct foreign investment. As important though was the question of the way in which integration should occur, and of central importance here was the fact that the US would be first among equals. European integration would take place in an Atlantic framework, through the Bretton Woods agreement, the Marshall Plan, the General Agreement on Trade and Tariffs and through NATO. While the US welcomed European military agreements, they did so with the condition that these would remain under the NATO umbrella. In the immediate aftermath of war, the main defeated powers were granted sovereignty in return for restrictions on military autonomy, and the US constructed bases in both Germany and Japan. It was also hoped that the development of multilateral organizations would lead to mutual constraints being placed on all the developed capitalist powers. All this was put in place under US leadership, but this was still a liberal hegemony in which the subordinate states had access to the dominant state, which would further cooperation and consensus rather than conflict (Deudney and Ikenberry 1999; Ikenberry 2006: part 1).

These developments of course do beg the question of whether the US can accurately be described as an empire, rather than merely being the primary or hegemonic nation. In what sense was the US imperialist after 1945, especially given its commitment to sovereignty for colonies? Part of this commitment undoubtedly reflected the US' own history of anti-colonial struggle. Indeed, given the simplistic anti-Americanism often found in Europe (among both left and right), a contrast between Europe's own colonial record (and barbarity within Europe) and the US' support for independence certainly undermines any claims that the former have to moral superiority.[4] However, it would also be naïve to explain US support for independence solely on the grounds of altruism, and in part it reflected the distinctive nature of the US hegemonic project after 1945. The US supported independence 'because it realistically calculated that the break up of other more formal kinds of empire was likely to decrease its' rivals power, while increasing its own weight in a reformed world system' (Cox 2003: 18; see also Williams 1972). This becomes clearer when we see how sovereignty was actually conditional, an issue discussed in the context of the Cold War in the next section. But it also reflected the fact that the kind of empire that the US supported was one in which the enclosed world of protectionism at home and exclusive trading relations with colonies abroad were rejected, in favour of an open-door policy. And such a policy meant a commitment, as we have seen, to sovereign states on the one hand, and to open economic relations on the other.

This was compromised by the contingencies of the post-war international order. As we have seen, this particularly applied in the case of security, where NATO played a leading role in contrast to say, the United Nations Security Council. Furthermore, multilateralism at the Security Council itself was compromised by permanent membership and veto powers for a handful of states. It was also clear in the case of the international economy. The agreement at Bretton Woods in 1944 did establish the ground rules for a multilateral international economic order, but this was compromised by the decision of the United States to establish the dollar as the main international reserve currency, rather than (as Keynes wished), a specifically international currency called the bancor, which would be used to automatically transfer reserves from capital surplus to capital deficit countries (Brett 1983). The US did not agree to this, and so the new International Monetary Fund (IMF) and International Bank for Reconstruction and Development (IBRD, of which the World Bank was the most important section) were comparatively weak institutions, and they had only a limited role to play in the post-war order. When they became more important in the 1980s, their weakness in relation to the US state was all too clear, as we will see in the next chapter.

In the late 1940s, capital was recycled from surplus to deficit countries, primarily through the vehicle of Marshall Aid to the European countries (and Japan), rather than through World Bank finance. At the same time, the US allowed space for European recovery, and so protectionist policies continued for a while. The US Congress voted against a formal International Trade Organization, committed to the promotion of free trade, mainly because of protectionist domestic pressures, especially in agriculture. The more informal General Agreement on Tariffs and Trade (GATT) was established, whereby each round of talks would try to establish more open trade and investment policies. While this led to considerable tensions, the GATT was reasonably successful in promoting increasingly free trade policies while allowing considerable room for manoeuvre for states who wanted to maintain protectionist policies (Brett 1985). In the context of the post-war boom, and together with US funds from Marshall Aid and increasingly from US foreign investment, this allowed Germany and Japan to recover and briefly challenge US hegemony by the 1970s, as we will see in the next chapter.

The Marshall Plan sharply contrasted with the initial plan for post-war reconstruction, the Morgenthau Plan, named after the US Secretary to the Treasury from 1934–45, Henry Morgenthau. This envisaged the post-war reconstruction of Europe, and especially Germany, taking place through free trade policies (Reinert 2006). This plan – which was very similar to neo-liberal policies adopted in the 1980s – was rationalized on the grounds that the war-ravaged economies could compete by attracting capital and trading their way out of poverty. In the case of Germany, this was backed up by the idea that it should cease to be a major industrial power, and should instead specialize in producing agricultural goods – though quite how this idea was consistent with the economic case made for recovery through open trade policies is another matter. In any case, the Plan was abandoned for Germany in 1947, and Marshall Aid allowed for considerable protection for European economies to allow themselves to recover from the war and promote industrial reconstruction.

The GATT was particularly useful for developing countries in that it allowed them to pick and choose which agreements they could support and which they could discard, and it effectively allowed them to practice the principle of asymmetric protection, protecting selected sectors from foreign competition without having to reciprocate. In this way, the international context allowed developing countries some space, which facilitated the development of import substitution industrialization policies. ISI was tolerated by the US as long as the regimes that carried it out did not become too nationalist and/or an ally of the Communist movement. Indeed, ISI was compatible in some respects with modernization theory (Rostow 1960), which developed after the Second World War. This theory argued that all societies passed through similar stages of development in the transition to a full mature, modern society (Rostow 1960). The United States was regarded as the highest stage of social development, a society based on meritocracy, opportunity and consensus, as opposed to traditional societies that were seen as hierarchical, static, and in need of change from outside. This view of history was essentially an update of John Stuart Mill's liberal theory of progress (Jahn 2007a), discussed in Chapter 3. Where it crossed over with ISI was the belief that Third World societies should endeavour to catch up with the modern West, and that this should be done through industrial modernization, which would include the adoption of western technology and (perceived) western values of progress through entrepreneurialism (McClelland 1961). Modernization theory thus regarded contact with the West as liberating for backward countries. ISI was implicitly more critical of the West, as the rationale for industrialization was to overcome the colonial division of labour that left some countries in a subordinate position in the world economy. But the solution to this problem was modernization through industrialization.

At the same time, modernization theory did give room for developmentalist policies which were designed to promote convergence with the West. It was therefore based on a liberal view of social change but not a neo-liberal one, as we will see in Chapter 7. Moreover, modernization theory was deeply embedded in the realities of international politics at the time. Rostow (1960: 166–8) argued that modernization of the Third World was necessary for the survival of the West, and his most famous book was sub-titled *A Non-Communist Manifesto*. He was also an adviser to President Johnson at the time of the escalation of the Vietnam war. In this regard it is no exaggeration to say that the theory was at the centre of US foreign policy after 1945, as it 'was not only a project of domestic transformation for Southern states but also a strategy of geo-political management as well as a vision of transformation for international order' (Bromley 2008: 9).

In terms of strategy, modernization theory saw democracy as the outcome of, rather than precondition for, modernization. Huntington's *Political Order in Changing Societies* (1968) argued that the transition to modernization carried important dangers, as participation by the ill-educated masses could erode the prospects for the emergence of a modern, and stable, liberal democracy. Modernization theory was thus caught up in the conflicts associated with the Cold War, and to an extent, liberal principles were compromised as the United States supported anti-communist, authoritarian regimes. On the other hand of course, this fear and distrust of 'the masses' was a central component of classical liberalism's distrust of democracy, as an overly politicized population could demand an erosion of market freedom and demand a tyranny of the majority (Tocqueville 1988). Although Tocqueville himself was suspicious of the free market on the grounds that this too could lead to a tyranny of the majority, economic liberalism has essentially argued that individual freedom is guaranteed by the existence of private property and the market exchange of the products of this property, and that this is far more important than democracy, which is dangerously collectivist, at least if it is not restricted (Hayek 2006).

This was a liberal international order, but one that was compromised, mainly by the actions of the US. It involved the export of dollars and the encouragement of reconstruction – in part through protectionism – in Europe and Japan, even if the US was not always the major beneficiary. Liberal policies in the developing world were also encouraged, alongside an acceptance that import substitution policies could be carried out. There was also the promotion of a managed transition to modernization, but one which often involved support for authoritarian regimes (Hoff 2008: ch.5). However, none of these features quite tells us what the precise nature of US imperialism effectively meant, and how this has changed over time. The rest of the chapter focuses on imperialism in the context of the post-colonial international order, and what came to be known as the North–South divide. First, the question of military imperialism is examined, and this is followed by consideration of new theories of imperialism that emerged in the post-war world, which focused on both military and economic imperialism with specific emphasis on the global 'South'.

The Cold War, Military Imperialism and the Third World

The Cold War played a central role in influencing the nature of imperialism after the Second World War. For realist writers (Waltz 1979), developed countries cooperated in the face of a common enemy, the Soviet Union, and thereby promoted a strategy of containment in the context of an anarchical state system. Many Marxist writers influenced by Lenin and Bukharin's emphasis on inter-imperialist rivalries, effectively argue along similar lines. Cox (1984) argues that the inter-systemic conflict between capitalism and communism had a functional role to play, serving to legitimize US or Soviet hegemony, both domestically and within their respective wider spheres of influence. For the capitalist world, this served to unite otherwise hostile imperialist rivals; indeed, the so-called Soviet threat actually facilitated capitalist restructuring (Cox 1984: 146).

This view derives from the development of Trotsky's theory that the Soviet revolution had degenerated, and a parasitic and highly authoritarian bureaucracy ruled over post-capitalist property relations. Trotsky (1980) argued that in terms of international relations, this would lead to the Soviet Union playing a contradictory role, in that if it supported the overthrow of capitalist social relations within other states (which was far from guaranteed), it would only be in such a way as to defend the interests of the Soviet bureaucracy. Later Marxist theories disagreed with the view that the Soviet Union remained a workers' state, albeit one deformed by the Soviet bureaucracy, and suggested that the development of a new bureaucratic stratum had led to the formation of a new class in a new social formation (Cox 1984; Ticktin 1992).

Another Marxist approach suggested that inter-imperialist rivalries continued after 1945, but these were between the liberal capitalism of the US and its allies, and the state capitalism of the Soviet bloc. This theory started from the correct premise that the Soviet Union did not conform to any recognizable principles of democratic socialism. It then made the far more contentious claim that it was a state capitalist regime. The main advocate of this theory, Tony Cliff (1974: 208–9) recognized that social relations within the Soviet Union were not capitalist, arguing that 'if one examines the relations within the Russian economy, abstracting them from their relations with the world economy, one is bound to conclude that the source of the law of value, as the motor and regulator of production, is not to be found in it'. He instead suggested that the Soviet Union was state capitalist because of its incorporation into a capitalist dominated world system. Trade between the Soviet Union and the capitalist world was limited, but Cliff (1974: 210) contended that 'the commercial struggle has so far been of less importance than the military. Because international competition takes mainly a military form, the law of value expresses itself in its opposite, viz., a striving after use values'. Indeed, he argued that military competition, which he regarded as competition over use values and not commodities, has 'become the main aim of capitalist production' (Cliff 1974: 212).

These arguments overlap with the theory of the permanent arms economy, which contended that the increasingly state interventionist capitalism of the post-1945 period had a particular effect on the nature of capital accumulation. This theory takes its cue from Hobson's argument that surplus capital can be disposed of in ways other than capital export. Writing from a social democratic perspective, Strachey (1959) suggested that redistributive policies associated with the welfare state have, contrary to Lenin's argument, resolved the problem of under-consumption. Baran and Sweezy (1966, see below) argued along similar lines from a more Marxist (though also still Keynesian) position, and suggested that military spending was one way of dealing with the problem of surplus capital. But it was Mike Kidron (1962; 1967; 1968) who most clearly developed a Marxist position, arguing that arms production was not commodity production, and so Marx's arguments concerning the tendency of profit rates to fall as the organic composition of capital rises, no longer applied. Put (too) simply, this broadly means that machinery increasingly replaces labour in the production process, undermining profit rates as labour is the source of surplus value. Arms production can counteract this tendency as it is outside the orbit of commodity production. But, like Cliff, Kidron suggested that this led to a new competition between militarized capitalist powers, led by the US and the USSR.

These views are attractive in that they held no illusions about the nature of the Soviet Union. However, they are also unconvincing.

Cox's view tends towards a functionalist account of the Cold War, reducing conflict between the superpowers to domestic problems of legitimization. Cliff's view is unconvincing, because it reduces competition to an externally generated phenomenon, outside the frame of specific social relations. In terms of arms production, this leads to the rather odd argument that the production of weapons functions to slow down the organic composition of capital, which in turn must mean that capital accumulation is itself slowed down. An advocate of Cliff's views, Binns (1975: 25; see also Callinicos 2009b: 175) argues this point explicitly, suggesting that armaments 'reduce the amount accumulated, and thus slow down the rise of the organic composition of capital. This leads to the rate of profit declining more slowly than otherwise, and causing the crisis to be delayed further'. The problem with this argument is that it itself tends towards the stagnationist view of capitalism that it is trying to correct, because if arms production slows down accumulation, then it is difficult to see why high rates of accumulation and the post-war boom occurred in the first place. Ultimately, the problem with this view is that arms production is not outside of commodity production; as Mandel (1975: 289) suggests, 'surplus value used to build arms factories and to produce weapons certainly is accumulated surplus value. The purchase of weapons must after all have been preceded by the production of weapons as commodities'. Moreover, arms production has a higher organic composition of capital than many other industrial sectors, so any diversion into this sector is unlikely to halt a decline in the average rate of profit (Mandel 1973: 36).

More broadly, in terms of international relations, these views are unconvincing, Cox because of the failure to see how radically different socio-economic systems influenced international relations, Cliff, for the denial of any difference between such systems and, like realism, a commitment to an ahistorical analysis of international competition (or anarchy). The Cold War was an inter-systemic conflict, as has been convincingly outlined in the work of Halliday (1983; 1989). But we need to be clear how these different systems influenced international relations, and how and why the Third World came to play a central role in this inter-systemic conflict. For unlike most accounts of the Cold War, we should not assume that the chain of causation ran from superpower interests to their clients in the Third World. Rather, inter-systemic conflict took particular forms, and had particular agents in the Third World, which were influenced by, but not reducible to, superpower rivalries and interests. Put bluntly, 'the Cold War emerged out of the crisis wrought by the uneven and differenti-ated nature of global capitalist development' (Saull 2005: 254). In this way, the Cold War did not simply influence imperialism; it was a central part of it.

In the period from 1917 to 1939, there was a Cold War between these two social systems, as the new Soviet state faced invasions from foreign powers in support of the counter-revolutionaries in the civil war. In this period, while capitalist powers showed a great deal of hostility to the Soviet Union, this was complicated by the rise and expansion of Nazi Germany. Indeed, while communist expansion in Europe was successfully resisted, one of the costs was the rise of European fascism. After the war, the centre of gravity of communist revolution shifted to the Third World, as Saull suggests:

> The 'resolution' of the social contradictions that had bedevilled European capitalism through the American post-war settlement highlighted in the projects of European integration and a managed liberal international economic order propped up by US political-military hegemony contrasted with the intensification of social conflict in the South. (2005: 256)

In practice then, the US' commitment to state sovereignty after the war was compromised by the threat of communism – and in some cases, nationalism – in the Third World. It should be stressed that this threat existed independently of the Soviet Union, as local social and political forces took the lead in revolutionary struggles. This was certainly the case in the most significant struggles in the period from 1950 to the early 1970s: in Korea, Vietnam and Cuba. In each of these cases, it was local forces and not the Soviet Union, who led revolu-tions. Soviet support for such forces was hesitant or, in the case of Cuba, non-existent, until revolutions had actually taken place. However, once these had occurred, they impacted on the wider super-power conflict in a number of ways. In particular, they boosted one superpower and thus provoked a response from the other.

Crucially however, these responses were very different, reflecting the different social structures that existed within the two social systems. In the case of the Soviet Union, it maintained firm control in Eastern Europe, and did so through what was effectively the only means available to it: armed intervention. Social relations within the

Soviet system, meant that 'because socio-economic production was centrally organized and co-ordinated by the bureaucratic apparatus of the Party-state both within and between communist revolutionary states, the dynamic of material accumulation and thus socio-economic expansion was always confined to the institutions of the state and determined by it' (Saull 2001: 60). Soviet intervention was always quite overt, but outside its immediate sphere of influence, it was also quite limited, unless Soviet-style social relations were directly transplanted to these new revolutionary states. These states did rely heavily on Soviet support, but this reflected less Soviet strength but rather the weaknesses of these states in the face of hostility from overwhelmingly more powerful capitalist states.[5]

US power over Third World states was qualitatively different. Rather, the United States '*could* expand its influence *without* direct military power, and involving a direct agency not directly identified or controlled by the US state' (Saull 2001: 23). The US could extend its influence through formally sovereign states, through the use of methods that were not directly 'political' or 'territorial'. This reflected the so-called separation of formal 'political' and 'economic' spheres that characterizes capitalist societies, a separation that is itself highly political. As we will see in the next section, an implicit recognition of this separation, and of the different ways in which the US (or other capitalist powers) may exercise power, was central to the development of new theories of imperialism in the context of an extra-territorial empire (Williams 1972; LaFeber 1963; Hoff 2008).[6]

It should be stressed however, that while the US did not *have to* use military power to extend its influence, it clearly did so on many occasions. There is a massive literature describing, though rarely explaining, such interventions (Chomsky 1968; 1994; 2007; Blum 2002). Intervention sometimes took place through the use of, and in collaboration with, local agents, such as in Iran in 1954, Chile in 1973, and in the 1980s under Ronald Reagan in (among others) Nicaragua and Afghanistan. Sometimes it was through more overt means, such as in Korea and Vietnam, and perhaps more symbolically, Grenada in 1983. In this sense, the US was clearly a military imperialist power, for in the capitalist world, what is clear is that '[o]nly the American state could arrogate to itself the right to intervene against the sovereignty of other states (which it repeatedly did around the world) and only the American state reserved for itself the "sovereign" right to reject international rules and norms when necessary. It is in this sense that only the American state was actively "imperialist"' (Panitch and Gindin 2003: 16).

However, the crucial point is that the dominant capitalist powers, and the US in particular, could influence the Third World through 'non-territorial' means. It was in this context that new theories of economic imperialism were developed in the post-war period, and it is to a consideration of these theories that I now turn.

Theories of Imperialism after 1945

In the post-war world, theories of imperialism tended to focus more on the question of North–South relations rather than relations between the advanced capitalist powers. This was not surprising, for as we have seen, relations between developed capitalist powers increasingly became cooperative, and much of the Cold War was effectively fought in the South. Moreover, what became known in this period as Third World nations were increasingly winning their independence, and so new theories had to be developed to explain relations of subordination in the context of state sovereignty, even if this was compromised by superpower intervention. What was needed, then, was a theory of 'imperialism without colonies' (Magdoff 1978: ch.4). Developing new theories of imperialism therefore became imperative, but equally what was needed were new economic theories which complemented the more overtly politico-military theories outlined above. This section examines these theories, first by putting them in the context of the growing internationalization of productive capital which occurred after 1945, and then examining a number of theoretical innovations that took place. This section therefore examines Soviet theories of imperialism before and after 1945, theories of under-development and world systems theory, dependency theories and theories of neo-colonialism, and the return of the idea that imperialism was progressive because it was the pioneer of capitalism.

The Internationalization of Capital

As we have seen, theories of imperialism had to deal with the fact that there was increasing cooperation among the developed capitalist countries after 1945, and the fact that the former colonies were becoming independent after 1945. The previous section focused on this latter question through an examination of military imperialism; this section concentrates on the question of the economics of imperialism. Central to the theories discussed here was the fact that capital was increasingly internationalized after 1945. Capital had of course been internationalized before this date, as merchant capital was involved in international trade and finance capital flows increased in the late nineteenth century. But what was distinctive about the post-Second World War era was the internationalization of productive capital through the multinational company.

There was some significant investment in production before 1945, with companies like Dunlop, Lever Brothers and General Electric all involved in direct foreign investment. But most foreign investment was in primary production, and much of this was in the developing world. In the post-1945 period, there was a substantial increase in direct foreign investment and increasing amounts of this was in manufacturing production (Jenkins 1987: ch.1; Dicken 2007). Initially this was led by US companies, but Europe and Japan quickly followed. This expansion was in part facilitated by new technologies in transport and communications, which meant that productive activity could increasingly be dispersed. The 1950s and 1960s saw the massive growth of subsidiaries of multinationals, and this included an increase in manufacturing investment in the developing world. For instance, from 1950 to 1984, the proportion of US direct foreign investment (DFI) in manufacturing to the Third World increased from 15 to 37 per cent (Jenkins 1987: 7). The increase in DFI to the developing world slowed down in the 1970s as some states placed limits on DFI, and turned to alternative sources of finance, and it continued to slow down in the context of structural adjustment and slow growth in the 1980s. However, as we will see in Chapter 7, by the 1990s, when limits to DFI were removed at a rapid pace, a new foreign investment boom took place.

Despite the growth of DFI in the developing world in the post-war period, it continued to concentrate in the developed world, and indeed in some respects this concentration actually intensified. Certainly, significant amounts of investment did go to developing countries, as multinationals invested in countries rather than face high tariffs on their exports from protectionist states carrying out ISI policies (Jenkins 1984a). When, from the 1960s onwards, Third World states also carried out export promotion strategies, they often did so by attracting foreign investment through setting up export processing zones which had tax holidays, labour controls and few limits on profit remittances. This again encouraged investment by multinationals eager to take advantage of low costs. Thus, the global pattern of investment demonstrated an increasing tendency to invest in manufacturing, accompanied by an increasing concentration of that investment in the already developed world. As a consequence, the Third World's share of direct foreign investment fell from 1975 to 1984: from Germany (27 per cent to 19 per cent), Japan (73 to 52 per cent) and Britain (19 to 16 per cent) and these figures include the East Asian newly industrializing countries as part of the Third World (Jenkins 1992: 35). But at the same time, while such concentration was significant globally, foreign investment was often very important from the viewpoint of individual developing countries, an issue discussed in more detail in Chapter 7.

Most of the theories of imperialism discussed below can be seen as responses, in part at least, to this internationalization of capital. In particular, most of them reflect the changing focus of such theories after 1945, from inter-imperialist rivalries in the developed capitalist world, to a much greater emphasis on the developmental impact of the internationalization of capital in the Third World. This latter issue was particularly contentious as we will now see.

Soviet Theories of Imperialism

New theories from the Soviet Union were not always directly influenced by the growing phenomenon of post-war capital internationalization, and indeed some pre-date 1945. But these are worthy of consideration for they did exercise some influence on the post-war theories which we will discuss in this section. We therefore start with these theories, and their development in the 1920s.

The (partial) derivation of Soviet theories of imperialism from Lenin can be attributed to his focus on the parasitic, decaying nature of monopoly or finance capital. He did however argue that the export of capital would still lead to capitalist development in the colonies and semi-colonies, but this part of his thought was forgotten as new theories generalized the emphasis on parasitism and stagnation. The 1920 'Theses on National and Colonial Questions' argued for a close alliance between Soviet Russia and national liberation movements in the colonies, and a resolution was passed declaring that 'European capitalism derives its strength less from the European industrial countries than from its colonial possessions' (cited in Mommsen 1981: 52). By 1923, with Lenin close to death, Stalin argued at the 12th Congress of the Communist Party that:

> Either we succeed in stirring up, in revolutionizing, the remote rear of imperialism – the colonial and semi-colonial countries of the East – and thereby hasten the fall of imperialism; or we fail to do so, and thereby strengthen imperialism and weaken the force of our movement. (Ibid.)

By 1924, imperialism reflected the division of the world into two camps: on the one side, the rich capitalist countries, and on the other, 'the camp of the oppressed and exploited people in the colonies and dependent countries' (cited in Mommsen 1981: 52–3). By the time of the Sixth Congress of the Comintern in 1928, all in the communist movement agreed that 'imperialism was economically retrogressive in the colonies' (Warren 1980: 107).

It is difficult to unpack the extent to which much of this was rhetorical self-justification, or simply bad analysis. Whatever the case, disastrous tactical errors were made as the Communist Party of the Soviet Union advocated tactical alliances against imperialism, only for indigenous forces to then turn against their former Communist allies. This was most clear between the wars in the case of China in the 1920s, when many Communists were killed by nationalist forces. The rhetoric at the time however stressed that national liberation was at the forefront of the defeat of international capitalism.

In the post-1945 period it became clear that this analysis was incorrect, and that international capitalism could survive the end of empire. Therefore new theories had to be developed to explain the changed situation, and the most influential within the official Communist movement was the theory of state monopoly capitalism. In this account, imperialism was still linked to a definite stage of capitalist development, but one in which the state functions as an outlet for surplus capital, rather than colonies and semi-colonies (see Mommsen 1981: 113–19). This was later tied to the Soviet promotion of peaceful coexistence with capitalist powers. Though this theory was often linked to the specific needs of the ruling group in the Soviet Union at the time, some of its claims were not entirely invalid, and it did overlap to some degree with other, more independent Marxist perspectives, that were developing at the time.

Under-Development and World Systems Theory

These theoretical approaches draw on some of the insights of the theories discussed above, but take them further. The theory is particularly associated with Paul Baran's *The Political Economy of Growth*, and even more with the 1960s and 1970s work of Andre Gunder Frank (1969a and b). It was further developed in the 1970s by Walter Rodney (1972), Samir Amin (1976) and Arghiri Emmanuel (1972b). The starting point for this analysis was the acceptance that capitalism and imperialism were indeed parasitic, and that this was most clear in the case of the underdeveloped world. In this respect it was not so different from the Soviet theories of the 1920s.

On the other hand, under-development theories departed from those Soviet theories in terms of political strategy, and this was because of their very different analysis of the social structures that existed in the poor countries. Paul Baran (1957: 197) argued that imperialism was based on the dominance of monopoly capital and is 'now directed not solely towards the rapid extraction of large sporadic gains from the objects of its domination, it is no longer content with merely assuring a more or less steady flow of those gains over a somewhat extended period. Propelled by well organized, rationally conducted monopolistic enterprise, it seeks today to rationalize the flow of these receipts so as to be able to count on it in perpetuity'. This account of under-development was part of what Baran (1957: 163–4) described as a stagnant, decaying, monopoly capitalism, which, 'far from serving as an engine of economic expansion, of technological progress and of social change' actually represents 'a framework for archaic technology, and for social backwardness'. The idea of a parasitic capitalism, as opposed to the dynamic competitive capitalism of Marx's day, was similar to Baran and Sweezy's (1966) argument, derived from Lenin, that monopoly capitalism had led to a mass of surplus capital that could not be used for accumulation in the rich countries. There was a tendency for the economic surplus, defined as the difference between total output and the socially necessary cost of producing total output, to rise, due to the growth of monopoly and the (supposedly) resultant decline in price competition. Baran and Sweezy identified several outlets for the surplus capital, including military and other government spending, advertising, and direct foreign investment. The last of these was only a short-term stop gap as it would lead to a further rise in surplus capital at home (although it could also be wasted on unproductive areas too), as surplus was extracted from the poor countries (Baran 1957: 22–4). This last point was the crucial difference between Lenin, who argued that surplus capital investment abroad could lead to capital expansion in the receiving country, and Baran and Sweezy. The latter essentially took the view developed in the increasingly Stalinist Comintern of the 1920s, that capitalism was now parasitic everywhere, as surplus extraction from the poor countries resulted in under-development. The capital that stayed in the Third World was wasted on luxury consumption by landlords and what Baran (1957: ch.6; also Frank 1969a: 168–9) called comprador administrations, tied and dependent on the imperialist countries.

Frank developed this theory further by particularly emphasizing the links between development and under-development. Like dependency theory (below), this theory was developed in the context of the perceived failures of import-substitution industrialization in the Third World, and a reflection on the ways in which this led to new forms of dependence, particularly on the import of capital goods, and on foreign investment by multinational companies. Frank developed this into a grand theory of development and under-development, which was used to explain the history of capitalism since at least the sixteenth century. This historical sociology of capitalism was critically discussed in Chapter 2, along with the problems associated with it. Here we need to focus much more on the utility of this theory for understanding the post-1945 international order.

The basic claim of Frank's theory is to argue that development and under-development are two sides of the same coin. Liberally borrowing from Baran's concept of economic surplus, Frank argued that the developed countries were developed because they extracted the economic surplus produced by the poorer countries. Frank argued that this process of surplus extraction occurred within countries too, but it was also clear that his hierarchy of metropoles exploiting satellites could be applied to rich and poor countries too. Thus, 'satellites remain under-developed for the lack of access to their own surplus' (Frank 1969a: 9), as capitalism 'has at all times and in all places ... produced both development and underdevelopment' (Frank 1969a: 240). For Frank, the whole world was capitalist irrespective of the relations of production that existed in a particular locality, whereas Baran argued that non-capitalist relations of production persisted, but were subordinated to the requirements of the wider capitalist-dominated international economy. Both agreed that this resulted in surplus extraction from satellite to metropolis. Walter Rodney (1972) argued along similar lines in his *How Europe Underdeveloped Africa*, but this work focused mainly on the colonial era.

Immanuel Wallerstein's world systems theory was very similar to these approaches. Indeed, he explicitly acknowledged his debt to Baran and Frank (Wallerstein 1979: 9) and argued that the world systems had been capitalist since at least the sixteenth century, and the basis for this was a division of the world into core, peripheral and semi-peripheral areas (Wallerstein 1974a, b). He argued that the core areas have since at least 1640 specialized in higher value production and appropriated a surplus from the periphery and semi-periphery (Wallerstein 1979: 18–19). In terms of the post-1945 era, Wallerstein suggests that a new semi-periphery has developed in southern Europe and East Asia, which acts as a buffer between core and periphery. This argument amounts to less an explanation and more a description of the rise of a number of countries out of peripheral status, though we will see below that a number of writers drew on world systems theory and dependency theory to try to explain the East Asian miracle. What is clear is that while Wallerstein added another layer to Frank's conception of metropolis and satellite, he essentially argued that under-development did indeed occur via a process of surplus transfer.

In many ways, under-development and world systems theory appear to be identical to those of Soviet Marxism in the 1920s. Both emphasized the parasitic nature of imperialism and the under-development of the colonies and semi-colonies. But they differed in one crucial respect. Stalinism argued that there could be a national alliance of almost all classes against imperialism in the oppressed nations, whereas under-development theory argued that this was impossible because the social structure in the under-developed countries was so strongly influenced by metropolitan interests. Frank (1969a: 343) argued that in Latin America, 'neo-imperialism and monopoly capitalist development are drawing and driving the entire bourgeois class ... into ever closer economic and political alliance with, and dependence on, the imperialist metropolis'. Baran (1957: 221) had earlier argued in a similar vein that '[u]nder such conditions the political independence barely won turns into a sham, the new ruling group merges with the old ruling group, and the amalgam of property-owning classes supported by imperialist interests uses its entire power to suppress the popular movement for genuine national and social liberation'.

In Frank's (1969b) case, this led to advocacy of socialist revolution to overcome under-development. Interestingly though, socialism came to mean an alternative way of promoting national development in a context where national capitalist development was no longer possible. In effect, socialism was conflated with de-linking from the world economy and promoting autarchy.

However, perhaps the main weakness of under-development theory was its failure to precisely explain the mechanisms of development and under-development. Indeed, the theory effectively constructed an ahistorical divide between metropolis and satellite, or core and periphery, which failed to explain changes within this structure, or how such a structure is maintained over time. The argument appeared to rest on the idea that a process of surplus extraction occurs through trade and investment relations between rich and poor world. Again, the mechanisms are not totally clear, but they could presumably refer to the fact that multinational companies may invest so much in a poor country, but they export more money in terms of profit repatriation. Added to this may be practices such as tax avoidance through transfer pricing, where two or more parts of the same parent multinational company trade across national borders, but declare their profits in the lower tax country (Murray 1981). Similarly, a process of surplus extraction may occur through unequal trade, in which the benefits of such transactions accrue to the rich country.

The problem with these arguments is that while such practices do indeed occur, they are not sufficient to establish as stark a dichotomy as that of development in one location, and under-development in another. Foreign investment may lead to some profit repatriation, but this is true in all locations where multinationals invest, not just poor countries. Furthermore, some investment will stay in the home country, and this will have some spin-offs in terms of income generation, employment, foreign exchange in the case of exporters, and so on, even if these may be more limited. Similarly, while trade relations may be unequal, they are not so unequal that the rich location accrues all the benefits and the poor location none at all.

These problems are most clear when we actually examine the nature and direction of capital flows and trade in the post-war international order. The internationalization of capital after 1945 was actually characterized by the increasing concentration of capital within the rich world, and most trade (measured in value terms) was between rich countries. This is not to deny the importance of foreign capital or trade to poorer countries, but it is to deny the starkness of a theory which suggests that the developed world only developed because it under-developed the poor world. If this was the case, then we would expect the direction of capital to flow from rich to poor world, and most trade to take place between these two regions, in order to facilitate the process of surplus extraction that is said to lead to development and under-development. Indeed, the richer developing countries in the period after 1945 tended to be those that received significant amounts of foreign investment, and who traded more with the developed world. This fact – and especially the rise of East Asia – was central to Marxist critiques of Frank which suggest that imperialism is the pioneer of capitalism (Warren 1973, and see below), but also neoliberal approaches discussed in the next chapter. On the other hand, the fact that capital does concentrate in established locations is problematic for these alternative theories, as we have already seen in earlier chapters, and which we will discuss in depth in Chapter 7.

The work of Emmanuel (1972b) and Amin (1974; 1976) are important in that they attempted to explain some of the mechanisms of under-development that were so clearly absent in the work of Frank. Emmanuel argues that poorer countries lose out in relative, rather than absolute terms (Frank's argument), due to a process of unequal exchange. Imperialist relations can therefore be derived from trade rather than the Leninist export of capital (Emmanuel 1972a). For Emmanuel (1972b), wage differentials between rich and poor countries are the main cause of unequal exchange. He makes a number of assumptions that challenge orthodox trade theory: he argues that capital is internationally mobile while labour is (relatively) immobile, and this leads to a tendency for profit rates to equalize across countries. In this context, an unequal exchange occurs because poor countries exchange goods in which more labour time is embodied for goods which are the product of less labour time. A transfer of surplus thus occurs from the poor to the rich countries because profit rates equalize in the context of international capital mobility. The result is that the ratio of advanced country prices to poor country prices is greater than the ratio of advanced country labour time to poorer country labour time, as embodied in specific commodities. Like Frank, the argument is that it is therefore through exchange that a transfer of surplus takes place from poor to rich country.

Amin adds to these arguments suggesting that there is an international division between central and peripheral capitalist formations. This involves two modes of accumulation, autocentric or self-generating accumulation in the centre and extraverted accumulation in the periphery. For the latter, this means three 'distortions' from central capitalism:

1   a crucial distortion toward export activities, which absorb the major part of capital arriving from the center;
2   a distortion toward tertiary activities, which arises both from the special contradictions of peripheral capitalism and from the original structures of the peripheral formations; and
3   a distortion in the choices of branches of industry, toward light branches, together with the utilization of modern techniques in these branches. (Amin 1976: 288)

In the post-war period, with the emergence of the multinational company and foreign investment in manufacturing, extraverted accumulation continues in new forms. These include concentration on the production of luxury goods, profit repatriation, and unequal exchange, which Amin also sees as being caused by low wages (Amin 1976: 193).

Clearly both Emmanuel and Amin make a more rigorous attempt to explain processes of surplus extraction which are ultimately only described by Frank. But their explanations are unconvincing. Amin's theory of autocentric accumulation is inconsistent with a theory that suggests foreign capital investment is important to capital expansion in the core countries (Bernstein 1979; Smith 1980). Both theories are also problematic in their assumption that unit labour costs are lower in the poorer countries than in the richer ones. Wages are undoubtedly lower, but this can be offset by higher productivity in the richer countries, which itself is a product of earlier rounds of capital accumulation. In Marxist terminology, the extraction of relative surplus value can more than offset the extraction of absolute surplus value, and so workers in the rich countries can be both better off (in terms of consuming use values) and more exploited, in relative terms (Bettelheim 1972; Dore and Weeks 1979). If it was the case that rates of surplus value were higher in poor countries, then one would expect capital to move from rich to poor countries, an expectation shared with orthodox theories of trade and investment, but one that does not conform to the realities of the international economy.

It may be true that the rate of extraction of *absolute* surplus value is greater in poorer, than in richer countries (Dore and Weeks 1979), but this is offset by higher rates of relative surplus value in richer countries. What this means is that rates of capital accumulation involve the extraction of surplus value through long hours and low wages in poorer countries, more than it does through increasing productivity and thus lowering the social reproduction requirements of labour, as is more common in richer countries (Bettelheim 1972). In the 1970s, some Marxists argued that this differential could be explained by the coexistence of a capitalist mode of production with non-capitalist modes (Wolpe 1980). This articulation of modes of production meant that the capitalist mode benefited from the coexistence of a non-capitalist mode, as the latter lowered the reproduction costs of labour, thus allowing capitalists to pay a lower wage than might otherwise be the case. Drawing in part on Rosa Luxemburg's work on imperialism, this theory usefully focused on relations of production rather than exchange (Laclau 1971). However, it also tended towards a functionalist account, whereby the preservation of non-capitalist social relations is explained by the functional needs of capital (Kiely 1995: ch.4). Moreover, the theory still tended to adopt a unilinear account of social change, as it was assumed that the break up of the non-capitalist mode would pave the way for a transition towards a more dynamic form of capital accumulation based on the extraction of relative surplus value. Instead, what tended to happen was that earlier rounds of accumulation led to further concentration within these spaces, and a relative marginalization of others, irrespective of the preservation or otherwise of non-capitalist social relations (Kiely 2008a and b). A convincing theory of imperialism thus needed to focus on the unevenness of global capital accumulation, and how its unequal *effects* generated cores and peripheries. We will argue in Chapter 7 that the recent neo-liberal era has intensified these tendencies.

What this discussion suggests then, is that there is a division of the world based on different rates of capital accumulation, and uneven development. Baran, Frank, Emmanuel and Amin are all attempting to grasp this reality, and this is an important part of any theory of (economic) imperialism. However, their explanations for why this occurs, and how it has changed over time, are unconvincing.

Dependency Theory and Neo-Colonialism

Many books, particularly those in English, tend to conflate under-development theory and dependency theory. In fact, the former is just one version of a broad church of dependency theories (Kay 1989). What unites dependency theories is the recognition that developing countries are in a subordinate position in the international economy, and in some senses their economies are strongly influenced by the core economies. Dos Santos (1970: 231) thus suggests that '(d)epen-dence is a conditioning situation in which the economies of one group of countries are conditioned by the development and expansion of others'. This notion of dependence could of course be applied to any country, as all countries are in some sense dependent on others (Bernstein 1979). But what dependency theories argue is that this inter-dependence is asymmetrical, so that the US' dependence on foreign capital is qualitatively different from another country's dependence on aid.

The question that then needs to be addressed is how this is the case. A wide range of theories have been developed which have attempted to demonstrate how dependence reflects some deeper sense of subor-dination. One of the most influential is Raul Prebisch's theory of unequal terms of trade. This is another theory of unequal exchange, but unlike Emmanuel (above), Prebisch (1959; also Singer 1950) argued that this was less a reflection of wage differentials and more one of the kinds of goods that were being produced. He suggested that there was a tendency for the terms of trade to decline as against those of manufactured goods, which was similar to the position taken by Josiah Tucker in his debates with David Hume (Chapter 3). Prebsich argued that this was because of the intense competition that existed between many primary goods producers, as opposed to the relatively few manufactured goods producers. This was also reinforced by a low income elasticity of demand for primary goods, so that as average incomes increased, people spent a proportionately lower amount of their income on primary goods. It was also further reinforced by higher wages in the core countries, an argument further (problemati-cally) made by Emmanuel. Prebisch argued that his theory provided the rationale for import substitution industrialization policies, which were a means to modernize 'backward' countries and reverse the colonial legacy of concentrating on primary products. Prebsich's rela-tionship to dependency theory is therefore an ambiguous one: on the one hand, he suggests that there are structured inequalities in the global economy which lead to dependent subordination; on the other hand, like modernization theory, he advocates industrialization in order to catch up with the developed countries. For dependency theory proper, the argument concerning structured inequalities was accepted, but the solution to this problem – ISI – was regarded as being part of the problem by later dependency writers.

The related theory of neo-colonialism, is usually associated with Kwame Nkrumah, who led Ghana to independence in 1957 but was eventually ousted in a coup in 1966. Nkrumah's bitter experience led him to argue that neo-colonialism was the last stage of capitalism, and it was one in which political independence was rendered problematic as a result of economic ties with metropolitan countries. Neo-colonialism effectively meant indirect exploitation by economic means, through unequal trade relations, capital export on unfavourable terms to the periphery, manipulation of the terms of trade by rich countries, and conditions associated with aid. Nkrumah therefore accepted Prebisch's theory of unequal terms of trade, and this influenced the thinking behind the United Nations Conference on Trade and Development (UNCTAD), which was formed in 1964. UNCTAD was made up of newly independent nation-states attempting to overthrow the economic legacies of colonialism, and in the 1970s, the call was made for a new international economic order, which would guarantee prices for Third World products of the market prices fell below a certain level (see Gill and Law 1988: ch.14). The UN General Assembly agreed to this principle in two votes in the mid 1970s, but in practice, little progress was made, and commodity price agreements were always limited in the real world of political economy.

Nkrumah's theory however also developed some additional features, beyond Prebisch's initial arguments. These related to social structures within peripheral societies, exploitation by multinational companies, and the self-interested way in which aid was dispensed. In terms of the first point, Nkrumah (see also Fanon 1967) argued that formally independent countries were often run by governments who were in effect puppets, acting in the interests of (usually white) capitalists. According to Nkrumah:

> In the days of old fashioned colonialism, the imperial power had at least to explain and justify at home the actions it was taking abroad.

In the colony those who served the ruling imperial power could at least look to its protection against any violent move by their opponents. With neo-colonialism neither is the case. (1965: xi)

The second point referred to the ways in which industrialization did not necessarily alleviate, but could in fact increase, dependence. This was because of the role of multinational companies in exploiting the Third World. As we saw above, under-development theory suggested a zero-sum game between multinational company and Third World state. Dependency theory however, unlike Frank, but perhaps in common with Amin, argued that it was possible for multinational companies to promote development in the Third World, but that this development remained dependent on the core countries. This argument could even be applied to the success stories in East Asia, as these were said to be the result of multinational companies relocating from First to Third World, in order to 'super-exploit' cheap labour in the latter countries. The result was unemployment in the rich world, and distorted or abnormal, and above all dependent development, in the newly industrializing countries (Frobel *et al.* 1980; Hart-Landsberg 1979; 1984). Third World industrialization was thus still development which ultimately reflected the interests of western (and Japanese) multinational companies, the main agents of economic imperialism. This was reinforced by dependent elites and national capital in the Third World, which showed little interest in promoting genuinely independent, national capitalist development, in opposition to imperialism. It was further reinforced by aid practices by the rich countries, which were often tied to strategic (Cold War) and/or commercial interests, so that for instance aid was often tied to the recipient country buying goods from the sending country. In this way, aid too, was a post-war manifestation of capitalist imperialism (Hayter 1971; 1985).

What is clear is that dependency theory and theories of neo-colonialism do recognize the reality of capitalist development in the Third World after 1945. It is the question of how this was distorted that is particularly contentious, and needs further interrogation. Before doing so, we would benefit from first examining a different interpretation of capitalist development in the periphery after 1945. This is associated with the idea that imperialism was progressively promoting capitalist development in the periphery.

Progressive Imperialism?

The final theory examined here is diametrically opposed to the idea that imperialism hold backs capitalist development in the Third World. Drawing on Marx's apologies for colonialism on the grounds that this led to capitalist development in the 'backward countries', Bill Warren (1980) argued that it was clear that in the post-1945 period, imperialism was indeed the pioneer of capitalism. For Warren (1973) and others influenced by his work (Schiffer 1981; Sender and Smith 1986), all the evidence pointed to rapid capitalist development in the so-called periphery, and this was aided by foreign capital invested. Indeed, Third World countries got capital investment on the cheap, as it gave them access to technology which took years of effort and expense to develop in the metropolitan countries (Warren 1973). It also led to higher per capita income, employment generation, and new skills, and indeed aided the development of political democracy as capitalism and development were 'Siamese twins' (Warren 1980). To be sure, such capitalist development took place in the context of massive inequality and uneven development, but these are intrinsic features of capitalist development. The crucial point is that the fact that capitalist development was taking place was indisputable, whatever one thinks of the social consequences of such development. Focusing on the ways in which imperialism allegedly held back capitalist development played into the hands of nationalist mythologies (Kitching 1982; 2001), which could become self-fulfilling prophecies as states adopted policies which held back further capitalist development in the name of a spurious anti-imperialism.

Warren's controversial thesis led to a number of attacks from other Marxists, some claiming allegiance to a version of dependency theory (McMichael *et al.* 1974), others focusing on uneven development (Lipietz 1982; Bernstein 1982; Kiely 1995). Its stark contrast, with many if not all of the theories discussed in this section, suggests that we need a fuller analysis of the relationship between imperialism and capitalist development in the period from the 1940s to the 1970s. Before doing so, a few comments specific to Warren need be made, which in turn will lead us into a more general analysis.

First, on one level Warren is correct. It is indeed the case that capitalist development took place on a rapid scale in the period from 1945 to the early 1970s. This 'Golden Age' (Glyn *et al.* 1990) applied not only to the developed countries, but also to Third World countries which experienced very high rates of growth. In the 1960s and 1970s, developing countries as a whole had an annual average per capita growth rate of 3 per cent, higher than the averages for developed countries in the nineteenth century (Chang 2002: 132). Moreover, while growth rates did diverge considerably among developing countries, with East Asia doing particularly well in this period, they were still high throughout the developing world. African countries averaged growth rates of between 1–2 per cent per capita per year in the 1960s and 1970s, which again compares favourably with the developed countries in their era of 'take off' (Chang 2007: tables 5 and 7). Indeed, it has been argued that the 1960s and 1970s can be described as one where there was an industrial revolution in the Third World. Baran's (1957: 197) argument that metropolitan capital's over-riding interest is 'to prevent, or, if that is impossible, to slow down and control the economic development of under-developed countries' thus seems absurd – though no more absurd than neo-liberalism's claim that this era showed the inherent inefficiency of ISI, or indeed the claim that colonialism was better for developing countries than independence. Each of these claims flies in the face of the capitalist development which was occurring at the time. In Baran's case, he also gives metropolitan capital an almost omnipotent power to determine the fate of Third World countries. Much the same point can be made about under-development theory.

However, can the same be said of dependency theories, which actually agreed that capitalist development was possible, and indeed was happening, in the periphery? The main point made by different versions of this theory was that capitalist development was taking place, but that it was somehow different from earlier phases of capitalist development in the developed countries. While this argument is not necessarily incorrect, it sometimes led to the unconvincing contrast between 'normal' and 'dependent' capitalist development. This begged the question of what was 'normal' and ironically came close to a adopting Eurocentric view of capitalism that regarded advanced capitalism as the norm and dependent variations as simply deviations from that norm.

On the other hand, Warren's conclusions themselves tended towards a view that there was a normal road to capitalism, and in contrast to dependency theory, suggested that this was occurring in the Third World. Warren also tended to move from a position of recognition that such a development is occurring, to one that uncritically endorsed such development, without any examination of the social forces and struggles involved in such processes (Seers 1978; Lipietz 1982). In many ways, Warren's view was simply an inversion, a mirror image of the dependency view: both constructed a norm, and then argued about whether or not Third World countries were conforming to that norm (Gulalp 1986). What both theories lacked was an account of specificity, and the different ways in which capitalism was developing in the Third World. This in turn meant that there was a need to concretize the relationship between imperialism and uneven development, both internationally, and within specific nation states. In contrast to Warren, this meant recognizing that uneven development was not simply a product of the backwardness of capitalism in some places, but was intrinsic to the way that capitalism functioned throughout the globe. Put this way, the idea of dependency as a concept designed to understand specific manifestations of uneven development, rather than a grand theory, does seem useful (Palma 1978; Leys and Saul 2006; Kiely 2007a).

Summary: Imperialism and Post-War Capitalism in the Third World

The critical discussion of the theories outlined in this section suggests that, in terms of the relationship between economic imperialism and capitalist development in the periphery, we need to recognize the following. First, capitalist development was occurring in the Third World in the post-war period. Second, this did not necessarily mean that such development was replicating earlier processes of capitalist development in the developed countries. Third, while there may be mechanisms of domination and subordination that arise out of the unevenness of capital accumulation, these need to be specified rather than read off from a general theory which has preconceived expectations about what these may be. We could also add a fourth, which has been of less concern in this section, which is how does the 'North–South' question of imperialism relate back to questions of rivalries between the advanced capitalist powers? This is a question discussed in depth in Chapter 6 and especially Chapter 9, but will also be touched on in the conclusion here.

The first issue then, is a recognition that capitalism was occurring in the developing world. We need not assume that this would lead to convergence with developed countries, but some comparison with the latter's own methods of promoting capitalism is useful. As we saw in

Chapter 4, the advanced capitalist countries developed in the late nineteenth century through import-substitution policies, designed to protect their 'national economies' from foreign, or British competition. These policies also occurred in the dominions (Canada, Australia, New Zealand), but were not implemented in colonies as colonial powers did not allow such policies to take place. They also did not occur in independent Latin America, where dominant classes happily imported manufactured goods and whose wealth was derived from the land.

In the post-war period (or in Latin America, in the 1930s), this changed as new social and political forces demanded new policies. Both the forces and policies involved varied from country to country, but there was a general pattern of alliances across different classes, committed to national development through industrialization, justified on the grounds that living standards would improve in the long term, and through appeals to nation building. This was the domestic social basis for ISI policies in the Third World, although this varied from state to state in terms of ideological justification, social cohesion, degrees of contestation, and economic effectiveness (Sandbrook 1985; Evans 1995; Chibber 2003). At the same time, as the first section in this chapter showed, these policies were further enabled by the compromises made after 1945, which meant a commitment to a liberal international order on the part of the hegemonic power, but acceptance by the US of some protectionist policies by other states, including in the developing world. The existence of the Soviet Union, and the capacity of states to play off one superpower against another, gave further impetus to ISI policies.

Alongside the defeat of the US in Vietnam, and the wave of revolutions that took place in the 1970s, imperialism was seriously weakened in the period from 1945 to the mid 1970s. However, the period from the 1970s, and especially the early 1980s onwards, saw a period of neo-liberal restructuring which altered the nature of imperialism, both in terms of relations between the developed capitalist powers, and especially in terms of the collapse of the Soviet bloc, and capitalist development in the Third World. These issues are examined in the next chapter, but we should briefly note that, in many respects imperialist relations became more overt from the 1980s, particularly in relation to the former Third World. Ironically, as they did so, the concept of imperialism was increasingly abandoned, in favour of the idea of globalization. This abandonment was certainly in part caused by the weaknesses of existing theories of imperialism, but they also reflect the success of the establishment of neo-liberal hegemony in the 1980s, and especially the 1990s.

For the moment however, we should emphasize that in terms of capitalist development in the Third World, this did occur on a substantial scale after 1945. Such development was highly unequal and often failed to resolve questions of poverty, but it was capitalist development nonetheless – and this included substantial, if uneven and unequal, advances in social development indicators such as life expectancy, health care and so on. What this suggests is that contrary to under-development theory, capitalist development was occurring, but contrary to Warrenite Marxism, it was not necessarily leading to convergence with the rich countries. There were structured inequalities in the international economy, even if countries dealt with them in different ways. There was also significant policy space which enabled countries to pursue development strategies of import substitution industrialization. These were compromised by the fact that states hoped to shift from ISI and promote exports in the world market, but they faced competition from already established producers in the rich countries. They were also undermined at times but US opposition to some forms of nationalism, especially when it was perceived that this might develop in a socialist direction. This era then, represented some success for Third World nationalism against imperialism. This was to change substantially in the 1970s and 1980s.

How then does this debate relate to the question of US imperialism after 1945? One way of thinking about this is to briefly re-examine the work of William Appleman Williams, and those associated writers who are sometimes described as the 'Wisconsin school' (Williams 1972; McCormick 1967). Williams argued that the open door policy was essential to the market needs of US capital. In one respect, this argument is unconvincing because it has been argued in this section that trade and DFI figures show that there is no clear cut link between political and military intervention on the one hand, and economic expansion on the other (Tucker 1971; Perkins 1984). For this reason, the economistic interpretation of open-door imperialism (McCormick 1967), which links it to the accumulation needs of US capital, is as unconvincing as those classical theories of imperialism which link expansion to the needs of surplus capital.

On the other hand, a more flexile and less economistic reading of open-door imperialism is compatible with the argument outlined in this section (Young 1968; Gardner and Young 2005). It is still the case that American capital, or indeed (foreign) capital in general, *may* benefit from an open-door policy, whether or not they choose to take advantage of such a strategy. In other words, open-door imperialism is contingently useful rather than a structural necessity. Moreover, the open door can still guarantee markets and/or supplies of raw materials and other goods, and this can benefit specific capitals. It will not necessarily be demonstrated by quantitative indicators such as shares of world trade or investment, but that does not mean that foreign capital does not benefit from these linkages. Indeed, given that I have suggested that the effect of the open-door policy has been to marginalize some parts of the international economy, low shares of world trade and investment are hardly surprising. As we will see in the next chapter, such marginalization has gone hand in hand with an intensification of an open-door policy.

Conclusion: Imperialism and International Relations, 1945–1989

The period from 1945 to the early 1970s and beyond was characterized by five features relevant to our concerns. First it was a period of (compromised) liberal internationalism under US hegemony, based on growing cooperation between the advanced capitalist powers, rather than inter-imperialist rivalries. Second, it was a period of intersystemic conflict between liberal capitalism on the one hand, and a highly authoritarian, non-capitalist system on the other. Third, this conflict both influenced, and was influenced by, social revolution in the South, which gave rise to military intervention on the part of both superpowers. Fourth, the capitalist superpower was also able to use other means to influence sovereign states, and this took place in the context of the internationalization of capital. This was led by the United States, but other states played a crucial role. This internationalization led to greater integration among the developed states, which in turn further fuelled cooperation, although as we will see, tensions increased from the late 1960s. Finally, the compromises made to the liberal international order included some leverage for newly independent states to promote 'development' through import substitution policies not dissimilar to those carried out by European powers in the period from 1880 to 1914. At the same time, the internationalization of capital promoted new forms of uneven development, based on the tendency of capital to concentrate in certain areas, mainly in the already developed countries. In this way, capital was internationalized but it did not promote convergence between countries. The (economic) theories of imperialism that were developed after 1945 were flawed attempts to come to terms with these continued hierarchies. The late 1960s and early 1970s saw the beginnings of a new period, in which US hegemony briefly came under threat, but was ultimately maintained, based on the shift towards neo-liberalism and globalization, and the end of the Cold War. This is the subject of the next two chapters.

6
Neo-Liberalism, Globalization and Geo-Politics in the Post-Cold War World

This chapter focuses on the transition from the Bretton Woods era and the Cold War to one dominated by neo-liberalism and a revived US hegemony. This examination takes in the breakdown of Bretton Woods, the neo-liberal turn from 1982, the relationship between this shift and the 'transnationalization' of capital, and the changing strategies of the US state in the context of the global crisis of capitalism in the 1970s. It then moves on to assess this transition, through an examination of theories of the state and restructuring, and the wider geopolitical implications that follow, particularly in the context of the end of the Cold War.

The chapter has four sections. The first outlines the restructuring of international capitalism in the 1970s and 1980s, linking this to growing rivalries between capitalist powers, the collapse of the Cold War, and the rise of globalization in the 1990s. The second looks at competing explanations for this reconstruction, and in doing so considers the relationship between US hegemony, capitalist restructuring and globalization. This theoretical account is developed further through an examination of theories of the state in the third section, and particularly theories of the state in the international capitalist order. Finally, the fourth section provides a preliminary account of geo-politics since 1989, reviving the so-called Lenin–Kautsky debate as outlined in Chapter 4.

From Bretton Woods to Neo-Liberalism

This section examines the movement away from the Bretton Woods system in the early 1970s, to the decade of globalization in the 1990s. It briefly examines the question of the revival of so-called inter-imperialist rivalries in the 1970s, the US shift away from the Bretton Woods order, the debt crisis of 1982 and the rise of neo-liberalism, and the decade of globalization in the 1990s. This discussion is then used to discuss the relationship between globalization and imperialism in the next section.

By the late 1960s and early 1970s, it was clear that the post-war boom was coming to an end. There were a number of tensions in the international order, which included rising social conflict in the developed countries, revolution in the South, falling rates of profitability, growth and increasing unemployment and inflation, and the rise of possible challengers to US hegemony (Mandel 1975; 1980; Armstrong *et al.* 1991; Brenner 1998). These developments all served to undermine the Bretton Woods order, which was based on fixed exchange rates and a gold-dollar standard. As we saw in the previous chapter, in the late 1940s there was a dollar shortage, which was resolved by the US exporting money through Marshall Aid and foreign investment. This enabled the US' competitors, especially Japan and Germany, to recover, but this was at the expense of the stability of the Bretton Woods system. This was because the value of the dollar was increasingly undermined, as the US ran not only payments but trade deficits from the early 1970s. This was seriously damaging to the Bretton Woods system, as it reflected a key contradiction in the post-war international capitalist order. This was the fact that the dollar was not only an international currency, it was the US' national currency too. Therefore, its value relative to other currencies ultimately depended on the competitiveness of the United States economy. If this was undermined, then US gold reserves would erode, and it would therefore have to devalue, as the dollar would no longer be as 'good as gold'. On the other hand, from 1944 onwards, the supply of international currency to the rest of the world depended on the US transferring dollars abroad – that is, it depended on the US running a balance of payments deficit. This contradiction was a consequence of this dual role of the dollar. The US' decision to run ongoing balance of payments deficits had the effect of undermining its value; the dollar shortage of the 1940s had become a problem of too many dollars by the late 1960s.

This problem of a dollar 'glut' was not inevitable, provided that the US maintained its lead in production over any competitors. However, its share of total manufacturing goods in the world market declined from 28 per cent in 1957 to 16 per cent in 1970 (Itoh 1990: 48), and this undermined the international demand for dollars.

So, the US resolved the problem of dollar shortage by providing international credit from the 1940s, thus allowing the restoration of international trade through payments in dollars (though this only came into full effect in 1958). However, this policy was at the long-term cost of undermining its own productive capacity and competitiveness. By the mid 1960s, the US had a constant trade deficit with its two main competitors, Japan and Germany (Brenner 1998: 119). The US' competitors no longer needed as many dollars to buy US goods, so dollars stockpiled in European banks.

The problem of the value of the dollar was intensified by the US' military commitments overseas, especially in Vietnam. This escalated the American deficit, so that it was in effect importing real goods in exchange for dollars, which were effectively increasingly worthless but which were accepted by other states according to the principles of the Bretton Woods agreement (Brett 1983: 165). The US' trade balance of $10 billion in 1947 and $6.6 billion in 1964, declined to $0.6 billion by 1968. The balance of payments was in constant deficit from 1950, but soared from $2.5 billion in 1968 to $19.8 billion in 1971. In that same year, the US ran a trade as well as payments deficit for the first time (Brett 1983: 173).

It should be clear then, that while the US dollar deficit was essential to the post-war economic recovery, it was at the long-term cost of undermining the competitive strength of the US economy. There was a basic contradiction between the dollar as the national currency of the US, and the dollar as the international currency. Its value relative to other currencies rested on the viability of the US economy, for if this became so weakened that it could not compete, or if the US government adopted inflationary policies, which increased its balance of payments deficit, its foreign exchange reserves would disappear and it would have to devalue. The basic problem then was that the supply of US dollars to the rest of the world depended on the US deficit, but the stability of the dollar depended on the US economy returning to surplus.

These problems cut across a number of competing interests, which some writers interpreted as reflecting the revival of 'inter-imperialist rivalries' (Mandel 1970; Rowthorn 1971). From the viewpoint of the US, the deficit guaranteed military supremacy, but also reflected a decline in US productive power located in the 'home economy', while at the same time guaranteeing expanded consumption without normal balance of payments constraints (because of the role of the dollar). From the viewpoint of the European powers, their surpluses meant that their foreign exchange reserves were constantly expanding, but these of course were mostly held in dollars. Devaluation would wipe out the value of some of these savings, but if the US deficit continued, there was the problem of growing inflation – existing side by side with slower rates of economic growth due to falling profit rates and declining productivity increases. In either case, the problem manifested itself as a dollar glut in which excess dollars in the international economy were increasingly worthless.

The erosion of US competitiveness and rise of Japan and Germany led to a dollar glut from as early as the 1960s, and this led to the growth of a new Eurocurrency market, which was basically a market in externally held currencies, and particularly dollars. These deposits fell outside the control of normal domestic banking regulations, and so banks that used Eurodollars could lend more cheaply, pay higher interest rates and still make more profits. While the growth of the eurodollar market in part reflected weakening US competitiveness (as these dollars would otherwise return to the US in payments for US goods), the US state also recognized that the growth of this market was in many respects a welcome development. In particular, these markets facilitated the overseas expansion of US capital. This included the expansion of US banks that took advantage of the lack of controls over these dollars, a policy that was tolerated or even encouraged by the US state (Helleiner 1994: ch.4). It also included the expansion of US transnational companies that set up production sites in Europe, in order to take advantage of market access and higher productivity, and which found the eurodollar markets a cheap source of finance. This investment further encouraged the development of Fordist mass production in Europe, and led to the intensification of the internationalization of capital flows, which increased further with the rise of European and Japanese foreign investment. These processes of internationalization – of both production and finance – were thus cautiously welcomed by the US state, not least because in terms of finance, they reinforced the role of the dollar as the main international currency, even though there were serious questions over the dollar's value.

These questions were addressed by the Nixon administration, which took the decision to abandon gold convertibility and allow the dollar to float downwards in 1971. The end of dollar–gold convertibility was followed by a number of planned devaluations from 1971 onwards, which in turn led to an abandonment of the system of fixed exchange rates and its replacement by a 'managed floating' system from 1973, and other countries followed. This movement away from the fixed exchange rates and capital control system of Bretton Woods, to a new system of floating rates and freer capital movement, changed the context of domestic economic policy. In the case of the former, the domestic and the international were reconciled by policies that maintained the value of a domestic currency relative to gold or dollars, and promoted sufficient expansion to maintain full employment, at least in the 'advanced' capitalist countries. Thus, interest rates could be directly used to slow or increase investment and consumption. However, with the development of the eurodollar market, followed by the end of fixed exchange rates, the context in which state monetary policy operated was increasingly internationalized. Policies designed to maintain growth and employment could now put pressure on the exchange rate and foreign exchange reserves, as financial speculators would sell local currency in favour of safer foreign currencies. The fall in reserves would have a deflationary effect on the economy. This shift represented the beginning of a shift to neo-liberal discipline in the developed countries.

The US government's decision to abandon the gold-dollar exchange standard and fixed exchange rates potentially gave the US enormous financial power. In particular it eliminated the need for the US to control its own balance of payments as the dollar remained the main source of international payment, and so (theoretically) unlimited amounts of dollars could be released into international circulation. However, this was at the cost of increasing inflation, and by the late 1970s it was clear that the expansionary policies of the Nixon, Ford and Carter presidencies could no longer hold. From the mid to late 1970s, the US ran record trade and current account deficits. At this point Saudi Arabia began to sell dollar reserves and leading European countries made plans for developing a new currency, which could potentially become an alternative to the dollar. It was clear that there was a real threat of a crisis of confidence in the dollar, and therefore the international system that relied largely on this currency as a means of payment was under threat.

From 1979 onwards under Carter, and especially after the 1980 election of Reagan, there was a shift in policy in the United States. Any imposition of capital controls was rejected, and instead a new policy of controlling inflation was introduced. This was mainly implemented through increases in interest rates, which had the effect of squeezing domestic demand, at least in the early period of the Reagan years. It also had the effect of undermining the US as a market for developing countries' exports, and increasing debt payment obligations in the developing world, as we will see below.

However, this tight monetary policy of controlling inflation and sustaining the dollar through high interest rates was accompanied by a growing 'military Keynesianism', in which demand was sustained by running massive budget deficits. These deficits occurred because the Reagan government massively increased military spending in the context of a renewed Cold War with the Soviet Union (Halliday 1983), while at the same time promoting a policy of reducing taxation. Both trade and budget deficits were instead financed by attracting capital from overseas, including from the Eurodollar markets and from capital-starved Latin America, and this capital was initially attracted by high rates of interest. The high dollar therefore had the effect of keeping domestic prices low, which helped to keep inflation rates low. Thus, the US went from being the largest creditor nation in the 1950s to the largest debtor and foreign capital recipient by the 1980s. These policies also had the side effect of lifting some other countries out of recession, as they stimulated demand for other countries' products. From 1980 to 1985, external demand generated one-third of Japan's and three-quarters of West Germany's GDP. In the case of Japan, this linkage was even more direct as around one-third of its total exports went to the United States (Schwartz 2000: 212, 216). Indeed, inter-dependence between the US and Japan was great, as the latter partly funded the former's deficits, and so effectively Japanese financiers provided the credit needed by the US government that continued to subsidize the continued growth of Japanese exports (Brenner 1998: 184). By 1991, the US budget deficit stood at $74 billion and the trade deficit at $4 trillion. The world's main creditor in the 1950s and 1960s had by the 1980s and 1990s become the world's largest debtor (Arrighi 1994: 316–17).

Meanwhile, in the developing world, a major 'debt crisis' emerged in 1982. In, 1973–4 the price of oil quadrupled as a result of the cut in oil supplies by OPEC countries in response to the 1973 Arab–Israeli war. Oil exporters now needed to find an outlet for their windfall profits, and oil importers faced potentially devastating import bills. The oil exporting countries deposited their windfalls in European banks (or European affiliates of US banks) and these petrodollars added to the already expanding Eurodollar market. Banks then loaned these dollars to a small number of countries, mainly located in Eastern Europe and especially Latin America (plus a few larger countries throughout the Third World). Thus, in the 1970s private bank lending became the major means by which some 'developing countries' gained access to capital, as opposed to official channels such as the IMF and World Bank, as was the case in the 1950s and 1960s.

Banks loaned money at low rates of interest and, in a competitive and 'unregulated' climate, often committed enormous sums to particular Latin American states – by 1982, the nine largest US banks had committed over twice their combined capital basis to a handful of developing countries. At this time, interest rates were low and repayment periods were relatively long term. However, from the late 1970s interest rates increased rapidly and repayment periods generally became shorter. The effect of interest rate rises on developing country debtors was devastating, adding perhaps a further $41 billion to their debt (based on average interest rates from 1961–80). Moreover, high interest rates in the US attracted capital from all over the world, including from high debt and low savings developing countries that needed this capital to help pay back debts. This combination of high interest rates and capital export from the indebted countries constituted a reversal of historic proportions. As Arrighi states:

> From then on, it would no longer be First World bankers begging Third World states to borrow their overabundant capital; it would be Third world states begging First World bankers to grant them the credit needed to stay afloat in an increasingly integrated, competitive, and shrinking world market. (1994: 323)

These problems were exacerbated by the general decline in commodity prices for many of the products of developing countries. There was a dramatic fall in average commodity prices of one-third from 1980–82 (Roddick 1988: 65), which further reduced the capacity of developing countries to meet their interest payments, a tendency which continued throughout the 1980s.

In 1982, Mexico was the first country to officially default on its foreign debt, and when non-payment threatened to spread to Brazil, there was a real danger that western banks – who had committed so much capital to Latin America – could fail. This was the start of the debt crisis. From the viewpoint of western banks, they faced the prospect that a number of high debt countries were in no position to pay back the interest on their loans. What was therefore needed was more money to be loaned to the high debt countries, but with some guarantee that these countries could meet their debt obligations. However, while it may have been rational from the viewpoint of all the banks to loan more money, in the context of 'unregulated' competition, it made no sense for any one individual bank to carry out this task (as there were no guarantees that all the other banks would follow).

The debt crisis was effectively policed through granting limited access to new loans provided that they met with the approval of international finance, and particularly the International Monetary Fund. The IMF therefore became a far more active agent in the international economy, effectively policing a whole series of economies that faced balance of payments difficulties throughout the 1980s. Thus, despite the relative lack of power given to the IMF in 1944, reflected mainly in terms of its small amount of financial resources, it became a highly visible institution throughout the developing world, particularly after 1982. It received new (though still quite low) financial resources to help it carry out this task – and, alongside the conditions attached to its loans, this visibility led to massive protests against the institution from the 1980s onwards (Walton and Seddon 1994).

For the IMF, countries that faced severe balance of payments deficits, and therefore difficulties in meeting their interest payment obligations, were said to have adopted incorrect policies. What this amounted to was the idea that they were consuming more than they were producing, and importing more than they were exporting. This in turn was caused by too much government intervention in these economies. What was therefore needed was a set of policies that would encourage countries to re-adjust their economies, and start to export more than they imported, and produce more than they consumed, therefore enabling them to earn foreign exchange to meet their debt obligations. The US state advocated a policy of 'managed neo-liberalism' in which the IMF would play a key role in policing debtor nations, in terms of approving loans made either by the IMF itself or more indirectly the (increasingly diminishing) new loans from banks, subject to certain conditions. The burden of adjustment was placed solely in the hands of the debtor countries, rather than surplus countries, and this meant that in practice enormous policy changes had to be undertaken.

The immediate policy required then was for countries to restore balance of payments equilibrium. In this respect, IMF management was a success, as for instance Brazil and Mexico quickly moved from current account deficits to small surpluses in just two years (1982–4). But these results were achieved simply by a massive cut in imports. From 1985 to 1987, the highly indebted countries transferred $74 billion to creditors – the equivalent of 3.1 per cent of the combined GNP of these countries in that period (World Bank 1989: xix). At great social cost, this guaranteed repayment to creditors, and indeed the profits of leading banks soared in this period. For the debtors, adjustment usually entailed a shift to neo-liberal, market friendly policies, which in practice often led to devaluation of a nation's currency (to make exports cheaper), a reduction in state spending (to combat inflation), wage cuts (to restore private sector 'incentives'/profitability), non-discrimination against exporters, and revision to (state controlled) pricing policy, particularly for agriculture. In other words, developing countries shifted policies from protectionist import substitution industrialization, to one where the market could be 'freed' from state constraints by policies of liberalization, privatization, and reform of the state. The basic assumption was that indebted countries had chosen economically inefficient policies, which have focused too much on states protecting domestic economies from the opportunities that global market forces can offer. In this interpretation, globalization came to mean countries operating open policies, which allow them to exercise their comparative advantage. While the results of the adjustment policies were poor in terms of both economic growth and social consequences in the 1980s, there was a shift in optimism in the globalization decade of the 1990s, as foreign investment grew and production became more 'globalized' (see Chapter 7).

This section has outlined a shift away from the Bretton Woods era to one of neo-liberal capitalism from the 1970s onwards. This involved economic crisis, US decline and increased competition from other developed countries, anti-inflationary policies and the liberalization of finance, the debt crisis, and the global shift towards market friendly neo-liberal policies. All these were further reinforced with the collapse of communism in the late 1980s and early 1990s. But the question that needs to be asked is how does this relate to theories of imperialism? This is investigated in the next section, which examines the relationship between US hegemony, capitalist restructuring and globalization.

Theorizing Restructuring, Hegemony and Globalization

This section provides a critical reflection on the narrative presented in the previous section. In particular, it examines various ways of interpreting the shift to a neo-liberal international order, and discusses how this might relate to the question of imperialism. But we must also introduce the concept of globalization, and begin to examine how this too might relate to the question of imperialism. We therefore need to focus on the question of US 'decline' and the rise of competitors, the US decision to shift to floating exchange rates, the anti-inflationary stance of the US from the late 1970s, and the resolution of the debt crisis in the South in the 1980s.

For a number of Marxists from various schools of thought, the growing tensions that existed in the international capitalist order in the early 1970s were expressions of the revival of inter-imperialist rivalries (Mandel 1970; 1975; Rowthorn 1971). Rowthorn (1971: 32) described this view as one in which 'the relatively autonomous states no longer perform the necessary organizing role, or perform it so badly that serious conflicts break out between them and the unity of the system is threatened. For this to happen the antagonisms between states must be severe'. Thus, the focus of theories of imperialism began to shift once again. In the context of the post-war boom, as we saw in the last chapter, the focus was overwhelmingly on the effects of imperialism on what had come to be known as the Third World. Implicit in such theories was the idea that the US was now a super-imperialist power, whose overwhelming power had rendered classical theories based on inter-imperialist rivalries redundant (Baran and Sweezy 1966). Rowthorn (1971: 31) argued that this view suggested that 'all other capitalist states are dominated by the United States and have comparatively little freedom to choose their policies and control their economies in ways opposed by the American state. America acts as the organizer of world capitalism, preserving its unity in the face of socialism. This domination may not, of course, operate smoothly – for antagonisms will not be eliminated but merely contained'. Finally, a third view revived Kautsky's theory of ultra-imperialist cooperation, and argued that this operated in the post-war period, albeit in the context of US leadership. However, alongside these explicitly Marxist theories in the 1970s, there developed other theories, both Marxist and non-Marxist, of globalization, and these will also be discussed in this section.

There is clearly evidence to support both the views of inter-imperialist rivalries and US super-imperialism. The dollar crisis and European and Japanese recovery both suggest that antagonisms between rival blocs had returned (Mandel 1970; Rowthorn 1971). But it is also clear that the US did play a leading role in restructuring capitalism in the 1970s, especially through financial domination, and despite the defeat in Vietnam, the US remained overwhelmingly dominant in military terms (Petras and Rhodes 1976). However, both these views are not without their problems, because they fail to capture the specificity of the nature of US imperialism, particularly in its relations with other advanced capitalist states, and the way that neo-liberal restructuring served to reinvigorate US hegemony.

The restructuring from the 1970s, and especially from 1979 onwards, must be put in the context of the nature of the Bretton Woods order. While this was a golden age in terms of growth rates, it was also a period of reconstruction, and in that sense it was also one of transition (Burnham 1990; Panitch and Gindin 2003; 2004; Konings 2005). Indeed, by the time European currencies became fully convertible in 1958, the order was already under threat. The viability of the system of fixed exchange rates rested on capital controls being maintained, but these were being undermined by growing trade and foreign invest-ment (as well as growing domestic competition, not least in finance), which all led to the expansion of a global financial market, which further undermined fixed rates and capital controls. Thus, just as it is mistaken to see the New Deal as the start of an era in which capital was unproblematically subject to social control, so too is it the case with the Bretton Woods era. The financial regulations associated with the New Deal were a product of social struggles from below, but the effect of new deal policies was to expand the integration of the US popula-tion into a wider network of financial relations, and the massive expansion of commodity production and consumption (Lacher 1999). Similarly, the effect of the Bretton Woods order was not a straightfor-ward system of financial repression, but rather the promotion of new forms of the internationalization of capital. This was less a case of global markets outgrowing national states, and more 'a process through which the dramatic expansion of American finance began to assume international dimensions. It was the externalization of American practices and institutions that during the 1960s began to transform a conservative system of international payments into an integrated system of expansionary financial markets' (Panitch and Konings 2008b: 10).

This process of internationalization did not lead to a new era based on competing national blocs of capital, as theorized by Bukharin, but rather a reorganization of US hegemony and an intensification of international integration, or what came to be called (economic) globalization. That these developments occurred was due to the fact that 'by the time of the crisis of the early seventies, American ideological and material penetration of, and integration with, Europe and Japan was sufficiently strong to rule out any retreat from the international economy or any fundamental challenge to the American state' (Panitch and Gindin 2003: 19; see also Poulantzas 1974: 81). The use of the notion of inter-imperialist rivalries thus hardly captured the very different realities that existed in the post-war order, both in 1945 and in the 1970s and 1980s. This was not only because of the overwhelming military power of the US, but also the radically different economic circumstances that existed alongside US hegemony. There was an increasingly open trading order, whereby average tariffs were increasingly lowered in the post-war period (with some exceptions), and direct foreign investment took on an increasingly significant role. This not only increased global integration, but affected 'domestic' class structures. There were no longer clearly demarcated territorial blocs of national capital, but national capitalist states whose reproduction 'was increasingly tied to the rules and structures of the American-led global order' (Panitch and Gindin 2003: 20). This meant that, from the 1970s onwards, 'all the nation states involved came to accept a responsibility for creating the necessary *internal* conditions for sustained *international* accumulation, such as stable prices, constraints on labour militancy, national treatment of foreign investment and no restrictions on capital outflows' (Panitch and Gindin 2003: 20; see also Poulantzas 1974: 47). This did not mean that all countries converged absolutely on policy, and domestic institutions and social and political forces continued to impact in different ways (Hay 2005b), but it did mean that the direction of change was in a neo-liberal direction (Albo 2005).

This of course leads us to the question of globalization. The literature on this subject is vast and one cannot hope to do it justice here (see Held *et al.* 1999; Scholte 2005; Held and McGrew 2007; Bisley 2007). Briefly, much of this literature has broken down debates over globalization into a number of camps: Held *et al.* (1999) discuss hyper-globalizers, sceptics, and transformationalists; Giddens (1999) discusses sceptics and boosters; McGrew (2000) discusses neo-liberal, radical and transformationalist views; and Hay and Marsh (2001) talks of three waves of globalization theory. Much of this debate concerns the extent to which globalization has occurred and how this can be measured: the hypers and the first wave both suggesting that the movement of flows, images and people has transcended, or at least transformed the nation state (Ohmae 1995), while the sceptics and the second wave both point out the limits on capital flows for example, and argue that the nation-state continues to be of great relevance (Hirst and Thompson 1999; Hay 2005a). The third wave suggests that the discourse of globalization has facilitated changes in state policies that effectively become self-fulfilling prophecies, which re-interpret contingent political and social change as a necessity, thus making globalization a political project more than an objective process (Hay 2000). The transformationalists argue that there have been considerable qualitative changes in the international order, such as increasing mobility (of capital, media, people) and the rise of international institutions of global governance (Held and McGrew 2007), a position endorsed by Giddens' support for globalization's boosters.

None of these positions had much to say about the particular role of the US state[1], or indeed the neo-liberal restructuring that took place from the 1970s. This partly reflects the ambiguous nature of much of the globalization debate, and the extent to which it is a concept used to explain certain phenomena, and that has causal status, or whether it is actually something that refers to certain phenomena that can be explained by other (social and political) factors (Rosenberg 2000; 2005; 2007; Kiely 2005a and 2005b; Axford 2007). Some Marxists have attempted to draw on the idea of globalization, regarding it as a new period of capitalist development that is closely linked to neo-liberal transformation. For Bill Robinson (2004: 9, 10; see also Sklair 2002; Becker and Sklar 1987), globalization's defining feature is '*the rise of transnational capital*', a central feature of which is 'the increasing globalization of the production process itself'. For Robinson:

Capital has become increasingly liberated from the spatial barriers of the nation-state as a result of new technologies, the worldwide reorganization of production, and the lifting of nation-state constraints to the operation of the global market taking place under globalization. (2004: 39–40)

As a result the nation-state 'is no longer the organizing principle of capitalism and the institutional "container" of social relations' (Robinson 2004: 40). The clear implication is that US hegemony is gradually being eroded by a new transnational hegemony, where the US state plays a leading role, alongside other institutions of a nascent transnational state (Robinson 2004: 77, 129). Robinson's work constitutes one of the more constructive Marxist attempts to come to terms with the globalization of production. He rightly challenges those views that hold on to some notion of inter-imperialist rivalries (Robinson 2004: 137), or which, in an attempt to partially defend the Lenin–Bukharin legacy, exaggerate the extent of geo-political competition in the international order (see below). But what is less satisfactory is his account of the relationship between the nation-state and transnational capitalism, and by implication, the shift towards a neo-liberal order. He tends towards a reductionist view of the state, regarding it as a mere transmission belt for an increasingly globalized capitalism (Robinson 2004: 141). This has echoes of Cox's (1996: 111) view of the internationalization of the state, where, 'as a consequence of international production, it becomes increasingly pertinent to think in terms of a global class structure alongside or superimposed upon national class structures'. Hardt and Negri (2000: 307) also share this view when they state that '[g]overnment and politics come to be completely integrated into the system of transnational command'. However, what in Cox's view is a mere description becomes, for Robinson, a substitute for an explanation, so that one spatial node simply sheds another when required by the needs of (global) capital. As Morton suggests, the problem for Robinson:

is the lack of appreciation of the articulation of capitalism through multi-scalar relations. Capitalism does not simply supplant one spatial scale for another but instead works across spatial scales within state forms and through geopolitics. The point is not to assume the supplanting of one spatial scale for another – or to take the dominance of one spatial scale over another as a given – but to appreciate the manner in which capitalism operates through nodal rather than dominant points. This means appreciating states as political nodes in the global flow of capital, whilst eschewing claims that the global system can be reduced to a struggle between states ... The transnational state thesis ... offers a *flattened ontology* that removes state forms as a significant spatial scale in the articulation of capitalism, levels out the spatial and territorial logics of capital accumulation, and elides the class struggles extant in specific locations. (2007: 148; see also Brenner 1999)

For our concerns here, what this means is that the transnational capitalism thesis tends to exaggerate the independence of 'transnational capital' from national state, and as a result, like liberal globalization theories, downplays the crucial role that some states played in deepening global integration (Rosenberg 2005). In particular, it underestimates the role of the US state in taking the lead in the promotion of neo-liberal policies. As was suggested in the previous section, the interest rate rises under Paul Volcker (Chair of the Federal Reserve) from 1979 were crucial in the promotion of policies of liberalization. As Gill suggests:

the US financial complex has been at the vanguard of restructuring and deregulation (or more accurately, liberal re-regulation) of the world financial system. This more liberalized system that emerged during the 1980s and 1990s helped recycle the trade surpluses of other nations (especially from China, Japan and South Korea, as well as from the European Union) to fund American expansion and massive US debts and payments deficits. (2004: 31–2)

This in turn has enabled the US to remain militarily hegemonic. The effect of these changes has been, among other things, the massive growth of trade and budget deficits in the US. In 2006, the US trade deficit stood at $838 billion, the equivalent of 6.4 per cent of US GDP (Rude 2008: 21). Whether this signals the erosion of US hegemony is an issue for debate in Chapter 9, but we should immediately question the view that this should be seen simply as the triumph of financial capital over industrial capital. As we saw in the discussion of British imperialism and gentlemanly capitalism, this view tends to set up too rigid a dichotomy between industry and finance. The Volcker shock was designed to retain existing capital in, and attract new capital to, the US, as part of a process which re-asserted US hegemony and successfully reorganized global capitalism. In attracting financial flows, the US also revived its productive base, as finance served to discipline firms in the promotion of shareholder value, in the process rapidly reallocating capital to more profitable sectors, financing risky new ventures, and new technological investment in older sectors. Of course the role of finance carried with it huge risks too, as capital tended to exaggerate profitable expectations and under-estimate risks (such as the US sub-prime mortgage market in 2007), and shift rapidly out of sectors (for example, the hi-tech stock market boom and bust 1996–2001) and countries (financial crashes in Latin America and East Asia) when it was clear that these would not be fulfilled. Indeed, financial liberalization has been accompanied by an increase in financial crises (Rude 2004).

However, this does not mean that finance is simply a parasite on industrial production, and for global capital and US hegemony, the restructuring process was successful. The US rate of growth from 1983 to 2002 was greater than in all the other G7 countries, and by the late 1990s, the real GDP of the US was 20 per cent higher than the total of the top 12 Western European economies, compared to relative parity in 1982 – and indeed a gap of only 13 per cent in 1950, at the beginning of the post-war boom. For France, Germany and Italy combined, the gap was 55 per cent in 1950; by 1982 it had narrowed to 37 per cent, but by 1998 it had increased once again, back up to 51 per cent (Panitch and Gindin 2005a: 151). But it was not only this revival that reflected its hegemony; in addition, the US provided a model for others wanting access to global flows, and further stimulated the global integration of capital, as well as increasing the productivity of capital (Dumenil and Levy 2004). This served to discipline other developed capitalist states who also wanted access to the increasingly global circuits of capital, including states in the developing world through more coercive means such as IMF and World Bank conditions attached to new loans and aid. These in turn reflected the capitalist nature of US imperialism, which did not need directly political, military or 'territorial' means to discipline other states (Saull 2005: 269).

These developments did in part reflect the growing 'transnationalization' of capital, as Robinson contends, but it should be clear by now that the US state played a leading role in the shift towards neo-liberalism. Perhaps it is better then, to regard this process, less as one in which transnationalization takes place 'above' the nation-state, and more one whereby increasingly internationalized capital came to depend on many states, and the US state in particular (Panitch and Gindin 2004: 54). The US state, as the hegemonic power, leads all capitalist states in the reorganization of global capitalism, although of course these other states were all active agents in the uneven and contested processes of neo-liberal transitions.

This can be seen if we look again at the effect of the Volcker shock of 1979–81. At the time, this was rationalized in terms of the monetarist idea that inflation could be controlled by the state limiting the supply of money. However, this could not occur because the supply of money is not determined solely by governments, but rather by the demand for private loans (and thus debt) in the private sector, and thus the creation of credit by private financial institutions. The interest rate rises from around 8 per cent in 1978 to 19 per cent in 1981 increased the price of, and therefore reduced short-term demand for, money. Though these very same rate increases helped to foster further financial instruments that had already developed in the 1960s and 1970s, and thus promoted a further longer term increase in the supply of money as credit, the short term effect was very significant. It led to a recession that increased unemployment and defeated organized labour, eroded welfare states, and simultaneously restored confidence in the dollar as the international reserve currency. This in turn allowed the US to run its national economy without large-scale foreign exchange reserves. The restructuring of global capitalism in a neo-liberal direction thus simultaneously led to a reinvigoration of US hegemony, whereby the US state could runs deficits financed by US Treasury bills, so long as there were buyers for these bills. Foreign capital soared into the US from the early 1980s, initially attracted by high interest rates and then by the fact that the dollar was a safe haven as the international reserve currency (Seabrooke 2001: ch.4). The US was now an imperialist power that relied heavily on capital imports to maintain its primacy, though whether this is sustainable after the economic shock of 2007–8 is subject to debate, and will be considered further in Chapter 9. In terms of theories of imperialism then, this represented a new configuration of relations between the developed capitalist states, that can be traced back to post-war reconstruction, and which represented far greater cooperation under US leadership than in the pre-war period. This continued, albeit in new ways, in the 1990s and beyond, and is also discussed further in the context of contemporary geo-politics, below and in Chapter 9.

But what is clear from the discussion on the transition to neo-liberal globalization is that nation-states, and the US state in particular, played a key role in the process. We therefore need a better understanding of the capitalist state, and this is discussed in the next section.

State Theory Revisited

Marxist debates on the state are essentially attempts to show why the state is not neutral in its dealings with different social classes in society. In other words, its essential task was to explain why the state in capitalist society ultimately represented the interests of the capitalist class. Marx and Engels (1964: 59) wrote in 1846 that the capitalist state is 'nothing more than the form of organization which the bourgeoisie necessarily adopt both for internal and external purposes, for the mutual guarantee of their property and interest'. However, there were also more sophisticated interpretations of states in specific periods, not least in terms of Marx's notion that the state had some autonomy from the bourgeoisie in France in the mid-nineteenth century (Marx 1979; Miliband 1977: 284–5).

Much of the debate since then has replicated these two views. The former, instrumentalist view regards the state as an instrument that is manipulated by dominant classes. This occurs 'either directly through the manipulation of state policies or indirectly through the exercise of power on the state' (Gold *et al.* 1975: 34), which in turn reflects close social ties between state managers and the capitalist class operating outside the state (Miliband 1969; 1983). Poulantzas (1969; 1978) on the other hand, offered a less agency-based and more structuralist account, which argued that the capitalist state's form and function was necessarily determined by the wider totality of capitalist social relations. In this way, the state was closer to what Engels (1978: 338) had described as an ideal collective capitalist, in which the state acts for the general interest of capital, rather than the particular interests of specific capitals (Altvater 1973).

Whether or not the positions in the Miliband–Poulantzas debate were necessarily incompatible is questionable (Barrow 2008). But alongside this debate, there was a further position, sometimes known as the state derivation debate. This focused more on the social forms of capitalism, with some contributions suggesting that only under the

totality of capitalist social relations was there the appearance of separate economic and political spheres (Clarke 1991). The 'economic'
did not determine, as crude economistic Marxism (and its detractors)
argued, but rather the whole notion of a separate economic sphere was
itself a product of historically specific social relations. It was this
argument that was developed by a number of 'open' and 'political
Marxists' (Clarke 1991; Wood 1995). One implication was that capital itself is not contained by any specific nation-state, and some
contributors from within this tradition suggested that there is no
intrinsic relationship between capital and the nation-state, in part
because the former preceded the latter (Teschke 2003; Lacher 2006;
Teschke and Lacher 2007).

While this undoubtedly was a valuable contribution to the debate,
what was missing was the relationship between state form and state
function, which in turn closely mirrored what was at stake in the structuralism of Poulantzas against the more agency-based account of
Miliband. It was all very well pointing out that the notion of a
distinctly political sphere was a form of appearance of capitalist social
relations, but this could only be the starting point, and not the end-
point of the analysis (Callinicos 2009b: 84). The separation of the two
spheres may have (unevenly) occurred through the development of
capitalist social relations, but this in itself said little about what actual
role or function the state played in this process. This left us with three
overlapping problems: the relationship between structure and agency,
between state form and state function, and between the general fact of
the capitalist state and the specific policy of governments that constitute part of that state.

Furthermore, what was often missing in much of this debate was
the fact that the state does not exist in isolation, but is actually part of
an international system of nation-states (Barker 1978; Ashman 2009).
As has already been suggested, in this regard there are three current
positions in the debate: the first emphasizes the continued utility of
nation-states and thus geo-political competition; the second, at the
other end of the spectrum, argues that nation-states are increasingly
irrelevant; and the third suggests that nation-states retain their relevance but their increasing internationalization under US hegemony
has eroded, but not eliminated, geo-political conflict of the kind theorized by classical Marxist theories of imperialism.

Callinicos (2007a; 2009a; 2009b: ch.2) has perhaps most clearly
shown how many of the current (Marxist) debates over imperialism

are simultaneously debates over the nature of the capitalist state in the international state system. He has attempted to theorize this relationship by critically drawing on realist theories of international relations. Like Harvey (at times), Callinicos (2007a: 539) suggests that imperialism 'is constituted by the intersection of, respectively, capitalist and territorial logics of power and economic and geo-political competition'. The inter-relation between these two logics is one based on mutual irreducibility but also one which demonstrates the close connections between the two. This is done by following Block's (1977; 1987) agency-based account of the state, which focuses on the relationship between capitalists and state managers, and how the rules of reproduction between these two social groups are based on both independence and mutual interaction (Ashman and Callinicos 2006; Callinicos 2007a). In particular, capitalists need state support to promote stability, protect property and provide infrastructure, while states are dependent on the resources promoted by capital accumulation. More broadly, Callinicos argues against the transnational state thesis and suggests that the maintenance of a number of capitalist states can be located in the context of the uneven and combined development of global capitalism (Callinicos 2007a: 545; 2009b: 89–92; see also Harman 1991; Harvey 2003a; Nachtwey and Brink 2008; Ashman 2006; 2009; Davidson 2009). Given the competition and conflict, and unevenness and incompatibility, associated with capitalist accumulation, the continued division of the world into nation-states remains inevitable. This is reinforced by 'contingencies' such as national identities, a pre-capitalist territorial past, and imperial legacies (Callinicos 2007a: 545).

The centrality of uneven and combined development to these accounts is in some respects a welcome development.[2] As much of this book has argued, the expansion of capitalism does not lead to a progressive diffusion of capitalist social relations and capital accumulation throughout the world; rather, general tendencies combine with specific manifestations of capitalism, both within and between nation states. This is reflected in an uneven and unequal international division of labour, in which capital concentrates in some locations and marginalizes others, and in the dynamic, uneven and unequal effects of capital accumulation. The unequal effects of imperialism has been a central theme of this book, and for instance dominated the thinking of various schools of dependency and modes of production theorists in the 1970s (see Chapter 5). It was also central to Trotsky's

(1969; 1977) original formulation of the theory of uneven and combined development, as it applied to Russia and other late capitalist developers (see Chapter 4). Whether or not the idea can usefully be applied to the international state system is more debateable, as we will see.

This approach is in marked contrast to the transnational state thesis and the theory of empire as outlined by Hardt and Negri (2000). Robinson's argument (2004: 99) that transnational capitalism represents an equalization of the conditions for the accumulation of capital is unconvincing, and owes more than a little influence to neo-classical theories of competition (see further below, p. 172). Teschke and Lacher (2007) replicate this error in their contention that uneven and combined development is a contingent feature of international capitalism. Moreover, it is also the case that while the nation-state system does indeed pre-date capitalism, such states have become a central feature of international capitalism. Particularly useful in this regard is Ashman's historical periodization of the state in the international capitalist order. She accepts the argument made by political Marxists that capitalism initially promotes an institutional separation of political and economic spheres, but then suggests that 'we need to move ... to the addition of further levels of determination that produce tendencies in the opposite direction – to the fusion of economics and politics' (Ashman 2009: 37). In other words, we could say that the forms of appearance of capitalist social relations led to a more visible apparent separation in the case of early capitalist developers like England/Britain and Holland. This was not, *contra* Anderson (Chapter 4), archaic capitalism but the first really dynamic capitalist development. Though of course the state still played a central role, the separation appeared to be more organic and spontaneous than later capitalist developers. But it was precisely the fact that these early capitalist developers emerged which made later capitalist development in Europe, and more ambiguously in the United States,[3] more consciously designed.[4] It had to be because geo-politics and economics effectively combined in processes of protected capitalist development at home and imperialism abroad (see Chapter 4). There was also of course working-class pressure for reform, but it is clear that the process of unequal capitalist competition also gave rise to the close inter-penetration of capitalist economics and geo-politics. Ashman puts the point clearly:

The state system develops prior to the dominance of capitalism but is incorporated into it and adapted to the capitalist mode, producing specifically capitalist geopolitics. Latecomers striving to overcome 'backwardness', then consciously seek to develop particular state forms and are drawn into capitalist forms of geopolitical competition. (2009: 42)

These insights are close to the argument already presented in this book, namely that the era of classical imperialism should be regarded as one of rivalries between an established capitalist power and those aiming to emulate Britain. In the case of Ashman (2009), and Callinicos (2007; 2009a and b), this is central to their defence of the idea that the international state system is still characterized by geopolitical competition between the advanced capitalist states. However, while this analysis is useful for accounting for the character of the state system in the era from 1882 to 1945, I have already suggested in earlier chapters that it is far more problematic when applied to the post-1945 era of greater cooperation between the advanced capitalist states. This point brings us back to the question of the Lenin–Kautsky debate, and the applicability of these theories after 1945, or even after 1989 or 2001. This will be discussed in the next section. Before doing so however, we need to briefly re-visit the question of the relationship between structure and agency, form and function, and particularly the general (the imperialist state system) and the specific (a particular government policy). This is important in its own right, but also as a warning about making sweeping over-generalizations based on particular government policies at a particular point in time.

Wood's (2003) work on imperialism was in part an attempt to think about the Bush doctrine, and specifically the doctrine of pre-emption, and how this related to global capital and the nation-state system. She argued that pre-emption was part of a strategy to declare war on all states that challenged US hegemony, and this would serve to discipline all states in the international order. In her words, as US hegemony comes under threat, so the US responds in a more coercive way, and thus '[i]t is this endless possibility of war that imperial capital needs in order to sustain its hegemony over the global system of nation states' (Wood 2003: 25).

Harvey (2007: 66) makes a number of convincing points against Wood, specifically focusing on the undoubted ambiguity in her treatment of the relationship between national states and global capital, capitalism and uneven development, and economic and military power. Wood (2003: 136–7) argues that (insofar as it exists) globalization is about 'preventing integration', as capital 'benefits from uneven development'. She then goes on to argue that capitalism 'requires military action', and suggesting that constant war is 'too disruptive to the economic order', while also asserting that capitalism needs 'this endless possibility' of war, and then arguing that war gets embedded in the 'doctrine of extra-economic, and especially, military coercion (Wood 2003: 144, 165; Harvey 2007: 144, 165, 164). These statements are more a set of assertions than an argument, with Wood suggesting that capital and/or the states system consciously promotes, and benefits from uneven development, and then attempting to suggest that war is too disruptive but also an endless possibility. Uneven development should in fact be theorized as an effect, rather than a rational strategy, of capital accumulation, and while war may be both disruptive and a possibility, this can only be explained through a more historically specific analysis than Wood suggests.

Harvey himself does not necessarily resolve the problems in Wood's analysis, but this may be a reflection of a wider problem with Marxist perspectives on imperialism, already hinted at in earlier chapters. Harvey (2007: 68) argues that the *specifics* of neo-conservatism do not form the basis for a *general* political economy of imperialism. Indeed, he argues that territorial and capitalist logics of power are constantly in flux, even at times coming close to the transnational capitalism position best represented by Robinson, or at least advocacy of a Kautskyite position (Harvey 2007: 67, 69). This highlights the problems of definitions of imperialism discussed in earlier chapters, and the issue of how one theorizes the relationship between the specific (such as the invasion of Iraq) and the general (a theory of imperialism).

Related to this point, Callinicos' use of Block's theory of the close interest between state managers and the interests of capital in general, may be useful, but ultimately it evades the question of whether or not the specific decisions made by state managers always coincide with, or deviate from, the interests of capital (Hay 2006: 74–5). And more relevantly for our purposes here, they do not tell us whether these will intensify rather than alleviate, geo-political conflict. This of course is a crucial question when looking at an issue like the decision to go to war with Iraq. Perhaps important in this regard is Jessop's (2002;

2008) development of Poulantzas' structuralism, and his argument concerning the strategic selectivity of states, which means that the structures and operations of the state are 'more open to some types of political strategy than others' (Jessop 1990: 260). The strength of this account is that it does not lose sight of the structured inequalities that influence state behaviour, but it also leaves room for particular contingencies that influence a specific decision or policy carried out by state managers.

The implication that follows is the possibility of a dialogue between Marxist and constructivist approaches, albeit one that situates the importance of ideas within the context of the generality of capitalist social relations (Bieler and Morton 2008), and the specificity of the changing evolution of the state within a changing international order. This brings us back to what Jessop (2008) calls the strategic-relational approach to the state, which does not read off particular actions by states (or governments) from either a preconceived capitalist or geo-political logic, but sees these in terms of the relations between different social forces, the nature of economic and/or geo-political crises, and popular perceptions of such crises (Hay 2006: 76). This is implicit in Stokes' (2007: 263) suggestion that while there are good economic grounds for the US to maintain and expand a liberal international order, 'this does not discount the very real potential for ideology to "over-determine" US policy, and there are a number of debates, arguments and disagreements, amongst US foreign policy planners as to the precise strategies that the American state should pursue to maintain US hegemony'. Such ideas are not free floating, and they must be located within the wider structure of the contemporary international state system and geo-politics. This is discussed further in the concluding chapter in the context of 'America' and 'empire' as a political project. For now, the next section examines geo-politics in more depth.

Post-Cold War Geo-Politics: Lenin and Kautsky Revisited

As we saw in the previous section, there are a number of theorists of contemporary imperialism who highlight the continued centrality of geo-political conflict in the current era. They do so, in part at least, by suggesting that a transnational state or even increased cooperation between nation-states, is impossible in the context of the uneven and combined development of international capitalism. Those that emphasize the continued centrality of geo-political conflict suggest that cooperation between advanced capitalist states occurred in the context of the Cold War, and with its ending, rivalries are likely to increase, and indeed have been increasing.

This very general debate has some parallels with the nature of US foreign policy in a post-Cold War world. Much of the debate since 1989 (and 2001) has been over how hegemony should be used in a unipolar world. Realists have generally been wrong-footed by contin-ued US engagement with the international order in this new context, while liberals have welcomed continued engagement, but argue that the hegemonic order can only be maintained provided that the US continues to use its power wisely, which amounts to working through international cooperation and multilateralism (Nye 2002; Ikenberry 2006). Much of the supposedly novel academic literature on global governance shares this view (Held and McGrew 2002; compare with Keohane and Nye 1973; 1977). As the last chapter showed, the neo-conservative position represents a further 'take' on the role of US primacy, arguing for international engagement in order to promote liberal expansion, but being far more prepared than liberal interna-tionalists to use hard, military power and unilateral methods in order to facilitate this process (PNAC 2000). The end of the Cold War was not an excuse for multilateral engagement but rather an opportunity for the US to use its military power to refashion the world in its image. President Bush argued in 2002, that:

> Competition between great nations is inevitable, but armed conflict in our world is not ... America has, and intends to keep, military strength beyond challenge, thereby making the destabiliz-ing arms races of other eras pointless, and limiting rivalries to trade and other pursuits of peace. (Cited in Smith 2007: 5)

What is clear in these perspectives is that they all share the view that US hegemony is largely concerned with the policing of those states that lie outside the core. In other words, imperialism is largely about US promotion of the expansion of liberal democracies and so-called free markets, and certainly not a return to the formal empires of old Europe (Mazarr 2003). While some neo-conservatives are more prepared than others to call this empire (Ferguson and Kagan 2003), and indeed a few on the fringes even openly advocate some return to formal colonialism (Boot 2003), this is exceptional and would anyway still involve 'free market' relations between states (or colonizer and colonized).

What is important to our concerns here is how this account of imperialism, which focuses on the ways that the 'North' effectively dominates (parts of) the 'South', relates to the question that dominated classical accounts of imperialism, namely that of geo-political relations between advanced capitalist states. Brenner (2006) usefully contrasts two contemporary accounts of imperialism. The first, paying some allegiance to Lenin and Bukharin (see Chapter 4), suggests that despite the changes that have occurred since 1914, geo-political competition remains significant. For Bellamy Foster (2003: 13), 'inter-capitalist rivalry remains the hub of the imperialist wheel'.

Rees (2006: 215), takes this argument one step further, and suggests that 'North–South' security considerations actually hide the deeper reality that 'interstate rivalry is now both more volatile and is actually resulting in more wars when compared to the relative stasis of Cold War imperialism'. Harman (2003: 65) appears to suggest something similar when he argues that developed capitalist states 'settle their differences in less industrialized parts of the world. Hence the years since 1945 have been marked by war after war, but away from Western Europe, North America and Japan. And often the wars have been "proxy wars" involving local regimes to a greater or lesser extent beholden to, but not completely dependent on, particular great powers'.

While he comes from a slightly different starting point, Kees van der Pijl has argued for a variant on this position. He accepts that capitalism has become increasingly transnational (van der Pijl 1984; 1998), but also argues that the state system means that geo-political conflict between the advanced capitalist powers retains a central place in any understanding of contemporary imperialism (van der Pijl 2006). In particular he identifies conflict between what he calls the Lockean heartland of Anglo-American liberal capitalism, and contender states, such as France, and later Germany and Japan (van der Pijl 2006: ch.1). He argues that while most contender states have been incorporated into the heartland, this has not entirely overcome tensions, and indeed 'with the world economy today apparently more integrated than ever, the west itself seems to be drifting from its post-war moorings before our eyes' (van der Pijl 2006: p.xii). In this analysis much is made over the rise of the euro, geo-political tensions over the war in Iraq and the rise of China (van der Pijl 2006: chs. 9 and 10).

This position, emphasizing the centrality of geo-political conflict between developed capitalist powers, is also endorsed by some of those discussed in the previous section. Callinicos recognizes the changes that have taken place since 1945, but simultaneously defends the continued importance of Lenin and Bukharin's theories of imperialism. He accepts that in earlier work (Callinicos 1994), he wrongly saw the potential of a return to older inter-imperialist rivalries, when it is clear that geo-political competition of a comparable form is unlikely in an era of greater economic integration between advanced capitalist states and overwhelming military dominance by one state (Callinicos 2005: 117; 2006). In his own words, he earlier wrongly endorsed 'a simple repetition of earlier historical patterns without taking into account the effects of the concrete forms taken by economic and geopolitical competition' (Callinicos 2005: 110). At the same time, he also argues that the Bukharin–Lenin approach is the theory that provides the best framework for understanding the contemporary American war drive' (Callinicos 2003: 104, 105), although he simultaneously qualifies this by rejecting the notion that states act in ways that reflect an easy 'fit' between economics and geopolitics, while recognizing that the Lenin and Bukharin view tends to collapse the two together (Callinicos 2002a: 262; 2007a: 539–42). On the other hand, Callinicos also appears to suggest that there was an important change with the Bush Doctrine, as it 'is based on an accurate reading of the long term *economic* and geopolitical threats facing US capitalism, and involves the decision to exploit 11 September and the US's current military supremacy to shift the global balance of *economic* and political power further to its advantage' (Callinicos 2002b: 30, my emphasis). Within these statements there are substantial qualifications to the view that simply uses Lenin and Bukharin's theories to understand contemporary realities, but equally they also read like someone wanting to hold on to the view that such theories remain an 'indispensable instrument for understanding the contemporary world' (Callinicos 2005: 116. As we have already seen, this means that he ultimately endorses the view that geo-political competition is more important than geo-political cooperation, because of the tensions that arise out of the uneven and combined development of international capitalism (Callinicos 2007a and b; 2009a and b).

The second, contrasting position is usefully summarized by

Brenner's (2006: 91) asking the following question: 'can the use of force among advanced capitalist states be advantageous for any of them, even the US, given the extraordinary degree to which the processes of economic internationalisation have rendered capitals inextricably interdependent, wherever they are located?' In other words, in the context of greater global integration that has resulted from the internationalization of capital, how effective is the use of force in promoting the interests of any single state? Brenner refers this back to the 'Kautskyan' view of imperialism, which suggests that cooperation between the advanced capitalist states is now greater than (geo-political) competition between them (Bromley 2008: ch.2). Today, this is associated with those who argue that geo-political competition has been eroded by globalization, or at least takes new, and less significant, forms which render the Leninist view redundant.

This view is utilized in slightly different ways by the theories of transnational capitalism (Sklair 2002; Robinson 2004; Harris 2005), empire (Hardt and Negri 2000; 2004), and post-imperialism (Becker *et al.* 1987). Although each view is distinctive, they all agree that the old era of inter-imperialist rivalries has come to an end. This is because nation-states no longer represent clear blocs of national capital, but rather are part of a new transnational, or global, capitalist order. Nation-states are still relevant, but for Robinson (2002: 210; 2007: 80–4) they are part of a nascent transnational state apparatus, which includes supranational bodies like the World Bank, but which also reflect the re-ordering of the functions of the nation-state in the new era of globalized capitalism. Hardt and Negri (2000: 9, viv) have also argued that the world is now post-imperialist as no single nation-state can exercise power in the way that European states did in the past. In the case of Hardt and Negri, little attempt is made to verify their thesis but Robinson's argument is clear. One cannot talk of imperialism in the sense of the inter-imperialist, zero sum, rivalries of old, because in the current period, neo-liberalism entails increased openness rather than the sealing off of colonized spaces from all but the colonizing power. In other words, neo-liberal imperialism involves very different economic *and* geo-political relations from those associated with older inter-imperialist rivalries. Robinson puts the point very usefully:

I know of no single IMF structural adjustment programme that creates conditions in the intervened country that favours 'US'

capital in any special way, rather than opening up the intervened
country, its labour and its resources, to capitalist from any corner of
the world ... therefore it is more accurate to characterise the IMF
(or for that matter, the World Bank, other regional banks, the WTO,
etc.) as an instrument not of 'US' imperialism but of transnational
capitalist exploitation. (2007: 83)

However, while one can accept that the international order is very
different from the era that concerned classical Marxist theorists of
imperialism, one can also argue that increased openness and global
integration is not necessarily incompatible with US hegemony. The
choice is not one of *either* imperialism based on advanced capitalist
rivalries, *or* transnational hegemony without one dominant nation-
state. This means that the US state has, unevenly and differently since
1945, promoted a liberal order in which it benefits, but in which other
developed capitalist powers have also reaped significant rewards
(Panitch and Gindin 2003; 2005b). This has certainly not eroded
points of contention between such states, which have concerned
economic and geo-political issues, but these have largely been over
who benefits from such an order, rather than representing systematic
challenges to it (Albo 2003). While the 1970s did see some challenges
as competitors began to undermine US hegemony, this was resolved
through neo-liberal restructuring, a recovery of US hegemony, and
sustained cooperation in the international order. This position then
suggests that tensions between states may remain important, but
rejects the idea that geo-political conflict is of such great significance
that we are actually (or potentially) witnessing a revival of anything
like the inter-imperialist rivalries of old.

It should be clear what is at stake in the debate over the significance
of contemporary geo-politics: the 'Leninists' interpret any sign of
disagreement between the major powers as evidence of heightened
conflict, while the 'Kautskyites' argue (to my mind, far more convincingly) that these conflicts exist alongside continued – and heightened
– cooperation. This debate is not simply one that replicates the views
of Lenin and Kautsky, but this remains a 'useful framework for
contrasting the positions staked out in the current Marxist discussion
of imperialism' (Callinicos 2007a: 535; see also Brenner 2006). What
needs to be addressed is the question of the significance of geo-
political conflict in the context of an international capitalist order that
is very different from the period from 1880 to 1914. Brenner again is

useful, suggesting a potentially very different scenario from that envisaged by contemporary 'Kautskyites'. For him, even if economic internationalization has undermined the utility of military power, 'in view of the abiding and still very major conflicts of interests among national capitals – and given how easily the mechanisms enforcing the dependence of the state on capital can malfunction – should we not expect attempts by powerful states, above all the US, to tip economic advantage in their own favour through the application of force short of war or through "limited war"' (Brenner 2006: 91).

This debate is also implicit in the work of David Harvey (2003a and b). In terms of the classical theories and his conception of the new imperialism, Harvey tends to vacillate between these two positions. He argues that the new militarized imperialism under George W Bush was rooted in capital's search for new spatial fixes in the context of over-accumulation, and acknowledges the related possibility of 'the ever-present danger of military confrontations (of the sort that gave us two world wars between capitalist powers in the twentieth century) lurking in the background' (Harvey 2003a: 124). In this work, Harvey argues that the war in Iraq was an attempt, in part at least, to discipline (potential) competitors such as China through controlling Iraqi (and wider) oil supplies. The war reflected the close interaction between accumulation and geo-political rivalries. In Harvey's words, 'whoever controls the Middle East controls the global oil spigot and whoever controls the global oil spigot can control the global economy, at least for the near future' (Harvey 2003a: 19). This is not dissimilar to the argument made by 'Retort' (2005: 52; also Nitzan and Bichler 2006), which claims that the post-2001 world is based on the shift in neo-liberalism from 'an epoch of "agreements" and austerity programmes to one of outright war'. Harvey uses the concept of accumulation by dispossession in order to explain the shift from neo-liberalism to a more militarized neo-conservatism. In the neo-liberal era, new mechanisms of accumulation have opened up including extended privatization of previously commonly held resources, the extension of intellectual property rights and of finance into more and more areas of social life (Harvey 2003b: 73–6; Harvey 2003a: ch.4). While this has been achieved largely by non-military means, through structural adjustment programmes and the creation of the World Trade Organization, Harvey suggests that this order is under threat as US hegemony is increasingly undermined by its twin deficits and the rise of potential competitors. The US has therefore become increasingly tempted to use its military might, 'looking to control oil supplies as a means to counter the power shifts threatened within the global economy' (Harvey 2003b: 80–1).

At the same time, Harvey (2007: 58, 59) also explicitly rejects the view that classical Marxist theories of imperialism are relevant in the early twenty-first century, or indeed were even of much use in the period before 1914. Moreover, it could be argued that the quotation above concerning control of Middle East oil is less about the revival of the inter-imperialist rivalries of old, and more about the US maintaining strategic influence in the context of global integration. Certainly there is greater global demand for oil with the rise of China and India, it is likely that Middle East oil will be the main source for this increased demand in the foreseeable future, and the oil industry in that region has since the 1970s largely been owned by state companies and not the oil majors, who control only a small fraction of world oil reserves. Moreover, some have argued that oil reserves are declining (Simmons 2005; Elhefnawy 2008), and in this context of growing scarcity there is an increased likelihood of military conflict between the US and China (Klare 2008). For the same reasons, the war in Iraq should be regarded as a war for oil (Klare 2004).

On the other hand, the *form* of control promoted by the US is not the same as that promoted by imperialist powers in the late nineteenth century who, except for Britain, upheld policies of territorially exclusive policies with their respective colonies. The context now is very different, and:

> [t]he key point is that whoever gets to set the terms of future bargains between the national oil companies of the producer states and the international oil companies of the consuming countries, it remains the case that three-fifths (and rising) of the world's oil is traded on highly integrated markets across national borders and the rest moves on national or regional markets in which prices are aligned with international movements. The actual route traveled from wellhead to final consumption by any given barrel depends primarily on economic decisions and circumstances beyond the control of governments. (Bromley 2006a: 429)

In other words, control of Middle East oil is not done to deprive others of access to such oil, but rather to maintain strategic power in the context of other countries' dependence on Middle East oil (see further below). Oil scarcity may change this context, but there are strong grounds for questioning the arguments concerning both scarcity and the inevitability of conflict. First, oil price rises have stalled with the move to global recession, and in any case such increases were less about depletion of reserves and more about the run down of excess capacity. The picture concerning future reserves is complicated by the OPEC system of allocating production quotas, and thus the politicization of decisions linked to reserve estimates which influence such quotas. But perhaps most important of all, there are still high levels of reserves, even if much of these are unconventional oil sources – oil sands, oil shale and heavy oil. The stumbling block in this case has been the high cost of production, but if scarcity of conventional sources drives up oil prices, then this makes production based on these sources more than viable. Fuel for transportation could then come from sources other than crude oil, including unconventional oil, natural gas or coal (Bromley 2008: 143–6).

Nonetheless, the wider argument that there has been a resurgence of geo-political competition has some, limited, merit – US neo-conservatives have clearly identified China, alongside various enemies in the Middle East, as a strategic competitor to the US, part of a clash between liberal states and autocracies (G. Schmitt 2002; 2003; Schmitt and Blumenthal 2005; Brookes and Shin 2006; Kagan 2008). But, as in the specific case of oil, this must still be situated in the context of a liberal international order. This is implicit in Harvey's (2007: 68–9) contention that the specifics of neo-conservatism do not substitute for a convincing political economy of contemporary imperialism. As we saw in Chapter 4, from 1880 to 1914 (and beyond), classical imperialism was linked to attempts to secure supplies of specific raw materials through territorial acquisition and relatively closed economic links between colonizer and colonized. In contrast, as Brenner (2006: 104) suggests, it is hard to see how such a strategy can work in the context of state sovereignty and open borders today.

Bromley's point above concerning world oil markets can be generalized, and, as he points out:

> the form of control that the United States is now seeking to fashion is one that is open to the capital, commodities and trade of many states and firms. It cannot be seen as an economically exclusive strategy, as part of a predatory form of hegemony. Rather, the United States is seeking to use its military power to fashion a

geopolitical order that provides the political underpinning for its preferred model of the world economy: that is, an increasingly open liberal international order. (Bromley 2005: 153; see also Stokes 2007: 249–50)

In other words, even if the US gained exclusive access to and control over Iraqi oil, this is not sufficient for them to exercise significant leverage over China, either economically or geo-politically. Even less does it mean depriving its rivals of access to oil. Indeed, as Stokes (2007: 251) points out, 'by underwriting transnationally-orientated political economies in the Middle East the US has (by default) guaranteed security of oil supply to *world* markets'. The US is actually far less dependent on oil supplies from the Middle East than Japan, the EU and China, and the US has made considerable efforts to diversify its energy sources in recent years. This was a key recommendation of the Cheney Report of 2001 (NEPDG 2001), and it has meant considerable (low intensity) military involvement in Latin America, Africa and Central Asia, in what would otherwise be described as rogue states (Kiely 2005b: 81–2; Stokes 2007). In this way, the so-called war on terror has become embroiled in the darker realities of real politics, and in the words of Dick Cheney, it has meant that the US will 'have on the payroll some very unsavoury characters' (cited in Stokes 2007: 264). While Cheney 's statement clearly suggests that there is a conflict between US energy strategy and the wider strategy of 'democratization', the broader point is that even if oil was a motive for the war in Iraq, it was one that was unlikely to lead to exclusive US control of Iraqi oil, irrespective of Iraqi opposition to the US-led occupation, or significant leverage over other territories more dependent on Middle East oil. The US is certainly diversifying its sources of oil, but this does not amount to an exclusive strategy that aims to prevent others from gaining access to oil supplies, and Iraq is unlikely to be a major source for a long time to come.

There was, of course, considerable disagreement among developed capitalists states over the decision to go to war in Iraq in 2003. For Callinicos (2005: 119; see also van der Pijl 2006: ch.10), these tensions reflected the fact that the conquest of Iraq was a pre-emptive strike, 'less against Saddam Hussein than against other leading powers', which both reflected and led to a deeper crisis in the transatlantic alliance. However, as Callinicos (2005: 119–20) himself notes, there have been considerable efforts to improve relations since 2003. These may have limits, especially as European states have resisted involvement in the occupation, but these tensions need to be put into context. The US invasion was retrospectively endorsed by these states through the United Nations, and in any case these tensions can hardly be regarded as a renewed manifestation of older inter-imperialist rivalries, which were concerned with access to closed markets. The disputes over Iraq were more about tactics and strategy over how to police a rogue state, rather than a manifestation of systemic geo-political rivalries. Indeed, as Robinson (2007: 91) points out, these disagreements were as sharp *within* the US state as they were between the US on the one hand, and France, Germany and Russia on the other. Certainly, the US plans post-invasion were to grant privileged access to US companies, but this was less a general trend than a specific response to non-cooperation by other capitalist powers. One can call this heightened geo-political conflict if one wishes, but this needs to be located within a longer term context of cooperation (alongside competition) led by the US state, and the promotion of global integration through open door policies.

In some respects, Russia is an exception to this trend. Since the collapse of communism, US-Russian relations have undergone a number of changes – from close ties between Clinton and Yeltsin, undermined by the break-up of Yugoslavia and shock therapy within Russia, to close cooperation in the war on terror, undermined by the US invasion of Iraq and a turn to authoritarianism under Yeltsin from 2003 (Rutland and Dubinsky 2008). But perhaps the main issue of contention is over the question of influence in the newly independent territories that were once part of the Soviet Union. This in turn overlaps with the question of oil in the region, and what some have called a new 'great game' (Kleveman 2004). This reflects continued geo-political conflict, and the US has provided aid to a number of regimes in the region such as Georgia and Uzbekistan (Stokes 2007: 258–9). In 2008, tensions between Russia and the US heightened over Russian military action in South Ossetia, a province within Georgia (Hewitt 2008). Moreover, Russian nationalists tend to regard economic and geo-political influence in the region as a zero-sum game between the US and Russia.

However, it is far from clear that access to oil reserves in the region would be exclusive to specific powers. It is best regarded less as a rival game between two (or more) great powers, and more one of regional influence between a global power and a regional power, one of which (Russia) has been in decline since 1989, although it has enjoyed a new lease of life through oil booms in the new century (Bromley 2008: 192). This in turn is part of a post-Cold War geo-political strategy of selective incorporation of zones of conflict into the so-called liberal zone of peace. Georgia has been targeted for inclusion in this incorporation by the US and NATO, which has led to tensions with (excluded) Russia, and this has indeed heightened geo-political rivalries. It is not however geo-political conflict in the same sense as the inter-imperialist rivalries of 1914 or 1939. Furthermore, these conflicts have local roots and should not be reduced to the geo-political rivalries of powers like the US or Russia. While these rivalries are important, nationalist conflicts cannot be reduced to 'great power' interests, as though local actors in such places were merely the puppets or playthings of imperialist powers (Halliday 2008). More broadly then, while accepting the continued significance of geo-political conflict, I am suggesting that the relationship between military and economic imperialism is far more complex than the 'Leninist' view suggests. This is because increased global integration through the internationalization of capital has severed an earlier closer link between economic and military imperialism.

The 'Leninist' response is that greater integration does not mean the end of geo-political conflict, even if this does not mean all out war (Callinicos 2007a: 535). Citing James' (2001) study of 'globalization' from 1880–1939, Callinicos (2007b: 72) suggests that the inter-dependence between advanced states in that period was not sufficient to prevent heightened geo-political conflict and ultimately war. Harman (2003: 65) makes a similar point when he states that '[t]he capitalist economy was highly internationalized in 1914, but this did not prevent all-out war. Again, in 1941, the presence of Ford factories and Coca-Cola outlets in Germany did not stop a US declaration of war after Pearl Harbor'. The clear implication is that just as earlier periods of globalization did not end geo-political conflict, so contemporary globalization is unlikely to have the same results.

This is an important question, not least because as we saw in Chapter 4, there was increased inter-dependence between core countries, as most trade and capital flowed between them and not between core and periphery. James' basic argument is that the era of openness from the 1860s to 1914 was eroded by the failure of institutions to tackle the problems of globalism, so that they can no longer organize effectively, and so they become 'the major channels through which the resentments against globalization work their destruction' (James 2001: 5). Interestingly, James' argument mirrors claims previously made by globalization sceptics like Hirst and Thompson (1996). While Hirst and Thompson (1996: 27) suggest that trade/GDP ratios in the late twentieth century were not unprecedented in order to show that national economic management remains a possibility, James (2001: 12) uses similar data to suggest that both eras had high levels of global integration, which were eroded by a backlash against institutions that had the task of managing globalization. This argument is strengthened by the fact that before 1914, some observers (Angell 2007) argued that the increased integration of the world economy meant that war between great powers was a thing of the past, a claim rendered redundant by war in 1914. Therefore, just as liberal peace theory was wishful thinking in 1910, so it may prove to be in the early twenty-first century.

But there are also problems with this argument. As we have already seen, the period from 1880 to 1914 was characterized by increasing rates of tariff protection in many of the imperialist countries, which were introduced in order to promote national industrial development and catch up with Britain. James' (2001: 12) argument that '[t]rade was largely unhindered, even in apparently protectionist states such as the German empire' is thus incomplete. The main claim made in James' book is that the period up to 1914 was one of free trade and open competition, only to be eroded by the protectionist policies of the inter-war years, an argument rejected in Chapter 4.

It remains true however that there was a significant degree of integration before 1914, irrespective of whether this was the result of neo-liberal or protectionist policies, not least between the core countries that eventually went to war with each other. But there is a qualitative difference in the form of integration between the two eras. For what is most significant are not changing or constant trade/GDP ratios, as suggested by sceptics like Hirst and Thompson and liberals like James, but increasing ratios between trade and value added goods, as 'the disintegration of production itself leads to more trade, as intermediate inputs cross borders several times during the manufacturing process' (Feenstra 1998: 34). There is a clear upward bias in the ratios of merchandise trade to merchandise value added as we can see in Table 6.1.

Table 6.1   Ratios of Merchandise Trade to Merchandise Value Added

Country	1913 %	1990 %
France	23.3	53.5
Germany	29.2	57.8
Japan	23.9	18.9
UK	76.3	62.8
US	13.2	35.8

Source: Feenstra 1998: 34

The UK and Japan are outliers from a clear tendency towards increased trade/value added ratios, the former reflecting its unusually high trade ratios, the latter an unusually low one. But what is clear is an upward tendency that reflects the rise of global networks of production, discussed further in the next chapter. This brings us back to the question of how, or whether, transnational capitalism has transcended the old national blocs of the advanced capitalist states. We therefore arrive back at three competing perspectives all derived from the Marxist tradition: first, Rees, Bellamy Foster, van der Pijl and Callinicos all point to the continued centrality of geo-political rivalries; second, at the other extreme, Robinson, Sklair, and Hardt and Negri all point to the erosion of nation-state based rivalries due to globalization and transnational capitalism; and in between these positions, Panitch and Gindin argue that globalization reflects changes in the nature of imperialism, but nation states – and the hegemonic US state in particular – continue to be of great significance, albeit in the context of greater cooperation between (developed) capitalist states. The same question can be asked with greater specificity, namely what is the geo-political significance of the rise of global production networks?

These networks are novel compared to the 1880–1945 period, and so the qualitative nature of inter-dependence has changed, and we can no longer speak of national blocs of capital in Bukharin's sense. Does this qualitative change mean that geo-political competition and conflict ceases to exist? Some neo-liberal writers argue that this is indeed the case, and that it is not only international trade that promotes 'liberal peace', but also the global inter-dependence that has arisen from the fragmentation of production (Friedman 2005a and

2005b.[5] For many writers who suggest that geo-political conflict is still the main characteristic of contemporary imperialism, the theory of liberal peace has its Marxist counterpart in Kautsky's theory of ultra-imperialism (Rees 2005: 5).

The liberal peace thesis is problematic, as it presents a linear account of transition from a zone of (non-liberal) war to that of liberal democratic peace, and conflates a correlation with causation. Instead of discretely separating zones of conflict and peace, we need to focus on the international system as a whole, which 'compels recognition of the mutually constitutive relations between so-called zones of war and zones of peace' (Barkawi and Laffey 1999: 404). This does not mean that the so-called zone of war is simply a function of, or can be read off from, the zone of peace (as the Rees quote on inter-imperialist rivalries earlier in the chapter does), but it does mean that we need to recognize interaction in these zones far more seriously than the democratic peace thesis allows. For instance liberal peace theory defines war in such a way that it excludes covert operations, often US led, that have led to the overthrow of liberal democracies (Patomaki 2008: 20–1).

But perhaps more important, and was argued in Chapter 4 in relation to Kautsky, we need to dispense with conceptualizing war or peace at such a general level of determination, a fault associated *both* with those that emphasize the inevitability of inter-imperialist war *and* those that point to inevitable democratic peace through closer ties of mutual dependence and the extension of liberal democracy. Once we dispense with such over-generalizations, then we are in a far better position to analyse the contemporary nature of international politics, and identify sources of tension and of cooperation in that order. We therefore need to look in more *empirical* detail at contemporary geo-politics (Callinicos 2007a: 537), rather than attempt to theorize these through the use of general abstractions such as inter-imperialist rivalries and democratic peace theory.

However, one final theoretical point needs to be made as it is central to the argument of this chapter, and indeed the book's overall argument that US imperialism after 1945 (and 1989) is very different from the era of classical imperialism from the 1880s to 1945. In a response to Davidson's (2009) argument that uneven and combined development takes place *within* as well as *between* nation states, Callinicos (2009a: 102) suggests that 'it is one thing to say that individual states can manage considerable geographical inequalities and quite another to suggest that a global state could'. In one respect this is a perfectly acceptable argument, and I have already suggested that there are considerable problems with the transnational state thesis. However, if global uneven and combined development makes a global state impossible, then how does national uneven and combined development 'allow' for the possibility of a nation-state? Or, put slightly differently, why is it possible for a nation-state to coordinate in the context of 'national' uneven and combined development, but not possible for a combination of nation-states to coordinate in the context of 'global' uneven and combined development? This of course is precisely what I have suggested since Chapter 5, namely the internationalization of advanced capitalist states under US hegemony. This is also the view of many of those who have suggested that the nature of imperialism and of global capitalism has changed enormously since the era of classical imperialism (Panitch and Gindin 2003; 2004; Albo 2004; Bromley 2008; Hirst *et al.* 2009: ch.8). Callinicos (2005: 110–11; 2007a: 546) does accept that significant changes have occurred to international capitalism since 1945, but ultimately he falls back on the idea that competition between states is more important than cooperation between them. But, in drawing too heavily on uneven and combined development, this would appear to be theoretically unsustainable. Capitalism's history is associated with a variety of territorial projects and geo-political relations (Teschke and Lacher 2007). In contrast, Callinicos' (2007a: 542) argument that realism provides some utility for those wanting to understand geo-political competition in the international order is problematic. He is clearly correct to argue that if the state is to be considered an actor in the international capitalist order, then its actions cannot be reduced to the logic of capital accumulation,[6] and therefore any focus on the state 'must take into account the strategies, calculations and interests of rival political elites in the state system' (Callinicos 2007a: 542). However, it is not clear that realism provides any help in this regard, at least in the form advocated by Callinicos.[7] This is because the structural realism that he wants to use, albeit critically, regards the actions of such elites as irrelevant, and their explanation for state behaviour is regarded as being a product of the international system of anarchy. Although Callinicos is at pains to avoid the reification of realist theory, his own approach replicates that particular theory's weaknesses; realism's ahistorical logic of international anarchy is replaced with Callinicos' over-generalized account of geo-political competition.[8]

However, the largely theoretical discussion in this chapter can only take us so far, and we need to look at contemporary issues more substantively. In terms of geo-political relations between major capitalist powers, this task is undertaken in Chapter 9.

Conclusion

The 1960s and 1970s saw the breakdown of the Bretton Woods order. Though some Marxists regarded this as giving rise to a new era of rivalries between capitalist powers, this chapter has suggested that in fact it instead led to an intensification of the liberal international order, and a reconfiguration of a US hegemony that was briefly under threat.

This is not to argue that geo-political competition has completely ended, but it is to argue against the view that this competition is automatically more significant than cooperation between states. It is perfectly possible to have increased state cooperation existing alongside uneven development between states – the European Union is just one example among others – just as a nation-state can play a coordinating role in the context of national uneven development. This position owes something to Kautsky's analysis of ultra-imperialism, albeit one where one state plays the leading role in coordinating global capitalism, and where uneven development persists.

However, what this chapter has not done is provide a comprehensive political economy of contemporary imperialism. What is needed is an account which shows how uneven development has given rise to new forms of marginalization in the world economy, and particularly how this very liberalization and restoration of US hegemony has given rise to new forms of domination in the international capitalist order, which are central to the book's rethinking of the idea of imperialism. This is the task of the next two chapters, which focus on the political economy (Chapter 7) and geo-politics (Chapter 8) of contemporary imperialism.

7
The Political Economy of Neo-Liberal Imperialism

This chapter follows the discussion of restructuring in the previous chapter to discuss the relationship between neo-liberalism and the political economy of imperialism. It does so by returning us to the question of free-trade imperialism, as discussed in Chapters 3 and 4, and the post-war radical accounts of dependency discussed in Chapter 5. The central argument of this chapter is that neo-liberalism is a form of free-trade imperialism that reinforces the division of the world into cores and peripheries of global capitalism.

This has taken place in a new context, one on which many peripheries have actually industrialized to some extent, and in which there has been some degree of integration into the global flows of capital. However, this has not eroded, and indeed in many respects has intensified, domination and marginalization in the international capitalist order.

The chapter demonstrates this in three sections. First, the recent phenomenon of the globalization of manufacturing production is discussed, and the potential implications for this eroding domination and subordination in the international order are noted. Second, a closer look at the evidence provides grounds for a more sceptical account, one which suggests that this globalization has not eroded uneven development, and alongside that, the subordination of some locations by others. Third, the argument is further developed by returning to the question of imperialism and the effects of uneven and combined development in the periphery.

170

The Globalization of Production: Capitalist Diffusion at Last?

The problems associated with discourses of globalization notwith-standing, it is an undeniable fact that in recent years, there has been a substantial globalization of production. This is potentially significant as the developing world has undergone a substantial process of industrialization, unlike the de-industrialization experienced by the colonies in the late nineteenth century. The first tier newly industrializing countries, particularly in East Asia, developed their successful processes via a strategy that combined export promotion with import substitution, led by a developmental state that governed the market (Wade 1990). But it is also the case that in the current period of (neo-liberal) globalization, an increasing proportion of the value of exports from developing countries comes from manufacturing. In 1970, 18.5 per cent of the total exports from the developing world were manufactured goods; by the late 1990s, this had risen to over 80 per cent (Baker *et al*. 1998; UNCTAD 2002b: 5).

One possible implication of this development is that the globalization of production alone is sufficient to aid the industrial development of the developing world, in contrast to older strategies of import-substitution industrialization that neo-liberals at least deem to have failed. In this way, the neo-liberal context of existing globalization actually serves to confirm the stagist views sometimes found in Marx (Chapter 3), and in the work of Bill Warren (Chapter 5). Kitching (2001: 267; see also Desai 2000: 44; 2002.) argues that:

> as capitalism passes from its imperialist phase to its globalization phase, it begins to *take revenge* (economic revenge) on that subgroup of the world's workers whose living standards have been artificially raised and sustained by a combination of national economic protection and imperial domination. In particular, the free movement of productive capital, which is a hallmark of the globalization phase, allows the poor workers of the world to play their economic ace card (the low cost of their labor's production and reproduction). It does so by eliminating the capital stock advantage that enabled the richer workers of the world to compensate – in global competition for the higher cost of their labor.

Such a view is also present in the 'post-imperialist' views of Becker and Sklar (1987: 14) when they argue that 'imperialism – the domination of one people by another – will be [is being] superseded by transnational class domination of the world as a whole'. It is also clear in Robinson's (2004: 99, my emphasis) contention that with the erosion of territorialized space, the 'particular spatial form of the uneven development of capitalism is being overcome by the globalization of capital and markets and the *gradual equalization of accumulation conditions this entails'*.

Such views concerning equalization of accumulation sound suspiciously like neo-liberal interpretations of the global economy, in which convergence takes place through liberalization policies. This is where many critical interpretations of globalization, based on liberal notions of 'flattened out' inter-dependence, easily converge with neo-liberal prescriptions, despite the intentions of the globalization theorists (see for instance Kaldor 2003: 138; compare with World Bank 2002). In fairness to Robinson, as we will see, he does mean something quite different from neo-liberals, but his effective rejection of continued uneven development is problematic. Related to this point, it is not at all clear that, leaving aside the exaggerated contention, the rise of transnational class domination must mean the end of 'the domination of one people by another.'

This globalization of production is often linked to liberalization policies since the early 1980s, which are said to have rendered ISI policies redundant. Following earlier neo-liberal work which attacked state-guided development in the Third World (Little *et al.* 1970; Krueger 1974; Lal 1984), a number of writers have suggested that export promotion of manufacturing has been a resounding success, and this is often linked to the case made for poverty reduction (Krueger 1998; Ben-David and Loewy 1998; Bhagwati and Srinivasan 1999; Bhagwati 2004). Following an argument consistently made, albeit with some qualifications, by the World Bank since at least 1987, the argument is that trade and investment (and perhaps capital account) liberalization allows developing countries to exercise their comparative advantage and attract foreign investment and savings (World Bank 1987; 1993, 1994). This is the position also taken by the World Bank's 2002 report, *Globalization, Growth and Poverty*, which suggests that there has been a decline in the number of people living in absolute poverty, from 1.4 to 1.2 billion (World Bank 2002: 30). This reduction in poverty is said to be caused by 'globalization friendly' policies, as the most successful countries promote openness, and thus access to the opportunities presented by global market forces, an argument previously made by those who saw the period from 1880 to 1914 as an earlier period of globalization or benign imperialism (see Chapter 4). Insofar as there remain significant poverty levels, this is a reflection of the fact 'not that there is too much globalization, but that there is too little' (Wolf 2003: 4), an argument which sees globalization as inherently integrating from the outset, so long as correct policy choices are adopted. This debate overlaps with the idea of a contemporary progressive US liberal imperialism replacing the progressive British liberal imperialism of the nineteenth century (Ferguson 2004; Lal 2004). For the Bank, the 'more globalized' a country, the higher the rates of growth and poverty reduction. Developing countries are therefore poor because they have not adopted the correct, globalization friendly, policies. What is therefore required is the incorporation of developing countries into a benign, US led globalization.

These contentions are questionable however (Milanovic 2005; Kiely 2007a: ch.7; 2007b; Wade 2007).[1] The alleged decline in poverty partly reflects a shift away from poverty counts made on the basis of international price comparisons in two different periods – 1985 in the case of the first figure, and 1993 in the case of the second, lower figure (Pogge 2004: Wade 2004). The World Bank's *World Development Report* on 1999/2000 was actually far more pessimistic than the optimistic assertions cited above, as it used the 1985 base year calculations to argue that absolute poverty had increased from 1.2 billion in 1987 to 1.5 billion in 1999 (World Bank 1999a: 25). The shift from the 1985 count to the 1993 count had the effect of lowering the poverty line in 77 out of 92 countries for which data were available, and these countries contained 82 per cent of the total population of the 92 countries (Pogge 2004: 42). The measure of absolute poverty is also questionable because of the method of calculation, based on purchasing power parity. This method attempts to factor in local variations in the purchasing power of particular goods, a laudable aim, but one that is particularly difficult when measuring poverty (Reddy and Pogge 2003). This is because the basket of goods that is used to make the comparison includes goods that are unlikely to be consumed by the poor, and which measure average income. This probably has the effect of under-estimating the numbers of people living in poverty, as consumers with rising income (above poverty level) spend a decreasing proportion of their income on food, and an average rise in income over time will therefore translate into smaller comparisons of those goods which the poor actually consume, and whose price differentials may be far more significant (Reddy and Pogge 2003). Moreover, there are serious question marks concerning the data on growth rates and poverty reduction for China (Milanovic 2007). Indeed, in 2007, the Asian Development Bank presented the first official results based on PPP measures for China, and suggested that China's economy is 40 per cent smaller than was previously suggested, and that the number of people living below the poverty line is 300 million, which is 200 million more than previous estimates. For India revised estimates suggest that the official poverty line is closer to 800 million rather than the previously suggested 400 million (Keidel 2007). The full implications of the latest International Price Comparison survey in 2005 have yet to be drawn, but the almost 40 per cent cut in PPP GDP of India and China broadly conforms to the argument that some of the claims made for poverty reduction are wildly exaggerated (Wade 2008).

Furthermore, the question of causality between policy, growth and poverty reduction is contentious. The Bank measures openness through trade/GDP ratios, and how these have changed in the period from 1977 to 1997. These ratios measure trade outcomes, not trade *policy*, and in any case, some of the poorest countries in the world actually have high trade/GDP ratios. Thus, in 1997–8, the trade/GDP ratio for 39 of the poorest, least developed countries averaged 43 per cent, around the same as the world average, but their share of world exports from 1980 to 1999 declined by 47 per cent (UNCTAD 2002a: 103, 112). In the period 1999–2001, trade/GDP ratios of the least developed countries averaged 51 per cent, which was actually *higher* than that in the most developed countries (UNCTAD 2004: 3). In terms of trade *policy*, over this same period, least developed countries actually went further than other developing countries in dismantling trade barriers (UNCTAD 2004: 113). Indeed, if nation states are weighted on a one-to-one basis, then the growth rate differentials between high and low globalizers is statistically very small (1.5 per cent a year for the former, 1.4 per cent for the latter – Sumner 2005: 1174).

But perhaps the most important point is that measuring *changes* in the trade/GDP ratio is inherently biased. The most globalized countries tend to be ones that initially had a low trade/GDP ratio in 1977, but whose ratios have increased since that time. This measurement therefore excludes countries with high but not rising trade/GDP ratios from the category of more globalized, particularly those very poor countries dependent on the export of a few primary commodities, and which have had very low and sometimes negative rates of growth (UNCTAD 2002b: part 2, ch.3). Indeed, a falling trade/GDP ratio may simply reflect falling prices for economies overly dependent on a small number of primary commodities, which in turn is exacerbated by the consequent need to cut imports in the face of ongoing trade deficits (Birdsall and Hamoudi 2002)

China and India count as more globalized countries, even though their trade and investment policies remain less open than some of the low globalizing countries. This is justified by the assertion that 'as they reformed and integrated with the world market, the "more globalized" developing countries started to grow rapidly, accelerating steadily from 2.9 per cent in the 1970s to 5 per cent through the 1990' (World Bank 2002: 30). But this claim does not conform to the reality of growth in China or India, which pre-dated their growing openness, and indeed in India, there was little change in growth rates once liberalization were implemented in the 1990s (Rodrik 2001). Moreover, despite liberalization, such as the lifting of some restrictions on foreign capital investment, they remain far from open economies. Like the first tier East Asian NICs, capital controls remain strong, subsidies still exist and there are still relatively high tariffs on selected imports. Average tariff rates in India did decline from 80 per cent at the start of the 1990s to 40 per cent at the end of the decade, while China's declined from 42.4 per cent to 31.2 per cent in the same period, but the latter figures remain higher than the average for developing countries (Rodrik 2001). Thus, the idea that growth has been caused by neo-liberal policies should be treated with suspicion, and it is clear that attempts to draw general conclusions from the policies of China and India is misguided. When we do attempt to generalize, it is clear that the Bank's own data suggest that if we measure openness not by trade/GDP ratios or changes in these ratios since 1975, and instead focus on trade and investment policies in 1997, allegedly high globalizers had higher average tariffs (35 per cent) than low globalizers (20 per cent) (Sumner 2005: 1174). The IMF index of trade restrictiveness measures trade policy through quantifying average tariff rates and non-tariff barriers, and there is no evidence of greater trade restrictiveness on the part of the poorest countries. So, we can at least question the view that poverty has been reduced and certainly seriously challenge the view that this is because of globalization-friendly policies.

Even if the case made for causality between trade liberalization, growth and poverty reduction is unconvincing, neo-liberals suggest a further factor. This is the argument that the liberalization of foreign investment policy, which in turn has facilitated the rise of direct foreign investment, including to the developing world, has led to growth and poverty reduction. It is undoubtedly true that there has been a significant rise of direct foreign investment, with an increase rise from $59 billion in 1982 to $202 billion in 1990, $1.2 trillion in 2000, down to $946 billion in 2005, and back up to $1.3 trillion in 2006 and $1.8 trillion in 2008 – though a substantial decline is predicted following the financial crisis (UNCTAD 2002b: 3–5; 2007: 9; 2008: 3). This investment is made by an estimated 77,000 multinational companies, with 770,000 affiliates throughout the globe. These companies account for around one-third of world trade directly (through intra-firm trade with affiliates), plus a further third through trade with third parties (UNCTAD 2006: 10).

The Reality of Global Uneven Development

For the developing world, the data above suggests that at long last, the division of the world between rich and poor, and core and periphery, is slowly eroding. Chapters 3 and 4 suggested that central to nineteenth-century imperialism was the prevention of industrialization in, or the actual de-industrialization of, the periphery. This has clearly changed. Thus, if we use OECD categories (UNCTAD 2002b: 65), we can divide exporters into at least 5 types of goods exported: primary commodities, labour intensive and resource-based industries, and products of low to medium, medium to high, and high levels of skill, technology and scale requirements. Developing countries' exports in the high level category increased from 11.6 per cent in 1980 to 31 per cent by 1998 of total developing country exports, and their share in this sector in total world exports increased from 20.2 per cent to 30.2 per cent over the same period (UNCTAD 2002b: 68).

However, if we break down these categories, then a rather different picture emerges. Based on a detailed study of 46 developing countries at different stages of industrial development, Shafaeddin (2005a and 2005b) suggests that around 40 per cent (20/46) of these countries have experienced rapid export expansion, and 11 of these countries have had high output growth. Of these 20 success stories, two had moderate output growth and seven had low output growth. The next twenty countries had moderate export growth and the bottom six had low levels of export growth. Fifty per cent of the sample actually experienced a level of de-industrialization, which could not be attributed to industrial maturity and diversification into services, but rather 'forced diversification', based on the decline of some industries. Where new industries had emerged, these were often in resource-based or labour intensive sectors, and where on paper, developing countries did see a considerable increase in participation in medium to high skill/technology/scale sectors, this was actually misleading as 'for the most part developing countries' involvement in skill and technology intensive products is confined to the labour intensive parts, frequently just assembly, of vertically integrated production systems', with the result that 'while developing countries are becoming increasingly similar to major industrial countries in the structure of their exports, this is not the case for the structure of their manufacturing value-added' (Kozul-Wright and Rayment 2004: 11–12) By the end of the 1990s, the fifteen fastest growing exports from developed countries were all in the top 20 of most dynamic global exports, while only eight of the top twenty exports from developing countries were in the top 20 list of most dynamic global exports – and in most of these cases (with the partial exception of east Asia), these were concentrated in the labour intensive, assembly stages of production (UNCTAD 2002b: 71). Perhaps most tellingly, since the reform period started in the 1980s, while the developed countries' share of manufacturing exports fell (from 82.3 per cent in 1980 to 70.9 per cent by 1997), its share of manufacturing value added actually *increased* over the same period, from 64.5 per cent to 73.3 per cent. Over the same period, Latin America's share of world manufacturing exports increased from 1.5 per cent to 3.5 per cent, but its share of manufacturing value added fell from 7.1 per cent to 6.7 per cent (Kozul-Wright and Rayment 2004: 14). For developing countries as a whole, manufacturing output's contribution to GDP has barely changed since 1960: it stood at 21.5 per cent in 1960, and increased to just 22.7 per cent in 2000. There was significant regional variation: sub-Saharan Africa saw a decline from 15.3 per cent to 14.9 per cent; West Asia and North Africa increased from 10.9 per cent to 14.2 per cent; Latin America saw a decline from 28.1 per cent to 17.8 per cent (with the southern cone decline being 32.2 per cent to 17.3 per cent); South Asia's increased from 13.8 per cent to 15.7 per cent; East Asia (excluding China) increased from 14.6 per cent to 27 per cent; and China's increased from 23.7 to 34.5 per cent (Kozul-Wright and Rayment 2004: 32). By the end of the 1990s, developing countries as a whole accounted for only 10 per cent of total world exports of goods with a high Research and Development, technological complexity and/or scale component (UNCTAD 2002b: 56). In many cases, participation in global production networks is negatively correlated with manufacturing value added, while some countries with substantial rates of manufacturing production but low rates of participation in global production networks have higher rates of manufacturing value added (UNCTAD 2002b: 78–80).

At this point it would be useful to re-visit the post-war theories of imperialism discussed in Chapter 5. It is indeed true that we are continuing to see some degree of capitalist development in what used to be called the Third World. However, this is not leading to the kind of convergence envisaged by Warren, as some of his followers (reluctantly) concede; indeed, contrary to the Kitching quote cited above, most Warrenites continue to envisage some kind of import-substitution policies as the way to promote capitalist development in the periphery (Sender and Smith 1985). Seen in this way, neo-liberalism hinders processes of capitalist development that may lead to convergence with the advanced countries (Weeks 2001). Weisbrot *et al.* (2005) compare rates of growth and social development improvements between 1960 and 1980 on the one hand, and 1980 to 2005 on the other. Their comparisons are based on five categories of countries at comparable levels of development over the two periods, and they show that in the latter period, four of the five categories had lower annual average rates of growth, and that in most cases, comparable rates of improvements in social development indicators such as life expectancy, reduced infant mortality, and education participation slowed down in the latter period. These outcomes do not conform to the static analysis of under-development theory, where no improvement would logically be the expectation. However, nor do they point to anything like convergence through neo-liberal modernization. Instead, it upholds the view that ' "developing" countries are not just "behind" the economically advanced countries but remain subordinated to them by various mechanisms' (Leys and Saul 2006: 9–10).

This is in contrast to Robinson's views on convergence. His argument that conditions of accumulation are becoming equalized as capitalism becomes more transnational is, on the face of it, similar to a neo-liberal view. However, like earlier theories of a new international division of labour, which were influenced by cruder dependency and world systems theories (Frobel *et al*. 1980), Robinson is actually arguing that convergence is occurring due to levelling down, rather then the neo-liberal view of a levelling up process. He argues that '(w)orldwide convergence, through the global restructuring of capitalism, means that the geographic breakdown of the world into north-south, core-periphery or First and Third worlds, while still significant, is diminishing in importance' (Burbach and Robinson 1999: 27–8).

But actually, what is happening is that the global restructuring of capitalism has not eroded uneven development, and has in many respects intensified it. The rise of East Asia shows that the notion of a static north–south divide is too simplistic, which was always the case, but it does not erode uneven development based on unequal conditions of accumulation, and most certainly does not mean convergence, either through a levelling up or levelling down process. In terms of understanding the relationship between globalization and contemporary imperialism, this analysis suggests that a revised and updated version of the Prebisch–Singer thesis (Singer 1950; Prebisch 1959), which argued that there was a tendency for the terms of trade to decline for primary producers against manufacturing exporters, may be useful (see Chapter 5). With the rise of manufacturing exports from the developing world, this argument could be regarded as out of date, but in fact it can be fruitfully used to look at the terms of trade between *different types* of manufacturing exports (UNCTAD 2002b: 118; Kaplinsky and Santos-Paulinho 2005). Based on a study of trade in manufacturing goods from 1970 to 1987, Sarkar and Singer (1991) have claimed the price of manufacturing exports from developing countries fell by an average of 1 per cent a year. This has been challenged on methodological grounds, and particularly the use of the category of non-ferrous metals when examining price movements (Athukorala 1993), but a further study has suggested that the price of this category made no difference to the overall movement of manufacturing prices (Rowthorn 2001). Other studies have supported the claim that the price of simple manufacturing exports from developing countries have tended to fall against more complex manufacturing and services from developed countries (Maizels *et al*. 1998). One study of Chinese exports suggests that the net barter terms of trade fell by 10 per cent against developed countries from 1993–2000, but improved as against other developing countries (Zheng 2002).

Essentially then, while manufacturing has been 'globalized', developed countries still tend to dominate in high-value sectors, based on high barriers to entry, high start up and running costs, and significant skill levels. This dominance has been reinforced and intensified in recent years by the extension of intellectual property rights, particularly through the World Trade Organization (WTO). These rights further concentrate information among established firms and forces developing countries to pay various kinds of extra payments for the use of the products associated with these ideas (Kiely 2005a: ch.5). In the developing world, where there are large amounts of surplus labour, barriers to entry, skills and wages are low. While this gives such countries considerable competitive advantages, the very fact that there are low barriers to entry means that competition is particularly intense and largely determined by cost price, which also means low wages. Thus, the clothing industry, where developing countries have achieved considerable increases in world export shares in recent years, has a very low degree of market concentration. In contrast, sectors like machinery and transport equipment have very high degrees of market concentration, and are mainly located in the developed world (UNCTAD 2002b: 120–3).

The neo-liberal argument is that production in these labour-intensive sectors is only a starting point, allowing countries to upgrade as more developed countries shift to higher-value production. This flying geese model is thus seen as a useful starting point for developing countries (Akamatsu 1962; Balassa 1989; for a critique, see Kasahara 2004). However, it assumes that upgrading is a more or less inevitable process, and one that can be driven by the 'natural' workings of the market. But as we have seen, upgrading has occurred by states deliberately protecting themselves from import competition from established producers, via a process of import substitution industrialization. In the context of a tendency towards free trade, upgrading is far from inevitable and indeed, faced with competition from established overseas producers, is unlikely to occur.

Furthermore, developing country exporters still face protectionism from developed countries. While there has been considerable liberalization, for instance in the textiles and clothing sectors, through the WTO, this has not eliminated practices such as the implementation of non-tariff restrictions, including subsidies and various products standards, some of which relate to safety issues, but some of which are open to abuse. Moreover, tariff barriers in some products remain in place and it is likely that 'the products of export interest to developing countries face the highest barriers in developed country markets' (UNCTAD 2006: 75). Perhaps above all, there is also the aforementioned expansion of intellectual property rights, so that the life span of and number of goods covered by patents has been extended enormously (Chang 2003: ch.8).

At the same time that developing countries faced protectionist policies abroad, import intensity at home has grown, encouraged by the high import content of global production networks, a shift to high income luxury goods as liberalization has intensified inequality, and cheap imports fuelled by (short-lived) consumer booms on the back of financial flows entering a country encouraged by high interest and exchange rates (Santos-Paulino and Thirlwall 2004; Saad-Filho 2005). As well as encouraging imports, these inflows do little to stimulate investment in the context of high interest rates, and so they eventually lead to deteriorating trade deficits, loss of confidence in local currencies and a flight of capital out of the country. In this sense then, the supposedly failed import substitution policies of the 1950s and 1960s have been replaced by policies of 'production substitution', based on new, short-lived neo-liberal 'models', rapidly replaced by financial crashes that are blamed on insufficient liberalization, when it is these very policies that contribute and exacerbate financial crises. Moreover, developing countries have increased their holdings of foreign exchange reserves, partly to insulate themselves against the worst effects of any rapid export of capital. Reserves have risen from about 6 to 8 per cent of GDP in the 1970s and 1980s to almost 30 per cent by 2004 (Rodrik 2006: 255). While in one respect this is a rational response to the possibility of financial crisis, it also has significant costs (Lapavitsas 2009). In particular, it erodes investment possibilities in these countries, leading to an estimated annual loss of almost 1 per cent of GDP (Rodrik 2006). Given that these holdings are mainly in dollars, it also integrates these societies ever more closely into US-led financial markets, an issue discussed further in Chapter 9. Furthermore, the financial crisis that broke out in 2007–08 intensified these contradictions. Foreign capital inflows which were used to finance consumer booms contracted, falling from $1.2 trillion in 2007 to $707 billion in 2008, with an estimated fall down to $363 billion in 2009 (Seager 2009). As a result, heavily indebted countries found that they had to return to the IMF, an institution that was generally regarded as being obsolete in the boom years, as capital flowed into so-called emerging economies. This was particularly the case in eastern Europe and some of the poorer developing countries that still had current account deficits (UNCTAD 2008: ch.3). IMF loans have been accompanied by similar conditions faced by developing countries since financial crashes became commonplace after 1982; namely, cuts in state budgets, increases in interest rates, and privatization (Brummer 2008; Stewart 2008). These policies have been promoted while primary commodity prices have fallen sharply, thus leading to the re-emergence of a yet another debt crisis (Brummer 2008). Indeed, while the financial crash of 2007 is usually linked to bad debts associated with the US mortgage market (see Chapter 9), it could equally be argued that Western European creditors faced their own toxic debt problems as a result of lending practices to emerging economies, particularly in Eastern Europe (MacWhirter 2008).

Furthermore, apart from East Asia, though foreign investment levels increased (before the 2007–8 crash), this had often reflected a shift in ownership from the state to private sector, rather than genuinely new, greenfield investment. Indeed, investment/GDP ratios were lower across the board since the reform process started in the early 1980s. Thus, investment/GDP ratios for sub-Saharan Africa fell from a peak of around 23 per cent in the early 1980s, down to around 15 per cent in 1985. By 2000, the figure stood at around 17 per cent. For the big Latin America five (Argentina, Brazil, Chile, Colombia and Mexico), the investment/GDP ratio of peak of close to 25 per cent in 1981 fell to 16 per cent by 1984. By 1989, just before the FDI boom, it stood at 19 per cent, and by 2000, it had only increased to 20 per cent (Kozul-Wright and Rayment 2004: 30).

For these reasons then, while the globalization of production does represent an important shift from the international division of labour of the era of classical imperialism, what has actually emerged is an international division of labour in which older hierarchies have developed new forms, alongside the development of new inequalities, which have led to new contradictions and new forms of uneven development. Therefore, while the globalization of production has led to important changes in the international division of labour, these have not led to anything like global convergence, or ended uneven, and unequal, development. The implications that follow are therefore different from Akamatsu's flying geese model (see above), or Raymond Vernon's (1966) product-cycle model, which both tend to imply that some form of convergence will eventually occur through industrialization, as early industrializers dispense with earlier forms of industrialization, thus allowing later developers to follow. It also differs from new trade theory, which suggests that the developed countries should specialize in highly skilled production, and draw on the state to promote skill and technology upgrading, while developing countries initially specialize in labour intensive production, which will eventually facilitate a process of industrial upgrading (Krugman 1986; Grossman and Helpman 1991). Such a theory lies at the heart of social democracy's current accommodation to neo-liberalism, and particularly the strategy of progressive competitiveness, which supposedly encourages win–win situations through free trade and the exercise of comparative advantage (for a critique, see Albo 2004). But the argument presented here suggests something else altogether. Even if we leave aside the limited development of skilled jobs in the developed countries, the fact is that an international division of labour of this kind is not one that is as mutually beneficial as this scenario suggests. The outcome may not be zero-sum, but it is highly unequal.

Drawing on Schumpeter's theory of innovation, Arrighi *et al.* (2003) suggest that early innovators have 'locked in' advantages over later developers, and so they tend to accrue a disproportionate amount of the benefits, for:

> it is the residents of the countries where the innovation process starts who have the best chances to win [Schumpeter's] 'spectacular prizes', that is, profits that are 'much greater than would have been necessary to call forth the particular effort'. The process tends to begin in the wealthier countries because high incomes create a favorable environment for product innovations; high costs create a favorable environment for innovations in techniques; and cheap and abundant credit creates a favorable environment for financing these and all other kinds of innovations. Moreover, as innovators in wealthy countries reap abnormally high rewards relative to effort, over time the environment for innovations in these countries improves further, thereby generating a self-reinforcing 'virtuous circle' of high incomes and innovations. (Arrighi *et al.* 2003: 17–18)[2]

In other words, we can re-interpret the claims of the flying geese model, product cycle theory, and new trade theory, on the grounds that convergence does not occur because the innovating country not only 'refuses' to stand still and instead continues to innovate, but also because the earlier process of innovation makes further innovation more likely in these locations. Once the innovations are diffused, that is, 'by the time the "new" products and techniques are adopted by the poorer countries', such products 'tend to be subject to intense competition and no longer bring the high returns they did in the wealthier countries' (Arrighi *et al*. 2003: 18).

It is therefore hardly surprising that the share of Africa and Latin America in world trade has fallen in recent years, precisely as the globalization of production has increased. Africa's share declined from 4.1 per cent in 1970 to 1.5 per cent in 1995, and Latin America's from 5.5 per cent to 4.4 per cent over the same period (UNCTAD 1998: 183). In 1960, Africa's share of total merchandise exports was 5.6 per cent, and Latin America's 7.5 per cent; by 2002, Africa's share had declined to 2.1 per cent and Latin America's to 5.4 per cent (UNCTAD 2004: 51). The share increased for Asia, from 8.5 per cent to 21.4 per cent, but this was the region that was most resistant to neo-liberal policies. Similarly, foreign investment figures are highly concentrated, with developing countries generally receiving around one-third, to the developed world's two-thirds, of global foreign investment. For example, between 1993 and 1998, 'developed countries' received 61.2 per cent of world DFI, developing countries 35.3 per cent, and the former communist European countries 3.5 per cent (UNCTAD 2002b: 3–5). For 1999–2000, foreign investment inflows to the developed world constituted 80 per cent of total DFI, and the proportion going to developing countries constituted only 17.9 per cent of the total (UNCTAD 2002b: 5). In 2001 developed countries received 68.4 per cent, developing countries 27.9 per cent and the former communist European countries 3.7 per cent. And by 2006, out of a total of $1.3 trillion, developed countries received $857 billion and developing countries $379 billion, with transition economies receiving $69 billion. As we have seen, since 2008, inflows to developing countries fell substantially. Thus, the direction of foreign investment is highly unequal, with developing countries as a whole receiving around one-third, and of this third, only a few developing countries receive the lion's share. Indeed, from 1990 to 2005, the top 10 developing country FDI recipients increased their developing country share from 60 to 70 per cent of the total (Rugraff *et al*. 2008: ch.1). The 49 least developed countries received just 2 per cent of the DFI inflows into developing countries and 0.5 per cent of total world

FDI in 2001 (UNCTAD 2002b: 9). This has increased since then, not least because of rising Chinese overseas investment, but it remains very small (UNCTAD 2007: 34).

These figures are in some respects misleading, as cross-border mergers and acquisitions count as foreign investment increases, and are more likely to occur between developed country companies. Moreover, the developing world may be integrated into globalization less through direct foreign investment and more through subcontracting. On the other hand, the concentration of trade figures shows that unevenness and inequality persist despite these practices, and the figures above on lower investment/GDP ratios as foreign investment increases, suggest that foreign takeovers in the developing world do not necessarily generate dynamic new investment. Given the concentration of population in the developing world, it can also be argued that the foreign investment figures actually underestimate concentration in the developed world, if measured on a per capita basis. The investment and trade figures cited here then, ultimately back up the inequality and unevenness associated with the globalization of production (Dicken 2007: ch.18).

Where does China fit into this analysis? Without denying the fact that it has experienced very high rates of growth, and poverty reduction, there are grounds for questioning some of the more upbeat interpretations of the Chinese miracle. Despite the efforts of the Chinese leadership, the country has not been particularly successful in developing major global companies. Indeed, 'in export markets, China's aspiring global giant corporations must content themselves mainly with selling lower end sophisticated products (for example, power stations, steel mills, fighter planes), mainly to other developing countries' (Nolan 2001: 91). Otherwise, these firms concentrate on the domestic market or export in low-value sectors such as bicycles and motor-bikes. This failure is less a result of the inherent inefficiencies of import substitution industrialization, and more a reflection of the difficulties faced by late developers in promoting high value production that can compete in world markets, or indeed can develop in an unprotected domestic market (Breslin 2007; Kiely 2007a: ch.9).

Furthermore, China's success in breaking into some export markets is a mixed blessing for other developing countries. China's percentage of manufacturing exports to the US increased from 9.1 per cent in 1992 to 22.9 per cent in 2000, and to the EU it increased from 9.5 per cent to 16.7 per cent for the same years. Over the same period,

Thai export shares to the US fell from 26.4 per cent to 22.9 per cent and to the EU from 21.3 per cent to 17.7 per cent, and South Korea's fell from 25.9 per cent to 23.9 per cent (US), and, although they showed a small increase in shares to the EU, far bigger was the share of exports to the rest of East Asia. With some small variations, there has been a significant increase in shares by East Asian exporters to the rest of the region, while EU and US shares (either taken together or individually) have generally fallen or stagnated (Athukorala 2003: 40–1). Even more significant has been the increase in shares in parts and components rather than finished goods. Indeed, between 1992 and 2000, these accounted for 55 per cent of the export growth of Indonesia, Thailand, Malaysia, Singapore, the Philippines and Vietnam (Athukorala 2003: 33). There was no clearly identifiable pattern in the share of components and parts in trade to the US or EU from East Asian countries, with some showing increases and some decreases, but generally the far bigger increases in shares of parts and components was in East Asian countries trade with China. By 2000, the shares were 50.6 per cent for Malaysia, 54 per cent for Thailand, 50.3 per cent for Singapore, 81.8 per cent for the Philippines, 26.7 per cent for South Korea, and 29.8 per cent for Taiwan. At the same time, parts and components in China's share of exports to the US (4.3 per cent to 9.1 per cent) and EU (2.9 per cent to 10.9 per cent) increased from 1992 to 2000, but from far lower bases and the total shares remained low (Athukorala 2003: 48–9). In the period from 1992 to 2003, parts and components accounted for 52 per cent (Taiwan), 44 per cent (Malaysia), 70 per cent (Philippines), 59 per cent (Singapore) and 31 per cent (Thailand) of the total manufacturing export growth for particular countries. For China, the figure was 17 per cent (Athukorala and Yamashita 2005: 33). Taken together, these figures suggest that China has increased its role as a manufacturer of final goods produced within the East Asian region, which are exported to the EU and US (and Japanese) market.

The inequalities associated with oligopolistic competition and buying practices alluded to above are reflected in the fact that firms 'focus on activities with low barriers to entry. Once the cost pressures become too intense, rather than moving upward into higher end activities or taking time to develop proprietary skills, the firms diversify into other low entry barrier markets' (Steinfeld 2004: 1976). Indeed, these tensions reflect a key contradiction in China's miracle, as the national champion policy is 'a story about a government claiming as its ultimate policy aim precisely the type of firms that its most high profile restructuring (and trade) policies militate against. In essence, the government is seeking to create the very firms that comparative advantage, not to mention global technological change, militate against' (Steinfeld 2004: 1980–1).

And this is ultimately a story about the political economy of neo-liberal imperialism. It is clear that, apart from the first tier East Asian NICs, industrialization since the 1970s and 1980s has been over-whelmingly concentrated in lower-value production characterized by low barriers to entry, intense competition and diminishing returns. It is in these sectors – clothing, textiles, toys, and so on – that develop-ing countries have a cost advantage, particularly in low wages. But precisely because they are characterized by low barriers to entry, they do not provide the basis for upgrading to sectors with higher barriers to entry, where rents can be accrued to the most dynamic producers (Kaplinsky 2005: Kiely 2007b; Reinert 2007). Indeed, since 1990, the growth of China's exports in absolute amounts has exceeded that of the rest of the top 10 leading manufacturing exporters from the devel-oping world, and since 2000, the latter nine countries combined export share has fallen whilst China's has risen (Eichengreen *et al.* 2004). This reflects the fact that competition in low-value sectors is particularly intense and not necessarily a springboard to further devel-opment. This is not lost on the Chinese Communist Party, which combines a policy designed to draw on foreign investment while at the same time trying to continue the promotion of industrial policy – ISI – in order to upgrade into higher value activity (Nolan 2001).

Imperialism, Neo-Liberalism and Uneven and Combined Development

The discussion in the previous sections has effectively brought us back to a re-consideration of the theories of imperialism discussed in earlier chapters. The export of capital to poorer countries has been important in financing short-lived consumer booms (followed by economic collapse, see above), but far more significant is the return of free-trade imperialism, which developed in the context of a short-lived British hegemony in the nineteenth century (Chapter 3), which was replaced by protectionist development, colonialism and inter-imperialist rivalries in the advanced capitalist countries (Chapter 4).

We now see the return of free-trade imperialism under US hegemony, which has serious implications for capitalist development in the periphery. And if we re-examine post-war theories of imperialism (Chapter 5), we can say that the concerns of theories of dependency – namely to show how capitalist development differs for later developers – is if anything, more relevant today than it was in the period from 1945 to 1982, even if many of the answers provided by such a theory were spurious. In particular, the most extreme branch of dependency theory, the under-development school, was concerned to show how under-development was the product of conscious agents promoting backwardness. However, what is being suggested here is that *uneven* development is the consequence of the way that markets operate, and in this sense it happens 'behind the backs' of conscious agency. This is not to say that nothing can be done about it, but rather the question is to search for agents that can alleviate and challenge neo-liberalism as a form of social rule (Albo 2005). This of course brings us back to the question of uneven and combined development, and the way in which capitalist diffusion 'develops some parts of world economy, while hampering and throwing back the development of others' (Trotsky 1970: 19).

The political economy of liberal imperialism today is less about sins of commission, and more about sins of omission – that is, contemporary economic imperialism can be defined as the act of *depriving developing countries of the right to develop protectionist industrial policies and thereby generate dynamic comparative advantage* (Kiely 2007a). In other words, it is less what advanced countries *do* to less developed countries, and more a question of what the former increasingly *do not* allow the latter to do, namely carry out industrial policies. This is crucial to the process of dynamic comparative advantage because of the high rates of productivity, linkages, and spin-offs that are generated by technologically sophisticated industries (Kitching 1982; Kiely 1998: ch.2). This takes us back to List's argument (1966: 295; see also Chang 2002; 2007) that '[i]t is a very common clever device that when anyone has attained the summit of greatness, he kicks away the ladder by which he has climbed up, in order to deprive others of the means of climbing up after him'.

This is most clear in the case of the World Trade Organization, which promotes the principle of one member, one vote and, in contrast to the GATT (see Chapter 5), the idea of a single undertaking, whereby states sign up to all agreements, rather than pick and choose.

In practice, votes do not take place and developing countries have consistently accused richer countries of making agreement behind their backs. But more important is the fact that the WTO gives considerable protection to *companies*, through more stringent trade-related intellectual property rights (TRIPS), and more liberal investment regimes both generally (trade-related investment measures, or TRIMS) and in services (General Agreement on Trade and Services, or GATS). Moreover, existing protectionism by developed countries tends to discriminate against developing countries (Oxfam 2002), although there have been some changes in this regard, in the clothing sector in particular (Heron 2006; Kiely 2008a, b). Furthermore, led by the US, developed countries called for significant reductions in, if not outright abolition of, industrial tariffs by 2015, at the 2001 Doha round of the WTO. In return, developed countries have promised to liberalize trade in agricultural goods (Wilkinson 2006). At the Hong Kong talks of 2005, both sides criticized insufficient degrees of liberalization (Lee and Wilkinson 2007).

However, it should be clear from the argument made in this book that liberalization is no solution even if carried out in a symmetrical fashion. Developed world liberalization of agriculture, could adversely affect developing countries that import currently subsidized products, and in the developing world, the winners are likely to be bigger producing countries, and/or larger landowners, and not poor countries or poor farmers. But perhaps most important, just as the unequal treaties and formal colonialism undermined industrial policies for developing countries in the nineteenth century, so industrial tariff liberalization, alongside earlier rounds of structural adjustment, prevents the poorer countries 'from using the tools of trade and industrial policies that they had themselves so effectively used in the past to promote their own economic development' (Chang 2007: 77).

But this argument concerning neo-liberal imperialism needs to be qualified. First, there remain some mechanisms which still give some room for protectionism, particularly for the poorest developing countries. These apply for example to some exemptions allowed through the WTO, and through European Union agreements with the poorest developing countries (Hurt 2003). Nevertheless, the direction of change is certainly towards, rather than away from, free trade and liberal foreign investment (Gallagher 2005). Second, it is a mistake to regard this as simply imposition by the developed over developing countries, or the US over other developed countries. Crucially for understanding contemporary imperialism, we must recognize that whatever its other faults, Robinson's argument that dominant classes are more 'transnational' today is convincing. Domination is not simply imposed by the US, but rather, in the context of global integration, dominant economic and political actors in the developing world and in Europe, want access to international circuits of capital, and therefore may support neo-liberal policies, even if they simultaneously adopt nationalist 'cultural politics' or resist the most blatant features of US unilateralism (Albo 2003; Greenfield 2004).

Furthermore, the rigid division of sins of omission from sins of commission underestimates the ways in which states have to be restructured, above all in developing countries, to conform to neo-liberal policies. To return to List, the ladder does not simply fall, it is kicked, and neo-liberal policies do the kicking. This may be done primarily through domestic actors in the developing world who support neo-liberal policies, but this is also accompanied by external sources, and particularly international institutions like the World Bank, IMF and WTO. While 1980s structural adjustment naïvely believed that restructuring simply occurred through 'freeing the market' from state regulation, the shift to the post-Washington consensus in the 1990s reflected a belated recognition that 'freeing the market' rested on wider process of reform, and particularly the development of enabling institutions to ensure successful neo-liberal reform (World Bank 1997). While such reform is often couched in the language of participation and empowerment, it remains clear that institutional change is still a means to the end of neo-liberal, or 'pro-globalization' policies. The shift towards 'pro-poor' policies after the publication of the 1990 *World Development Report* led to renewed attention being paid to increasing agricultural opportunities, alongside training to promote labour skills, and social safety nets (World Bank 1990). All these factors would supplement the market. The state would also be reformed and good governance would be based on respect for the rule of law, transparency and accountability in decision making, and good human rights practices, which in effect often meant the encouragement of liberal democracy, particularly through bilateral aid conditions (World Bank 1992). The market would also be supplemented by civil society, which was re-defined as a space that allows for the development of entrepreneurial initiative, thereby promoting the social capital necessary for the promotion of development. However, this turn away from neo-liberalism was largely cosmetic, reflecting a new technocratic fix whereby the correct balance was to be achieved between the state, private sector and civil society, in a context in which neo-liberal policies were effectively taken for granted. This culminated in the 1999 Comprehensive Development Framework, which drew on older themes in development economics, but did so in an eclectic and largely inconsistent way.[3] The older 1980s agenda of macroeconomic stability, liberalization and privatization remained in place, but were now enhanced by a whole new set of policy instruments, which represented a more 'holistic' approach based on social transformation (Stiglitz 1998). However, in practice, these policies were a means to an end, and were still ultimately designed to ensure that the neo-liberal policies of the 1980s could be implemented more effectively (Fine *et al.* 2001; Jomo and Fine 2006; Williams 2008). Indeed, for all the talk of participation, empowerment and partnership, in many respects the post-Washington Consensus entailed a *more* interventionist stance than its 1980s predecessor, as supposedly temporary stabilization and adjustment measures are replaced by attempts to embed neo-liberalism within the institutions of 'governance states'. As Graham Harrison (2004: 77) suggests, 'post-conditionality politics does not mean an end to donor intervention; rather, it [means] ... that intervention is not exercised solely through conditionality and adjustment, but to a significant degree through a closer involvement in state institutions and the employment of incentive finance'.

Most crucially, the technical fix promoted by the post-Washington consensus envisaged social transformation and the shift to a more 'developed' capitalism. But like the Washington consensus before it, the post-Washington consensus precluded the return of the kind of developmental state that existed in nineteenth-century Europe and the US, and in the developing world, particularly East Asia, in the 1960s and 1970s. The post-Washington consensus therefore promoted market-friendly intervention, and not interventions that more explicitly governed the market through developmental states (World Bank 1993).

This section has therefore suggested that contemporary economic imperialism is based on the erosion of ISI policies and their replacement by neo-liberal policies in the developing world. However we should be careful about what implications can be drawn from this analysis, as it is far from clear that a simple reversion of ISI would (on its own at least) be a progressive alternative to neo-liberalism. First,

ISI polices were often carried out by authoritarian methods that were far from socially progressive. Second, in any case it is unclear that dominant classes and political actors in the developing world would want to go back to ISI – in the ISI period support for such policies was always ambiguous (Chibber 2004b). While Chang (2002) provides a powerful critique of neo-liberalism as an ideology of development, he is less convincing in accounting for the changes in the global economy and the fact that neo-liberalism is also a form of social rule. Dominant classes in the developing world do want access to global circuits of capital, but are far less inclined to use this access to promote 'developmentalist' policies. Furthermore, the context in which 'developmental', pro-industrialization policies take place is now very different. For as industrialization (and now post-industrialization) has swept the globe, measured in terms of proportion of total employment, the absorption of labour forces by manufacturing has gradually declined. A movement out of agriculture into manufacturing, in which the latter was characterized by increasing returns, linkages and higher productivity, and was reinforced by the rise of organized labour as production was socialized, was a recipe for some form of progress, albeit with many social costs along the way. Later industrialization, including in contemporary China, has seen far less absorption of labour by manufacturing, and so the dynamic potential for progress has been seriously eroded (Evans and Staveteig 2006). The pattern we now see is one of urbanization without high rates of industrialization, and the development of cities of slums (Davis 2004; Bernstein 2004; Kiely 2008a). Unless accompanied by radically different social policies, ISI is unlikely to alter this growing trend. This bleak analysis is further reinforced by the fact that in a growing number of economic sectors, value added is a product of ideas that are increasingly concentrated in the developed world and reinforced by the expansion of intellectual property rights. In this way, we can also identify a 'knowledge imperialism' that reinforces global hierarchies in the world today.

Conclusion

This chapter has outlined and theorized the political economy of neo-liberal imperialism, with a particular focus on capitalist development in the South. It was shown that one facet of globalization has been the rise of manufacturing production in what used to be called the Third World. However, it was also shown that this dispersal of capital was also accompanied by continued concentration of capital, and particularly of high value production in the advanced capitalist countries, and financial flows into the US (which in turn has reinvigorated US hegemony, as Chapter 9 will further argue). Indeed, it was argued that liberalization polices served to undermine the prospects for the emergence of a more dynamic capitalism in the South, which ISI policies were designed to foster. Instead, a great deal of manufacturing in the South faces low returns, intense competition, and developed world protectionism. For this reason we can characterize the current era as one based on the imperialism of free trade. Indeed, restructuring intensifies this situation by opening domestic markets in the South to competition from established producers. This restructuring is also clear in the most extreme form of neo-liberal intervention, namely military intervention against so-called rogue or failed states, an issue discussed in depth in the next chapter.

Finally, the world economic downturn of 2007–08 has seen changes in policy in the developed world so that some have argued that we are now witnessing the end of neo-liberalism (Mason 2009). Whether or not these amount to the end of neo-liberalism is a contentious point, and we return to this question in Chapter 9. What we have seen though is that in the developing world at least, and particularly in Eastern Europe, management of the crisis has fully accorded with neo-liberal – and therefore imperialist – practices.

8
Liberalism and 'Humanitarian Imperialism'

This chapter examines the other main feature of contemporary (liberal) imperialism, that of humanitarian intervention. The rise of this doctrine is traced to the end of the Cold War, and the resurgence of the cosmopolitan idea that the rights of individuals are more important than the sovereignty of nation-states, an argument also heard to justify military intervention in Afghanistan and Iraq after 2001. The chapter therefore starts by outlining the case for liberal imperialism and specifically, humanitarian intervention. It then critically examines these arguments, both generally and in relation to the debates over the Iraq war of 2003, to demonstrate the problems of the case for liberal imperialism. This section suggests that, notwithstanding important differences, (some versions of) contemporary cosmopolitanism and neo-conservatism share a commitment to liberal imperialism. The basic argument made in this section, and in the chapter as a whole, is that the case for a so-called cosmopolitan imperialism is unconvincing, undemocratic and self-contradictory. Indeed, it will be argued that exposing neo-conservatism's contradictions can be broadened to show that these same problems lie at the heart of the case for a benign liberal imperialism.

The Rise of the Discourse of Humanitarian Imperialism

This section examines the case for liberal imperialism, both generally, and more specifically in relation to the case for humanitarian military intervention. This case is examined through comparing and contrasting what would appear to be two very different political positions: cosmopolitanism and neo-conservatism. It will be argued that while there are significant differences between the two, there are also important similarities. These in part reflect the ambiguities of contemporary cosmopolitan thought, but more important for our purposes, it will be argued that the similarities reflect some broader assumptions that are shared with the idea of the need for a progressive liberal imperialism, and that these highlight weaknesses common to both perspectives.

Contemporary cosmopolitanism basically argues that the rights of individuals are more important than the sovereignty of states. Moreover, current advocates suggest that a cosmopolitan order is more likely in a post-Cold War world, where nation-states can be influenced more by ethical considerations than old-fashioned power politics (Cooper 2003; Held 2004; Beck 2006; Kaldor 2006). This argument is often backed up by an older theme in international relations theory, that of liberal democratic peace theory. Its advocates argue that war is less likely to take place between liberal democracies, as these states are more likely to promote collective international interests, and to respond to their electorates in accountable and transparent ways which further undermine the likelihood of war (Doyle 1984; Russett 1993; Starr 1997). This theory can be traced back to Kantian notions of perpetual peace, based on the idea of a world republic of peaceful nation-states which champion a spirit of commerce and a 'universal community' (McGrew 2002). The case for liberal peace was (unsuccessfully) re-made in the inter-war period, particularly by Woodrow Wilson, and has been revived in the context of the post-Cold War world of globalization, above all by contemporary advocates of cosmopolitanism. The basic argument made is that with the end of the Cold War, and the increase in inter-dependence between (and beyond) states, the prospects for cooperation between states has increased. In other words, globalization enhances the prospects for liberal democratic expansion and peaceful relations between states (Held and McGrew 2003).

One of the major problems faced by theories of liberal peace is how one deals with the question of non-liberal states in the international order. An argument that has been commonly made is that because liberal democracy represents a more progressive form of government than, say, Ba'athist dictatorship, then under certain conditions there may be a case for liberal democracies to intervene in the affairs of non-liberal states. Indeed, in some accounts the domestic structure of liberal democracies, and the implications this has for (peaceful) international relations, is itself sufficient for such states to have established the moral high ground. For instance, at the more academic end of the debate, Michael Doyle (1999) argues that power politics may be necessary to protect the liberal zone of peace and that military intervention may sometimes be justified.

These arguments are not identical to neo-conservative claims, but equally, they are not entirely incompatible with them, nor with liberal versions of cosmopolitanism. In his famous Chicago speech of 1999, former British Prime Minister Tony Blair (1999) set out a number of principles that must be met for a war to be considered just. These included: certainty that war was the only means, that diplomatic options had been exhausted, that there had been a practical assessment of military operations, that intervention was prepared for a long term haul, that national interests were being met (but equally that these were new in the context of globalization), and that the United Nations would be the central pillar of promoting international norms. Whether or not Afghanistan and especially Iraq met these criteria is highly questionable, but for Blair at least, there was clearly some continuity between the interventionist principles of 1999 and the Iraqi invasion of 2003.

Blair also accepted the view that US hegemony is desirable, and that, while UN authority for interventions is preferable, it is not a necessity. US hegemony and the global good are considered inseparable, as US hegemony promotes liberal democratic expansion and therefore long term peace. Blair's case for the war in Iraq may have changed frequently, but one justification was humanitarian and indeed cosmopolitan, namely that the human rights of oppressed Iraqis 'trumped' the sovereignty of the Iraqi state (Cushman 2005). Moreover, in Blair's eyes at least, this was deemed to be good not only for the Iraqi people, but for the wider 'international community' as it rid the world of a major rogue state, and thus potentially expanded the liberal zone of peace.

These views were the basis for the liberal case for war in Iraq in 2003, and form part of a wider liberal case for imperialism. On the other hand, the main proponents of the Iraq war in the US were neo-conservatives who, on the face of it, are hostile to liberalism. Part of this hostility can be explained by the different meanings given to liberalism. But there is also some important overlap between liberalism and neo-conservatism, which needs discussion, not least because it gives us some clue to exploring the problems with liberal imperialism, both in the current period and in the past, and therefore the nature of US imperialism.

The influence of neo-conservative ideas on the Bush II administration is a matter of some debate (Williams 2004; Hurst 2005; Drolet 2007). While it would be a mistake to talk about a neo-conservative coup within US policy-making circles, neo-conservatives did have some considerable political influence after 2001. At the same time, it would also be a mistake to assume that the rise of neo-conservative influence represents a radical break from previous US administrations (see Kiely 2005b). This is because neo-conservative ideologues have become increasingly influential, especially (but not only) in the Republican Party, since the 1960s, and because many neo-conservative ideas can be traced back to the foundation of the Republic. In terms of the former, briefly, these links developed from the late 1960s in the context of Johnson's Great Society welfare programme at home, and what was regarded as vacillation over Vietnam and the Cold War abroad. A number of prominent neo-conservatives joined the staff of Democrat senators such as Henry 'Scoop' Jackson and Daniel Patrick Moynihan, and developed a critique of the foreign policies of Nixon and Kissinger. Republicans like William Kristol, Elliot Abrams, Gary Schmitt, Paul Wolfowitz and Francis Fukuyama also aligned themselves with an older architect of the Cold War, Albert Wohlstetter, and challenged the ideas and policies associated with *détente,* such as arms limitations and a balance of power with the Soviet Union. Many neo-conservatives were also associated with Team B under George Bush senior in the 1970s, which gathered 'alternative' intelligence to that provided by the 'mainstream' in the CIA. In 1976, the Committee on the Present Danger promoted the idea of a military build up and a rejection of the appeasement of the Soviet Union. Thirty-three members of this Committee were appointed to the Reagan administration, twenty of them in national security positions. Many of these re-surfaced under Bush junior in 2000, to restore what Kristol and Kagan (1996) regarded as a 'neo-Reaganite foreign policy'.

Many neo-conservatives believed that it was Reagan's confrontational policies which led to US victory in the Cold War, though many of these same people were disappointed by his 'soft' stance towards

Gorbachev. The end of the Cold War led to considerable debate – and some dismay – that there was no longer an identifiable enemy, though for some Saddam Hussein came to function in this way. Bush senior's failure to overthrow Saddam led to disillusionment with that particular president. There were however still some neo-conservatives in the Bush I administration, and Defense Secretary Dick Cheney, in collaboration with the likes of Wolfowitz and Libby, called for the expansion of US military power in order to re-shape the world. The neo-conservatives were thus unsurprisingly hostile to the Clinton administration, despite the latter's willingness at times to use military power. The neo-conservatives made a comeback in the Bush II administration, and their influence was most clearly felt after the events of September 2001 – but equally neo-conservatism has had some considerable influence at least since the Reagan years of the 1980s.

The rise of prominent neo-conservative thinkers within and beyond the Republican party is therefore an important issue. It is also significant for the specific reason that Bush II was often portrayed as an isolationist president before 9/11, when in fact his foreign policy team of interventionists, including neo-conservatives, was put in place before the terrorist attacks (Smith 2007: ch.1). However, we should be careful not to reduce the significance of the rise of neo-conservatism to the growing prominence of certain personnel within the Republican Party or the US state apparatus, as some conservative Republicans and some Marxists tend to do (Halper and Clarke 2004; Gowan 2005). As Kristol (2003) argues, neo-conservatism is a persuasion more than a unified ideology, and part of its success must be examined in terms of the ways in which it coincides with wider ideas about the American nation (which in turn has implications for the US under Obama). In other words, we need to examine how neo-conservatism overlaps with wider views about America today, both domestically and internationally. This involves an engagement with aspects of US popular culture (Croft 2006), but also with the views of the supposedly despised liberals, many of whom have increasingly adopted a similar position on foreign policy to that of their neo-conservative 'adversaries' (Smith 2007: 79).

We therefore need to examine in some detail neo-conservative ideas, and how these relate to liberalism and neo-liberalism, US hegemony and 'the American nation'. Neo-conservatism has a relationship to neo-liberalism that is at one and the same time supportive and critical. As one of its most astute critics notes, neo-conservatives accept the economic, administrative and technological components of modernity, but reject modern morality and aesthetics (Habermas 1985). Neo-conservatives therefore support the 'free market', individual freedom, private property and so on, but are equally suspicious of the cultural consequences of modernity (Bell 1988), but also develop their own particular critique of the alienation, anomie and rationalization of modern life. To alleviate these problems, neo-conservatives propose that while the so-called free market should be supported, in contrast to classical liberals like Hayek, this must be embedded in a morality that goes beyond liberal individualism. Morality cannot be reduced to the individual, whether or not he or she is a rational utility maximizer (neo-classical theory) or the only appropriate unit of analysis in a world of imperfect knowledge (Hayek 1996).

The state can therefore never simply be limited to enabling the market to operate efficiently. For Irving Kristol (1995: 186), this is a recipe for nihilism, as no common purpose can be established in society, and this is necessary for the effective maintenance of a capitalist social order. Up to this point, many contemporary 'egalitarian liberals' would agree, and this has led to the development of a more interventionist form of liberalism. But for Kristol, this is part of the problem because egalitarian liberalism is simply another version of rational individualism, whereby the state intervenes to provide for group as well as individual interests. In this respect, while Kristol supports neo-liberal economics, he also argues that there is a need to pursue values that transcend neo-liberal economism. This leads him to advocate a position where the state plays the role of a moral teacher, which enforces individual responsibility, hard work and family values. The state is thus not a night-watchmen as envisaged by classical liberals and contemporary neo-liberalism, but rather an institution designed to promote particular values. Indeed, the argument is made that the Scottish Enlightenment was, in contrast to its European counterpart, concerned with the question of virtue as much, if not more than, individual self interest (Himmelfarb 2008). This emphasis on the importance of virtue leads to a rejection not only of the neo-liberal state, which reduces politics to the pursuit of individual or group interests, and thus regards the state as simply a vehicle for the pursuit of such interests. This is a recipe for nihilism, perhaps best exemplified for neo-conservatives by the cultural particularisms associated with identity politics, which promote fragmentation and therefore social disintegration. While liberalism is undoubtedly critical of some of the irrationalities that sometimes accompany identity politics, neo-conservatives regard such politics as being symptomatic of a wider social malaise caused by a lack of clear values in liberal democracies. In this way, neo-conservatism has had a particularly abrasive role to play in the culture wars that have dominated the United States since the 1960s.

For neo-conservatives, the view that the state should act as a moral leader carries over directly into the neo-conservative view of the international sphere. Just as there is a domestic crisis at home, and the need for cultural reconstruction, so too is there a need for a more virtuous foreign policy. This involves the promotion of a 'future oriented conservatism' (Williams 2004: 314), whereby neo-conservatives attempt to recover virtue from the limits of neo-liberalism. This is done by recovering a specifically American, republican virtue, which attempts to combine liberal individualism with public responsibility. In domestic politics, the state plays the role of reconnecting the individual to the community through the promotion of republican virtue, but the state should also lead in foreign affairs as well. As we saw in Chapter 5, this is not new, but is part of a historical narrative of American empire, based on the exceptional, but universal nature of American nationalism, which is differentiated from the particular nationalisms of Europe. In the words of two prominent neo-conservatives:

> American nationalism – the nationalism of Alexander Hamilton and Teddy Roosevelt – has never been European blood and soil nationalism ... Our nationalism is that of an exceptional nation founded on a universal principle, on what Lincoln called 'an abstract truth, applicable to all men at all times.' Our pride in settling the frontier, welcoming immigrants and advancing the cause of freedom around the world is related to our dedication to our principles. (Kristol and Brooks 1997: 31)

In other words, both foreign and domestic policy is central to US national identity, and the national interest. This is an argument that is distinctive from both conservative realism and liberal internationalism, but has some common ground with the latter more than the former. Realist theories of international relations suggest that there are potential enemies in an anarchical world order made up of self-interested nation-states. This is true but insufficient for the neo-conservatives because it does not clearly identify actual, as opposed to potential, enemies. Indeed, a realist analysis too easily accepts that the national interest is best preserved by a policy of isolationism, something strongly rejected by neo-conservatives, who explicitly promote the need to identify enemies, both at home and abroad. As Kristol suggested in early 2001, '[i]n politics, being deprived of an enemy is a very serious matter. You tend to get relaxed and dispirited. Turn inward' (cited in Drolet 2007: 274). Furthermore, realists suffer from the same problems as those associated with the neo-liberal state, which is that they both sever values from interests, and specifically the national interest. But just as self-interested material calculation is never enough for the neo-liberal state at home, nor is it sufficient for the state in the international arena. Michael Williams suggests that:

> In this vision, the national interest cannot be reduced to an analytical concept of foreign policy or a narrowly defined material interest. It is a political principle – a symbol and requirement of the political virtue needed for a healthy modern polity. A clear, commonly shared understanding and commitment to the national interest is the sign of a healthy social order domestically and a basis for a strong and consistent action internationally. (2004: 321)

Neo-conservatives argue that there is something almost decadent about realism and modern liberalism, in that both fail to provide the basis for social stability. This crisis lies at the heart of liberal modernity, and has led to social breakdown at home and US decline and international disorder abroad. Despite this bleak scenario, neo-conservatives argue there are also grounds for optimism, and that these have increased since September 2001. This is because it is asserted that the views of neo-conservatives resonate with those of the 'average American', who similarly regards republican virtues as central to American values (Brooks 2004). This focus on the centrality of values allows neo-conservatives to reach out to wider constituencies, not least those of the religious right, in their attempt to promote a backlash against what they consider to be a liberal, intellectual elite (Laurent 2004; George 2008). Neo-conservatives therefore suggest that '[j]ust as "average" Americans are victimized by a culture that systematically misunderstands them and attacks their lifestyle and values, so too America is victimized by a world that is irrationally, decadently, or perfidiously hostile towards it' (Williams 2007: 117).

The events of 9/11 are therefore regarded as irrational attacks that literally came out of nowhere, without context and one that bore no relation to the history of US foreign policy in the Middle East. At the same time, the attacks were also an opportunity for the US to rethink its responsibility in the international arena and promote a more abrasive US foreign policy. The Project for the New American Century publication, 'Rebuilding America's Defenses' (PNAC 2000), suggested that a more aggressive US foreign policy, based on massive military expansion, would be a transformation 'that is likely to be a long one, absent [*sic*] some catastrophic and catalyzing event – like a new Pearl Harbor'. Similarly, Kristol (1995: 486) has argued that '[t]here is no "after the Cold War" for me. So far from having ended, my Cold War has increased in intensity', while Norman Podhoretz had earlier welcomed the 1991 Gulf War as an opportunity for the re-moralization of the US in the post-Cold War order, as it had a new foreign demon to unite the nation (cited in Hurst 2005: 183). This rationalizes the view that the US must exercise its proper role in the international arena, as well as at home.

The strategy that follows from such a world-view is most effectively formulated by Thomas Barnett (2003; 2005). He talks of a 'functioning core' and a 'non-integrating gap', and argues that the latter should be integrated into the former, in part by expanding the sphere of 'globalization'. State Department director of Policy Planning Richard Haass argues that these divisions mean that the core, functioning states have an obligation to intervene into non-functioning states that have limited rights of sovereignty, a duty that has increased since the attacks on 11 September , 2001 (Mazarr 2003: 508). This is not so dissimilar to Wilsonian liberal internationalism and indeed nineteenth-century liberal imperialism (Mazarr 2003: 509). Paul Wolfowitz (2000) has similarly argued that 'nothing could be less realistic than the version of the "realist" view of foreign policy that dismisses human rights as an important tool of American foreign policy ... [W]hat is most impressive is how often promoting democracy has actually advanced American interests.'

Seen in this way, neo-conservatism may be hostile to some aspects of liberal thought, but it also has considerable elements of continuity with the (liberal) 'empire of liberty'. Indeed, like liberal imperialists and contemporary cosmopolitan thinkers, neo-conservatives are, inconsistently, committed to liberal democratic expansion. But what *is* different about neo-conservatives are the methods they are prepared to use to implement such a project. While Clinton was prepared to use hard power at times, neo-conservatives regard this as far more of a necessity, based on the idea that politics must include the identification of enemies – as in George W. Bush's axis of evil. This is an important difference between neo-conservatives and contemporary cosmopolitans, as many of the latter rightly point out that the idea of a *war* on terror is completely misplaced. Held (2004: 195) thus rightly argues that '[t]he terrorists must be treated as criminals and not glamorized as military adversaries'. In contrast, neo-conservatives (and Tony Blair) have treated terrorism as an evil that threatens civilizations, less a Huntingtonite clash of civilisations and more a war for civilization.[1] This elevates the nature of the threat posed by terrorism, but fully accords with the neo-conservative emphasis on a politics that stresses the need to identify enemies and eliminate evil. Clinton of course talked about rogue and failed states, and the need for the indispensable nation to intervene in order to police such states, but the neo-conservatives see this military reconstruction as part and parcel of a cultural revolution. Unconcerned with issues of multilateralism and international cooperation, neo-conservatives elevate the widespread belief of US manifest destiny to the point where the US acts as a heroic, benevolent hegemon, policing the world for a global good that is self-evident and in no need of external institutional legitimacy. For the neo-conservatives, this cultural revolution is crucial to the strengthening of democracy, both within and beyond the United States. In this respect neo-conservatism is very different from contemporary cosmopolitanism. But there are also important overlaps, and, among other things these will be emphasized in the next section, which looks at the case against liberal imperialism.

The Case against Liberal Imperialism

The arguments outlined in the previous section are important and go to the heart of the question of whether or not US imperialism is one that is to be supported on the grounds that it is benevolent. This section challenges this idea, first by making some general statements about liberalism and neo-liberalism, and then shows how the neo-conservative resolution of these dilemmas is inconsistent with a commitment to democracy. In other words, I will argue that there can be no such thing as a cosmopolitan or democratic imperialism – the two are simply incompatible.

The first point that needs to be made is that liberal democratic expansion, no matter how desirable, and irrespective of the (flawed) military means to promote it (see Dalby 2009), is not as straightforward as liberals and neo-conservatives imply. As we saw in the previous chapter, the reconstruction of states in the developing world (and beyond) since the 1980s has involved the promotion of liberal democracy and so-called free markets, which are often said to be mutually reinforcing. States can enter the liberal zone of peace through economic growth and development, and this in turn is said to be best achieved through pro-free market policies carried out by enabling institutions which respect accountability, transparency and the rule of law (World Bank 1997). As we have seen, the rationale for intervention and 'humanitarian empire' (Mallaby 2002; Power 2003; Chesterman *et al.* 2005) was not exclusively neo-conservative, and had a lot in common with advocacy of the idea of liberal imperialism. Indeed, this notion of liberal or benevolent imperialism was not a movement away from, so much as a new strategy within, neo-liberalism. Military intervention could be regarded as the most extreme manifestation of neo-liberalism, a kind of military structural adjustment (Dodge 2005; 2006; Kiely 2007a: ch.8), linked to older processes of pro-market reform and institutional shock therapy (Cammack 2004). This idea of a 'liberal peace makeover' (Cramer 2006) following peaceful reconstruction (including in cases of US-led intervention) rested on the idea that policies of liberalization and privatization, backed by democratization and the promotion of civil society, will lead to growth, prosperity, development and security. This would mean security would be enhanced, not only within the state in question, but also more widely as a zone of conflict was progressively integrated into the liberal zone of peace.

But, as should be clear by now, capitalist development has consistently occurred when states have only selectively drawn on the world market, while simultaneously protecting 'national economies' through tariffs, restrictions on the movement of capital, subsidies and even state planning. This applies to the US and developed European powers (see Chapter 4), and later industrializers such as South Korea and Taiwan (Amsden 1989; Wade 1990; Kiely 1998). It also applies, albeit in more ambiguous ways, to China (Bramall 2000; Nolan

2001). Like all other successful capitalist developers, these countries have selectively protected themselves from higher productivity economies, so that domestic producers would not face bankruptcy in the face of cheaper imports from established competitors (Chang 2002). Moreover, their success in breaking into export markets has often been subsidized by the state precisely because of the competition faced by established, more efficient, overseas competitors. Indeed, as we argued in the last chapter, the economics of contemporary imperialism can largely be explained by the *prevention* of such policies taking place in developing economies today, even if domestic elites in those countries are happy with this arrangement. So the first point is that the economic policies designed to promote incorporation into the non-integrating gap are more likely to intensify marginalization ('non-integration') rather than inclusion (or 'integration').

Interesting in this regard is Bromley's (2008: ch.1) argument that US hegemony has been based on the idea that the diffusion of economic power is central to US security, and thus there is an integrating imperative to US imperialism. While much of Bromley's argument focuses on relations between the core capitalist powers, it is also applied to the developing world. He argues – as I did in Chapter 5 – that modernization theory was a central component of US foreign policy after 1945. Bromley (2008: 2) argues that 'it was always envisaged that the long-run decline of US economic preponderance was both cause and consequence of its attempt to transform the international order. It was precisely because *relative* economic decline was seen as inevitable that the imperative to transform the rest of the world in America's image was so strong'. He then goes on to argue that:

the imperative to transform the rest of the world in an American direction was all the more urgent, yet difficult, as it became evident that liberalism was by no means the only, or even the best, vehicle for the diffusion and replication of economic development. This predicament established an enduring tension between unilateral impulses to remake the world in the US image, if necessary alone and by force (American nationalism as liberal imperialism), in an attempt to fashion cooperative international management (an ever growing number of) liberal capitalist powers, and worries that overseas entanglements would threaten the domestic order. (Bromley 2008: 2)

This quotation usefully captures some of the dilemmas and tensions that exist between the geo-politics and the economics of US imperialism, but it does not go far enough. This is because – the reference to non-liberal paths to modernity notwithstanding – Bromley underestimates the ways, whatever US intentions, in which neo-liberal policies serve to undermine the diffusion of economic power, and thus how the hegemonic side of US imperialism undermines the diffusionist side.

Related to this point, the idea that liberal democracies can simply be introduced as a kind of quick fix solution to dictatorship is highly problematic. Not least in those places where liberal democracies are already established, this has come about through a long process of often bloody conflict (Mazower 2001; Mann 2004). The liberal discourse of failed states may *describe* with some degree of accuracy the characteristics of such states, but it does not explain how these have come about or how they may be sustained. Liberal imperialism instead tends to regard such states as deviations from a liberal democratic norm, waiting to be liberated by an enlightened West from chaos or rule by a dysfunctional tyrant. This betrays a complete lack of historical or sociological understanding as to why such states have arisen in the first place.

This is not to say that all states in the South are exactly the same, and state formation has shown considerable variation within this wider context. Among many other classifications, different states have been identified as rentier (which rely heavily on revenue from the export of one primary product, most obviously oil, rather than local taxation), bureaucratic authoritarian (usually highly repressive, combining state nationalism with import substitution policies), and shadow states (where authority is in the hands of warlords and private armies), often linked to foreign investment by multinationals operating in economic enclaves (Bromley 1994; Allen 1995; Reno 1999; Dannreuther 2007). But what *is* clear is that, despite these differences, there is no automatic path to a liberal democratic political order.

This is a crucial point, for as Berger and Borer (2007: 209) point out, some neo-conservatives believed that all that was needed in Iraq was 'the breaking of the Ba'athist apparatus, capturing or killing Saddam and his henchmen, and letting a mass inspired "good government" of loyal Iraqis spontaneously emerge from the ostensibly minimal wreckage of the US military's "shock and awe" campaign'. While

Berger and Borer are certainly correct, they underestimate the extent to which this was the belief of a considerable number of liberals too (Smith 2007).

Neo-conservatives make much of the success of nation-building in post-war Japan and West Germany, but crucial to those successes was the existence of domestic social and political forces that led the democratic transition, a previous history of liberal democracy (in Germany), fewer ethnic divisions once the Nazis were removed, remnants of opposition to the Nazis, and fewer contested territorial boundaries (Smith 2007: ch.5). The situation in Afghanistan and Iraq is very different, and in both cases failure can be attributed to the misplaced belief that liberal democracy could easily be imposed through foreign intervention.

Indeed, the neo-conservative approach to post-war reconstruction can be traced back to the normative assumptions of a great deal of liberal theory. Much liberal theory is excessively moralistic, based on a conception of what Rawls (1993: 285) calls 'ideal theory', which is said to have primacy in the normative liberal approach. The argument here is that without an idea of 'a perfectly just basic structure ... the desire to change lacks an aim' (Rawls 1993: 285). However, in the real world of politics, based on interests, power and unpredictable contingencies, this a recipe for disaster, seeking as it does to provide an ideal model completely devoid of social and political context, and therefore reality (Geuss 2008). The idea of a liberal subject, in which a public arena of individual interests coincides with, but for political purposes, subsumes the private arena of irrationalism and faith, is one that is historically constructed (Williams 2007: chs.2 and 4). The question of whether or not individual self-interest is sufficient for a public sphere to operate is certainly debatable, but this is not the issue here. Rather, it is that the construction of the liberal self is not a natural state of affairs, but it is assumed to be so by those carrying out liberal wars of intervention – and indeed, as we saw in the previous chapter, by those advocating 'good governance'. It is for this reason – this conflation of the natural and the constructed – that liberal wars have such 'unforeseen' consequences. And it is ultimately for this reason that those who promote liberal wars then turn to their 'good intentions' as justification for such wars. Indeed, the liberal emphasis on good intentions and lack of self-interest can and does lead to the subtle exercise of power, for as Williams suggests, it:

can be transformed into a stress on the *responsibility* of those others to exercise that right in a legitimate way in order to be respected. By making membership in the community a matter of universal right, withholding entry into the community can be cast as the result of either the wilful unworthiness of these others, or as evidence of their as yet insufficient progress towards meeting the standards of discipline to which they ought to aspire. Either way, the onus is placed upon those outside to live up to the principles and actions that would merit inclusion – a process which they ought to recognize as their *own responsibility*. The failure to recognize and work towards this goal is evidence of a lack of self-discipline and moral responsibility on their behalf. This failure can be cast as all the more disappointing (and recalcitrant outsiders as morally/politically culpable), since liberal states had so conspicuously set aside the narrow pursuit of their material self-interest and advantage in favour of recognizing the claims of others, despite the latter's manifest material-strategic inferiority. (2007: 59)

This is where liberal ideology comes up against the question of political reality. Ignatieff's (2003) statement that the human rights movement's strength 'has been its moral perfectionism, its refusal to allow trade-offs between principle and power, rights and expediency' is interesting in this respect. For as Ignatieff (2003: 79) is all too aware, in practice, the US state has made such trade-offs, but has sought to explain them away by intrinsic good intentions. But the issue is not just one of double standards (see below), but also one of poorly made strategic choices. Interesting in this regard is the comment made by former National Security Adviser Brent Scowcroft on Paul Wolfowitz (cited in Smith 2007: 147), that 'Paul's idealism sweeps away doubts'. In other words, facts simply get in the way of ideologies and can be dismissed in those terms – not just because of liberal good intentions, but because liberal imperialism is simply 'the right thing to do', a statement constantly repeated by Blair after 2003 (Webster 2007). For Blair 'a sense of subjective certainty is all that is needed for an action to be right. If deception is needed to realize the providential design, it cannot be truly deceitful' (Gray 2008: 142). A sense of how this can blind neo-conservative ideologues to political reality can be seen from the statement that concludes Kristol and Kaplan's *The War over Iraq: Saddam's Tyranny and America's Mission*:

The mission begins in Baghdad, but, it does not end there ... America cannot escape its responsibility for maintaining a decent world order. The answer to this challenge is the American idea itself, and behind it the unparalleled military and economic strength of its custodian. Duly armed, the United States can act to secure its safety and to advance the cause of liberty – in Baghdad and beyond. (2003: 140)

As Owens (2007: 125) argues, according to this perspective, 'factual truths about the nature of Iraqi society, about the ambiguity of pre-war intelligence, about the limits of the power of high-tech warfare possess no inherent right to be as they are'. Even if the chaos that ensued following the defeat of Saddam was predictable, for liberal imperialists this is irrelevant because critics simply fail to see that Saddam Hussein was 'uniquely evil'. This was how Blair described Saddam Hussein to a number of Iraqi experts who met him in November 2002, and warned him of the dire consequences of war (George *et al.* 2004). One (anonymous) expert commented on the meeting that he was 'staggered at Blair's apparent naïvety, at his inability to engage with the complexities. For him, it seemed to be highly personal: an evil Saddam versus Blair–Bush' (George *et al.* 2004). This simple-mindedness is derived from a world-view in which liberal society is the norm, and any deviations from it can be explained by the actions of a few evil men. For this reason, liberal imperialism's excessive moralism opens the way to double standards (below) *and poor strategy.*

This argument does not endorse an 'anything goes' relativism, as though it were a choice between a de-historicized liberal model on the one hand, and endorsement of dictatorship on the other. Politics does indeed involve making choices and having preferences, but it also involves a realization that these exist in real world situations that cannot be wished away by high minded ethical principles. It is in this regard that these principles can easily end up as a rationale for impe-rialist practices, the 'justification' derived from the good intentions of those with such principles (Horton and Lee 2006; Runciman 2006; Owens 2007). We have already met this argument in Chapter 4.

The liberal imperialist response to these issues is to claim that liberal hypocrisy is a lesser evil (Hitchens 2003; Ignatieff 2005), which is preferable to human rights violations committed by, or within, failed or rogue states (Brown 2003; Isaac 2002). Thus, even if the war on terror involves some compromises with liberal principles, these are justified on the grounds that western liberals have good intentions, unlike evil terrorists. However, this begs the question, as it leads to the circular argument that bad outcomes can be excused by good intentions, and good intentions can be proved by the fact that these bad outcomes were not intended in the first place (Runciman 2006). In this way, strategy is removed as an issue altogether. However, it also evades a wider issue, which is that politics – in this case, liberal hypocrisy – must be assessed on the basis of actions and outcomes, not intentions (Bernstein 2005; Owens 2007: ch.6). Unaccountable unilateralism, Abu Ghraib, Guantanamo bay, extraordinary rendition and the use of torture, ongoing alliances with authoritarian regimes, and civilian deaths through military action must be assessed on the basis of those actions, not the claimed good motives that lie behind them. The Downing Street memo, in which 'the intelligence and facts were being fixed around the policy', should be seen in this light. Ultimately, the case for war made in 2003 by both liberals and neo-conservatives rested on a simplistic assumption that the world could be divided into good and evil (see Gregory 2004), and that this *a priori* division could excuse behaviour that deviated from those high-minded liberal principles which supposedly established the case for war in the first place. While this view accords with Mill's double standards based on different levels of development (discussed in Chapter 3), Kant (1957: 7, 8) was far more consistent, arguing that one must first observe moral laws for their own sake and apply them to oneself before judging others, and even suggested that 'no state shall by force interfere with the constitution or government of another state ... regardless of circumstance'. Kant's argument rested on his concern that such actions violate the very claims made for a higher political order in the first place.[2]

This gap between words and actions grows wider when we note the fact that western liberal-democratic states have often supported authoritarian regimes, in the colonial era, in the Cold War, and indeed in the post-Cold War era (Hoff 2008). Moreover, democratic expansion has itself been limited and has essentially left unchallenged social structures that guarantee high levels of social and political inequality, which neo-liberal reforms have often intensified. This is important because it undermines the formal equality associated with the principle of one person, one vote, because social and political power is concentrated in such a way that the influence of such votes is limited. Moreover, given the influence of the Washington institutions in heavily indebted developing countries, democratic states have limited scope for choosing different policies. In this way, the 'empire of liberty' may promote only a 'low intensity democracy' (Robinson 1996; Evans 2001).

In any case, neo-liberals distrust democracy as it can lead to the erosion of what they consider to be freedom, which is ultimately exercised in the context of a free market. As we have seen, for neo-conservatives this sphere of freedom is never enough because it is a recipe for social fragmentation, and it is here that they locate the current crisis of liberal democracy. But their resolution is to expand the power of unaccountable elites who can act as a moral tutor on behalf of 'the masses'. In other words, the crisis of democracy is 'resolved' by the 'democratic' extension of undemocratic principles. Domestically then, while neo-conservatives want to revive the ideal of citizenship alongside the neo-liberal individual, they simultaneously fear too active a citizenry, which could undermine both the free-market economy and the role played by an unaccountable elite in acting as a moral tutor, and therefore determining what the ideal citizen should be (Krauthammer 1990; also Strauss 1968).[3]

In explicitly acknowledging an intellectual debt to Leo Strauss, Irving Kristol has argued that truth could never set all of the people free, and that indeed telling the truth to the masses was fraught with danger because 'the popularization and vulgarization of these truths might import unease, turmoil and the release of popular passions hitherto held in check by tradition and religion' (Kristol 1995: 8–9). For these reasons, the US needed to focus on what the Declaration of Independence called 'self evident truths', which were the preserve of cultural elites, acting for the good of the masses.[4] One of these truths was the idea that the US was the indispensable nation, and it is a short step from this notion to the unquestioned assumption that US hegemony, in acting as a moral tutor to the rest of the world, is benevolent, *no matter what it does*. William Kristol and Robert Kagan make this link particularly clear:

> The re-moralization of America at home ultimately requires the re-moralization of American foreign policy. For both follow from Americans' belief that the principles of the Declaration of Independence are not merely the choices of a particular culture but are universal, enduring, 'self-evident' truths. That has been, after

all, the main point of the conservatives' war against a relativistic multiculturalism. (1996: 31)

Tony Blair's attempt to justify the war in Iraq follows directly from this principle. As is well known, the concept of a just war (Walzer 1992)[5] usually involves adherence to the principles of just cause, right intention, proper authority, proportionality, and last resort, at least some of which were not met in the case of Iraq. But Blair's justification effectively collapsed just cause (*jus ad bellum*) and proportionality and restraint in the exercise of war (*jus in bello*), so that the latter can somehow be justified solely by reference to the good intentions of the former. Blair's case is not that of the just war tradition, which differentiates between good and bad wars, but rather between those (well-intentioned) states or people deemed to be good, as against those deemed to be bad, or evil, and for Blair this is to be decided on an *a priori* basis (Runciman 2006; Gray 2008: 140). Indeed, in some respects Blair has turned the just war tradition on its head, as war is seen by him as 'no longer a last resort against the worst evils, but an instrument of human progress' (Gray 2008: 140). For liberal imperialists, international law can be used to serve a particular purpose, or if that fails, how it can be circumvented by appealing to a higher justice outside of the law.

Once again then, we arrive back at an imperialism justified by the principles of liberalism, and not so far from the ideals of neo-conservatism. As we have seen, the evasions, half truths, lies and contingent 'justifications' and evasions such as the idea of an 'unreasonable veto' at the United Nations should be seen in this light. These were all necessary for 'good' to be implemented, but as already argued, this is self-justification without accountability, and it is all too easy to see how the international vigilantism of Bush II follows. As Singer (2004: 192) notes, the good that is said to follow is that of democratic expansion under US hegemony, but this is inconsistent 'since such principles and ideals are incompatible with the imposed, unelected global dominance of any single nation'.

Indeed, neo-conservatives are guilty of exaggerating not only the capacity of the US to expand liberal democracies, but also the strength of US power more generally. For all its other faults, realist theory (among other approaches) has usefully focused on the limits of American power. Hans Morgenthau was acutely aware of the authoritarian implications of a politics that emphasized the twin strategies of moral regeneration at home and the promotion of national greatness abroad. According to Michael Williams (2004: 326; see also Mearsheimer 2005), '[f]ar from providing the basis for a robust and responsible foreign policy, Morgenthau worried that the uncritical assertion of national greatness and the *assumption* of legitimacy on the basis of an *a priori* claim to virtue actually risked undermining the legitimacy and power of the United States'. This argument is of great relevance to understanding aspects of both US domestic and foreign policy since 2001, and how democratic principles have been eroded and not expanded.

It is clear then that neo-conservatism draws on elements of liberal imperialism, but adds a strong dose of conservative elitism to justify its politics. Where then does this leave contemporary cosmopolitanism? This section has suggested that elements of a cosmopolitan approach have been incorporated by those advocating a new liberal imperialism, including neo-conservatives. For all its criticisms of US power since 2001, contemporary cosmopolitanism is characterized by ambiguity. Although suspicious of the role of the United States in international affairs, Robert Cooper (2002), also endorses what he sees as a 'cosmopolitan imperialism', albeit one where the European Union would play a more active role. Not unlike Thomas Barnett, he divides the world into three kinds of states: post-modern states, which are basically advanced liberal democracies, committed to peace and compromise and beyond the power politics of the old state system; modern states, such as China, which are stable but self-interested; and pre-modern, failed states, which are sources of instability. Echoing John Stuart Mill, Cooper argues that post-modern states should intervene in pre-modern states in order to preserve order, even if this means the promotion of double standards and colonial power. In his words (Cooper 2002: 17):

> The challenge of the post-modern world is to get used to the idea of double standards. Among ourselves, we operate on the basis of laws and open cooperative security. But when dealing with more old fashioned kinds of states outside the post-modern continent of Europe, we need to revert to the rougher methods of an earlier era – force, pre-emptive attack, deception, whatever is necessary to deal with those who still live in the nineteenth century world of every state for itself. Among ourselves, we keep the law but when we are operating in the jungle, we must also use the laws of the jungle.

This advocacy of double standards has the merit of honesty and as we have seen already it lies at the heart of all ideological justifications for imperialism. It is also where neo-conservatism and (some versions of) cosmopolitan do overlap. Tony Blair, like neo-conservatives, has consistently spoken of the need to combat evil, but this is never grounded in any social or political reality. And it is this lack of grounding in social and political reality that is precisely the general problem with contemporary cosmopolitanism. This can be seen for instance when Kaldor (2006: 146–7) simplistically promotes 'islands of civility' in the context of so-called new wars, or even more in the case of Beck's simplistic dichotomy of support for military humanism and the war on terror against ethnic cleansing and/or crimes against humanity (Beck 2006: 146–7, 154). But even in the case of more sophisticated advocates of cosmopolitan principles, such as Habermas, there are problems. Certainly the cosmopolitan principle can be a 'useful ideological instrument of imperialist expansion', as Schmitt (1996: 154) famously argued. In fairness, Habermas and Beck are aware of this problem. It is not clear however that the tensions are satisfactorily resolved. Thus, Habermas, a strong opponent of the illegal war in Iraq, supported the intervention over Kosovo, regarding it as a 'step on the path from the classical international law of nations towards the cosmopolitan law of a world society' (cited in Douzinas 2007: 207). Interestingly, a number of prominent international lawyers accepted that the NATO bombing of Serbia in 1999 was illegal, but, echoing the view of the Independent International Commission on Kosovo (2000; see also Douzinas 2007: 204–6), it was also legitimate. However, classical liberal cases for the rule of law rest on the argument that ethics should be considered separate from law, as it was the very disinterestedness of law which gave it authority. If subjective values are used in the interpretation of law, then it becomes a recipe for chaos on the one hand, or the abuse of power on the other. The latter of course was precisely Schmitt's objection to international law, as Habermas is acutely aware (1998: 198–9). Indeed, he condemned the invasion of Iraq on precisely these grounds, condemning the 'moralization of international politics' over its 'juridification' (Habermas 2006: 116). We are thus left with the paradox that for the international lawyers supporting the war over Kosovo, 'morality saves politics from [inadequate] law', while 'for Habermas, law saves politics from [potentially problematic] moralisation. The sleight of hand is evident: morality and human rights are identified in their form and content but separated in their action' (Douzinas 2007: 208). Indeed, one has some sympathy with Robert Kagan's (2004: 129) condemnation of European inconsistency when comparing Kosovo in 1999 and Iraq in 2003: 'They scuttled away from the moralistic principles they used to justify Kosovo and began demanding a much more rigid adherence to the UN charter.'

This leaves contemporary cosmopolitanism caught in the same problematic identified above; namely, that (assumed) intentions matter more than actions. This leads to the assumption that the liberal democratic West is characterized by peaceful inter-state relations, in contrast to a realm of conflict, where the potential still exists for barbaric wars to take place. Thus, contemporary cosmopolitanism – like the democratic peace thesis, liberal imperialism and neo-conservatism – not only constructs a divide between state sovereignty and human rights, but also sets up a dichotomy between pacific and war-like spheres of interaction. The effect of such a division is to reduce western interventions to a question of policy, which may be either defensible (Kosovo–Serbia) or misguided (Iraq), but never evil.

On the other hand, this view sees wars and human rights abuses in the 'zone of conflict' as a product of (an ungrounded notion of) evil. This is the thinking that lies behind the claim made by pro-war cosmopolitans, against the anti-war position that the latter were effectively happy to see Saddam Hussein remain in power, and thus appease evil (Cushman 2005). But this argument suffers from the construction of a rigid dichotomy between advocating support for war on the one hand, against an anti-war apology for Saddam Hussein on the other. It is a large step to take from opposition to war to support for a dictatorship, and there are anti-war cosmopolitan positions which also attempt to provide a basis for solidarity without military intervention (Shaw 2002; and see Chapter 10). Indeed, the burden of proof must surely lie with the pro-war position which suggests that solidarity is most effective through military attack. This is bound to lead to the slaughter of innocents, and no conception of collateral damage can alter this fact. Indeed, the whole idea of collateral damage is based on the fallback position already rejected above, namely that the West is virtuous because of its intentions rather than its actions. This idea of collateral damage is part of a long liberal tradition of dividing violence into objective as against subjective forms of violence (see Zizek 2008). Subjective violence is part of the discourse of evil, and is the main way in which violence is assumed to occur. It is easily associated with evil because it can easily be attributed to agents, be they communist dictators, Ba'athist tyrants or terrorists. Objective violence – such as the slaughter of indigenous people in the former colonies, or of Iraqis after 2003 – is deemed to 'have just happened as the result of an objective process, which nobody planned and executed' (Zizek 2008: 13). Once again this lets liberals off the hook as against the evil instigators of subjective violence.

Alternatively, if the United States government is measured not by its intentions but its actions, then a new charge can be made; namely that it is not simply an issue of the absence of war allowing Saddam Hussein to stay in power, but also that the presence of war has the danger of reinforcing American (imperialist) power. For if we focus on action rather than motive, then the US military intervention in Iraq is ethically comparable to that of Saddam Hussein's tyranny. The only way in which it cannot be is to excuse actions on the basis of good intentions, but this leads to the circular argument that 'you can tell we mean well from the fact that we didn't mean to kill those people; you can tell we didn't mean to kill those people from the fact that we mean well' (Runciman 2006: 46; see also Owens 2003). And it is precisely this belief that leads to some convergence between neo-conservatism and at least some interpretations of contemporary cosmopolitanism, as both effectively endorse the Bush approach that 'you are either with us' (on the side of good) 'or against us' (on the side of evil).

Indeed, perhaps the most prominent liberal advocate of war, Paul Berman, has argued that the world can be divided into those who resist, and those who collaborate with, Islamist totalitarianism (Berman 2005; Cohen 2006). Cushman (2005: 22) similarly argues that '(i)f one agrees with Paul Berman that the West is at war with the forces of Islamofascism, then those who do not recognize this point or take it seriously are, objectively, part of the problem of fighting successfully against it'. Moreover, as the quotation from Kristol and Kagan (above) makes clear, neo-conservatives regard themselves as cosmopolitans precisely because they see the United States as exceptional but universal, and thus the cosmopolitan nation.

This kind of thinking is an abuse of the term evil, because 'instead of inviting us to question and to *think*, this talk of evil is being used to stifle *thinking* ... In the so-called "War on Terror", nuance and subtlety are (mis)taken as signs of wavering, weakness and indecision. But if we think that politics requires judgment, artful diplomacy and judicious discrimination, then this talk about evil is profoundly anti-political' (Bernstein 2005: 11). However, we can go further than this, because it is not only the case of how current notions of evil lead us to indiscriminate and counter-productive initiatives against terrorism. It is also the case – and this is crucial for challenging contemporary imperialism – that simplistic good–evil dichotomies blind us to violent actions taken by imperialist states, which are assumed to be on the side of good and therefore incapable of evil actions. The idea of collateral damage thus serves 'as an authorization. It plays on the narrow sense of liability disconnected from common notions of moral responsibility – the idea that we are responsible for the reasonably predictable consequences of our actions. With the removal of accountability from the equation the risks of warfare are justified because no one in power saw nor wanted their consequences' (Owens 2007: 88). This has the effect of rendering small massacres acceptable as they are deemed to be the unintended consequence of the supposedly just action of the forces of good (Shaw 2005).

The argument in this section is perhaps best summed up by two statements made on the American satirical comedy, *The Daily Show*. In an obvious reference to the reporting on *Fox News*, mock reporter Rob Corddry commented on the treatment of prisoners in Iraq and at Guantanamo Bay, that '[t]here's no question that what took place in that prison was horrible. But the Arab world has to realize that the US shouldn't be judged on the actions of a … well, we shouldn't be judged on actions. It's our principles that matter, our inspiring, abstract notions. Remember: just because torturing prisoners is something we did, doesn't mean that it's something we *would* do.' Another *Daily Show* episode, perhaps echoing Donald Rumsfeld, reported that 'Everything we do is legal. Torture is not legal. Ergo … we do not torture' (cited in Stam and Shohat 2007: 32) These are the ideological fallacies of empire, and are quite explicit in the neo-conservative support for an unquestioned US hegemony, but also in a good deal of contemporary liberal cosmopolitanism. Both are complicit with a liberal imperialism which supports domination by unaccountable political actors. Agents of imperialism often regard themselves as unquestionably good, and thus regard their actions as being subject to different kinds of laws from the perpetrators of evil, but then empires are all to often devoid of self-awareness. In terms of both the invasion itself, and the conduct of the war, the US and Britain have been accused of violating international law and committing war crimes (Bowring 2008: 61–7). For advocates of liberal imperialism, this is excusable as it is the unintended outcome, the collateral damage, of the well intentioned. For critics of imperialism, this is the most naked exercise of imperialist power. Although it is less likely to be used in the post-Bush II era, it is still likely to be used, an issue taken up in the concluding chapter.

Conclusion

Good intentions are not incompatible with imperialism. However, good intentions can involve bad actions and have bad outcomes and these are a constituent feature of contemporary liberal imperialism, and indeed liberal imperialism in the nineteenth century (see Chapter 3). This chapter has argued that the promotion of liberal humanitarian wars of intervention can be imperialist, and deserve condemnation. Liberal imperialists of all shades tend to ignore the historical, social and political realities of the countries in which they intervene. This is not an argument made to support the current order in such countries, but it is an argument that liberal imperialists are often woefully naïve about the potential for military intervention to not only limit the deaths of innocents, but also to promote liberal democracy and free market solutions that supposedly lift such countries out of the 'zone of conflict'. This ignores domestic political realities and the ways in which neo-liberal free trade and free-market policies actually hinder capitalist development in an unequal international order. It also ignores the historical realities of capitalist development, which has been conflict ridden and violent, particularly in its early stages.

This leads to the second point, which is that perhaps these conflict-ridden and violent wars can provide the basis for a long-term social transformation which will promote capitalist development and a movement from the zone of conflict to the zone of peace. This is unlikely to occur and in any case this is not the rationale for such wars in the first place. If it was to occur, it would be one that was at odds with the Western self-image as the source of good fighting evil, and providing quick-fix solutions to countries deemed to have deviated from liberal normality. Rather, it would reflect capitalist development in which might trumped right. But the more important point is that while 'progressive' capitalist development may arise out of conflict, it is far less likely to emerge because of foreign military intervention. Rather, such development could emerge as part of a process of anti-imperialist resistance to an imperialist military intervention; in other words, it would occur *despite* rather than because of the intervention. Moreover, as we have seen, military intervention should be regarded as the most extreme form of institutional shock therapy, and thus an intrinsic part of the process of neo-liberal structural adjustment, and free trade imperialism is not conducive to capitalist development in poorer countries. Perhaps above all though, this chapter has challenged the view that the United States, or any other imperialist power, has an unquestioned right to intervene in other states. The claim that they hold the moral high ground cannot be accepted once we move from the question of intention to action, from motive to reality. When confronted with ugly reality, liberal imperialists can only fall back on the question of intention, and this is irrelevant and dangerously self-justificatory.

On the other hand, this does leave us with some uncomfortable questions concerning intervention, and the undoubted desirability of social and political change in countries deemed to be rogue or failed states. This in turn leads us to consider once again questions of cosmopolitanism and anti-imperialism. More broadly, it also forces one to confront the issue of the nature of all social and political change, and how this might be brought about, for this chapter has suggested that neo-conservatives, and liberal imperialists more generally, are guilty of adopting evolutionary models of social change that stand apart from social and political reality (Gray 2008). The purpose of this chapter has however been to question the benign nature of contemporary liberal imperialism, and not to examine the question of anti-imperialist alternatives. We will return to this question in Chapter 10.

9

The End of US Hegemony? Contemporary Hegemonic Challenge and World Economic Crisis

The previous three chapters provided detailed discussion of the *reality* of contemporary imperialism, focusing on continued cooperation between advanced capitalist states in the post-Cold War world (Chapter 6), the political economy of neo-liberal imperialism (Chapter 7), and the geo-politics of neo-liberalism and humanitarian imperialism (Chapter 8). This final substantive chapter addresses the question of the *future* of imperialism, with particular reference to the question of US hegemony. It does so by focusing on the rise of China and, to a lesser extent, the European Union, and the potential for heightened economic and/or geo-political competition, or even the rise of new hegemonic challengers to US imperialism. The first section sets out the debate in general terms, and this is followed by a second section that examines the argument with specific attention paid to the world economic crisis that started in 2007–8.

Geo-Political Competition and Hegemonic Challenge? China and the European Union

This section examines in more concrete detail the nature of geo-politics in the twenty-first century. It does so through a particularly close examination of the significance of the rise of China, and of the

European Union. It will further develop the argument outlined in the last chapter, that while some geo-political tensions remain important in the international order, these exist in a new context, which undermines the utility of a 'Leninist' mode of analysis (see Chapter 6).

The rise of China can be considered in at least two ways. First, its rise will inevitably lead to an intensification of geo-political rivalries. Second, and distinct but not completely unrelated to this first argument, China's rise will be at the expense of the US; that is, it is a new hegemonic challenger. This may result in new conflicts as the first position contends, or it may simply lead to US hegemonic decline without conflict. As we saw in earlier chapters, contemporary US neo-conservatives are concerned with the rise of China and were dismayed by Clinton's policy of treating it as a strategic partner rather than competitor. There have also been considerable sources of tension, ironically perhaps greater in the Clinton years than in the period since 2001. These include closer US ties to Taiwan from 1995, culminating in a US show of force in the Taiwan Strait area, the Asian financial meltdown of 1997 and particularly the IMF's management of this crisis, the NATO intervention over Kosovo and especially the bombing of the Chinese embassy in Serbia in 1999, and in the Bush II era, the US spy plane incident over Hainan. Also in the Bush II era, China opposed the war in Iraq and joined the G-20 at the WTO, but in both cases as more of a silent partner, rather than an active player (Foot 2006; Narlikar and Tussie 2004). The US continues to maintain a huge naval presence in the Pacific, and especially close to the coast of China. This has led some to argue that the rise of China represents a revival of older great power conflicts. For Hore (2004: 24–5), 'as economic ties deepen between the US and China, so too will political and military tensions. It is glaringly obvious that the neo-liberals' dream of global economic integration leading to a decrease in military competition is precisely the reverse of reality. We still live in the world of imperialism as Bukharin and Lenin described it almost 100 years ago, where greater economic integration and competition lead to a greater, not a lesser danger of wars.' This position is not dissimilar to that of 'offensive realists', who also argue that the US should 'do what it can to slow the rise of China. In fact, the structural imperatives of the international system, which are powerful, will probably force the United States to abandon its policy of constructive engagement in the near future' (Mearsheimer 2001: 402). The war on terror led to the expansion of US bases in Central Asia, not so far from the Chinese

border. Moreover, the National Security Strategy argued that the war
on terror would have an effect on those countries that were not the US'
immediate enemies, deterring them 'from pursuing a military build up
in the hope of surpassing, or equaling the power of the United States'
(NSS 2002). There are also economic tensions over trade, market
access, and what the US regards as an undervalued Chinese currency,
which exacerbates the US trade deficit with China. China's current
account surplus with the rest of the world increased from $30 billion
in 1997, to $69 billion in 2004, to $161 billion in 2005 (Morgan 2007:
3; and see further below).

In a distinct but related argument, it has also been claimed that
'China's new ideas are having a gigantic effect outside of China.
China is marking a path for other nations around the world who are
trying to figure out not simply how to develop their countries, but also
how to fit into the international order in a way that allows them to be
truly independent, to protect their way of life and political choices in
a world with a single massively powerful centre of gravity' (Ramo
2004: 3). Unlike western involvement in the region, China's tends to
come with no strings attached and advocacy of the principle of non-
interference in domestic affairs and respect for the principle of sovereignty. There is also something of a new 'scramble for Africa' led by
competing US and Chinese interests. Certainly China has turned to
Africa in search of resources, particularly oil, and has engaged in
foreign investment with national petroleum and gas interests in
Sudan, Angola, Algeria and Gabon (Alden 2007: 14; Rogers 2006;
2007). China's trade with Africa tripled between 2000 and 2005, and
in the latter year China overtook Britain as Africa's third largest trading partner (Carmody and Owusu 2007: 505). Around a quarter of
China's oil is imported from the Gulf of Guinea, while, at the same
time, the US has increasingly turned to (among others) West Africa as
a potential source of oil supplies. There is also now considerable
Chinese investment in Africa. This has increased from zero to an estimated $12 billion in 2005, though this remains a small proportion
(around 3 per cent) of total Chinese direct foreign investment
(Crabtree and Sumner 2008).

Giovanni Arrighi (2007) suggests that none of these developments
adds up to a simple replication of the inter-imperialist rivalries of the
nineteenth century, but rather the replacement of one hegemonic state
– the US, with another– China. Indeed, he argues that the more valid
comparison to be made (in terms of the early twentieth century) is not

with Anglo-German relations, but rather with Anglo-US relations. Taking in a broad historical approach which, like the global historians discussed in Chapter 2, suggests that Asia was ahead of Europe until around the eighteenth century, Arrighi argues that, led by China, Asia is likely to soar ahead in the near future. By around 1950, European and North American dominance was under strain, as the western capital and energy intensive path of industrial development reached its limits, and the East Asian labour intensive and energy saving 'industrious revolution' began to challenge western hegemony and restore Asia's position as the central region in the world economy. In effect, the virtuous circle of capitalism, industrialism, and militarism driven by inter-state competition was eroded by a crisis of legitimacy, a new Asian hybrid of industrious and industrial revolutions, nationalism in the Third World, and, in the context of increased global integration, the erosion of the synergy between financial and military capabilities which had served to keep West ahead of East. US-led military attempts to overcome these problems backfired 'and created unprecedented opportunities for the social and economic empowerment of the peoples of the global South' (Arrighi 2007: 95). These opportunities varied across regions, and much of the South was constrained by a new era of indebtedness and neo-liberal restructuring, which served to further 'integrate' these economies into the world economy, but without promoting sustained development. In Asia, and especially East Asia, things were different, however, and this region is now set to challenge US hegemony, which is in decline, and which has further been eroded by the military adventurism of the Bush II administration.

Drawing on themes developed in his earlier work (Arrighi 1994), Arrighi argues that an ongoing sequence of capital accumulation has historically been accompanied by the rise and fall of hegemonic powers. Thus, from the Italian city states up to the era of US hegemony, via Dutch and then British hegemony, 'the same sequence of declining and emerging capitalist centers that, according to Marx, were linked to one another by a recycling of surplus capital through the international credit system. In both sequences, the states that became identified with capitalism … were larger and more powerful than their predecessor' (Arrighi 2007: 93). Arrighi thus argues that the industrial capitalism of the West came to challenge and surpass East Asia, only to then be challenged by the latter in the second half of the twentieth century.

This argument usefully (but only partially) challenges the older idea of inevitable inter-imperialist rivalries, and the view that China's rise will inevitably give rise to heightened geo-political competition. Arrighi (2007: 9) however suggests that US hegemony is now on its last legs, and the Iraq war represents its final curtain, the 'terminal crisis of US hegemony'. The expense of the war on terror, coupled with the ongoing twin deficits in the US has meant that it is increasingly dependent on foreign capital, including Chinese capital. In 2005, the US imported goods and services from abroad of a value of $2 trillion, of which $243 billion came from China. By early 2006, China held $263 billion in US Treasury bonds, and had accumulated foreign currency reserves of $875 billion. China is now the second largest exporter to the US (after Canada), the second largest holder of US Treasury bonds (after Japan), and the largest holder of the dollar as a foreign currency (Morgan 2007: 4). This is regarded as part and parcel of the terminal crisis as 'the national wealth and power of the United States [is] ever more dependent on the savings, capital, and credit of foreign investors and governments' (Arrighi 2007: 9, 146–61).

Arrighi thus suggests that China's rise will not necessarily lead to heightened conflict. His views do however closely parallel the claims of neo-realist hegemonic stability theory (Kindleberger 1973; Gilpin 1983), which contends that a liberal international order can only be maintained by a strong hegemonic power, and periods of instability coincide with the fall of hegemonic powers, which in turn undermines liberal international order. In this way, there is something of a family resemblance between theories that emphasize heightened geo-political conflict and those that focus on hegemonic stability and instability. Most important, these theories suggest that with the economic slowdown in the US in 2007, and the geo-political problems associated with Iraq, we are witnessing a period of transition in the international order, and China (or Europe, see below) may be the most significant challenger.

However, Arrighi's evidence does not necessarily reflect East Asia's rise and the US decline. Chapter 7 showed that much of the rise of manufacturing in the developing world concentrates on low value production characterized by intense competition and diminishing returns. Arrighi believes that China's rise represents an erosion of this trend. However, it could be argued that it is fully compatible with it. Of the patents that apply in the US, Japan and the European union,

China accounts for just 0.1 per cent of them (Hutton 2008). The shares of TNC manufacturing affiliates in China's exports increased from 17.4 per cent in 1990, to 55 per cent in 2003 (Hart-Landsberg and Burkett 2005: 125). As Chapter 7 demonstrated, China's growth in manufacturing exports must in part be explained through its (subordinate) role in East Asian production networks, and it essentially concentrates on exporting the lower value end of such goods. The Communist Party leadership appears to be simultaneously promoting export-led growth in low value sectors while attempting to develop 'national champions' through import-substitution policies. In this respect, China is attempting to repeat the successes of earlier East Asian industrialization strategies, particularly Taiwan and South Korea (Wade 1990; Amsden 1989), but also earlier capitalist development trajectories in the West (Chang 2002).

The problem the Party faces however is that the wider international context has changed, and many nation-states are increasingly hemmed in by neo-liberalism (though it should also be stressed that now many 'national capitals' actively support this wider commitment to neo-liberalism – see Chibber 2003; 2004b; Pirie 2006). In the case of China, it is difficult to see how their national-champion policy is compatible with WTO membership, and there have been some expressions of discontent within the US about continued protectionism in the Chinese domestic market. According to the annual US Congressional-Executive Commission on China report in 2005, '(t)he Chinese government has also proposed and implemented new measures that appear to protect and promote domestic industry and disadvantage foreign business, sometimes in contravention of its WTO commitments' (cited in Breslin 2007: 100). China's flouting of WTO commitments could be regarded as a sign of strength on its part (Arrighi 2007: 277), but in fact there is great concern in China about the impact of liberalization on domestic industry (Nolan 2001), as this is likely to erode a development strategy based on the promotion of national champions.

One brief example illustrates this point. In the early 2000s, mercantilists within the Communist Party, and particularly within the Ministry of Science and Technology and the Ministry of Information, attempted to impose specifically Chinese standards for information technology infrastructure. The proposed Wireless Authentication and Privacy Infrastructure (WAPI) would have meant that foreign capital would have had to produce one product for China, and one for the rest of the world. An alliance within the party-state apparatus between nationalists and 'new leftists' suspicious of liberalization criticized the impact of trade liberalization on the industrial policy associated with building national champions, and the ability of foreign capital to extract rents on products made in China which have to conform to global standards. Thus, for every Chinese DVD player made, around US$12 to $13 is paid in royalties to conform to European or Japanese standards, which rise to $21 if exported, and patents and conforming to standards – which go to the likes of Microsoft and Intel – make up more than half the manufacturing cost of a personal computer made in China (Bell and Feng 2007: 54). This attempt to localize standards failed as China succumbed to pressure from US state representatives and business interests, but ultimately because Intel publicly stated that it would not support WAPI, and so China faced the prospect of having no wi-fi-equipped computer systems from the second half of 2004. The Chinese state backed down, though this 'retreat' was certainly supported by sections of a fragmented Chinese state, particularly those at the Ministry of Commerce (MOFCOM).

Arrighi is certainly correct that China cannot by any stretch of the imagination be described as a neo-liberal miracle. However, we need to distinguish between neo-liberal ideology which is based on the fallacy that capitalist development can take-off through neo-liberal policies, and neo-liberalism as a form of social rule (Albo 2005), in which there are strong pressures, domestic and international, that make states increasingly conform to neo-liberal norms. This is true even if this rule serves to subordinate some states and localities in the international order, including in some respects China. For as Kerr (2007: 92) argues, China 'is doing well from export earnings, but the added value and technological lead of US, Japanese and European transnationals is not being significantly eroded'. For Nolan (2004: 204), 'none of China's leading enterprises had become a globally competitive giant corporation, with a global market, a global brand, and a global procurement system'. Indeed, in the FT 500 leading companies based on market capitalization in 2007, China had eight companies compared to the US' 184. In the top 20, the US had 13 companies and China (including Hong Kong) just two, one of which was China's national bank (www.ft.com).

So, it is largely in low-value, labour-intensive sectors that China has played a major role in out-competing other developing countries. This has promoted a synergy between Chinese exports and the US domestic market. In 2004, Wal-Mart imported $18 billion in goods from China, making it the national equivalent of the fifth largest 'national' importer of Chinese goods. The US Centre for Strategic and International Studies has estimated that China's low cost exports makes the US better off by about $70 billion a year, though of course such an estimate rests on a number of assumptions. Nevertheless, it is clear that in the context of falling average real wages and growing wage inequality, consumption levels have been maintained in part through increasing high income consumption, but also through a combination of increasing debt and low cost imports consumed by lower income consumers (Morgan 2006).

Furthermore, US deficits with China need to be situated in a specific context, namely that China's build up of foreign-exchange reserves in part reflects the continued *strength* of US hegemony. The dollar remains the main international reserve currency, and this gives the US considerable leverage over other countries. It allows the US considerable autonomy in terms of financing trade deficits, thus further facilitating high consumption levels. Of course other states could switch from the dollar, thus causing devaluation as has periodically occurred since the collapse of Bretton Woods. However, as the main international reserve currency, 'the dollar acts as a form of risk insurance since it provides the opportunity to generate capital movements in financial markets towards US assets' (Morgan 2006: 32). The US thus gains as the main site of financial trading, through profits from speculation and through flows of investment capital. This is reinforced through the 'structural power' of the US as it acts as a market of last resort for the world economy, thus further extending US leverage over other states (Gill 2004). China's accumulation of dollar reserves should be seen in this light, as 'it is China who bares the risk of the gambler's scenario of generating large dollar reserves and the purchase of dollar-denominated assets because it is China that must accept the losses of a sudden dollar destabilization or of a speculative attack on its own currency' (Morgan 2006: 32).

In this sense then, though of course the US twin deficits do matter, and reflect uneven development in the international order, they also reflect the fact that the US manages to maintain its hegemony in part because of the capital inflow that finances such deficits (Panitch and Gindin 2004). The so-called European challenge (Leonard 2005) must also be seen in this context. The idea that the European Union represents a new challenger to the US, or that its rise represents heightened geo-political conflict, is an influential one (Wallerstein 2003; Haseler 2004). It is also sometimes associated with the view that the so-called European project, based on a social model that incorporates labour and welfare rights into a social democratic model, is a more progressive challenger to US neo-liberal capitalism (Clark 2008).

These views are problematic however. As we saw in Chapter 5, the US encouraged European integration after 1945, partly to discipline Germany, but also as part of a project of global integration through the internationalization of capital. At the same time, security issues were kept separate from economic integration through the creation of NATO, where US leadership was far more open and direct. In this period of what Cafruny and Ryner (2007) call US integral hegemony, various social democratic and corporatist, 'national capitalisms' were promoted in Europe, aided by the export of US capital. However, in the second, post-1980s period, which is one of minimal US hegemony, the project of European integration is 'based on the assumption uniting parties of the center-right and center-left that a decade of stagflation and failed attempts at European monetary coordination after the collapse of Bretton Woods system meant that there is "no alternative" to national and regional neo-liberalism' (Cafruny and Ryner 2007: 4). This period started with the retreat from Keynesian policies in France in 1983, and includes the Single European Act (1987), the Maastricht Treaty (1993), the creation and extension of the euro, and the failed attempts to implement the Constitutional Treaty from 2004 onwards. This second project is often regarded as an extension of the European social model, but in fact the single market and monetary union 'have greatly reduced national prerogatives without giving rise to the pan-European democratic polity necessary to lend stability and cohesion to these radical developments' (Cafruny and Ryner 2007: 4–5).

The second European project then, represents a break from, rather than an extension of, the European social model. It is not a progressive alternative to US hegemony. Is it then an alternative of some sort, progressive or not? There are strong grounds for answering this question in the negative as well, and this relates back to the question of the character of European integration. As Gill (2001: 47–8) suggests, Maastricht and European monetary union 'seek to minimize the threat of currency turbulence by moving to a single currency and by "locking in" political commitments to orthodox market-monetarist fiscal

and monetary policies that are perceived to increase government credibility in the eyes of financial market players'. In practice, this means
the euro and the move to strict fiscal discipline are intended to maintain investor confidence in a way that essentially copies the US
model. Crucially however, this following of the US model occurs in a
very different context for the European Union, as the US benefits
from a financial hegemony that Europe does not have. Grahl (2004:
291) argues that 'the primacy of the dollar rests on the scale and
liquidity of North American financial markets and, measured by this
yardstick, the preponderance of the US economy, far from giving way
to competitive challenge, is greater than ever before'.

US primacy in part then rests on financial hegemony, though as we
have suggested this cannot be separated from industrial capital as 'the
dollar denominated markets increasingly determine the terms and
conditions for corporate finance, and the resulting pressures tend to
create a corporate world in the image of the US itself' (Grahl 2004:
292). But this leads to a further question, which is whether the euro
can sustain a challenge to the dollar as the world's most important
reserve currency, and in this way challenge US hegemony. It should
be clear by now that a global currency does confer certain advantages
to states that also happen to issue the same currency, as is the case with
the dollar. These include political issues such as international prestige
and the ability to pursue foreign objectives without constraint, but
these ultimately derive from the practice of seigniorage, which is 'the
implicit transfer, equivalent to an interest free loan, that goes to the
issue of money that is widely used and held abroad. Because it may
remain in foreign circulation indefinitely, an international currency is
like a claim that might never be exercised. But because it is virtually
costless to produce, it enables the issuer to acquire vast amounts of
goods, services and assets from the rest of the world at little or no
sacrifice' (Cohen 2003: 578). This in turn facilitates the ability to rely
on one's own money to help finance external deficits which, as we
have seen, has been common practice in the United States since the
early 1980s. The key question then is this: does the euro's rise mean
an undermining of the US' ability to carry out such practices?

Certainly there is some evidence of the euro's rise as a global
currency, particularly in the context of the economic problems faced
by the United States from 2007 onwards (Kirshner 2008). Russia and
a number of Middle East states increased their holdings of currencies
other than the dollar from 2001 onwards, and the euro accounted for

25 per cent of all global financial reserves in 2008, compare to 18 per cent in 1999 (McNally 2008: 16). The euro was involved in 49 per cent of all cross-border transactions in 2006, compared to 43 per cent for the dollar, and in international bond markets in the same year, 49 per cent of all debt was held in euros compared to 37 per cent for the dollar (McNally 2008: 16). The rise of the euro is regarded by some as evidence of US economic decline, and the idea discussed above that financial hegemony is short-lived and ultimately unsustainable (Brenner 2002; Arrighi 2007). In particular the US state faces a dilemma between sustaining the advantages associated with the dollar being the international reserve currency, and carrying out policies which would strengthen the national economy but undermine dollar hegemony.

As we have seen, the advantage of dollar hegemony is that it gives the US the capacity to issue its national currency to pay for debts. In effect then, Asian central banks, in investing in the US (through DFI, stocks and Treasury bonds) have returned to the US those dollars that the US has used to pay for its current account deficit. However, critics suggest that this cannot go on indefinitely and recycling back to the US fuels speculative bubbles (in stock markets, housing, and so on), which once they come to an end, makes the US a less attractive place to invest. The US may respond (as in 2007 onwards and periodically since 1982) by lowering interest rates to manage the damage caused by the end of a speculative bubble, but this makes dollar-denominated assets less attractive as finance is attracted to areas of higher interest rates, and thus higher returns. The argument is that this will lead to a speculative flight away from the dollar, which will further encourage even more of a movement away from the dollar. The end result will be a decline in the dollar and ultimately, the end of US hegemony (see the next section). The US state could increase interest rates to halt the decline of the dollar, but this would be at the cost of an increase in the intensity of recession in the US, thus undermining further the strength of the US national economy (Brenner 2002). It is precisely for these reasons that the euro is said to represent a hegemonic challenge to the dollar, and hence the United States. Although the argument is not made so explicitly, it is implied that the shift from one hegemonic power to another is bound to lead to heightened economic and geo-political conflict, particularly as the existing hegemonic power is unlikely to relinquish its status without some form of resistance.

On the other hand, there are strong reasons for suggesting that the euro's challenge to the dollar is limited. Between February 1985 and November 1987, the value of the yen and the mark both doubled against the dollar, but it was the US that had the most successful economy in the 1990s and the dollar was ultimately unchallenged as the primary international reserve currency (Gindin 2008). Of course the euro is a currency that is used in more than one national territory, so it could be argued that it represents a greater threat than the yen or the mark. However, this may not be the case. Certainly in the years immediately after monetary union, the euro's involvement in financial transactions was not very impressive, at least when compared to the involvement of all the currencies that the euro replaced. For example, by 2001, the euro was involved in 38 per cent of all foreign currency transactions, which compared to the dollar's 90 per cent. Perhaps most strikingly, 53 per cent of such transactions involved European currencies on the eve of their replacement by the euro (Cohen 2003: 580).

Since then, as we have seen, the euro has become far more significant. The dollar accounted for 70.9 per cent of official foreign exchange reserves in 1999, and 65.7 per cent by 2006; the euro's share increased from 17.9 per cent to 25.2 per cent over the same period (MacNamara 2008: 444). However, while this growth is significant, the dollar's dominance remains striking and in any case it can be argued that the euro is limited by a number of factors. The most important are the measures that restrict growth even as they ensure financial stability, such as European Central Bank policy and the Growth and Stability Pact, which limits deficits to 3 per cent of GDP. The fact that this pact has been ignored in recent years does not mean that the anti-growth bias of the European Union has been over-turned, but rather that the European project is increasingly fragmented (MacNamara 2008). Such fragmentation has been exacerbated by some countries rejecting European integration treaties, largely on the grounds of support for retention of those social models that are increasingly undermined by the integrationist project. Moreover, the economic crisis from 2007 exposed tensions in the European project (Gamble 2009: 124–8), as weaker economies have no room for manoeuvre within the context of a European wide currency as opposed to a national currency that might float downwards and potentially aid exports (assuming that markets can be found for the goods). Some commentators have suggested that a number of countries, including Italy, may leave the Eurozone in the near future.[1]

While there has been an increase in the purchase of alternative currencies to that of the dollar, this has largely been a practice adopted by developing countries, whose dollar holdings as a percentage of total foreign exchange reserves decreased from 70 per cent in 1995 to 60 per cent in 2007 (Aquanno 2008: 19). This has not however meant an absolute decline on dollar holdings, and in the period from December 2006 to September 2007, foreign purchases of US Treasury debt increased by \$132 billion to a record \$2 248 billion (Aquanno 2008: 19). Moreover, among developed capitalist countries, the percentage of dollars held as a proportion of reserve assets increased from 60 per cent in 1995 to 69 per cent in 2007 (Aquanno 2008: 19). The shift to the euro is certainly not insignificant, but the practice of holding assets in more than one currency, is not unusual and does not in itself constitute a challenge to the hegemony of the dollar.

Moreover, focusing simply on US deficits does not capture the significance of the changed context in which capital operates today. The foreign income of US investors increased from 11.1 per cent of total US capital income in 1960, to 38.1 per cent in 2006. The income paid to foreign investors accounted for 3 per cent of total US capital income in 1960, but as much as 35.6 per cent in 2006 (Rude 2008: 22). In 2006, the foreign sales of US transnational companies stood at \$4 225 billion, and US exports stood at \$1 283 billion. The total sales for non-US transnationals operating in the US stood at \$2 761 billion, and US imports of foreign TNCs totalled \$1 997 billion. The combined figure for the first set of figures – representing US transnational capital is \$5 508 billion, while for the latter the figure is \$4 758 billion (Rude 2008: 24). Thus, US transnational capital maintains a strong surplus, even as the US territorial economy runs deficits. This does not mean that the deficits are irrelevant. However, it does mean that we cannot 'map' US capital onto the US territorial state, or vice versa, and talk about national blocs of capital in the way that Bukharin used the term. Indeed, these figures reflect the increased globalization of production as outlined in Chapter 7. It is also worth repeating (see Chapter 6) that the US rate of growth from 1983 to 2002 outstripped all the other G7 countries, and that the real GDP of the US was 20 per cent higher than the total of the top 12 Western European economies by 1999, compared to relative parity in 1982, and a gap of only 13 per cent in 1950 (Panitch and Gindin 2005a: 151). This strength of the US economy, relative to rivals also puts any simplistic notions of US over-reliance on finance at the expense of industry into perspective. There has been considerable decline in industrial employment in the US, but this is in part because of corporate strategies which have shed some production activities while maintaining others, including higher value production (Whitford 2005). This analysis accords with that in Chapter 7, which showed that in recent years, developing countries' share of manufacturing output increased while their share of value added declined.

In terms of economics then, my argument suggests that a significant European challenge to the US is exaggerated. Instead, the evidence points to Europe as a junior partner in a neo-liberal international order still dominated by the United States. This applies equally to the question of geo-politics. Though, as we have seen, much has been made of the conflicts that emerged over Iraq in 2003 (see Callinicos 2005; van der Pijl 2006; Layne 2008), and specifically German, French and Russian opposition to the invasion, these tensions coincided with substantial cooperation over the conduct of the war. This included collaboration on the part of French and German intelligence services with the US, the use by US forces of European airspace during the war, and collaboration with the CIA over flights carrying alleged terrorists to secret torture centres (Cafruny and Ryner 2007: 106). The much vaunted plan for a European Common Security and Defence Policy is regarded by both the US and major European powers – with the partial exception of France – as a supplement, rather than an alternative, to NATO and US leadership. As things stand, the EU's military capability is round about one tenth of that of the US (Cafruny and Ryner 2007: 117–19). There is of course the question of what exactly NATO stands for in a post-Cold War world, and some have argued that it will eventually decline (Layne 2008). However, this view underestimates the ways in which NATO has altered its self-identity, shifting from a Cold War alliance to one based on the expansion of the so-called liberal peace, and incorporation of new, or potential, liberal democracies into the alliance (Williams 2007: ch.4).

In terms of geo-political relations between the US and China, the picture is also far from clear cut. Cooperation has increased in the war on terror, and the Chinese political elite tend to pursue a strategy that cannot be easily accommodated by theories which suggest an inevitable intensification of geo-political conflict. In particular, the Chinese leadership has moved towards a strategy which accepts, albeit reluctantly, the fact of US primacy, and wants to find ways of accommodating to it. While the most significant section of the Chinese leadership remains pessimistic about such prospects, they are also resigned to it, and an influential minority regards cooperation as both desirable and feasible (Gong 2004). This is part of the strategy of stressing China's *heping jueqi*, or peaceful rise, which is contrasted to the violent rise of previous powers (Alden 2007: 115). While pursuing a strategy that attempts an increase in cooperation with the US, such as the construction of a common counter-terrorist stance, the Communist Party elite has simultaneously hedged against the prospects of failure by developing bilateral and regional ties with the different parts of the developing world, which has been facilitated by closer trade and investment ties and increased aid (Alden 2007). These relationships are therefore of some significance, but at present at least, they do not constitute a new coalition of forces united by a challenge to US hegemony at the level of the international state system (Foot 2006). In short, while there is considerable evidence of conflict for the 'Leninists' to emphasize, there is much to back the 'Kautskyite' view which emphasizes cooperation. Thus, growing inter-dependence between China and US does give rise to tensions, but equally provides the impetus for cooperation. How these operate in a particular period is far more contingent than (Leninist, or indeed realist) theories which suggest inevitable conflict, or indeed liberal theories which suggest growing pacification as commercial relations expand.

These comments should not be misinterpreted. I am not suggesting that the growth of China is economically or indeed geo-politically irrelevant. Leaving aside the question of calculations, China's growth rates have been impressive, and combined with its size, have great implications. But equally, China's miracle cannot be theorized simply in terms of its national development, and in part at least reflects the transnationalization of capital, and the changing forms of uneven development that have arisen out of this process.

This brings us back to the 'modernizing' and 'Leninist' theories of imperialism. The idea that imperialism is either based on the export of surplus capital and intensified inter-imperialist rivalries, or it is a modernizing force based on capitalist diffusion is implicit in much of the interpretations of China's rise. The radical view sees China's rise as inevitably provoking intense (geo-political and economic) conflict between new great powers, while the liberal view sees China's rise as evidence of the modernizing force of neo-liberal globalization. The interpretation here suggests that China's rise must be situated in a very different context, based on new patterns of global capitalism and uneven development, and these must be related to an imperialism of free trade, and not the imperialism identified by classical Marxists at the turn of the nineteenth century. Put bluntly, China's rise can be accounted for, less by reference to the rise of (Bukharin's) national blocs of capital, and more by the reconstruction of capital on a global scale.

US Decline Revisited: the Global Economic Crisis of 2008 Onwards

The argument so far in this chapter has shown a considerable degree of scepticism concerning predictions of US hegemonic decline. However, in 2007–8, the US economy suffered a serious economic downturn. What are the implications of this for the future of US imperialism? Does it mean that we are now entering a new period of capitalism, in which both US primacy and neo-liberalism are in terminal decline? This book has argued that to understand the period from the 1980s to the 2000s, the most useful historical comparison to be made in the history of capitalist imperialism is less with the era of classical imperialism from 1882 onwards, and more the era of free trade British hegemony from around 1846 to 1870. Is it now the case that some more useful parallels can be drawn from the later period? These could include the economic downturn and the deflation of 1873–96, which in turn coincided with, and extended, inter-imperialist rivalries, saw the beginning of the end of British hegemony, and culminated in war. In other words, just as the 'internationalism' of the 1860s gave way to the rivalries of the 1880s, in the context of the depression that started in the 1870s, so might the 'globalization' of the 1990s (and beyond) give rise to the rivalries (or hegemonic challengers) of the 2010s, in the context of the depression that started in 2007–8? (Patomaki 2008: chs.7 and 8) A full answer to these questions can only really be made over the years to come. What this section attempts to do is briefly examine the crisis and some of the possible implications for the future.

In 2007, the US housing market went into free fall as the high risk, sub-prime mortgage market collapsed as over 2 million people fell behind with their mortgage repayments, and the total foreclosure rate for all mortgages reached its highest ever level of 0.83 per cent (Lapavitsas 2009; Gamble 2009: ch.1). This had an impact way beyond the housing market because the financialization of the US economy included the securitization of these loans; that is, the breaking up of these loans into small amounts and then placing them in larger composites and selling them on (Ingham 2008: 168–9). In the context of stagnant real wages (itself a product of neo-liberalism), consumption in the US has been maintained by debt financing, including of mortgages. Personal savings collapsed from 9–10 per cent of disposable personal income in the 1970s to around 0.4 per cent by 2007, the lowest ever level for a developed capitalist economy. In the context of lower savings and debt fuelled consumption, the trade deficit reached record levels ($762 billion) in 2006. The housing boom of the 1990s onwards was fuelled by cheap credit, which in turn was a product of the ability of the US to borrow cheaply in international capital markets. The expansion of home ownership was thus intimately connected to contemporary imperialism, and particularly the fact that the central banks of oil exporters and East Asian surplus countries were prepared to finance US current account deficits. This was reinforced by financialization which, in terms of the housing market, meant that the US economy expanded in part because of the housing boom. The US housing market was characterized by relatively high levels of home ownership, high levels of mortgage debt relative to GDP, easy and cheap re-financing of mortgages, and the securitization of mortgage loans. All these factors served to stimulate the US and other economies, such as Britain, which had similar housing markets (Schwartz 2008).

However, in 2007 the boom came to an end as the ongoing expansion of the housing market collapsed in the face of unsustainable debts, caused by increases in the (increasingly common) variable rates of interest in mortgages and the inability of debtors to meet these new obligations. Given the securitization of mortgage loans, the crisis quickly spread throughout the economy. From August 2007, the interbank money market collapsed as banks found it difficult to obtain liquidity from each other to meet short-term debt obligations, and instead banks held large volumes of mortgage-backed securities, or supported financial institutions which held them. With the growth of mortgage failures, these securities became far more difficult to sell, depriving banks of liquidity, and consequently putting bank solvency into doubt. This further exacerbated the problem, as trust between banks collapsed and they began to hoard rather then lend money. In a turbulent month in September 2008, the crisis deepened as the investment bank Lehmann Brothers collapsed, other investment banks changed their status so that they were more tightly regulated, AIG, the largest insurer in the world was nationalized, and the US treasury bought up $700 billion of toxic securities (Mason 2009: ch.1; Gamble 2009: ch.1).

This is undoubtedly a major crisis for neo-liberal capitalism, though as we saw in Chapter 7, in parts of the developing world and Eastern Europe, management of the crisis has replicated the IMF programmes that were implemented in the 1980s. More broadly, what is clear is that it is a global crisis that goes way beyond the United States. In terms of the sub-prime crisis in the US, this has exposed not only US banks but other financial institutions in both Asia and Europe, reflecting their integration into the Dollar–Wall Street regime (Gowan 1999). The question that follows is how does this global crisis of neo-liberalism impact on US hegemony? The US decline thesis suggests that the US economy is weak and it is now in terminal hegemonic decline. The second, related argument is that US weakness reflects a global crisis of over-accumulation, and with the onset of recession, an increase in economic and geo-political tensions will undoubtedly arise. Thus, because of the uneven and tension ridden process of capital accumulation, a shift away from geo-political cooperation is likely to give way to an era in which geo-political and economic tensions predominate – the 'Leninist' view thus trumps the 'Kautskyite' position.

Tensions *may* increase in the next few years, particularly given the severity of the crisis of 2008–9, but this is not inevitable. Since the breakdown of Bretton Woods, states in the developed capitalist world have proved to be remarkably resilient in cooperating, even when some have paid far more costs than others in managing the financial crises and/or recessions. This is true for example of Germany and Japan in the early 1990s and some East Asian states after 1997. And this point applies equally to the issue of US hegemonic decline, because here too it is the United States that has successfully managed global instability, and in ways where others have paid much of the costs. Similarly, in 2008 the Eurozone itself faced what appears to be the start of a deep recession, with a contraction of 0.2 per cent in the second and third quarters of that year, and as much as a 3 per cent (predicted) contraction for 2009 (Kollewe 2008; Gow 2009).

Germany alone experienced an annual fall of 6.7 per cent in GDP from early 2008 to early 2009 (Connolly 2009). Beyond the Eurozone, Japan suffered an annualized 15.2 per cent fall in GDP for the first three months of 2009 (McCurry 2009).

Although far from a recession, the many tensions within China's own economic miracle have been exacerbated by the downturn from 2008 onwards. China's industrial expansion has occurred through localized growth which has made sense for each particular locality, but has also resulted in massive over-capacity. At the same time, banks have continued to loan money to finance further expansion, so that by 2005, about $900 billion (the equivalent of around 40 per cent of China's GDP, and more than its foreign exchange reserves) were effectively non-performing loans (Hung 2008: 161–2). These problems are reinforced by increasing inequality and the erosion of state welfare measures, which together mean that the share of wage income in China's GDP has fallen from an estimated 53 per cent in 1998 to 41.4 per cent in 2005 (Hung 2008: 162). While there is a high rate of household savings, much of this is to cover formerly socialized services, such as health, education and retirement expenses. Moreover, much of this household saving is unequally distributed, with 80 per cent held by less than 20 per cent of the population, who tend to import luxuries rather than buy domestic goods. In sum, China has a particularly high ratio of gross fixed capital formation (investment) to final expenditure (consumption), one comparable to the US on the eve of the great depression, and this is based on excess industrial capacity, asset inflation and sluggish domestic demand. China thus remains highly dependent on exports, particularly to the US market which (when re-exports via Hong Kong are included) account for 30 per cent of China's total exports (Hung 2008: 169). The US is also the largest source of foreign direct investment inflows into China (Nolan 2008: 196).

The economic crisis that developed in 2007–8 is thus not only a crisis for the US, but also for China. The idea that China has 'decoupled' from the advanced capitalist countries (implicit in Arrighi's analysis), and could somehow lead the world out of recession and simultaneously challenge US hegemony is unconvincing. We have already seen that China essentially finishes goods for exports, and it is these exports that have suffered since demand fell in Europe and the US (Kiely 2008a and b; Brannigan 2008). Indeed, the global financial crisis has exacerbated the contradictions of Chinese development, as the stock market and property prices have collapsed, non-performing loans have increased, factories have closed in the Pearl river delta region, unemployment has increased, and growth rates fallen (Hutton 2008). It is therefore not surprising that the recession has affected China adversely. In the month of January 2009 exports plummeted by 17.5 per cent on a year on year basis, the biggest monthly fall for over ten years, and unemployment has soared as at least 20 million migrant workers have lost their jobs since the global downturn (Brannigan 2009a; Fenby 2009). Thus, rather than seeing China's growth as a sign of a hegemonic challenge to the US, it could be regarded as one that reflects the increased integration between the two economies, as already argued in more general terms earlier in the chapter. Specifically then, any recession in the US will adversely affect the Chinese economy, and indeed has done.

These points however only directly challenge the US decline thesis, and whether or not any global recession will lead to heightened tensions is ultimately an open question. Chapter 6 rejected 'inevitablist' positions from both sides of the debate on economic and geo-political conflict. But the increased inter-penetration of capitals does provide a very different context from earlier periods of imperialism. If there is a crisis in the US economy, then this is less a crisis of US hegemony and more an economic crisis for global capitalism. For, as Panitch and Konings suggest:

> it is the distinctive characteristic of modern imperialism that America's financial problems are not just its own problems. That is to say, foreign investors cannot engage in a wholesale dumping of dollars on to the world market without destabilizing the system as a whole and doing serious damage to their own interests in the process. For the foreseeable future, therefore, the question is not so much how the US state will ward off an external threat but rather how it will manage and stabilize global financial markets – on behalf of domestic and foreign capital. (2008b: 18)

Much of this discussion overlaps with contemporary Marxist debates over the nature of economic crisis. While it is certainly clear that there has been a substantial increase in financial crises since financial liberalization was introduced, these have been successfully managed through international cooperation. However, it could be argued that the 2007–8 crisis is a more serious one, and may not be successfully managed in the same way. This in turn depends in part on how one explains the causes of the crisis and how these lead to various likely consequences. Brenner (1998; 2002) has argued that capitalism has not successfully resolved its crisis of the 1970s, and that neo-liberalism did not lead to a new era of sustained accumulation. The crisis is therefore one of over-capacity and low profits, rooted in the failure of firms to exit from sectors where competition is particularly intense, which in turn is due to the sunk costs associated with high rates of investment (Brenner 1998). Neo-liberalism may have periodically alleviated some of the effects of the crisis, but has not been successful in promoting a new boom to match that of the post-war period. Instead, full-scale crises have been averted by increases in consumer debt through the massive expansion of credit, while rates of profit and capital accumulation have been sluggish. Ultimately then the causes of the 2007–8 recession lie in the failure to resolve a crisis of capitalist production. This approach points to the reality of global imbalances, and particularly the recycling of East Asian surpluses built up in response to the financial crash of 1997. These were recycled to the US and Britain in particular, and used to finance consumer spending and, particularly when interest rates were lowered after 2001, financed asset price booms, including in the housing market.

Panitch and Gindin, on the other hand, argue that the crisis is one of financialization. As we have seen, they argue persuasively that the 1970s crises of US hegemony and global capitalism were resolved by the restructuring of the US state through the Volcker shock. While it is true that average growth rates in the neo-liberal era have been lower than they were in the post-war Golden Age, it is the latter, rather than the former, which has been exceptional in this regard. Despite the disasters in much of the developing world, annual average growth rates in the neo-liberal era compare favourably with previous periods stretching back to the 1820s, apart from the exceptional Golden Age (Maddison 2001: 265).[2] Panitch and Gindin also suggest that while Brenner's account can point to diminishing profit rates in particular sectors, it cannot explain why competition will drive down profit rates for the economy as a whole, an argument we first encountered in the context of Ricardo's theoretical advances over Adam Smith in Chapter 3 (see also Fine *et al.* 1999). The argument that profit rates have fallen due to a rise in the organic composition of capital is also problematic, as it ignores the defeat of organized labour and resultant low real wages, the increase in capital productivity that finance in part promotes, and the fact that profit rates have increased substantially since the crisis of the 1970s (Dumenil and Levy 2004: 24; Glyn 2006; Moseley 2008). Panitch and Gindin also make the point that the idea that capitalism has been in crisis for twenty-five years begs the question of when, from this perspective, is capitalism not in crisis?

Nevertheless, capitalism is indeed prone to crisis, and it is a constituent part of its dynamism (Clarke 1999; Gindin 2000), and this has been reinforced by the financialization associated with neo-liberalism. What we have seen in recent years is a massive expansion of credit and debt, but this in itself does not constitute a crisis for capitalism, in which finance simply replaces a stagnant monopoly capitalism as some argue (Baran and Sweezy 1966; Bellamy Foster and Magdoff 2009). Financial expansion should be regarded as a sign of *both* capitalism's expansion *and* its (increasingly) crisis-prone nature. Seen in this way, the credit crunch is a sign of both capitalism's strength (its success in converting people into debt-led consumers) and weakness (its related capacity to extend this conversion too far). Important in this regard is the work of Hyman Minsky (1982: 36), who argued that financial instability was an intrinsic feature of capitalism. He argued that the business cycle involved an initial phase of expansion based on increased revenue through expanded production, which gave rise to further periods of expansion. This culminated in the extension of Ponzi finance, named after Charles Ponzi's pyramid selling scheme of the 1920s, in which money paid to early financial investors was financed by purchases made by later investors (see Kindleberger 2000: ch.5). While such schemes are often associated with 'rogue individuals' who break the law, Minsky argued that financial expansion was inextricably linked to such schemes, even if they remained legal. Financial firms borrow to acquire financial assets (such as sub-prime mortgages) in order to sell them on. This can work effectively so long as asset prices continue to expand, but such expansion comes up against the limits of finding secure income streams that could effectively guarantee these loans, culminating in exposure to bad loans and toxic debts, which were managed by state bail-outs and nationalizations. Minsky's argument echoed Keynes' (1973: 159) observation that '[s]peculators may do no harm as bubbles on a steady stream of enterprise. But the position is serious when enterprise becomes the bubble on a whirlpool of speculation. When the capital development of a country becomes the by-product of the activities of a casino, the job is likely to be ill-done.'

The crisis of 2007–8 should be seen then, as a crisis that originated in the financial sector, which expanded enormously in the neo-liberal era. However, in contrast to Keynes (as well as Hobson, Cain and Hopkins),[3] this financial expansion should not be regarded as one that is entirely separate from the productive economy. As we have seen, finance has helped to fuel a new era of capitalist expansion, albeit one that is increasingly crisis-prone precisely because finance plays such as central role. Much the same point can be made about US hegemony. Financialization is not a reflection of a last desperate attempt by a declining hegemonic power to retain its primacy, as some have argued (Arrighi 1994; 2007; Bellamy Foster and Magdoff 2009). While this may have been true of British hegemony, which faced increasing erosion in terms of its competitiveness, the picture is far less clear in the case of the US. As we have seen, the US has been committed to some kind of diffusion of economic activity throughout the globe, while retaining its competitive edge in key sectors. As well as increasing its lead in terms of GDP shares over European rivals (see above), the US has maintained its share of high-tech production, and the growing share from China and South Korea has been at the expense of Europe. The US has also increased its volume of exports more rapidly than any other of the Group of 7 countries since the neo-liberal turn of the early 1980s (Panitch and Gindin 2005b: 6).

In terms of its deficit, US national debt stood at $3 076 billion in December 2008, and this was owned predominantly by Asian economies, with (mainland) China accounting for $727.4 billion and Japan $626 billion of US Treasury securities. While Japan's amount has shown a small but fluctuating increase since the financial crisis gathered pace, China's has increased from $477 billion a year earlier in December 2007 (www.treas.gov/tic/mfh/txt). These holdings reflect increased inter-dependence between internationalized capitalist states, but they are also bound to generate some concerns as well. Certainly, Chinese premier Wen Jiabao expressed concerns about the growing US deficit, particularly in the context of stimulus packages introduced in the early days of the Obama presidency (Brannigan 2009b). There has also been some talk, led by China, France, India and Russia, of building an alternative international reserve currency (Bardeesy 2009). However, such diversification away from the dollar would undermine the value of those creditors holding dollar-denominated assets. At the G-20 summit in April 2009, there were also clear differences over how to resolve the crisis, with the US (and the UK) more committed to a stimulus package and Europe more concerned with measures designed to promote measures controlling the banks and thus promote a new era of what Keynes called financial repression. Also there were some calls for China to use its enormous surpluses to provide a financial stimulus to the International Monetary Fund, and China in turn demanded a change in the voting at the IMF. Domestically, and echoing Hobson's arguments which focused on imperialism as the export of capital (see Chapter 4), there has been some pressure for China to divert its resources into stimulating domestic demand, ironically so that it can become less dependent on the main imperialist power. But even this supposed challenge to US hegemony is limited. A recent proposal to write a World Bank[4] *World Development Report* on income inequality was opposed by Executive Directors from Russia and China on the grounds that such an issue was too openly political (see Wade 2008).

Perhaps more serious has been the growth of financial protectionism, whereby banks are increasingly reluctant to lend outside their national borders (Gamble 2009: 34–5). This may be a temporary phenomenon, reflecting a lack of willingness to lend in the context of the credit crunch, but it is likely to have longer-term implications as well. However, even in this context the willingness of foreign capital to purchase US debt has been quite resilient (see above), reflecting the dollar's role as a relatively safe haven for international investors. This may cause some conflict, for instance as state-backed Sovereign Wealth Funds from China, Russia and the Middle East threaten to take over US assets, but (insofar as takeovers of US companies is resisted) it also reflects the US' ability to pick and choose when it is committed to neo-liberal principles. Whether or not these conflicts add up to a new era of international capitalism, in which neo-liberalism comes to an end and new geo-political as well as economic tensions emerge, is thus debateable. The G-20 meeting in London in the spring of 2009 saw some much trumpeted differences over how to manage the crisis, with the US emphasizing fiscal expansion and Europe a more multilateral approach, with an emphasis on some degree of financial repression (Stewart and Elliot 2009). But this hardly amounts to a new era of heightened (economic or geo-political) competition, rather than one of tactical (and rather small) disagreements over how to resolve the crisis, as the eventual agreement made clear (Stewart 2009). More generally, the US has successfully maintained its hegemonic position while increasing its deficits, and indeed the latter in part is a reflection of the former, even if the extent of such debts has to be managed. As things stand, the crisis is best seen as first a crisis of global capitalism, more than a crisis between national capitalisms and their respective states.

Conclusion

This chapter has argued that there remain important sources of conflict between states in the international order, and that there may even be the potential for an increase in the context of global crisis. However, in keeping with arguments in earlier chapters, it has also been suggested that these tensions are radically different from the period before 1945. This reflects the success of US imperialism in promoting the internationalization of capital and global integration which has eroded inter-imperialist rivalries based on states representing national blocs of capital. This integration is of course highly uneven and unequal, and for this reason (among others) tensions are bound to persist. But there are also strong tendencies which promote cooperation between states. In terms of geo-politics, the most significant source of geo-political tension in the world today is between some Northern and some Southern states, rather than between the advanced capitalist states. The rise of China, and to an extent the EU, could potentially alter this situation, but I have suggested that there are strong grounds – global integration, the role of the dollar, and an acceptance of the fact that US hegemony is here to stay – for arguing against this scenario.

Of course, the picture may be changing, and some writers have identified a terminal decline in US hegemony (Mann 2003; Arrighi 2007). The key – closely interlinked – factors identified by these writers are the ongoing deficits, the quagmire in Iraq, the recession from late 2007, and imperial overstretch brought on by too many military commitments combining with economic decline. These are all important issues and problems for the US, but this chapter has suggested some reasons to be sceptical about the declinist thesis. This is not only because of the problems (EU) or limits (China) of potential hegemonic challengers, but also because US problems need to be put into context. Defence spending has certainly increased as a result of the war on terror, but as a proportion of GDP, it is far lower now than it was in the Reagan years, and at the height of the Cold War. Related to this point, the US has faced recessions in the post-Bretton Woods era, but has actually come out of these stronger than potential rivals. While the recession that started in 2008 appears to be more serious, it is a global crisis and not simply a crisis of US hegemony. Finally, defeat in Iraq would be damaging to US hegemony in some respects, but it is hard to sustain the view that it would be more damaging than the defeat in Vietnam. In the case of the latter, there was still some kind of socio-political alternative to capitalism, namely state socialism. This is not the case in Iraq. Similarly, it is certainly the case that the presidency of Bush II did a great deal to undermine US legitimacy in the international arena, and has probably exacerbated economic problems in the United States. However, in the case of the former, a reversion to a more multilateral version of liberal imperialism is likely, particularly with the election of Obama in late 2008. The full implications of this victory are too early to call, but we have seen multilateral 'moments' followed by further unilateral turns, a recurring feature of US imperialism since 1945 (Gamble 2009: 120–4).

This final point does lead to a further, related question. The US has been a liberal hegemonic power, which has promoted the idea that international order can best be achieved through the development of other parts of the world. This is as true of policies of modernization during the Cold War (Chapter 5) as it is of expansion of the liberal zone of peace in the 1990s and the policing of rogue states after (and indeed before) 2001, even if the means to achieve modernization has changed from developmentalist to neo-liberal policies. The question that then arises is this: what is the relationship between US hegemony and the economic diffusion that is supposed to occur as a result of modernization? Put slightly differently, is the US prepared to tolerate the rise of other powers, provided that these are liberal and 'Americanized', even if this leads to a partial erosion of US (economic) power. And related to this point, if this erosion does – or indeed, as some claim, *has* – come about, how does the US react to this situation? The answer to this question takes us back to the debates addressed in this chapter, with those arguing that geo-political conflict between developed capitalist powers remains central to understanding the international order, against those who suggest that military adventures such as those in Iraq are unlikely to work if they are intended to restore US hegemony. The latter position can then lead to advocacy of a position of US decline (Arrighi 2007), or adoption of the position of the limits of military power without necessarily suggesting that the US is in decline. One response to this issue, as suggested above as well as in earlier chapters, is to point out that the neo-liberal policies that are currently endorsed throughout much of the world are not conducive to the kind of diffusion envisaged by modernization, and indeed in some respects serve to entrench the power of already developed countries. This is one reason, as Chapters 7 and 8 suggested, why military imperialism will not work if its aim is to incorporate 'non-integrating economies' into globalization. This is reinforced by the role of liberalized finance, which encourages capital flows into the US, and away from poorer countries.

But, in the case of the already developed countries, is the US prepared to accept a multi-polar system of core liberal states, and thus a kind of self-erosion of its own hegemony, or is this multi-polar system somehow compromised? There is no straightforward answer to this question, not least because it highlights some of the ambiguities of a US-led international order. From slightly different starting points, Zakaria (2008), Anderson (2007) and Bromley (2008) appear to accept the view that the US is happy to relinquish hegemony provided that the rest of the world is increasingly 'Americanized'; that is, provided other developed countries are liberal, market democracies. This would amount not so much to a hegemonic challenge, but rather to the creation of a multi-polar world without any single hegemonic power, with the US as 'first among equals'. This is the vision for 2025 presented by the US National Intelligence Council (2008), though it stresses that this will depend on the actions taken by state actors over the next fifteen years.

In practice though this is not anywhere near to being met; as we have seen, contemporary geo-political divisions are more about policing non-integrating rogue and failed states, and (from the viewpoint of the US) dealing with the rise of non-liberal powers like China. Economically we have argued that there are still grounds for seeing the US as the dominant power, even if the current period is one of great uncertainty. For all the economic problems that arose with the crisis of 2008 onwards, and the differences about how to resolve this crisis, it was equally clear that any resolution ultimately rested on the power of the US state to coordinate a global capitalism in crisis. Moreover, even in a world dominated by liberal, market democracies, it is questionable that the US would *entirely* dispense with its leading role in the international order. This is because the US does not only promote the expansion of the liberal international order; rather, its leaders 'claim the power to decree national and international rules, laws and norms, whist reserving "exceptional powers" for themselves' (Gill 2004: 24). This state of exception (Agamben 2005) does not only apply to military hegemony, but also international law, international economic agreements, and so on. Thus, whilst the US has been very successful in securing cooperation among developed capitalist states since 1945, and indeed since 1989, this is always qualified by some degree of tension stimulated by US unilateralism, as occurred from 2003 to 2008. In this respect those that emphasize geopolitical conflict point to a real issue of fracture in the international order. But at the same time, this issue should be regarded less as European or Japanese opposition to US hegemony in itself, and more one of disagreement about the way that the US may exercise its primacy at a particular point in time. And, as Chapters 5 onwards have suggested, this fact is a reflection of the very real changes that have occurred in that US-led international order since 1945.

10
Imperialism and Anti-Imperialism Today

This extended concluding chapter summarizes the argument made throughout the book and then tries to draw out some wider political implications. It does so by focusing on the reality of liberal and US imperialism today, how this relates to wider questions of liberalism and America, and how these in turn relate to the question of anti-imperialism. The first section develops further a theme briefly alluded to in the first section of Chapter 6, namely the utility of a critical focus on constructivist approaches to international relations. It does so by examining the questions of 'America' and 'empire', less as social realities, and more as political, or hegemonic projects. The second section then moves on to broadly summarize the nature of imperialism today, and provide some critical reflection on the nature of anti-imperialism. While suggesting that imperialism should indeed be rejected, the discussion suggests that anti-imperialism *per se* is not an intrinsically progressive alternative. This point leads to a much wider discussion, which draws on current debates concerning the crisis of ideological politics, the end of utopia, the utility of cosmopolitanism, and the question of solidarity.

Discourses of Americanization and Empire

Traditional 'anti-imperialist' critiques of America have been, and remain, strongly influenced by the idea of cultural imperialism (Dorfman and Mattelart 1971; Sardar and Wyn-Davies 2003). Briefly, this thesis contends that the US economic and political dominance in the international order also guarantees its cultural dominance. Often linked to studies that show the concentration of ownership in media industries, the theory of cultural imperialism argues that the culture industries serve to promote American hegemony through the dissemination of American values throughout the world.

There are a number of problems with this argument however. It too easily assumes that cultural power is determined by economic power, and tends to reduce consumers of US goods into passive victims, easily manipulated by the propaganda of American companies, even when they are owned by non-Americans (Tomlinson 1991; 1999). But more relevant for our purposes is the way that 'America' is constructed by the cultural imperialism discourse. American culture is regarded as singular, fixed and vulgar. There is no sense in the cultural imperialism thesis that American culture may itself be dynamic, and most crucially, contested, both *within* and *beyond* America.

This is a very significant observation, with much wider political implications. As we saw in Chapter 8, neo-conservatives are a central part of the culture wars in the United States, and particularly concerned with the promotion of what they call a culture of virtue. Much of the attacks in the culture wars are made against contemporary liberals, who are blamed for the social malaise that is said to have inflicted the United States. This is because liberalism focuses too much on rationalism and individualism, neither of which can provide the basis for social cohesion. Moreover, liberal decadence is said to be out of touch with the views of 'ordinary Americans', marginalized by a liberal cultural elite. Indeed, these liberals are said to be anti-American, as perhaps best exemplified by protests against the war in Vietnam (Kirkpatrick 2004). Neo-conservatives are thus part of a prominent cultural backlash, which aims to put culture at the centre of political debate. The focus on republican virtue and American identity 'provides a point around which a large range of positions and concerns can coalesce, and has been central to the role and influence of neo-conservatism in American politics over the last decade' (Williams 2007: 111). Thus, rather than seeing Americanization as static and fixed, it can be regarded as something that is open to debate, contestation and conflict. Particular political actors may want to fix its meaning, but this itself should be regarded by social scientists as part and parcel of a hegemonic project, which attempts to promote a common sense among 'ordinary Americans' (Frank 2004). In some respects it has succeeded too, though as with all theories of hegemony, there is a need for care in not exaggerating the degree to which certain ideas have taken hold within the general population.[1]

This can be seen in the case of the focus on how the defence of property was converted in the neo-liberal era into the expansion of home ownership. This in part was fuelled by the influx of credit from the foreign central banks of surplus countries, and thus of contemporary imperialist relations. In a context in which neo-liberalism led to the erosion of the welfare state, real wages and job security, it was the expansion of home ownership which was regarded as crucial as a means of promoting financial security (Schwartz 2008). In this way the hegemonic project of neo-liberalism within the US was closely linked to US hegemony in international relations. In the context of falling house prices alongside increased employment insecurity, it may be the case that neo-liberal hegemony in the US is now under threat. Ultimately this will depend on political opposition, not least because neo-liberalism has successfully revived itself in the context of periodic crises.

What should be clear though is that the broader question of 'what is America' is partly a question of America as a political, hegemonic project. And this in turn is a question of how America's enemies are themselves constructed, and indeed who these enemies are. This can be seen in the speeches of President Bush (2001) after the terrorist attacks in 2001, and in particular his asking of the question 'Why do they hate us?' His answer was that 'They hate our freedoms – our freedom of religion, our freedom of speech, our freedom to vote and assemble and disagree with each other.' A freedom-loving United States is thus contrasted to an irrational, evil, terrorist other, that simply hates America. An innocent, reactive United States is thus contrasted to evil others, who threaten the state that most represents good in the global order. As we saw in Chapter 8, this idea of a clear divide between those with good intentions and those with evil ones is then used to close off debate. For example, if one points to the fact that the US' current enemies were once its allies, the argument is dismissed because it allegedly appeases radical Islamists. The significance of this argument is addressed in the next section, but what is important at this point is how it can be used to hinder debate. We saw this in the cases of Paul Berman and Thomas Cushman in Chapter 8, but perhaps the most extreme example can be found in the case of David Horowitz (2006), a former leftist now on the far right of the American political spectrum. He has claimed that politicized

American universities, and certain liberal academics in particular, effectively 'identify with the terrorists' (www.mediamatters.org/research, 16 October 2009). This kind of argument thus dismisses liberal decadence, very much like neo-conservatism, while simultaneously claiming to uphold US values of liberal freedom. Indeed, neo-conservatism feeds into the idea that America is a victim, of modern liberal elites at home and terrorist enemies abroad (Kristol 1995). Values are needed in the face of a liberal, pluralism, the latter of which is not only relativist but also anti-American. Re-moralization is thus part of a project to rekindle a true, authentic America in the face of liberal and left threats at home and terrorist threats from abroad. And it is precisely this argument that has been so successfully employed by neo-conservatives in the aftermath of 2001. However, as we have seen, it is an argument that draws heavily on specific traditions of American (and liberal) freedom, and in this way forms part of a political project of Americanization. Indeed, neo-conservatism transcends party lines, and prominent and influential Democrat neo-conservatives have included Jeane Kirkpatrick and Henry 'Scoop' Jackson. Moreover, for all the criticisms made of liberalism, many prominent liberals support the interventionist positions taken by neo-conservatives in the name of a humanitarian, ethical and indeed liberal foreign policy which has the virtue of moral clarity (if not consistency) in terms of its values (see further below).

Neo-conservative views can be traced back to post-war discontent with big government at home and hostility to a soft line on communism abroad. While this often involved acceptance of economic liberal arguments such as those associated with Hayek's *The Road to Serfdom* (2001) and *The Constitution of Liberty* (2006), and Friedman's *Capitalism and Freedom* (2002), it also usually meant the promotion of virtue beyond the free market and the relativism and subjectivism of individual choice, as in Richard Weaver's *Ideas Have Consequences* (1984). In terms of wider appeal, the nomination of Barry Goldwater as Republican candidate for the President in 1964 was important, even though he was heavily defeated (and his libertarian views subsequently did not always coincide with other US conservatives). Goldwater revived the theme of a divine mission for the United States, arguing that God had intended 'this mighty republic to be ... the land of the free' (cited in Foner 1999: 313), and envisaged a free and inter-dependent world of prosperity under US leadership. But it was the economic crisis of the 1970s and the intensification of the

Cold War from the late 1970s that brought Reagan to power and paved the way for a neo-liberal turn in economics and a conservative turn in social and cultural policy. Even here though, the lines of opposition are not without ambiguity as the Democrats have essentially embraced neo-liberal economic policies, albeit with a less conservative social and cultural policy and some attempt to promote communitarian values (Kiely 2005a: ch.4).

This mixture of difference and similarity are most clear in the case of the idea of US hegemony and a project of Americanization. Neo-conservatives argue that there must be greater clarity about American values at home and abroad, and suggest that the self-evident nature of US benevolence is sufficient justification for unilateralist policies, including military intervention. This is clearly different from a more multilateral approach, in which the US works through international institutions, and military power is regarded as a last resort and limited in its utility. But at the same time, even those advocating multilateralism still regard the US as the leading – and benevolent – nation, and promote policies fully compatible with neo-liberal, free trade imperialism. As we have seen, the notion that the US is the exceptional but also universal nation is one that is hardly exclusive to neo-conservatism, and reaches deep into American political culture, transcending mainstream party divisions. The election of Barack Obama is likely to lead to some changes, particularly in terms of the most visible manifestations of US imperialism, such as Guantanamo Bay, extraordinary rendition and the use of torture. These are important and their significance should not be under-estimated. But whether an Obama presidency will lead to the end of free-trade imperialism is unlikely. Indeed, multilateralism may actually serve to re-secure US hegemony in regions where it has eroded, such as in Latin America. It is also clear that the idea of humanitarian imperialism will not simply fade away under Obama, even if the means to carry this out will differ from neo-conservative ones. The think tank, the Princeton Project on National Security (PPNS 2006) is interesting in this regard. It claims to be committed to a liberal internationalist alternative to the Bush Doctrine but essentially criticizes only the latter's means, suggesting that the export of liberal democracy and high growth free market democracies, and thus the extension of the liberal zone of peace, can indeed be better promoted through multilateral rather than unilateral policies (see Parmar 2009).

But it is not just 'America' and 'Americanization' that can be regarded as political projects. As we saw in Chapter 4, Niall Ferguson has made the case for progressive empire, in which liberal empires – Britain and now the United States – are seen as progressive forces in history. Ferguson (2004: 96) is more than aware that there was – and is – a dark side to empire, even suggesting in the case of Vietnam that '[w]ithin a short time, the reality – that imperialists are seldom loved – began to sink in'. He also points to the failures of British colonialism but explains these away by suggesting that colonialism was insufficiently interventionist, an argument that echoes those made by humanitarian imperialists for the early twenty-first century. However, as was suggested in earlier chapters, this is less a sophisticated analysis of what empire was – and is – and more one based on what empire might be. This ultimately means that Ferguson is less interesting as a historian of British or American empire, and more as an advocate of *empire as a political project*. And this ultimately brings us back to the conceit of empire, be it liberal or non-liberal, altruistic or self-interested. For as Howe suggests, Niall Ferguson's world view revolves around two basic assertions:

> Some people – mostly poor and dark-skinned ones – need to recognize that they are conquered, accept the fact, indeed realize that it's in their own best interests to be so. And other people, especially Americans, must know and accept that they are conquerors and imperialists, shoulder the accompanying burdens, understand that such a role benefits everyone. (2004: 1)

What this suggests then is that both America and empire can be regarded as political projects, and thus so too can anti-Americanism and anti-imperialism. Anti-Americanism *may* be part of a political project that incorporates hostility to freedom, equality and democracy (and Ferguson at his most sweepingly ahistorical is very keen to talk up the reactionary politics of anti-imperialists, from independence movements through to bin Laden), but equally it may not. This in part depends on what 'Americanization' means in the first place, as we have seen. If we understand Americanization in this way then, it is clearly not unrelated to debates over the relationship between liberalism and imperialism. It is to a final consideration of the relationship between US-led liberal imperialism, and its anti-imperialist enemies, that we now turn.

Liberal Imperialism, Anti-Imperialism and the End of Ideology

This final section examines debates over the nature of anti-imperialist politics, and how this relates to wider debates over contemporary politics more generally. It does so first by summarizing the arguments that the book has made against liberal imperialism. It then moves on to an analysis of the politics of anti-imperialism, initially by addressing one of the most compelling cases made against the Iraq war, by the political philosopher John Gray. An exposition of his argument is used to re-examine the debate between liberal imperialism's advocates and its detractors, which in turn is then used to discuss how questions of anti-imperialism are deeply implicated in broader debates over the end of ideology and the global crisis of politics, and how these debates relate back to the issues of imperialism today. These very wide debates are then used to discuss the dilemmas of embracing a progressive, as opposed to a blanket, anti-imperialist politics today.

This book has 're-thought imperialism' by suggesting that there are good reasons for largely dispensing with (most) classical Marxist theories (Chapters 4, 5, 6 and 9), and instead focusing on the relationship between imperialism and at least some forms of liberalism (Chapters 3, 5, 7 and 8). It has been suggested that fruitful comparisons can be made between the current era and the nineteenth century, but less to argue for the continued relevance of Lenin and Bukharin, and more to show how British imperialism at least, was associated with free trade and discourses of humanitarianism (Chapters 3, 4 and 8). The book has rejected the idea that liberal imperialism is a progressive force for three main, closely related, reasons.

First, free trade imperialism undermines capitalist development for later developers by kicking away the ladder, and undermining the potential to promote protectionist policies that are necessary to first build up a dynamic and competitive economy. This was true throughout the nineteenth century, until European and North American developers established protectionist industrial policies, and remains true in the current era of neo-liberalism. Related to this point, Blackburn (2005: 131) puts Ferguson's liberal case for colonialism into context, when he points out that he 'cites the disappointing performance of most ex-colonies as part of his case for empire, when it would be more logical to conclude that the empires, did not, in fact, really equip the colonized with survival skills'.

As this book has argued, empires may not have created uneven development in a capitalist world, but they did much to consolidate this, and this point remains true in a post-colonial, but still ultimately imperialist world, *particularly in the era of neo-liberal globalization* (Chapter 7). The neo-classical idea that free trade tends towards convergence between countries based on each specializing in their respective comparative advantage is an absurdity, but so too is the more flexible liberal position that states are better off promoting free trade polices because the alternative of protectionism will make matters worse. Countries can specialize at different stages of development and gains can be made for both, even if these are distributed unequally. This is the basis for some liberal theories of international relations, which suggest that absolute gains between states are more significant than relative gains between them – though the more sophisticated theories emphasize that states make decisions based on some kind of trade-off between the two games (Grieco 1993: 127). A similar case is made by economic liberals who regard neo-classical theories of equilibrium as misguided, but still suggest that, whatever the unequal outcomes, the gains made from free trade outweigh the losses (Lal 1984). But this argument ignores the cumulative nature of uneven development, so that capital can overwhelmingly concentrate in certain locations, and the historical fact that all developed capitalist countries have counteracted this tendency by adopting protectionist, industrial and *market unfriendly* policies (Chang 2002; Reinert 2007). Seen in this light, the most valid distinction in terms of gains is less one between absolute and relative gains between states, and more one between static and dynamic gains based on the kinds of goods produced, and the shift towards producing goods that generate Schumpeterian rents (see Chapter 7). In this way then, we have a theory of imperialism based on uneven development and the distinction between static and dynamic kinds of gains in terms of goods produced, something that is under-estimated by some of the most convincing accounts of imperialism today (such as Panitch and Gindin 2003; Bromley 2008). Of course state intervention to generate dynamic gains has often been counter-productive, especially in so-called failed states, but this is less a product of insufficient market-led intervention, and more one of specific historical and social factors, including international ones related to colonial and imperialist legacies. In a nutshell then, liberal imperialism endorses an imperialism of free trade (Shaikh 2005).

Second, liberal, humanitarian military interventions are based on the mistaken belief that liberal–democratic societies are the norm, and these can be introduced through quick-fix social engineering, which in turn will promote 'westernization'. This is wrong because it abstracts from the (often violent) ways in which already developed capitalist countries emerged, and indeed democratized, and ignores political realities on the ground in countries where intervention takes place. Liberal imperialism thus 'naturalizes' the liberal individual, liberal polity, and liberal society. As Jahn argues, liberal imperialists:

> start with optimistic assumptions about a natural development of humankind towards liberal market democracies – embodied in short-term democracy aid, peace-building operations and interventions designed to trigger this natural development. The failure of these policies are then blamed on the greater than expected developmental shortcomings of Third World societies leading to calls for long-term interventions designed to reconstitute every aspect of the target society in the image of liberal market democracies. And these state-building policies involve the conscious denial of the right to self-government domestically and the right to self-determination internationally. The denial of these rights, in turn, provides the basis for resistance to such liberal foreign policies in the developing world and this achieves exactly the opposite from their initial aims: they turn the targets of American altruism into enemies. (2007b: 223)

Third, in the process, this leads the imperialist power to betray and practise political action which undermines its own claim to hold the moral high ground. As Runciman (2008: 183) argues, '[i]mperial hypocrisy is rendered self-defeating ... since the sword cannot remain in the scabbard, and will be deployed for the supposed benefit of the people it is being used to coerce, by people who are unable to be honest with themselves about the nature of the coercion'. Moreover, this is not just a case of condemning the violence associated with liberal military intervention, but also one of thinking far more carefully about different kinds of violence. This brings us back to the contrast made between individual accounts of violence, where agents can easily be identified, and more systemic accounts of violence, where people suffering is a product of particular social relations, but no specific individual agency can be identified. Much of the case for humanitarian military intervention rests on an individualized account of violence and the idea that people can be saved from rule by evil individuals. But this ignores objective violence, associated with liberal military intervention and global social relations. For all three reasons then, capitalist economics and geo-politics may not be reducible to each other, but they are far from completely separate, and thus (liberal) imperialism should be rejected.

The question that needs to be addressed now then, is what of 'America's enemies', and more specifically, what of the politics of anti-imperialism? To examine this question, we will first look at a particularly powerful case against the Iraq war, made by British political philosopher John Gray. Gray's argument against the Iraq war of 2003 is linked to a wider understanding of politics which essentially embraces a rejection of radical social change. Thus, according to Gray:

> History was significant only as a record of human advance. To turn to it to chasten current ambitions was unthinkable, even immoral. Like Bush, Blair viewed history as the unfolding of a providential design, and a feature of their view is that the design is visible to the faithful. Others may be blind to the unfolding pattern, and in that case they may have to be guided. (2008: 142)

This world view was central to the conduct of Blair's premiership in the run up to the war on Iraq, for Blair was unique 'in viewing the shaping of public opinion as government's overriding purpose. The result was that whereas in the past lies were an intermittent feature of government, under his leadership they became integral to his functioning' (Gray 2008: 147). For Gray, this can be explained by Blair's liberal imperialism which as we have seen, closely mirrors Ferguson's idealization of empire:

> It is not so much that he is economical with the truth as that he lacks a normal understanding of it. For him truth is whatever serves the cause, and when he engages in what is commonly judged to be deception he is only anticipating the new world he is helping to bring about ... Blair's stance on these issues must by ordinary standards be judged to be thoroughly dishonest, but it is clear he believes that ordinary standards do not apply to him. Deception is justified if it advances human progress – and then it is not deception. (Gray 2008: 146)

As we have seen, the brutalities of empire are recognized by Ferguson, but are regarded as inconveniences in his projection of the political project of empire, and so too are the facts for Tony Blair.

Gray's critique of the decision to go to war with Iraq is convincing. However, it is also deeply troubling for those anti-imperialists who are committed to radical social change. This is because Gray's specific critique is part and parcel of a fundamentally conservative ideology that anti-imperialists reject. Gray's argument is that the decision to go to war in Iraq was part of a neo-conservative (and liberal) ideology which believed that there is an inevitable path in history, and that all societies will eventually become liberal democracies and grow through free market policies. This is not only linked to Fukuyama's (1992) account of the end of History, but also to other radical ideological projects that embrace dangerous utopias such as Marxism (Gray 2008: ch.2). Although Gray (1995: 160; 2008: 74–5) is suspicious of Karl Popper's rationalism, there is clearly an overlap with the latter's critique (Popper 1957) of historicist theories such as Marxism, which are said to embrace a theory of historical inevitability, and which lead to oppressive practices against those that stand in the way of the inevitability of history. We thus face the potential paradox that one of the best 'anti-imperialist' arguments against the Iraq war has been made by those like Gray that are highly suspicious of all progressive political projects. This point applies equally to those international relations theorists that have argued against the Iraq war on realist grounds (Mearsheimer 2005).

We can go further than this however, because these paradoxes lie at the heart of a current crisis in politics *per se*, and once again, we return to the reasons why liberal imperialism has made such a strong revival in recent years. The end of the Cold War and triumph of US and liberal hegemony, has led the revival of the case for liberal imperialism and hegemony, not least by those often critical of US imperialism in the past (Hitchens 2003; Cushman 2005). What is central to the arguments made by contemporary liberal imperialists who were formerly on the left is that the end of the Cold War has led to, or at least coincided with, a shift towards a relativism that rejects universal values and any notion of truth. Indeed, one 'left liberal' case for the war in Iraq explicitly links this to his earlier support for the Soviet invasion of Afghanistan (Ree 2006: 184). The context for this shift then is both the end of the Cold War, and the rise of a dangerous cultural relativism. In the case of the end of the former, the argument is sometimes made that in the absence of a competitor superpower, the US can behave in a more enlightened, and liberal way, in contrast with the realist polices of the likes of Henry Kissinger. This liberal argument is fully compatible with neo-conservative views, and in terms of international relations, it means that in contrast to the Cold War, the US can expand liberal democracy, rather than hinder it through the support of undemocratic, authoritarian but ultimately anti-communist regimes. This has meant considerable continuity among neo-conservatives (though they have been and remain inconsistent about supporting liberal democracies), but it does represent a significant change for some former leftists.

One reason for the crisis of the left since the Cold War is indeed that it is much harder to condemn US foreign policy. The standard criticism made by the left during the Cold War was that the US claimed to support freedom and democracy, but in fact supported many undemocratic regimes and indeed was often involved in the overthrow of liberal democracies. Since the end of the Cold War, while this charge can still be made (as the US still counts many authoritarian regimes as its allies), it is more difficult to make. The likes of the Taliban and Saddam Hussein cannot be regarded as allies of the left, even if they may to some degree be considered anti-imperialist. This leads to the second, related point, which is that the post-Cold War fallout has seen the move by sections of the left towards adoption of a dangerous relativism, which feeds into effective support for reactionary anti-imperialists. This argument became prominent in the debate over the Rushdie affair, when some anti-imperialists were reluctant to condemn the Ayatollah Khomeini's so-called *fatwa*. Some former leftists regarded this as an unnecessary concession to identity politics, and it became a meeting point for anti-imperialism and cultural relativism (Cohen 2006; Anthony 2007). This led some former leftists to embrace their former Cold War enemy, the United States, because it was the only state that promoted universal values in the face of such reactionary identity politics. As part of this discourse, the amorphous idea of totalitarianism has been revived and applied in new ways. While Arendt (1973) related the idea of total state control to the practice of nineteenth-century imperialism, Cold War ideologues regarded totalitarianism as a danger to the norms and ideals of freedom in the West. In the post-Cold War world, some liberal imperialists have argued that 'Islam' represents a new totalitarian threat (Harris 2006). In this way, the current liberal imperialist borrows parts of Huntington's (1996) thesis concerning a clash of civilizations. Huntington talks about fairly homogenous civilizations and then tries to find ways for these to co-exist with each other. Liberal imperialists, particularly of the neo-conservative variety, regard this as another instance of a dangerous relativism (see Chapter 8). But they do tend to (implicitly) accept Huntington's views about relatively homogenous cultures, but instead draw the conclusion that western culture must defeat these other, barbaric cultures (Kaplan 2006).

While for some former leftists, the Soviet Union was never seen as a bastion of socialism, it was still regarded as an important beacon of universalist hope, even if it had been usurped within that state by a highly repressive bureaucracy. With the collapse of communism, the US became seen as the only agent that could promote change, and much of this case was made with reference to the revolutionary ideals of Thomas Paine (Hitchens 2007a). That this view was shared by these former leftists' Cold War adversaries among US neo-conservatives was one of the ironies of the new era of politics.

At the same time, many other leftists remained committed to anti-imperialist politics, but this directed them into an opportunist politics that did indeed lead to silences on the practices of various 'anti-imperialist' movements. This could be said to reflect a fetishization of imperialism, in which all the evils in the world are ultimately traceable to an omnipotent and malign US. Critics argue that this approach takes the short step of embracing a relativist outlook based on its silences concerning the practices of various dictatorships and movements, particularly those that embrace radical Islamism (Euston Manifesto 2006). Sometimes this argument is extended so that secular values are embraced against religious ones, though in practice the denunciation of religion is used to attack Islam more than say, the influence of right-wing Christians in the United States (Hitchens 2007b).

The argument of those advocating liberal imperialism then, is that there is a need for a robust defence of universal values, and the Iraq war should be seen in this light. But for Gray, this is precisely the problem, as these supposed universal values lead to dangerous and counter-productive attempts to impose values on other societies. This is bound to end in tears, as Fukuyama (2006) for one, accepts in his belated rejection of the utopian thinking of neo-conservatives. For the liberal imperialists, this is a position that simply embraces the relativism that they oppose. On the other hand, it is unclear how Gray can give his support to any values or practices that exist in the present, as these are the product of radical ideas in the past that conservatives previously had rejected. While Gray (1995: 109) is insistent that conservatism has no relevance in the global age, and that we cannot go back to a mythical golden age, his work still seems to be caught in a conservative dilemma. This is that we need to adapt to current values and use this as the basis to carry out piecemeal change, but his own position would have previously led him to reject such values or practices, on the grounds that they were then associated with radical ideologies, dangerous utopias, and a clear vision of progress. Gray's response would presumably be that it is not his job to advocate social change, but rather to adapt to it, but then it becomes unclear how any social change can take place in the first place – or at least it can only take place through the action of those that reject a conservative world-view, and are indeed likely to be repudiated by thinkers such as John Gray. This is why his political philosophy is ultimately self-defeating. It also does tend towards a relativist, and perhaps even nihilist view, for as Colls (1998: 68–9) asks, '[c]an *rational* incommensurability exist in a world of indigenous cultural traditions where human rights and the democratic project, for some, have no special status? ... Gray decentres the world only to reposition it with a host of new ethnocentrisms.'

The specific issue then, is this: how does one, *contra* Gray, embrace radical social change, without, *contra* Hitchens *et al.*, embracing liberal imperialism? Put in terms of the liberal thought discussed in Chapter 3, how do we, *contra* (to some extent) Bentham, embrace the idea of human self-improvement, without, *contra* John Stuart Mill, apologizing for imperialism? More specifically, how does one reconcile acceptance of Gray's specific case against the Iraq war, with rejection of the wider political implications he makes? And, following on from this point, what is the relationship between anti-imperialist politics on the one hand, and solidarity with the 'rights and needs of distant strangers' on the other?

This brings us back to the question of cosmopolitanism, which argues that the rights of individuals are more important than the sovereignty of nation-states. As we saw in Chapter 8, cosmopolitan thought has enjoyed a revival in the context of the end of the Cold War and debates about how global interconnectedness make such ideals more likely to be realized. The appeal of this approach is that it seems to overcome the dilemma faced by an anti-imperialist position that easily falls into adopting the principle that 'my enemy's enemy is my friend'. This is precisely the problem of double standards condemned by contemporary liberal imperialists, whereby one condemns the actions of imperialist powers – and the United States in particular – while turning a blind eye to the abhorrent practices and reactionary politics of states or movements that happen to be the enemies of the US.

On the other hand, if we simply condemn states in the developing world, we then face the problems that liberal imperialists fail to resolve, namely the tendency to naturalize the liberal individual (and liberal democratic society), to support unaccountable hegemonic power, and to promote economic policies that marginalize rather than incorporate poorer states (and many people within those states). This in turn too easily leads to the view that the US is the only agent capable of liberating people from oppression, a mirror image of the crude anti-imperialist view that also reifies the US, only this time the US is regarded as benign rather than evil as in the case of the crude anti-imperialist view. In the case of many contemporary liberal imperialists, the attention paid to a so-called 'Islamic totalitarian threat' is based on a *naïveté* not only about US benign imperialism, but also the supposed Islamic threat to the international order. In a great deal of anti-Islamist rhetoric, there is an easy slippage from a recognition that there are Islamist political movements, to an assumption that these movements all have similar goals, and indeed that ultimately these movements can be understood solely by reference to the religion of Islam. There is no singular Islamist political movement (Gerges 2005), still less a homogenous Islamic religion (Halliday 2003). Apart from Samuel Huntington, the only people who believe that such singularity exists are the Islamists themselves in their political rhetoric, and contemporary liberal imperialists who betray their ignorance. To attempt to explain the actions of the wide variety of Islamist militants by sole reference to their religion is to ignore the social and political context in which such actions take place. This is *not* a move into the realm of apologetics – as Chapter 8 argued, this charge is an abuse of the concept of evil, one used to close down debate (Bernstein 2005). For example, the practice of suicide bombing was, before 2000, most commonly carried out by secular nationalists and Marxists, and not by Islamists (Pape 2005). It is precisely this kind of fact that is dismissed by liberal imperialists like Hitchens (2001). But as Seymour argues:

To dismiss conclusions based on solid empirical data as 'evil nonsense', and to insist dogmatically on those that are incompatible with that evidence, surely betrays an attitude more befitting a fundamentalist preacher than a secular humanist intellectual. (2008: 14)

Of course today's liberal imperialists sometimes qualify their hostility to Islam. When confronted by Yasmin Alibhai-Brown over his repellent comments that 'there is a definite urge – don't you have it? – to say that the Muslim community will have to suffer until it gets its house in order', Martin Amis referred to her Shia identity, which he described 'as the more dreamy and poetic face of Islam, the more lax and capacious' (cited in Seymour 2008: 14). Like some of the more romantic colonial administrators briefly discussed in Chapter 4, Amis went on that Alibhai-Brown's Shia identity was such that it 'endeared you to me, and made me feel protective' (cited in Seymour 2008: 17). This kind of nonsense is simply the reverse side of the Orientalist coin, combining a mixture of hostility on the one side, patronage on the other, and ignorance on both.

On the other hand, while it is quite proper and correct to reject current stereotypes about Islam, Islamism and the notion of a unified civilizational Islamic or Islamist threat to the West (Halliday 2003), and to situate these in their proper and specific contexts, it is also the case that whatever their differences, Islamist movements do have overwhelmingly reactionary political programmes (Halliday 2006; 2007). And this of course brings us back to the more general dilemma of how one opposes imperialism without embracing all anti-imperialist alternatives.

For cosmopolitanism, this dichotomy presents a problem, as it does not so much resolve the dilemma of supporting or opposing imperialism, but rather evades it. And, as was suggested in Chapter 8, this is because cosmopolitanism – no matter how desirable in the abstract – is too 'thin' a principle for political engagement. One can find cosmopolitan cases for and against war, free trade and US hegemony, which suggests, whatever some may wish (Beck 2006), that embrace of the cosmopolitan principle is no substitute for a wider politics. Moreover, cosmopolitanism lacks a convincing account of political agency, and it is this question which is central to how we may transcend the liberal imperialism versus crude anti-imperialism debate. As we have seen in the case of Gray, the issue could be constructed as one of the universalism of liberal imperialism versus the relativism of anti-imperialism. But this may be something of a red herring, and the difference between pro- and anti-war left liberals is less one about the debate between universalism and relativism, and more one about understanding the nature of power in the current imperialist order (Beetham and Devine 2006) – and the failure of liberal imperialists today to answer the three objections outlined above. But this still leaves the problem as to how one concretely combines an anti-imperialist critique with a rejection of relativism? The answer to this question is similar to the response to Popper's critique of historicism, which is that there is no meaning to history outside of the social and political agents that give it meaning in particular periods of history. In this way, Marxism is less 'a philosophy or transcendental account of the necessary course of history but is concerned with history in the sense that it constructs the concepts necessary to render historical processes intelligible' (Larrain 1986: 98). What this implies is that the movement for social and political change must ultimately be made from within those societies that are undergoing change. Wholesale interventions from outside, such as those associated with military imperialist powers, always carry the dangers of authoritarian social engineering that Gray identifies. Rejection of imperialist agency does not however mean endorsement of relativism or of simply turning a blind eye to the need for change, but rather one of realizing the limits of change from the outside, and finding ways that promote (anti-imperialist and cosmopolitan) solidarity within these limits. The rejection of intervention need not mean rejection of solidarity. Parekh (1995: 96) makes the point well when he suggests that:

> This does not mean that cultures could not, or should not be criticized and changed, but rather that demands for changes must come from within them, and that changes do not take roots unless they are grafted onto the critically teased out resources of the cultures concerned. The task of civilizing other societies is deeply problematic, and rests on dubious assumptions. (Parekh 1995: 96)

Related to this point is the example of E. H. Carr's (2001) writings on the inter-war period (Lawson 2008). He was critical of liberal internationalism which attempted to promote utopian projects of social and political change in the absence of any meaningful account of specific political realities. This sounds not unlike Gray's powerful critique of the neo-conservative project in Iraq. But unlike Gray, this is not the basis for a pessimistic political philosophy that rejects radical change *per se*. Rather, Carr argued that without such a vision of change, politics is reduced to a technocratic project of problem solving. Given that such problem solving would exist in the context of neo-liberal hegemony, Gray's world view reads less like a challenge to the neo-liberalism that he wants to reject, and more like an accommodation to it (Schwarzmantel 2008: ch.9).

However, the pro-liberal imperialism side is itself full of problems. Richard Bernstein (1983: 16–24) identifies what he calls the 'Cartesian anxiety' among such thinkers, in which a rigid dualism is constructed where we can only have either absolute knowledge or total relativism. Current varieties of liberal imperialism, as well as arguments that favour US imperialism as a benevolent force, fit into this category of thinking. For many advocates of the war in Iraq dismissed opponents as being guilty of propagating a spurious relativism, that was hopelessly inadequate at best, and supportive of terrorism or dictatorship at worst (see Cohen 2006). But as we have seen, this argument falsely equates opposition to war with support for dictatorship and/or terrorism, and evades the three reasons why liberal imperialism should itself be rejected (see above).

The approach advocated here then, suggests something between the pro- and anti- imperialist positions discussed above, combined with a healthy dose of realism where cosmopolitanism generally founders. It is not that opposition to war in Iraq meant support for Saddam Hussein, or a cultural relativism which rejects all forms of progress. What it does suggest is that while one can happily embrace the principle that liberal democracy is indeed a more progressive political system than others, even if this is limited by neo-liberal policies, one can also be sceptical about any attempt to social engineer such a system into being through war. As was argued earlier, this is because the intervention itself undermines in part the claims made for liberal democracy's moral superiority, because it is strategically likely to provoke nationalist resistance (and to point this out is not necessarily to apologize for that resistance), because of the nature of political and social forces within particular countries, and because the effects of war are unpredictable (except for the fact that they kill innocent people) and not easy to control.

Put bluntly, to speak of solidarity with distant strangers while simultaneously bombing them, even by 'accident', is perhaps the most violent form of representation. On the other hand, ignoring the plight of these strangers is less a form of solidarity, and more one of disengagement. This takes us into much wider debates about the nature of politics, for contrary to the claims of some radical thinkers (Reid 2005; Tormey 2006), politics (including solidarity) without representation is an impossibility (Parfitt 2002; Kiely 2005a: ch.6; Thomassen 2007). The question then, is what forms of (cosmopolitan) solidarity are possible, feasible, and desirable, or, to return to Carr, what does it mean in the current political context to talk of realistic utopias[2] and progressive anti-imperialism?

This is a very broad question, and a full answer is certainly beyond the concerns of this book. But it should be clear that a commitment to both anti-imperialism and genuine democratic advancement is part of an answer. In particular cases it might mean endorsing a policy of sanctions against particular regimes, provided these are properly targeted and it is clear that these sanctions are supported by democratic forces in the particular nation-states concerned. But it would be naïve to believe that there are easy answers to these questions. For instance, if we return to the question of political economy, but this time focus on *anti*-imperialism rather than imperialism, then we might get a sense of the dilemmas involved. This book has argued that the current neo-liberal order undermines the potential for capitalist development in the developing world, as it precludes, or at least makes more difficult, those policies initially adopted by richer countries when they first developed. But progressive anti-imperialism does not necessarily mean support for a return to ISI policies in opposition to neo-liberal imperialism. ISI policies were often carried out by brutal regimes and had enormous social costs, and progressive politics cannot simply endorse these as part of a supposed process of historical necessity. One has to recognize them, *contra* liberal humanitarianism, in terms of political strategy but this does not entail endorsement. This is true not only for moral reasons, but also because it is historically flawed. As was suggested in Chapter 7, any process of capitalist industrialization today faces the prospect of a failure to absorb labour and secure livelihoods through high rates of employment.

This brings us back once again to the question of agency, as well as progress, in the debate over the politics of anti-imperialism. Solidarity does imply some form of intervention, but we need an approach 'which is more modest in recognizing its limitations, but more ambitious in terms of recognizing what needs to be done' (Foley 2008: 235). The liberal emphasis on human rights is both too ahistorical (hence the need for limitations) and too narrow (hence the need for more ambition). An alternative perspective would be based on a genuine dialogue about different kinds of rights, which links to questions of global inequality and global injustice. It is clear that contemporary imperialism reinforces hierarchy, exploitation and marginalization in the international order. On the other hand, many contemporary anti-imperialist political movements fail to challenge these hierarchies, or insofar as they do, propose reactionary alternatives. The challenge for those proposing a progressive alternative is to forge a genuinely democratic path between these two dead ends.

Notes

3 Liberal Imperialism and Capitalist Expansion

1. Burke's attempted impeachment of the first Governor General of India, Warren Hastings, was based on this belief. However, in contrast to some sympathetic accounts of Burke's view (see for instance Mehta 1999), it remains the case that Burke was guilty of a romantic view of Indian society, not necessarily so different from Hastings. Both saw cultural difference as central to their case, the latter arguing that Indian society was so different that it excused behaviour by the East Indian Company that would have been unthinkable in Europe. What both views shared was the belief that colonialism could be exercised in a way that was compatible with Indian tradition, but they both failed to see how this tradition was a self-invention. This was not so different from some late nineteenth-century views of colonialism (discussed briefly in Chapter 4), which were more suspicious of the liberal transformationalism advocated by the Mills. Moreover, Burke's views on the New World were based on the standard colonial notion of a civilizing mission (see Kohn and O'Neill 2006).

4 Classical Imperialism, 1882–1945

1. Kautsky's 'Ultra-Imperialism' was completed before war broke out, but the theory was further developed once war had started. The English translation (Kautsky 1970) includes some passages that were written after the breakout of war.
2. Even those who argue that there was considerable factor price convergence in the nineteenth century accept that commodity price convergence can only explain a small part of this process. See O' Rourke, Taylor and Williamson (1996). On the Heckscher-Ohlin model, see Ohlin (1933). For critiques, see Shaikh (1979/80) and Kiely (2005a: ch.2).
3. On 'insufficient globalization', see Anthony Giddens (2002), and on 'insufficient American intervention', see Max Boot (2003). The former idea is discussed in Chapter 7, the latter in Chapter 8, and both (in relation to liberalism) in Chapter 10.
4. This interpretation of Britain as a developed capitalist imperialism is contentious, and I return to it further in the chapter.
5. The quote within the quote is from Anderson (1992: 143).

5 The Cold War, Post-War Boom and New Theories of Imperialism

1. This comment does not mean that protectionism was the cause of the Great Depression. Chapter 3 showed that high rates of protection in the developed world pre-date the

268

1930s depression, and in the period from the 1890s to 1913, was associated with high growth rates, including of world trade. A more plausible explanation for the contraction of world trade is the decline in demand across countries, though it may be true that within this context, increasing protectionist pressures, including competitive devaluations, exacerbated the problem. Protectionism did not however, cause the Great Depression.

2. NSC-68, 1950 (declassified in 1977), available at www.fas.org/irp/offdocs/nsc-hst/nsc-68.htm.

3. Among many others, see Morgenthau (1992) and Waltz (2001).

4. Though this of course is not to deny the US' own bloody history. It is however to deny any claims made for European superiority.

5. It should be stressed that this is an argument about the power of different states. The point is not made to excuse the authoritarian nature of such states, and especially the disastrous policies of 'primitive socialist accumulation' that existed in many of these states. For a critique of these policies, see Kiely (1998: ch.4).

6. This account of the Cold War is sometimes associated with the 'revisionist' school, which usefully countered the orthodox notion that the Cold War was simply caused by the US' defensive reaction to Soviet expansionism (Bailey 1950). However, this school tended to simply construct a mirror image of this position, replacing Soviet aggression with passivity, and US reaction with one-sided aggression (Saull 2001).

6 Neo-Liberalism, Globalization and Geo-Politics in the Post-Cold War World

1. But see the reflections on the limits of US military power in Chapters 8 and 9.

2. This should be qualified: first by the surprise that Marxist theories of international relations had not more widely engaged with such accounts earlier than it did (see for instance Novack 1972; Post 1978; Lowy 1981; Dunkerley 1988; Munck 1988; Kiely 1995; 1996); and second, because some of the attempts to use this idea as a transhistorical account of international or inter-societal history (Rosenberg 2006) are very limited in their utility. Indeed, Rosenberg's critique of 'globalization theory' – that it conflates description with explanation – could equally be applied to his transhistorical usage of the concept of uneven and combined development.

3. The US was more ambiguous, because, as we saw in Chapters 4 and 5, it combined ISI policies with an ideology of the individual expansion of frontiers through the empire of liberty, which gave rise to a distinctively US antipathy to the state.

4. This separation of spontaneous and designed orders pervades the work of classical liberalism. Hayek was the main advocate of the notion of a spontaneous market order as against a designed social order. Such a distinction is a fallacy but its basis lies in the fact that Britain was the first successful capitalist power and so set the terms on which later developers more consciously designed capitalist development. For all its insights, political Marxism tends to replicate this distinction (but see Wood 1991), which may be one reason for Teschke and Lacher's (2007) break from understanding capitalism in terms of the 'separation' of economics and politics. However, they do so by tending to embrace contingency wholesale.

5. The same writer has also made the much quoted claim that there 'can be no McDonald's without McDonnell-Douglas' (cited in Rees 2005: 5). However, this quotation does not add up to a new theory of (military) imperialism, and indeed was made to illustrate how

liberal states had to continue policing non-liberal states, rather than referring to rivalries between advanced capitalist states. It is therefore a statement far more compatible with the approach to geo-politics outlined in this and the previous chapter.

6. Callinicos does however tend to reduce the plurality of nation states to the reality of uneven and combined development, as we have seen.

7. This chapter has already hinted at the utility of more constructivist accounts, some of which are compatible with realism (see Williams 2005). This is further discussed in Chapter 10, and see also the next footnote.

8. Related to this point, realism suffers further because what constitutes a 'realist policy' is only ever suggested after the fact, as it is assumed that states will always act, in the context of international anarchy, in their national interest. But this of course begs the question – which more interesting, constructivist accounts of realism incorporate into their analysis (Williams 2005) – of what is the national interest, how this is constructed at a particular point in time, how this changes over time, and how different social forces may influence this construction at a particular point in time. This is discussed further in Chapter 10, but this is a very different take on realism than those suggested by Callinicos. Indeed the utility of a constructivist dialogue with realism is precisely one way of integrating the particular to the general, and agency to structure, as discussed in the first section of this chapter. This is hinted at by Allinson and Anievas (2009), Davidson (2009), and even to some extent Callinicos (2009b: 93–100) himself. See more generally Bieler and Morton (2008).

7   The Political Economy of Neo-Liberal Imperialism

1. The following five paragraphs draw heavily from Kiely (2007: ch.7).
2. The quote within the quote is from Schumpeter (1954).
3. World Bank (1999).

8   Liberalism and 'Humanitarian Imperialism'

1. Indeed, neo-conservatives dismiss Huntington as a right wing 'anti-American', as he is reluctant for the US to intervene in other nations (such as Iraq), and instead find ways of peacefully co-existing with other cultures. For a neo-conservative critique of right-wing anti-Americanism, see L. Kaplan (1998).

2. It is precisely this focus on the behaviour of liberal states in isolation from the activities of non-liberal states, which arouses such furious hostility to Chomsky's work among contemporary liberal imperialists (Collier and Horowitz 2004; Kamm 2005; Cottee and Cushman 2008). Certainly as a fully rounded explanation for particular actions by the US state, Chomsky's work is inadequate and indeed one dimensional. However, it could be argued that this is not its real purpose. Rather, it is an attempt to hold state actors to account *on their own terms*, and thus it works less as a fully rounded argument about US imperialism (or political agents in the developing world, of which he says very little), and more as an exposé of hypocrisy based on the enormous gap between words and actions, and not words and motives (Chomsky 2001; Owens 2007: chs.6–8).

3. Not all agree that Strauss is a particularly strong influence. See for instance Fukuyama (2006: 21–31), and note 4.

4. This of course leads to the question of the Straussian influence on neo-conservativism, and how it may have played a role in the case for the war in Iraq (see Drury 1997; George 2005). Briefly, Strauss' concerns were with ways in which democracies could be preserved in the context of the relativism promoted by liberal individualism. But this did not necessarily mean he would have endorsed straightforward lies by supposedly wise neo-conservatives, and in any case he was suspicious of ambitious foreign policy projects, which would presumably have included the democratization of the Middle East (Fukuyama 2006; Smith 2007: 30).

5. This brief list does not imply endorsement of Walzer's position on just war, which he himself somewhat selectively tried to apply to Iraq. More generally, it tends to separate a state-centric just cause (*jus ad bellum*) from a more individualistic understanding of the rules of conduct (*jus in bello*) for a just war. For a good critique, see Caney (2005: 197–8).

9   The End of US Hegemony? Contemporary Hegemonic Challenge and World Economic Crisis

1. A further, equally problematic argument, concerning the euro, focuses on the invasion of Iraq, which some see as being linked to the regime's switch from dollars to euros in foreign exchange earnings (Clark 2005). This is a particularly weak explanation for the war, for while it may have been possible to enforce a switch back to dollars in Iraq, the costs of the war would in all likelihood undermine the prospects of other countries continuing to hold dollars. Indeed a far easier way to maintain the attractiveness of the dollar would be for the US to cut its budget deficit, while the war in Iraq massively increased it (Kirshner 2008: 428).

2. Callinicos (2009b: 205) refers to the long downturn since 1973, a 'protracted period of slow growth', but earlier (2009b: 60) cites figures from Maddison which show that annual average global rates of growth have been higher in the post-1973 period than any period except for the post-war Golden Age.

3. Financialization should also be contrasted to Hilferding's understanding of finance capital, which essentially suggested that there was a close merger of banks and industrial capital, with the former financing the latter, in what came to be regarded as a German model of capitalist development (see Coates 2000). The financialization outlined in this and in previous chapters suggests something much closer to an Americanization of finance (Panitch and Konings 2008b).

4. This report eventually became the rather tame *World Development Report 2006* (World Bank 2006).

10   Imperialism and Anti-Imperialism Today

1. In this specific case cited here, Davis (2007: 42–60) questions the view that the white working class are simply voting against their economic interests by abandoning the Democrats. He suggests that this abandonment is more to do with the Democrats shift away from New Deal politics to neo-liberalism. This is convincing though it does not necessarily undermine, rather than complicate, Frank's case.

2. The idea of realistic utopias is also present in Rawls (1999), but as Chapter 8 argued, this is unconvincingly used because it abstracts from real relations of power.

References

Abu-Lughold, J. (1989) *Before European Hegemony: The World System AD 1250–1350* (New York: Oxford University Press).

Agamben, G. (2005) *State of Exception* (Chicago: University of Chicago Press).

Akamatsu, K (1962) 'A historical pattern of economic growth in developing countries', *Journal of Developing Economies* 1(1), pp.3–25.

Albo, G. (2003) 'The Old and New Economics of Imperialism', *The Socialist Register 2004* (London: Merlin), pp.88–113.

Albo, G. (2004) 'A World Market of Opportunities? Capitalist Obstacles and Left Economic Policy', in L. Panitch, C. Leys, A. Zuege and M. Konings (eds) *The Globalization Decade* (London: Merlin), pp.111–52.

Albo, G. (2005) 'Contesting the "New Capitalism"', in D. Coates (ed.) *Varieties of Capitalism, Varieties of Approaches* (Basingstoke: Palgrave Macmillan), pp.63–82.

Alden, C. (2007) *China in Africa* (London: Zed).

Allen, C. (1995) 'Understanding African Politics', *Review of African Political Economy*.65, pp.301–20.

Allen, R. (1992) *Enclosure and the Yeoman: The Agricultural Development of the South Midlands, 1450–1850* (Oxford: Clarendon).

Allen, R. (2000) 'Economic Structure and Agricultural Productivity in Europe, 1300–1800', *European Review of Economic History* 3, pp.1–25.

Allinson, J. and A. Anievas (2009) 'The uses and misuses of uneven and combined development: an anatomy of a concept', *Cambridge Review of International Affairs* 22(1), pp.47–67.

Altvater, E. (1973) 'Notes on Some Problems of State Interventionalism', *Kapitaliststate* no.1, pp.97–108.

Amin, S. (1974) *Accumulation on a World Scale* (New York: Monthly Review Press).

Amin, S. (1976) *Unequal Development* (New York: Monthly Review Press).

Ambrosoli, M. (1997) *The Wild and the Sown* (Cambridge: Cambridge University Press).

Amsden, A. (1989) *Asia's Next Giant* (Oxford: Oxford University Press).

Anderson, P. (1992) *English Questions* (London: Verso).

Anderson, P. (2007) 'Jottings on the Conjuncture', *New Left Review* II/48, pp.5–37.

Angell, N. (2007) *The Great Illusion* (London: Cosimo, first published 1910).

Anthony, A. (2007) *The Fallout: How a Guilty Liberal Lost his Innocence* (London: Jonathan Cape).

Aquanno, S. (2008) 'The Dollar Standard in Crisis?', *Relay* no.22, pp.17–18.

Arendt, H. (1973) *The Origins of Totalitarianism* (New York: Harcourt, first published 1951).

Armstrong, P., A. Glyn and J. Harrison (1991) *The World Economy since the War* (Oxford: Blackwell, 2nd edition).

Arneil, B. (1994) 'Trade, plantations and property: John Locke and the economic defense of colonialism', *Journal of the History of Ideas* 55(4), pp. 591–609.

Arrighi, G. (1994) *The Long Twentieth Century* (London: Verso).

Arrighi, G. (2007) *Adam Smith in Beijing* (London: Verso).

Arrighi, G., B. Silver and B. Brewer (2003), 'Industrial convergence, Globalization, and the Persistence of the North–South Divide', *Studies in Comparative International Development* 38(1), pp.3–31.

Ashman, S. (2006) 'Editorial Introduction', *Historical Materialism* 14(4), pp.3–7.

Ashman, S. (2009) 'Capitalism, uneven and combined development and the transhistoric', *Cambridge Review of International Affairs* 22(1), pp.29–46.

Ashman, S. and A. Callinicos (2006) 'Capital Accumulation and the State System: Assessing David Harvey's *The New Imperialism*', *Historical Materialism* 14(4), pp.107–31.

Athukorala, P. (1993) 'Manufactured exports from developing countries and their terms of trade: A re-examination of the Sarkar-Singer thesis', *World Development* 21(10), pp.1607–13.

Athukorala, P. (2003) 'Product Fragmentation and Trade Integration: East Asia in a Global Context' (Australian National University Working Paper 2003/21), pp.1–67.

Athukorala, P. and N. Yamashita (2005) 'Product Fragmentation and Trade Integration: East Asia in a Global Context' (Australian National University paper), pp.1–41.

Axford, B. (2007) 'In at the Death: Reflections on Justin Rosenberg's Postmortem on Globalization', *Globalizations* 4(2), pp.171–91.

Bacevich, A. (2002) *American Empire* (Boston: Harvard University Press).

Bagchi, A. (2009) 'Nineteenth century imperialism and structural transformation in colonized countries', in H. Akram-Lodhi and C. Kay (eds) *Peasants and Globalization* (London: Routledge), pp.83–110.

Bairoch, P. (1993) *Economics and World History* (London: Harvester-Wheatsheaf).

Bairoch, P. and R. Kozul-Wright (1996) *Globalization Myths: Some Historical Reflections on Integration, Industrialization and Growth in the World Economy* (Geneva: UNCTAD Discussion Paper no.113)

Balakrishnan, G. (2006) 'States of War', *New Left Review* II/36, pp.5–32

Balassa, B. (1989) *New Directions in the World Economy* (New York: New York University Press).

Baran, P. (1957) *The Political Economy of Growth* (New York: Monthly Review Press).

Baran, P. and P. Sweezy (1966) *Monopoly Capital* (New York: Monthly Review Press).

Bardeesy, K. (2009) 'Calls grow to supplant dollar as global currency', *Globe and Mail*, July 6.

Barkawi, T. and M. Laffey (1999) 'The Imperial Peace: Democracy, Force and Globalization', *European Journal of International Relations* 5(4), pp.403–34.

Barker, C. (1978) 'A note on the theory of the capitalist state', *Capital and Class* no.4, pp.118–26.

Barnett, T. (2003) 'The Pentagon's New Map', *Esquire*, March.

Barnett, T. (2005) *The Pentagon's New Map* (Berkeley: Berkeley Publishing Group).

Barone, C. (1985) *Marxist Thought on Imperialism* (Armonk, NY: M. E. Sharpe).

Barratt-Brown, M. (1970) *After Imperialism* (London: Merlin).

Barratt-Brown, M. (1974) *The Economics of Imperialism* (Harmondsworth: Penguin).

Barratt-Brown, M. (1988) 'Away with all Great Arches: Anderson's History of British Capitalism', *New Left Review* I/167, pp.22–51.

Barratt-Brown, M. (2000) 'Imperialism Revisited', in R. Chilcote (ed.) *The Political Economy of Imperialism* (Boston: Kluwer), pp.41–63.

Barrow, C. (2008) 'Ralph Miliband and the Instrumentalist Theory of the State: The (Mis)Construction of an Analytic Concept', in P. Wetherly, B. Barrow and P. Burnham (eds) *Class, Power and the State in Capitalist Society* (Basingstoke: Palgrave Macmillan), pp.84–108.

Beck, U. (2006) *Cosmopolitan Vision* (Cambridge: Polity).

Becker, D. and R. Sklar (1987) 'Why Postimperialism?', in D. Becker, J. Freiden, S. Schatz and R. Sklar, *Postimperialism: International Capitalism and Development in the Late Twentieth Century* (Boulder: Lynne Rienner), pp.1–18

Becker, D., J. Frieden, S. Schatz and R. Sklar (1987) *Postimperialism* (Boulder: Lynne Rienner).

Beetham, D. and P. Devine (2006) 'Left on the Platform', *Red Pepper* 142.

Bell, D. (1988) *The End of Ideology* (Boston: Harvard University Press, 1st edition 1960).

Bell, D. (2006) 'Empire and International Relations in Victorian Political Thought: Historiographical Essay', *Historical Journal* 49(1), pp.281–98.

Bell, S. and H. Feng (2007) 'Made in China: IT infrastructure policy and the politics of trade opening in post-WTO China', *Review of International Political Economy* 14(1), pp.49–76.

Bellamy Foster, J. (2003) 'The New Age of Imperialism', *Monthly Review* 55(3), pp.1–14.

Bellamy Foster, J. and F. Magdoff (2009) *The Great Financial Crisis* (New York: Monthly Review Press).

Ben-David, D. and B. Loewy (1998), 'Free trade, growth and convergence', *Journal of Economic Growth* 3(1), pp.143–70.

Bentham, J. (n.d.) *Emancipate Your Colonies!*

Berger, M. and D. Borer (2007) 'The Long War: insurgency, counter-insurgency and collapsing states', *Third World Quarterly* 28(2), pp.197–215.

Berman, P. (2005) *Power and the Idealists* (New York: Soft Skull Press).

Bernstein, H. (1979) 'Sociology of development versus sociology of underdevelopment', in D. Lehmann (ed.) *Development Theory: Four Critical Essays* (London: Frank Cass), pp.77–106.

Bernstein, H. (1982) 'Industrialization, development and dependence', in H. Alavi and T. Shanin (eds) *An Introduction to the Sociology of Developing Societies* (London: Macmillan), pp.218–35.

Bernstein, H. (2004) '"Changing before Our Very Eyes": Agrarian Questions and the Politics of Land in Capitalism Today', *Journal of Agrarian Change* 4(1/2), pp.190–225.

Bernstein, R. (1983) *Beyond Objectivism and Relativism* (Philadephia: University of Pennsylvania Press).

Bernstein, R. (2005) *The Abuse of Evil* (Cambridge: Polity).

Bettelheim, C. (1972) 'Appendix I: theoretical comments', in A. Emmanuel (1972) *Unequal Exchange* (London: New Left Books), pp.271–322.

Bhagwati, J. (2004) *In Defence of Globalization* (Oxford: Oxford University Press).

Bhagwati, J. and T. Srinivasan (1999), 'Outward Orientation and Development: Are revisionists right?', Yale University Economic Growth Center Discussion Paper no.806, pp.1–40.

Bieler, A. and A. Morton (2008) 'The Deficits of Discourse in IPE: turning base metal into gold?', *International Studies Quarterly* 52(1), pp.103–28.

Bilgin, P. and A. D. Morton (2004) 'From "Rogue" to "Failed" States? The Fallacy of "Short-Termism"', *Politics* 24(3), pp.169–80.

Bin Wong, R. (1997) *China Transformed* (Ithaca: Cornell University Press).

Binns, P. (1975) 'The Theory of State Capitalism', *International Socialism* I/74, pp.20–5.

Birdsall, N. and A. Hamoudi (2002) 'Commodity dependence, trade and growth: when "openness" is not enough', Centre for Global Development Working Paper, no.7 (available at www.cgdev.org/rp/publications.html).

Bisley, N. (2007) *Rethinking Globalization* (Basingstoke: Palgrave Macmillan).

Blackburn, R. (1997) *The Making of New World Slavery* (London: Verso).

Blackburn, R. (2005) 'Imperial Margarine', *New Left Review* II/35, pp.124–36.

Blair, T. (1999) 'Doctrine of the international community', available at www.number10. gov.uk/Page1297

Blaut, J. (1993) *The Colonizers Model of the World* (New York: Guilford).

Blaut, J. (2000) *Eight Eurocentric Historians* (New York: Guilford).

Block, F. (1977) 'The Ruling Class does not Rule', *Socialist Revolution* vol.7, no.33, pp.6–28.

Block, F. (1987) *Revisiting State Theory* (Philadelphia: Temple University Press).

Blum, W. (2002) *Rogue State* (London: Zed).

Boot, M. (2003) 'The Case for American Empire', *Weekly Standard*, October 15.

Bowring, B. (2008) *The Degradation of the International Legal Order?* (London: Routledge).

Bramall, C. (2000) *Sources of Chinese Economic Growth, 1978–1996* (Oxford: Oxford University Press).

Brannigan, T. (2008) 'Chill wind blows through China's manufacturing heartland', *The Guardian*, October 31.

Brannigan, T. (2009a) 'China's exports fall for third month', www.guardian.co.uk (accessed 19 February 2009).

Brannigan, T. (2009b) 'China is worried about its US assets says premier', *The Gaurdian*, March 13.

Braudel, F. and F. Spooner (1967) 'Prices in Europe from 1450 to 1750', in E. Rich and C. Wilson (eds) *The Cambridge Economic History of Europe IV* (Cambridge: Cambridge University Press), 378–486.

Brett, E. (1985) *The World Economy since the War* (London: Macmillan).

Brendon, P. (2007) *The Decline and Fall of the British Empire* (London: Jonathan Cape).

Brenner, N. (1999) 'Beyond state-centrism? Space, territoriality and geographical scale in globalization studies', *Theory and Society* 28(2), pp.39–78.

Brenner, R. (1977) 'The Origins of Capitalist Development: A Critique of Neo-Smithian Marxism', *New Left Review* no.104, pp.25–92.

Brenner, R. (1998) 'The Economics of Global Turbulence', *New Left Review* I/229, pp.1–265.

Brenner, R. (2002) *The Boom and the Bubble* (London: Verso).

Brenner, R. (2006) 'What Is, and What Is Not, Imperialism?', *Historical Materialism* 14(4), pp.79–105.

Brenner, R., and C. Isett (2002) 'England's Divergence from China's Yangzi Delta: Property Relations, Microeconomics and Patterns of Development', *Journal of Asian Studies* 61(2), pp.609–2.

Breslin, S. (2007) *China in the Global Political Economy* (Basingstoke: Palgrave Macmillan).

Brett, E. (1983) *International Money and Capitalist Crisis* (London: Macmillan).

Brewer, A. (1990) *Marxist Theories of Imperialism* (London: Routledge, 2nd edition).

Bromley, S. (1994) *Rethinking Middle East Politics* (Cambridge: Polity).

Bromley, S. (2005) 'Oil and United States Hegemony', *Government and Opposition* 40(2), p.225–55.

Bromley, S. (2006) 'Blood for Oil', *New Political Economy* 11(3), pp.419–34.

Bromley, S. (2008) *American Power and the Prospects for International Order* (Cambridge: Polity).

Brooks, D. (2004) *On Paradise Drive* (New York: Simon & Schuster).

Brookes, P. and J. Shin (2006) *China's Influence in Africa: Implications for the United States* (Washington: The Heritage Foundation).

Brown, C. (2003) 'Selective Humanitarianism: In Defence of Inconsistency' in D. Chatterjee and D. Scheid (eds) *Ethics and Foreign Intervention* (Cambridge University Press, Cambridge), pp. 31–50.

Brummer, A. (2008) 'The Fund is Back in Town', *New Statesman*, October 27.

Brunt, L. (1999) *Estimating English Wheat Production in the Industrial Revolution* (Oxford: Oxford University Discussion Papers in Social and Economic History), pp.1–22.

Bukharin, N. (2003) *Imperialism and World Economy* (London: Bookmarks, first published 1914).

Burbach, R. and B. Robinson (1999) 'The Fin de Siecle Debate: Globalization as Epochal Shift', *Science and Society* 63(1), pp.10–39.

Burnham, P. (1990) *The Political Economy of Post-War Reconstruction* (Basingstoke: Macmillan).

Bush, G. (2001) 'Speech by George Bush, 7 December 2001', available at www.whitehouse.gov (accessed 24 November 2005).

Bush, G. (2002) 'Remarks by the President at the 2002 Graduation Exercise of the US Military Academy, West Point, New York', available at www.whitehouse.gov/news/releases/2002/06/20020601-3.html

Cafruny, A. and M. Ryner (2007) *Europe at Bay: In the Shadow of US Hegemony* (Boulder: Lynne Rienner).

Cain, P. and A. Hopkins (1987) 'Gentlemanly Capitalism and British expansion overseas II: new imperialism, 1850–1945', *Economic History Review* (second series), XL(II), pp.1–26.

Cain, P. and A. Hopkins (1993) *British Imperialism* (London: Longman, 2 volumes).

Callinicos, A. (1994) 'Marxism and Imperialism Today', in Callinicos, A., C. Harman. M. Gonzalez and J. Rees *Marxism and the New Imperialism* (London: Bookmarks), pp.11–66.

Callinicos, A. (2002a) 'Marxism and Global Governance', in D. Held and A. McGrew (eds) *Governing Globalization* (Cambridge: Polity), pp.249–66.

Callinicos, A. (2002b), 'The grand strategy of the American empire', *International Socialism* 97, pp.3–38.

Callinicos, A. (2003) *The New Mandarins of American Power* (Cambridge: Polity).

Callinicos, A. (2005) 'Imperialism and global political economy', *International Socialism* no.108, pp.109–27.

Callinicos, A. (2006) 'Making sense of imperialism: a reply to Leo Panitch and Sam Gindin', *International Socialism* no.110, pp.196–203.

Callinicos, A. (2007a) 'Does Capitalism need the State System?', *Cambridge Review of International Affairs* 20(4), pp.533–49.

Callinicos, A. (2007b) 'Globalization, Imperialism and the Capitalist World system', in D. Held and T. McGrew eds., *Globalization Theory* (Cambridge: Polity), pp.62–78.

Callinicos, A. (2009a) 'How to solve the many state problem: a reply to the debate', *Cambridge Review of International Affairs* 22(1), pp.89–105.

Callinicos, A. (2009b) *Imperialism and Global Political Economy* (Cambridge: Polity).

Callinicos, A. and S. Ashman (2006) 'Capital Accumulation and the State System: Assessing David Harvey's *The New Imperialism*', *Historical Materialism* 14(1), pp.107–31.

Cammack, P. (2004) 'What the World Bank means by poverty reduction, and why it matters', *New Political Economy* 9(2), pp.189–211

Caney, S. (2005) *Justice Beyond Borders* (Oxford: Oxford University Press).

Cannadine, D. (1995) 'The Empire Strikes Back', *Past and Present* no.147, pp.180–94.

Cardoso, F. H. (1972) 'Dependency and Development in Latin America', *New Left Review* I/74, pp.83–95.

Carmody, P. and F. Owusu (2007) 'Competing Hegemons: Chinese vs. American Geo-Economic Strategies in Africa', *Political Geography* 26(5), pp.504–24.

Carr, E. H. (2001) *The Twenty Years Crisis, 1919–39* (Basingstoke: Palgrave, first published 1939).

Cesaire, A. (1955) *Discourse on Colonialism* (New York: Monthly Review Press).

Chang, H. J. (2002) *Kicking Away the Ladder* (London: Anthem).

Chang, H. J. (2003) *Globalisation and the Economic Role of the State* (London: Zed).

Chang, H. J. (2006) 'Trade and Industrial Policy During the Age of Imperialism', in Jomo, K. S. (ed.) *The Long Twentieth Century: Globalization under Hegemony* (Delhi: Oxford University Press), pp.278–99.

Chang, H.J. (2007) *Bad Samaritans* (London: Random).

Chesterman, S., M. Ignatieff and R. Thakur (eds) (2005) *Making States Work: State Failure and the Crisis of Governance* (New York: United Nations University Press).

Chibber, V. (2003) *Locked in Place* (Princeton: Princeton University Press).

Chibber, V. (2004a) 'The Return of Imperialism to the Social Sciences', *European Journal of Sociology* 45(3), pp.427–41.

Chibber, V. (2004b) 'Reviving the Developmental State?: The Myth of the "National Bourgeoisie"', in L. Panitch and C. Leys (eds) *The Socialist Register 2005* (London: Merlin), pp.144–65

Chomsky, N. (1968) *American Power and the New Mandarins* (New York: Random House).

Chomsky, N. (1994) *World Orders, Old and New* (London: Pluto).

Chomsky, N. (1999) *The New Military Humanism* (London: Pluto).

Chomsky, N. (2001) *A New Generation Draws the Line* (London: Verso).

Chomsky, N. (2007) *Interventions* (London: Hamish Hamilton).

Clark, D. (2008) 'European Foreign Policy and American Primacy', *International Politics* 45(3), pp.276–91.

Clark, G. (1991) 'Farm wages and living standards in the Industrial Revolution: England, 1670–1869', *Economic History Review* 54(3), pp.477–505.

Clark, G. (2001) 'Yields per acre in English agriculture', *Economic History Review* 44(3), pp.445–60.

Clark, W. (2005) *Petrodollar Warfare: Oil, Iraq and the Future of the Dollar* (Gabriola Island: New Society).

Clarke, S. (ed.) (1991) *The State Debate* (London: Macmillan).

Clarke, S. (1999) 'Capitalist competition and the tendency to overproduction', *Historical Materialism* 4(1), pp. 57–71.

Cliff, T. (1974) *State Capitalism in Russia* (London: Pluto).

Coates, D. (2000) *Models of Capitalism* (Cambridge: Polity).

Cobden, R. (1903) *Speeches on Free Trade* (London: Macmillan, speeches from 1840s).

Cohen, B. (1973) *The Question of Imperialism* (London: Macmillan).

Cohen, B. (2003) 'Global Currency Rivalry: Can the Euro Ever Challenge the Dollar?', *Journal of Common Market Studies* 41(4), pp.575–95.

Cohen, N. (2006) *What's Left? How Liberals Lost Their Way* (London: Fourth Estate).

Colas, A. (2007) *Empire* (Cambridge: Polity).

Collier, P. and D. Horowitz (eds) (2004) *The Anti-Chomsky Reader* (San Francisco: Encounter Books).

Colls, R. (1998) 'Ethics Man: John Gray's New Moral World', *Political Quarterly* 69(1), pp.59–71.

Connolly, K. (2009) 'Germany economy hits the brakes', *The Guardian*, May 15.

Cooper, R. (2002) 'Why we still need empires', *The Observer* April 7.

Cooper, R. (2003) *The Breaking of Nations* (London: Atlantic).

Corrigan, P. and D. Sayer (1985) *The Great Arch* (Oxford: Blackwell).

Cottee, K. and T. Cushman (eds) (2008) *Christopher Hitchens and his Critics* (New York: New York University Press).

Cowen, M. and R. Shenton (1996) *Doctrines of Development* (London: Routledge).

Cox, M. (1984) 'Western Capitalism and the Cold War System', in M. Shaw (ed.) *War, State and Society* (London: Macmillan), pp.136–94.

Cox, M. (2003) 'The empire's back in town; or America's imperial temptation again', *Millennium* 32(1), pp.1–27.

Cox, M. (2006) 'The imperial republic revisited: the United States in the Bush era', in A. Colas and R. Saull (eds) *The War on Terrorism and the American 'Empire' after the Cold War* (London: Routledge), pp.114–30.

Cox, M. (2007) 'Still the American Empire', *Political Studies Review* 5(10), pp.1–10.

Cox, R. (1981) 'Social Forces, States and World Orders: Beyond International Relations Theory', *Millennium* 10(2), pp.126–55.

Cox, R. (1987) *Production, Power and World Order* (New York: Columbia University Press).

Cox, R. (1996) 'Gramsci, Hegemony and IR: An Essay in Method', in R. Cox and T. Sinclair (eds) *Approaches to World Order* (Cambridge: Cambridge University Press), pp.124–43.

Crabtree, A. and A. Sumner (2008) 'Chinese Outward FDI in Africa: How Much do We Know?', in E. Rugraff, D. Sanchez-Anchodea and A. Sumner (eds) (2008) *TNCs and Development Policy* (Basingstoke: Palgrave Macmillan), pp.137–54.

Crafts, N. (1989) 'The Industrial Revolution: Economic Growth in Britain, 1700–1860', in A. Digby and C. Feinstein eds. (1989) *New Directions in Economic and Social History* (Chicago: Lyceum), pp.64–75.

Cramer, C. (2006) *Civil War is Not a Stupid Thing!* (London: Hurst).

Croft, S. (2006) *Culture, Crisis and America's War on Terror* (Cambridge: Cambridge University Press).

Cumings, B. (1999) 'Still the American Century', *Review of International Studies* 25(5), pp.271–99.

Cushman, T. (2005) 'Introduction: the Liberal Humanitarian Case for War in Iraq', in T.Cushman, (ed.) *A Matter of Principle* (Berkeley: University of California Press).

Dalby, S. (2009) 'Geopolitics, the revolution in military affairs and the Bush doctrine', *International Politics* 46(2/3), pp.234–52

Dannreuther, R. (2007) *International Security* (Cambridge: Polity).

Darwin, J. (2002) 'Globalism and Imperialism: the Global Context of British Power, 1830–1960', in S. Akita (ed.) *Gentlemanly Capitalism, Imperialism and global History* (Basingstoke: Palgrave Macmillan), pp.43–64.

Daunton, M. (1989) 'Gentlemanly Capitalism and British Industry, 1820–1914', *Past and Present* 122(1), pp.119–58.

Davidson, N. (2009) 'Putting the nation back into international', *Cambridge Review of International Affairs,*. 22(1), pp. 9–28.

Davies, G. (1994) *A History of Money* (Cardiff: University of Wales Press).

Davis, M. (2001) *Late Victorian Holocausts* (London: Verso).

Davis, M. (2004) 'Planet of Slums', *New Left Review* II/26, pp.5–34.

Davis, M. (2007) *In Praise of Barbarians* (Chicago: Haymarket).

Desai, M. (2000) 'Seattle: A Tragi-Comedy', in B. Gunnell and D. Timms (eds) *After Seattle* (London: Catalyst), pp.41–45.

Desai, M. (2002) *Marx's Revenge* (London: Verso).

Deudney, D. and J. Ikenberry (1999) 'The nature and sources of liberal international order', *Review of International Studies* 25(2), pp.179–96.

Dicken, P. (2007) *Global Shift* (London: Sage, 5th edition).

Dodge, T. (2005) 'Iraqi Transitions: from regime change to state collapse', *Third World Quarterly* 26(4/5), pp.705–21

Dodge, T. (2006) 'The Sardinian, the Texan and the Tikriti: Gramsci, the Comparative Autonomy of the Middle East State and Regional Change', *International Politics* 43(4), pp.453–73.

Dore, E. and J. Weeks (1979) 'International Exchange and the Causes of Backwardness', *Latin American Perspectives* 6(2), pp.62–78.

Dorfman, A. and A. Matellart (1971) *How to Read Donald Duck* (New York: International General).

Dos Santos, T. (1970) 'The structure of dependence', *American Economic Review* vol.60, May, pp.231–36.

Douzinas, C. (2007) *Human Rights and Empire* (London: Routledge).

Doyle, M. (1984) 'Kant, liberal legacies and foreign affairs: Part One', *Philosophy and Public Affairs* 12(3), pp.205–35.

Doyle, M. (1986) *Empires* (Ithaca: Cornell University Press).

Doyle, M. (1999) 'A liberal view: preserving and expanding the liberal pacific union', in T. Paul and J. Hall (eds) *International Order and the Future of World Politics* (Cambridge: Cambridge University Press), pp.41–66.

Drolet, J. F. (2007) 'The Visible Hand of Neo-Conservative Capitalism', *Millennium* 35(2), pp.245–78.

Duchesne, R. (2001/2) 'Between Sinocentrism and Eurocentrism: Debating Andre Gunder Frank's *Re-Orient: Global Economy in the Asian Age*', *Science and Society* 65(4), pp.428–63.

Duchesne, R. (2004) 'On The Rise of the West: Research Kenneth Pomeranz's Great Divergence', *Review of Radical Political Economics* 36(1), pp.52–81.

Duchesne, R. (2006) 'Asia First?', *Journal of the Historical Society* VI(1), pp.69–91.

Dumenil, G. and D. Levy (2004) *Capital Resurgent* (Boston: Harvard University Press).

Dunkerley, J. (1988) *Power in the Isthmus* (London: Verso).

Eichengreen, B. Y. Rhee and H. Tong (2004) 'The Impact of China on the Exports of Other Asian Countries' (Washington: NBER Working Paper no.10768).

Elhefnawy, N. (2008) 'The Impending Oil Shock', *Survival* 50(2), pp.37–66.

Elvin, M. (1973) *The Pattern of the Chinese Past*, Stanford: Stanford University Press.

Emmanuel, A. (1972a) 'White Settler Colonialism and the Myth of Investment Imperialism', *New Left Review* no.73, pp.35–57.

Emmanuel, A. (1972b) *Unequal Exchange* (London: New Left Books).

Engels, F. (1978) *Anti-During* (Moscow: Progress, first published 1878).

Engerman, S. (1994) 'Mercantilism and Overseas Trade, 1700–1800', in R. Floud and D. McCloskey (eds) *The Economic History of Britain since 1700: Vol. 1: 1700–1860* (Cambridge: Cambridge University Press, 2nd edition), pp.182–204.

Etherington, N. (1984) *Theories of Imperialism: War, Conquest and Capital* (London: Croom Helm).

Euston Manifesto (2006), available at http://eustonmanifesto.org/the-euston-manifesto (accessed on 3 April 2009).

Evans, P. (1995) *Embedded Autonomy* (Princeton: Princeton University Press).

Evans, P. and M. Staveteig (2006) '21st Century Industrialization and Development in the Global South: The Chinese Case in Historical-Comparative Perspective', unpublished paper.

Evans, T. (2001) 'If Democracy, Then Human Rights?', *Third World Quarterly* 22(4), pp.623–42.

Fanon, F. (1967) *Black Skins, White Masks* (New York: Grove).

Feenstra, R. (1998) 'Integration of Trade and Disintegration of Production in the Global Economy', *Journal of Economic Perspectives* 12(4), p.31–50.

Feinstein, C. (1998) 'Pessimism Perpetuated: Real Wages and the Standard of Living in Britain during and after the Industrial Revolution', *Journal of Economic History* 58(3), pp.625–58

Fenby, J. (2009) 'China's cast offs', www.guardian.co.uk (accessed on 9 February 2009).

Ferguson, N. (2003) *Empire* (London: Penguin).

Ferguson, N. (2004) *Colossus* (London: Allen Lane).

Ferguson, N. and R. Kagan (2003), 'The United States Is and Should Be, an Empire: A New Atlantic Initiative Debate', Washington: American Enterprise Institute for Public Policy Research, available at www.aei.org/events.

Fieldhouse, D. (1961–2) 'Imperialism: an historiographical revision', *Economic History Review* 14(2), pp.187–209.

Fieldhouse, D. (1973) *The Economics of Empire* (London: Weidenfeld & Nicolson).

Fieldhouse, D. (ed.) (1967) *The Theory of Capitalist Imperialism* (London: Longman).

Fine, B. (2001) *Social Capital versus Social Theory* (London: Routledge)

Fine, B., D. Milonakis, C. Lapavitsas (1999) 'Analysing the World Economy: Two Steps Back', *Capital and Class* no.67, pp.21–47.

Fine, B. C. Lapavitsas and J. Pincus (eds) *Development Policy in the Twenty First Century* (London: Routledge).

Foley, C. (2008) *The Thin Blue Line* (London: Verso).

Foner, E. (1999) *The Story of American Freedom* (New York: Norton).

Foot, R. (2006) 'Chinese strategies in a US-hegemonic global order: accommodating and hedging', *International Affairs* 82(1), pp.77–94

Frank, A. G. (1969a) *Capitalism and Underdevelopment in Latin America* (New York: Monthly Review Press).

Frank, A. G. (1969b) *Latin America: Underdevelopment or Revolution?* (New York: Monthly Review Press).

Frank, A. G. (1978) *World Accumulation, 1492–1978* (New York: Monthly Review Press).

Frank, A. G. (1998) *Re-Orient* (Berkeley: University of California Press).

Frank, A. G. and B. Gills (eds) (1993) *The World System: Five Hundred Years or Five Thousand?* (London: Routledge).

Frank, T. (2004) *What's the Matter with America?* (London: Vintage).

Friedman, M. (2002) *Capitalism and Freedom* (Chicago: University of Chicago Press, first published 1962).

Friedman, T. (2005a) 'Global is good', *The Guardian*, April 21.

Friedman, T. (2005b) *The World is Flat* (New York: Allen Lane).

Frobel, F., J. Heinrichs and O. Kreye (1980) *The New International Division of Labour* (Cambridge: Cambridge University Press).

Fukuyama, F. (2006) *After the Neocons* (London: Profile).

Gallagher, J. and R. Robinson (1953) 'The Imperialism of Free Trade', *Economic History Review* VI(I), pp.1–15

Gallagher, K. (ed.) (2005) *Putting Development First* (London: Zed).

Gamble, A. (1994) *Britain in Decline* (London: Macmillan, 3rd edition).

Gamble, A. (2009) *The Spectre at the Feast* (Basingstoke: Palgrave Macmillan).

Gardner, L. (1984) *A Covenant with Power: America and the World from Wilson to Reagan* (London: Macmillan).

Gardner, L. and M. Young (eds) (2005) *The New American Empire* (New York: New Press).

Gardner, R. (1956) *Sterling Dollar Diplomacy: Anglo-American collaboration and the Reconstruction of Multilateral Trade* (Oxford: Clarendon).

George, A., R. Whitaker and A. McSmith (2004) 'Revealed: The Meeting that could have changed the history of Iraq', *Independent on Sunday*, October 17.

George, J. (2005) 'Leo Strauss, Neo-conservatism and US Foreign Policy: Esoteric Nihilism and the Bush Doctrine', *International Politics* 42(2), pp.174–202.

George, S. (2008) *Hijacking America* (Cambridge: Polity).

Gerges, F. (2005) *The Far Enemy* (Cambridge: Cambridge University Press).

Gerschenkron, A. (1962) *Economic Backwardness in Historical Perspective* (Boston: Harvard University Press).

Geuss, R. (2008) *Philosophy and Real Politics* (Princeton: Princeton University Press).

Giddens, A. (1999) *Runaway World* (Cambridge: Polity).

Giddens, A. (2000) *The Third Way and its Critics* (Cambridge: Polity).

Giddens, A. (2002) *Which Way for New Labour?* (Cambridge: Polity).

Gill, S. (2001) 'Constitutionalising Capital: EMU and Disciplinary Neoliberalism', in A. Bieler and A. Morton (eds) *Social Forces in the Making of the New Europe* (Basingstoke: Palgrave Macmillan), pp.47–69.

Gill, S. (2002) *Power and Resistance in the New World Order* (Basingstoke: Palgrave Macmillan).

Gill, S. (2004) 'The Contradictions of US Supremacy' in L. Panitch and C. Leys (eds), *The Socialist Register 2005* (London: Merlin), pp.23–45.

Gill, S. and D. Law (1988) *The Global Political Economy* (London: Pearson).

Gilpin, R (1983) *War and Change in World Politics* (Cambridge: Cambridge University Press).

Gilroy, P. (2000) *Between Camps* (London: Allen Lane).

Gindin, S. (2000) 'Turning points and starting points', in L.Panitch and C. Leys (eds), *The Socialist Register 2001* (London: Merlin Press), pp. 343–66.

Gindin, S. (2008) 'Decline of the Dollar, Decline of Empire?', *Relay* no.22, pp.26–8.

Glyn, A. (2006) *Capitalism Unleashed* (Oxford: Oxford University Press).

Glyn, A., A. Hughes, A. Lipietz and A. Singh (1990) 'The Rise and Fall of the Golden Age', in S. Marglin and J. Schor (eds) *The Golden Age of Capitalism* (Oxford: Clarendon), pp.39–125.

Gold, D., C. Lo and E. Olin Wright (1975) 'Recent Developments in Marxist Theories of the Capitalist State: Part I', *Monthly Review* 27(5), pp.29–43.

Gong, G. (2004) 'The international strategy of China's new leaders', in Y.-H. Chu, C.-C. Lo and R. Myers (eds) *The New Chinese Leadership: Challenges and Opportunities after the 16th Party Congress* (Cambridge: Cambridge University Press), pp.156–79.

Goodman, J. and K. Honeyman (1988) *Gainful Pursuits: The Making of Industrial Europe, 1500–1800* (London: Hodder & Stoughton).

Gow, D. (2009) 'New year nightmare brings spectre of 1930s style depression to eurozone', *The Guardian*, January 1.

Gowan, P. (1999) *The Global Gamble* (London: Verso).

Gowan, P. (2002) 'The American Campaign for Global Sovereignty', in C. Leys and L. Panitch (eds) *The Socialist Register 2003* (London: Merlin), pp.1–27.

Gowan, P. (2005) 'American Grand Strategy', *Critical Asian Studies* 37(1), pp.128–39.

Grahl, J. (2004) 'The European Union and American Power', in L. Panitch and C. Leys (eds) (2004) *The Socialist Register 2005* (London: Merlin), pp.280–96.

Gray, J. (1995) *Enlightenment's Wake* (London: Routledge).

Gray, J. (2008) *Black Mass* (Harmondsworth: Penguin).

Greenfield, G. (2004) 'Bandung *redux:* anti-globalization nationalisms in South-East Asia', in L.Panitch and C. Leys (eds), *The Socialist Register 2005* (London: Merlin), pp. 166–96.

Gregory, D. (2004) *The Colonial Present* (Oxford: Blackwell).

Grieco, J. (1993) 'The Relative Gains Problem for International Cooperation', *American Political Science Review* 87(3), pp.729–35.

Greenfield, (2004) 'Bandung Redux: Imperialism and anti-globalisation nationalism in South East Asia', in L. Panitch and C. Leys (eds) *The Socialist Register 2005* (London: Merlin), pp.166–96.

Grossman, G. and E. Helpman (1991) *Innovation and Growth in the Global Economy* (Cambridge: MIT Press).

Gulalp, H. (1986) 'Debate of capitalism and development: the theories of Samir Amin and Bill Warren', *Capital and Class* 28, pp.39–59.

Habermas, J. (1985) *The New Conservatism* (Cambridge: MIT Press).

Habermas, J. (1998) *The Inclusion of the Other* (Cambridge: Polity).

Habermas, J. (2006) *The Divided West* (Cambridge: Polity).

Hall, J. (2007) 'Review of *The Eastern Origins of Western Civilisation*', *English Historical Review*, 63(495), pp. 149–51.

Halliday, F. (1983) *The Making of the Second Cold War* (London: Verso).

Halliday, F. (1989) *Cold War, Third World* (London: Hutchinson Radius).

Halliday, F. (2002) 'The pertinence of imperialism', in M. Rupert and H. Smith (eds) *Historical Materialism and Globalization* (London: Routledge), pp.75–89.

Halliday, F. (2003) *Islam and the Myth of Confrontation* (London: I. B. Tauris, 2nd edition)

Halliday, F. (2006) 'The left and the jihad', www.opendemocracy.net (accessed on 8 September 2006).

Halliday, F. (2007) 'The left and the jihad: a "liberal" riposte', www.opendemocracy.net (accessed on 12 January 2007).

Halliday, F. (2008) 'The miscalculation of small nations', www.opendemocracy.net (accessed on 26 August 2008).

Halper, S. and J. Clarke (2004) *America Alone: The Neoconservatives and the Global Order* (Cambridge: Cambridge University Press).

Halperin, S. (1997) *In the Mirror of the Third World* (Ithaca: Cornell University Press).

Halperin, S. (2004) *War and Social Change in Modern Europe: The Great Transformation Revisited* (Cambridge: Cambridge University Press).

Halperin, S. (2007) 'Re-envisioning Global Development: Conceptual and Methodological Issues', *Globalizations* 4(4), pp.543–58.

Hamilton, A. (2007) *Report on the Subject of Manufactures* (New York: Cosimo, first published 1791).

Hardt, M. and T. Negri (2000) *Empire* (Cambridge: Harvard University Press).

Hardt, M. and T. Negri (2004) *Multitude* (New York: Penguin).

Harman, C. (1991) 'The state and capitalism today', *International Socialism* 51 (second series), pp.3–57.

Harman, C. (2003) 'Analysing Imperialism', *International Socialism* 99 (second series), pp.3–81.

Harris, J. (2005) 'The Military Industrial Complex and Transnational Class Theory', in R. Appelbaum and W. Robinson (eds) *Critical Globalization Studies* (London: Routledge), pp.141–52.

Harris, S. (2006) *The End of Faith: Religion, Terror and the Future of Reason* (New York: Free Press).

Harrison, G. (2004) *The World Bank and Africa* (London: Routledge).

Hart-Landsberg, M. (1979) 'Export-led industrialization in the third world: manufacturing imperialism', *Review of Radical Political Economics* 11(4), pp.63–84.

Hart-Landsberg, M. (1984) 'Capitalism and third world economic development: a critical look at the South Korean miracle', *Review of Radical Political Economics* 16(4), pp.112–25.

Hart-Landsberg, M. and P. Burkett (2005) *China and Socialism: Market Reforms and Class Struggle* (New York: Monthly Review Press).

Harvey, D. (2003a) *The New Imperialism* (Oxford: Oxford University Press).

Harvey, D. (2003b) 'The New Imperialism: Accumulation by Dispossession', in L. Panitch and C. Leys (eds) (2003) *The Socialist Register 2004* (London: Merlin), pp.63–87.

Harvey, D. (2007) 'In What Ways is "The New Imperialism" Really New?', *Historical Materialism* 15(3), pp.57–70.

Haseler, S. (2004) *Super-State: The New Europe and its Challenge to America* (London: I. B. Tauris).

Hay, C. (2005a) 'Globalization's impact on states', in J. Ravenhill (ed.) *Global Political Economy* (Oxford: Oxford University Press), pp.235–62.

Hay, C. (2005b) 'Two Can Play at that Game … Or Can They? Varieties of Capitalism, Varieties of Institutionalism', in D. Coates (ed.) *Varieties of Capitalism, Varieties of Approaches* (Basingstoke: Palgrave Macmillan), pp.106–21.

Hay, C. (2006) '(What's Marxist about) Marxist State Theory?', in C. Hay, M. Lister and D. Marsh (eds) *The State: Theories and Issues* (Basingstoke: Palgrave Macmillan), pp.59–78.

Hay, C. and D. Marsh (2000) 'Introduction: Demystifying Globalization', in C. Hay and D. Marsh (eds) *Demystifying Globalization* (Basingstoke: Palgrave Macmillan).

Hayek, F. (1996) *Individualism and Economic Order* (Chicago: University of Chicago Press, first published 1948).

Hayek, F. (2001) *The Road to Serfdom* (London: Routledge, first published 1944).

Hayek, F. (2006) *The Constitution of Liberty* (Chicago: University of Chicago Press, first published 1960).

Hayter, T. (1971) *Aid as Imperialism* (London: Penguin).

Hayter, T. (1985) *Aid: Rhetoric and Reality* (London: Pluto).

Held, D. (2004) *Global Covenant* (Cambridge: Polity).

Held, D. and A.McGrew (2002) 'Introduction', in D.Held and A.McGrew (eds), *Governing Globalization* (Cambridge: Polity), pp. 1–22.

Held, D. and A. McGrew (2003) 'The Great Globalization Debate: An Introduction', in D. Held and A. McGrew (eds), *The Global Transformations Reader* (Cambridge: Polity).

Held, D. and T. McGrew (2007) *Globalization/Anti-globalization* (Cambridge: Polity).

Held, D., A. McGrew, D. Goldblatt and J. Perraton (1999) *Global Transformations* (Cambridge: Polity).

Helleiner, E. (1994) *States and the Re-emergence of Global Finance* (Ithaca, NY: Cornell University Press).

Heron, T. (2006) 'The Ending of the Multi-Fibre Agreement: A Development Boon for the South?', *European Journal of Development Research* 18(1), pp.1–21.

Hewitt, G. (2008) 'Abkhazia and South Ossetia: heart of conflict, key to solution,', www.opendemocracy.net (accessed 18 August 2008).

Hilferding, R. (1981) *Finance Capital* (London: Routledge, first published 1910).

Hilton, R. (1976) 'A Comment', in R. Hilton (ed.) *The Transition from Feudalism to Capitalism* (London: Verso), pp.109–17.

Himmelfarb, G. (2008) *The Moral Imagination* (London: Souvenir Press).

Hirst, P. and G. Thompson (1996) *Globalization in Question* (Cambridge: Polity).

Hirst, P. and G. Thompson (1999) *Globalization in Question* (Cambridge: Polity, 2nd edition).

Hirst, P., G. Thompson and S. Bromley (2009) *Globalization in Question* (Cambridge: Polity, 3rd edition).

Hitchens, C. (2001) 'The Fascist Sympathies of the Soft Left', *The Spectator*, September 29.

Hitchens, C. (2003) *Regime Change* (London: Penguin).

Hitchens, C. (2007a) *Thomas Paine's Rights of Man* (New York: Atlantic).

Hitchens, C. (2007b) *God is not Great* (New York: Atlantic).

Hobsbawm, E. (1987) *The Age of Empire* (London: Weidenfeld & Nicolson).

Hobson, J. A. (1988) *Imperialism* (London: Unwin Hyman, first published 1902).

Hobson, J. M. (2004) *The Eastern Origins of Western Civilisation* (Cambridge: Cambridge University Press).

Hobson, J. M. (2006) 'Explaining the Rise of the West: A Reply to Ricardo Duchesne', *The Journal of the Historical Society* VI(4), pp.579–99.

Hochschild, A. (2006) *King Leopold's Ghost* (London: Pan).

Hoff, J. (2008) *A Faustian Foreign Policy* (Cambridge: Cambridge University Press).

Hore, C. (2004) 'China's Century?', *International Socialism* no.103, pp.3–48.

Horowitz, D. (2006) *The Professors: The 101 Most Dangerous Academics in America* (Washington: Regnery).

Horton, J. and Y.-L. Lee (2006) 'Iraq, political reconstruction and liberal theory', in A. Danchev and J. Macmillan (eds) *The Iraq War and Democratic Politics* (London: Routledge), pp.181–200.

Howe, A. (1999) *Free Trade and Liberal England, 1846–1946* (Oxford: Clarendon).

Howe, A. (2007) 'Free trade and global order: the rise and fall of a Victorian vision', in D. Bell (ed.) *Victorian Visions of Global Order* (Cambridge: Cambridge University Press), pp.26–46.

Howe, S. (2002) *Empire: A Very Short Introduction* (Oxford: Oxford University Press).

Howe, S. (2003) 'American Empire: the history and future of an idea', available at www.openDemocracy.net (accessed 20 July 2004).

Howe, S. (2004) 'An Oxford Scot and King Dubya's Court', www.opendemocracy.net (accessed 22 July 2004).

Hung, H. (2008) 'Rise of China and the Global Overaccumulation Crisis', *Review of International Political Economy* 15(2), pp.149–79.

Huntington, S. (1968) *Political Order in Changing Societies* (New Haven: Yale University Press).

Huntington, S. (1996) *The Clash of Civilisations and the Remaking of World Order* (New York: Simon & Schuster).

Hurst, S. (2005) 'Myths of Neoconservatism: Geirge W. Bush's "Neoconservative" Foreign Policy', *International Politics* 42(1), pp.75–96.

Hurt, S. (2003) 'Co-operation and Coercion? The Cotonou Agreement between the European Union and ACP States and the End of the Lome Convention', *Third World Quarterly* 24(1), pp.161–76.

Hutton, W. (2008) 'Don't expect China to get the West out of this mess', *The Observer*, 26 October.

Ignatieff, M. (2003) *Empire Lite* (London: Vintage).

Ignatieff, M. (2005) *The Lesser Evil* (New Jersey: Princeton University Press).

Ikenberry, J. (2001) 'American Power and the Empire of Democratic Capitalism', *Review of International Studies* 27(2), pp.191–212.

Ikenberry, J. (2004) 'Liberalism and empire: logics of order in the American unipolar age', *Review of International Studies* 30(4), pp.609–30.

Ikenberry, J. (2006) *Liberal Order and Imperial Ambition* (Cambridge: Polity).

Independent International Commission on Kosovo (2000) *Kosovo Report* (New York: Oxford University Press).

Ingham, G. (1984) *Capitalism Divided* (London: Macmillan).

Ingham, G. (2008) *Capitalism* (Cambridge: Polity).

Inikori, J. (1987), 'Slavery and the Development of Industrial Capitalism in England', in B. Solow and S. Engerman (eds) *British Capitalism and Caribbean Slavery* (Cambridge: Cambridge Univeristy Press), pp.79–101.

Isaac, J. (2002) 'Hannah Arendt on Human Rights and Exposure, or Why Noam Chomsky is Wrong about the Meaning of Kosovo', *Social Research* 69(2), pp.263–95.

Itoh, M. (1990) *The World Economic Crisis and Japanese Capitalism* (London: Macmillan).

Jahn, B. (2007a) 'The Tragedy of Liberal Diplomacy: Democracy, Intervention, State Building, Part I', *Journal of Intervention and State-Building* 1(1), pp.87–106.

Jahn, B. (2007b) 'The Tragedy of Liberal Diplomacy: Democracy, Intervention, State Building, Part II', *Journal of Intervention and State-Building* 1(2), pp.211–29.

James, H. (2001) *The End of Globalization* (Cambridge: Harvard University Press).

Jenkins, R. (1984a) *Transnational Corporations and the Industrial Transformation of Latin America* (London: Macmillan).

Jenkins, R. (1984b) 'Divisions over the International Division of Labour', *Capital and Class* no.22, pp.28–57.

Jenkins, R. (1987) *Transnational Corporations and Uneven Development* (London: Methuen).

Jenkins, R. (1992) 'Industrialization and the global economy', in T. Hewitt, H. Johnson and D. Wield (eds) *Industrialization and Development* (Oxford: Oxford University Press), pp.13–40.

Jessop, B. (1990) *State Theory: Putting the Capitalist State in its Place* (Cambridge: Polity).

Jessop, B. (2002) *The Future of the Capitalist State* (Cambridge: Polity).

Jessop, B. (2008) *State Power* (Cambridge: Polity).

Jomo K. S. and B. Fine (eds) (2006) *The New Development Economics* (London: Zed).

Kagan, R. (2004) *Paradise and Power* (London: Atlantic).

Kagan, R. (2008) *The Return of History and the End of Dreams* (London: Atlantic).

Kagan, R. and W. Kristol (eds) (2000) *Present Dangers: Crisis and Opportunity in American Foreign and Domestic Policy* (San Fancisco: Encounter)

Kaldor, M. (2003) *Global Civil Society* (Cambridge: Polity).

Kaldor, M. (2006) *New and Old Wars* (Cambridge: Polity, 2nd edition).

Kamm, O. (2005) *Anti-Totalitarianism: The Left Wing Case for a Neoconservative Foreign Policy* (London: Social Affairs Unit).

Kang Chao (1986) *Man and Land in Chinese History* (Palo Alto: Stanford University Press).

Kant, I. (1957) *Perpetual Peace and Other Essays on Politics, History and Morals* (Indianapolis: Hackett, first published 1895).

Kaplan, L (1998) 'Leftism on the Right: Conservatives Learn to Blame America First', *The Weekly Standard*, February 9.

Kaplan, R. (2006) *Imperial Grunts* (New York: Vintage).

Kaplinsky, R. (2005) *Globalization, Poverty and Inequality* (Cambridge: Polity).

Kaplinsky, R. and A. Santos-Paulinho (2005) 'Innovation and Competitiveness: Trends in unit prices in global trade', *Oxford Development Studies* 33(3/4), pp.333–55.

Kasahara, S. (2004) 'The Flying Geese Paradigm: A Critical Study of its Application to East Asian Regional Development', UNCTAD Discussion Paper no.169, pp.1–34.

Kautsky, K. (1970) 'Ultra-Imperialism', *New Left Review* I/59, pp.41–6 (first published 1914).

Kay, C. (1989) *Latin American Theories of Development and Underdevelopment* (London: Routledge).

Kay, G. (1975) *Development and Underdevelopment* (London: Macmillan).

Keidel, A. (2007) 'The limits of a smaller, poorer China', *Financial Times*, November 13.

Kemp, T. (1967) *Theories of Imperialism* (London: Denis Dobson).

Keohane, R. and J. Nye (1973) *Transnational Relations and World Politics* (Cambridge: Harvard University Press).

Keohane, R. and J. Nye (1977) *Power and Interdependence: World Politics in Transition* (Boston: Little, Brown).

Kerr, D. (2007) 'Has China abandoned self-reliance?', *Review of International Political Economy* 14(1), pp.77–104.

Keynes, J. M. (1973) 'The General Theory of Employment, Interest and Money', in *The Collected writings of John Maynard Keynes*, vol.7 (London: Macmillan, first published 1936).

Kidron, M. (1962) 'Imperialism: Highest Stage but One', *International Socialism* no. 9 (first series), available at www.marxists.org/archive/kidron/works.

Kidron, M. (1967) 'A Permanent Arms Economy', *International Socialism* no.28 (first series), pp.8–12.

Kidron, M. (1968) *Western Capitalism since the War* (London: Weidenfeld & Nicolson).

Kiely, R. (1995) *Sociology and Development: The Impasse and Beyond* (London: UCL Press).

Kiely, R. (1996) *The Politics of Labour and Development in Trinidad* (Mona: UWI Press).

Kiely, R. (1998) *Industrialization and Development: A Comparative Analysis* (London: UCL Press).

Kiely, R. (1999) 'Globalization: Established Fact or Uneven Process?', in S. Ismael (ed.) *Globalization: Policies, Challenges and Responses* (Calgary: Detselig), pp.45–64.

Kiely, R. (2004) 'The World Bank and "global poverty reduction": good policies or bad data?', *Journal of Contemporary Asia* 34(1), pp.3–20.

Kiely, R. (2005a) *The Clash of Globalisations: Neo-liberalism, the third way and 'anti-globalisation'* (Leiden: Brill).

Kiely, R. (2005b) *Empire in the Age of Globalisation* (London: Pluto).

Kiely, R. (2005c), 'Capitalist Expansion and the Imperialism–Globalisation Debate', *Journal of International Relations and Development* 8(1), pp.27–56.

Kiely, R. (2006) 'United States hegemony and globalization', *Cambridge Review of International Affairs* 19(2), pp.205–21.

Kiely, R. (2007a) *The New Political Economy of Development* (Basingstoke: Palgrave Macmillan).

Kiely, R. (2007b) 'Poverty reduction through liberalization, or intensified uneven development?: Neo-liberalism and the myth of global convergence', *Review of International Studies* 33(4), pp.415–34.

Kiely, R. (2008a) 'Poverty through "insufficient exploitation and/or globalization"? Globalized production and new dualist fallacies', *Globalizations* 5(3), pp.419–32.

Kiely, R. (2008b) ' "Poverty's Fall" /China's Rise: Global Convergence or New Forms of Uneven Development?', *Journal of Contemporary Asia* 38(3), pp.353–72.

Kiernan, V. (1972) *The Lords of Humankind* (London: Penguin, revised edn).

Kiernan, V. (1980) *America: The New Imperialism* (London: Zed).

Kindleberger, C. (1973) *The World in Depression* (London: Penguin).

Kindleberger, C. (2000) *Manias, Panics and Crashes* (New York: Wiley, 4th edition, first published 1978).

Kirkpatrick, J. (2004) 'Neo-conservatism as a Response to the Counter Culture', in I. Stelzer (ed.) *Neoconservatism* (London: Atlantic), pp.233–40.

Kirshner, J. (2008) 'Dollar primacy and American power: what's at stake', *Review of International Political Economy* 15(3), pp.418–38.

Kitching, G. (1982) *Development and Underdevelopment in Historical Perspective* (London: Methuen).

Kitching, G. (1989) *Development and Underdevelopment in Historical Perspective* (London: Methuen, 2nd edition).

Kitching, G. (2001) *Seeking Social Justice through Economic Globalization* (Pennsylvania: Penn State University Press)

Klare, M. (2002) *Resource Wars* (Basingstoke: Palgrave Macmillan)

Klare, M. (2004) *Blood and Oil* (London: Hamish Hamilton).

Klare, M. (2008) 'Sino-American energy consumption', *Survival* 50 (4), pp. 68–74.

Kleveman, L. (2004) *The New Great Game* (London: Atlantic).

Knafo, S. (2006) 'The Gold Standard and the Origins of the Modern International Monetary System', *Review of International Political Economy* 13(1), pp.418–38.

Knafo, S. (2008) 'The state and the rise of speculative finance in England', *Economy and Society* 37(2), pp.172–92.

Kohn, M. and D. O'Neill (2006) 'A Tale of Two Indias', *Political Theory* 34(2), pp.192–228.

Kolko, G. (1968) *The Politics of War* (New York: Pantheon).

Kolko, G. (1969) *The Roots of American Foreign Policy* (New York: Beacon).

Kolko, G. (1985) *Anatomy of a War: Vietnam, the US and the Modern Historical Experience* (New York: New Press).

Kollewe, J. (2008) 'Eurozone officially enters recession', *The Guardian*, November 14.

Konings, M. (2005) 'The United States in the Post-war Global Political Economy: Another Look at the Brenner Debate', in D. Coates (ed.) *Varieties of Capitalism, Varieties of Approaches* (Basingstoke: Palgrave Macmillan), pp.189–210.

Kozul-Wright, R. (2006) 'Globalization, Now and Again', in Jomo, K. S. (ed.) *Globalization Under Hegemony* (New Delhi: Oxford University Press), pp.100–32.

Kozul-Wright, R. and P. Rayment (2004) 'Globalization Reloaded: an UNCTAD Perspective, UNCTAD Discussion Papers no.167, pp.1–50.

Krauthammer, C. (1990) 'The unipolar moment', *Foreign Affairs* 70(1), pp.23–33.

Kristol, I. (1995) *Neo-Conservatism: The Autobiography of an Idea* (New York: Free Press).

Kristol, I. (2003) 'The Neoconservative Persuasion', *The Weekly Standard*, August 25.

Kristol, W. and D. Brooks (1997) 'What Ails Conservatism?', *Wall Street Journal*, September 15.

Kristol, W. and R. Kagan (1996) 'Toward a Neo-Reaganite Foreign Policy', *Foreign Affairs* 75(4), pp.18–32.

Kristol, W. and R. Kagan (2000) *Present Dangers* (San Francisco: Encounter Books).

Kristol, W. and L. Kaplan (2003) *The War over Iraq: Saddam's Tyranny and America's Mission* (San Francisco: Encounter).

Krueger, A. (1974) 'The Political Economy of the Rent Seeking society', *American Economic Review* 64(3), pp.291–303.

Krueger, A. (1998) 'Why trade liberalisation is good for growth', *The Economic Journal* no.108, pp.1513–22.

Krugman, P. (1986) *Strategic Trade Policy and the New International Economics* (Cambridge: MIT Press).

Lacher, H. (1999) 'Embedded Liberalism, Disembedded Markets: Reconceptualising the *Pax Americana*', *New Political Economy* 4(3), pp.343–60.

Lacher, H. (2006) *Beyond Globalization: Capitalism, Territoriality and the international Relations of Modernity* (Basingstoke: Palgrave Macmillan).

Laclau, E. (1971) 'Feudalism and Capitalism in Latin America', *New Left Review* I/67, pp.19–38.

LaFeber, W. (1963) *The New Empire: An Interpretation of American Expansion, 1860–1898* (New York: Cornell University Press).

LaFeber, W. (1993) *America, Russia and the Cold War* (New York: McGraw-Hill, 7th edition).

Lake, A. (1994) 'Confronting Backlash States', *Foreign Affairs* 73(2), pp.72–80.

Lal, D. (1984) *The Poverty of 'Development Economics'* (London: Institute of Economic Affairs).

Lal, D. (2004) *In Praise of Empires* (London: Palgrave).

Landes, D. (1969) *The Unbound Prometheus* (Cambridge: Cambridge University Press).

Lapavitsas, C. (2009) 'Financialised Capitalism: Crisis and Financial Expropriation', *Historical Materialism* 17(2), pp. 114–48.

Larrain, J. (1986) *A Reconstruction of Historical Materialism* (London: Allen & Unwin).

Larrain, J. (1989) *Theories of Development* (Cambridge: Polity).

Laurent, E. (2004) *Bush's Secret World* (Cambridge: Polity).

Lawson, G. (2008) 'A realistic utopia? Nancy Fraser, cosmopolitanism and the making of a just world order', *Political Studies* 56(4), pp.881–906.

Layne, C. (2008) 'It's Over, Over There: The Coming Crack-up in Transatlantic Relations', *International Politics* 45(3), pp.325–47.

Lee, D. and R. Wilkinson (eds) (2007) *The WTO after Hong Kong* (London: Routledge).

Lenin, V. (1977) 'Imperialism: The Highest Stage of Capitalism', in *Selected Works* (Moscow: Progress, first published 1916).

Lenin, V. (2003) 'Introduction', in N. Bukharin (2003) *Imperialism and World Economy* (London: Bookmarks), pp.9–13.

Leonard, M. (2005) *Why Europe Will Run the 21st Century* (London: Fourth Estate).

Leys, C. and J. Saul (2006) 'Dependency', in J. Saul, *Development after Globalization* (London: Zed, 2006), pp.9–17.

Limqueco, P. and B. MacFarlane (eds) (1983) *Neo-Marxist Theories of Development* (London: Macmillan).

Lindert, P. and J. Williamson (2001) 'Does globalization make the world more unequal?', (Cambridge, Mass.: NBER Working Paper, no.8228).

Lipietz, A. (1982) 'Marx or Rostow?', *New Left Review* I/132, pp.48–58.

List, F. (1966) *The National System of Political Economy* (New York: Augustus Kelley, first published in English, 1885).

Little, I., T. Scitovsky and M. Scott (1970) *Industry and Trade in some Developing Countries* (Oxford: Oxford University Press)

Locke, J. (1980) *Second Treatise of Government* (Indianapolis: Hackett, first published 1690).

Lowy, M. (1981) *The Politics of Combined and Uneven Development* (London: Verso).

Lugard, F. (1965) *The Dual Mandate in British Tropical Africa* (London: Frank Cass, first published 1922).

Lundestad, G. (1998) *'Empire' by Integration: The United States and European Integration, 1945–1997* (Oxford: Oxford University Press).

Lundestad, G. (2003) *The United States and Western Europe since 1945* (Oxford: Oxford University Press).

Luxemburg, R. (1951) *The Accumulation of Capital* (New York: Monthly Review Press, first published 1913).

Luxemburg, R. (1972) 'The Accumulation of Capital: An Anti-Critique', in K. Tarbuck (ed.) *Imperialism and the Accumulation of Capital* (London: Allen Lane, first published 1921), pp.45–150.

MacNamara, K. (2008) 'A Rivalry in the Making? The Euro and international monetary power', *Review of International Political Economy* 15(3), pp.439–59.

Macwhirter, I. (2008) 'Europe's looming crisis', *New Statesman*, November 3.

Maddison, A. (1998) *Chinese Economic Performance in the Long Run* (Paris: OECD Development Centre).

Maddison, A. (2001) *The World Economy: A Millennial Perspective* (Paris: OECD Development Centre).

Magdoff, H. (1978) *Imperialism without Colonies* (New York: Monthly Review Press).

Maizels, A., T. Palaskas and T. Crowe (1998) 'The Prebisch Singer Hypothesis Revisited', in D. Sapford and J. Chen (eds), *Development Economics and Policy* (London: Macmillan, 1998), pp.95–110.

Makdisi, S. (1998) *Romantic Imperialism* (Cambridge: Cambridge University Press).

Mallaby, S. (2002) 'The reluctant imperialist: Terrorism, failed states and the case for American empire', *Foreign Affairs* 81(2), pp.2–7.

Mamdani, M. (1996) *Citizen and Subject* (London: James Currey).

Mandel, E. (1970) *Europe vs. America* (London: New Left Books).

Mandel, E. (1973) 'The Mystifications of State Capitalism', in International Marxist Group, *Readings on State Capitalism* (London: IMG), pp.33–40.

Mandel, E. (1975) *Late Capitalism* (London: New Left Books).

Mandel, E. (1980) *The Second Slump* (London: Verso).

Mann, M. (2001)'Globalization and September 11th', *New Left Review* II/11, pp.51–72.

Mann, M. (2003) *Incoherent Empire* (London: Verso).

Mann, M. (2004) *The Dark Side of Democracy* (Cambridge: Cambridge University Press).

Mantena, K. (2007) 'The crisis of liberal imperialism', in D. Bell (ed.) *Victorian Visions of Global Order* (Cambridge: Cambridge University Press), pp.113–35.

Marable, M. (1983) *How Capitalism Underdeveloped Black America* (Boston: South End Press).

Marchal, J. (2008) *Lord Leverhulme's Ghosts* (London: Verso).

Marx, K. (1976) *Capital* vol.1 (Harmondsworth: Penguin).

Marx, K. (1977) 'Speech on Free Trade', in D. McLellan (ed.) *Karl Marx: Selected Writings* (Oxford: Oxford University Press, first 'published' 1848), pp.269–70.

Marx, K. (1979) *The Eighteenth Brummaire of Louis Bonaparte* (Peking: Foreign Languages Press).

Marx, K.(1984) 'The reply to Zasulich', in T.Shanin (ed.), *Late Marx and the Russian Road* (London: Routledge), pp. 123–6.

Marx, K. and F. Engels (1964) *The German Ideology* (London: Lawrence & Wishart, first published 1846).

Marx, K. and F. Engels (1974) *On Colonialism* (Moscow: Progress).

Mayer, A. (1981) *The Persistence of the Old Regime, Europe to the Great War* (New York: Pantheon).

Mazarr, M. (2003) 'George W. Bush, Idealist', *International Affairs* 79(3), pp.503–22.

Mazower, M (2001) *Dark Continent* (Harmondsworth: Penguin).

Mazower, M. (2008) *Hitler's Empire: Nazi Rule in Occupied Europe* (London: Allen Lane).

McClelland, D. (1961) *The Achieving Society* (New York: The Free Press).

McCormick, T. (1967) *China Market: America's Quest for Informal Empire, 1893–1901* (New York: Quadrangle Books).

McCurry, J. (2009) 'Japan suffers record fall in GDP', *The Guardian*, May 20.

McDonagh, O. (1962) 'The Anti-Imperialism of Free Trade', *Economic History Review* 14(3), pp.489–501.

McGrew, A. (2000) 'Sustainable globalization? The global politics of development and exclusion in the new world order', in T. Allen and A. Thomas (eds) *Poverty and Development into the Twenty First Century* (Oxford: Oxford University Press), pp.345–64.

McGrew, A. (2002) 'Liberal internationalism: between realism and cosmopolitanism', in D. Held and A. McGrew (eds) *Governing Globalization* (Cambridge: Polity), pp.267–89.

McMichael, P., J. Petras and R. Rhodes (1974) 'Imperialism and the Contradictions of Development', *New Left Review* I/85, pp.83–104.

McNally, D. (2008) 'Global Finance, the Current Crisis, and Challenges to the Dollar', *Relay* no.22, pp.13–17.

Mearsheimer, J. (2001) *The Tragedy of Great Power Politics* (New York: Norton).

Mearsheimer, J. (2005) 'Hans Morgenthau and the Iraq War: Realism versus Neoconservatism', www.opendemocracy.net (accessed 19 May 2005).

Mehta, U. (1999) *Liberalism and Empire* (Chicago: University of Chicago Press).

Milanovic, B. (2005) *World's Apart* (Princeton: Princeton University Press).

Milanovic, B. (2007) 'Globalization and Inequality' in D. Held and A. Kaya (eds) *Global Inequality* (Oxford: Blackwell), pp.26–49.

Miliband, R. (1969) *The State in Capitalist Society* (London: Weidenfeld & Nicolson).

Miliband, R. (1977) *Marxism and Politics* (Oxford: Oxford University Press).

Miliband, R. (1982) *Capitalist Democracy in Britain* (Oxford: Oxford University Press).

Miliband, R. (1983) *Class Power and State Power* (London: Verso).

Mill, J. (1810) 'Voyages aux Indes Orientales', *The Edinburgh Review* 15, pp.363–84.

Mill, J. (1976) *History of British India* (Chicago: University of Chicago Press, first published 1817)

Mill, J. (2006) *Selected Economic Writings* (New York: Transaction).

Mill, J. S. (1890) *Considerations on Representative Government* (London: Longmans, Green & Co., first published 1861).

Mill, J. S. (1974) *On Liberty* (Harmondsworth: Penguin, first published 1859).

Mill, J. S. (1984) 'A Few Words on Non-Intervention' in *Collected Works* vol.18, J. Robson (ed.) (Toronto: University of Toronto Press, first published 1859), pp.109–24.

Minsky, H. (1982) 'The financial instability hypothesis' in C. Kindleberger and J. P. Lafarge (eds) *Financial Crises* (Cambridge: Cambridge University Press), pp.13–38.

Mintz, S. (1986) *Sweetness and Power* (London: Penguin).

Mitchie, J. and M. Kitson (1995) 'Trade and growth: An historical perspective', in J. Mitchie and J. Smith (eds) (1995) *Managing the Global Economy* (Oxford: Oxford University Press), pp.3–36.

Mommsen, W. (1981) *Theories of Imperialism* (London: Weidenfeld & Nicolson).

Morgan, J. (2007) 'The US–China Trade Assymetry in Context', Helsinki: University of Helsinki Centre of Excellence in Global Governance, Working Paper no.2, pp.1–68.

Morgenthau, H. (1992) *Politics Among Nations* (New York: McGraw Hill, first published 1948).

Morton, A. D. (2007) *Unravelling Gramsci* (London: Pluto).

Moseley, F. (2008) 'Some notes on the crunch and the crisis', *International Socialism* 119, pp. 89–92.

Murray, R. (ed.) (1981) *Multinationals Beyond the Market* (London: Harvester).

Nachtwey, O. and T. Brink (2008) 'Lost in Transition: The German World Market Debate in the 1970s', *Historical Materialism* 16(1), pp.37–70.

Nairn, T. (1964) 'The British Political Elite', *New Left Review* I/23, pp.19–25.

Narlikar, A. and D. Tussie (2004) 'The G20 at the Cancun ministerial: developing countries and their evolving coalitions in the WTO', *The World Economy* 27(4), pp.947–66.

National Intelligence Council (2008) *Global Trends 2025* (Washington: National Intelligence Council).

NEDPG (2001) 'National Energy Policy', available at www.whitehouse.gov/energy, accessed 16 February 208.

Nitzan, J. and S. Bichler (2006) 'New Imperialism or New Capitalism?', *Review* 29(1), pp.1–86.

Nkrumah, K. (1965) *Neocolonialism: The Last Stage of Imperialism* (New York: International Publishers).

Nolan, P. (2001) *China and the Global Economy* (Basingstoke: Palgrave Macmillan).

Nolan, P. (2004) *China at the Crossroads* (Cambridge: Polity).

Nolan, P. (2008) *Capitalism and Freedom* (London: Anthem).

Nowell, G. (2002/3) 'Imperialism and the era of falling prices', *Journal of Post-Keynesian Economics* 25(2), pp.309–29.

Novack, G. (1972) *Understanding History* (New York: Pathfinder).

NSC-68, (1950) (declassified in 1977), available at www.fas.org/irp/offdocs/nsc-hst/nsc-68.htm.

NSS (2002) 'The National Security strategy of the United States of America', available at www.whitehouse.gov/nsc/nss.html

Nye, J. (2002) *The Paradox of American Power* (Oxford: Oxford University Press Affairs).

Nzula, A., I. Potekhin and A. Zusmanovich (1979) *Forced Labour in Colonial Africa* (London: Zed).

O' Brien, P. (1982) 'European Economic Development: The Contribution of the Periphery', *The Economic History Review* 35(1), pp.1–18.

O' Brien, P. (1988) 'The Costs and Benefits of British Imperialism, 1846–1914', *Past and Present* no.120, pp.163–99.

O'Brien, P. (1991) 'The Foundations of European Industrialization: From the Perspective of the World', *Journal of Historical Sociology* 4(3), pp.288–317.

O'Brien, P. (1996) 'Path Dependency, or why Britain Became an Industrialized and Urbanized Economy Long Before France', *Economic History Review* 49(2), pp.213–49.

O'Brien, P. (1999) 'Imperialism and the Rise and Decline of the British Economy', *New Left Review* I/238, pp.48–79.

O'Brien, P. (2004) 'Colonies in a Globalizing Economy, 1815–1948' (London: LSE Working Paper no.08/04).

O'Brien, P. (2006) 'Colonies in a globalizing economy, 1815–1948', in B. Gills and W. Thompson (eds), *Globalization and Global History* (London: Routledge), pp. 223–64.

O'Brien, P. and S. Engerman (1991) 'Exports and the Growth of the British Economy from the Glorious Revolution to the Peace of Amiens', in B. Solow (ed.) *Slavery and the Rise of the Atlantic System* (Cambridge: Cambridge University Press), pp.177–209.

O'Rourke, K., A. Taylor and J. Williamson (1996), 'Factor price convergence in the late nineteenth century', *International Economic Review* 37(4), pp.499–530.

Ohlin, B. (1933) *Inter-regional and International Trade* (Cambridge: Harvard University Press).

Ohmae, K. (1995) *Borderless World* (London: Fontana).

Overton, M. (1998) *Agricultural Revolution in England: The Transformation of the Agrarian Economy 1500–1800* (Cambridge: Cambridge University Press).

Owens, P. (2003) 'Accidents Don't Just Happen: The Liberal Politics of high-Tech Humanitarian War', *Millennium* 32(3), pp.595–616.

Owens, P. (2007) *Between War and Politics* (Oxford: Oxford University Press).

Oxfam (2002) *Rigged Rules and Double Standards* (Oxford: Oxfam).

Palma, G. (1978)'Dependency and development: a formal theory of underdevelopment or a methodology for the analysis of concrete situations of underdevelopment?', *World Development* 6, pp.881–924.

Panitch, L. and S. Gindin (2003) 'Global Capitalism and American Empire', *The Socialist Register 2004* (London: Merlin), pp.1–42.

Panitch, L. and S. Gindin (2004) 'Finance and American Empire', *The Socialist Register 2005* (London: Merlin), pp.46–81.

Panitch, L. and S. Gindin (2005a) 'Euro-Capitalism and American Empire', in D. Coates (ed.) *Varieties of Capitalism, Varieties of Approaches* (Basingstoke: Palgrave Macmillan), pp.139–59.

Panitch, L. and S. Gindin (2005b) 'Towards a Theory of the Capitalist Imperial State', mimeo.

Panitch, L. and S. Gindin (2006a) 'Imperialism and Global Political economy: a reply to Callinicos', *International Socialism* no.109, pp.194–99.

Panitch, L. and S. Gindin (2006b), 'Theorizing American Empire', in A. Bartholomew (ed.), *Empire's Law* (London: Pluto), pp.21–43.

Panitch, L. and S. Gindin (2008) 'The Current Crisis: A Socialist Perspective', *Socialist Project e-bulletin* no.142, pp.1–8.

Panitch, L. and M. Konings (2008a) 'US Financial Power in Crisis', *Historical Materialism* 16(4), pp.3–34.

Panitch, L. and M. Konings (2008b) 'Demystifying Imperial Finance' in L. Panitch and M. Konings (eds) *American Empire and the Political Economy of Global Finance* (Basingstoke: Palgrave Macmillan), pp.1–13.

Parekh, B. (1995) 'Liberalism and colonialism: a critique of Locke and Mill', in J. N. Pieterse and B. Parekh (eds) *The Decolonization of Imagination* (London: Zed), pp.81–98.

Parfitt, T. (2002) *The End of Development* (London: Pluto).

Parmar, I. (2009) 'Foreign policy fusion: Liberal interventionists, conservative nationalists and neoconservatives – the new alliance dominating the US foreign policy establishment', *International Politics* 46(2/3), pp.177–209.

Patomaki, H. (2008) *The Political Economy of Global Security* (London: Routledge).

Perkins, B. (1984) 'The Tragedy of American Diplomacy: Twenty Five Years After', in W. A. Williams (1999) *The Tragedy of American Diplomacy* (New York: W. W. Norton, revised edition), pp.313–30.

Petras, J. and R. Rhodes (1976) 'The Reconsolidation of American Hegemony', *New Left Review* I/97, pp.37–53.

Phillips, A. (1987) *The Enigma of Colonialism* (London: James Currey).

Pirie, I. (2006) 'Economic Crisis and the Construction of a Neo-Liberal Regulatory Regime in Korea', *Competition and Change* 10(1), pp.49–71.

Pitts, J. (2003) 'Legislator of the World? A rereading of Bentham on India', *Political Theory* 31(2), pp.200–34.

Pitts, J. (2005) *A Turn to Empire: The Rise of Imperial Liberalism in Britain and France* (Princeton: Princeton University Press).

Pitts, J. (2007) 'Boundaries of Victorian international law', in D. Bell (ed.), *Victorian Visions of Global Order* (Cambridge: Cambridge University Press), pp.67–88.

Platt, D. (1968) 'The Imperialism of Free Trade: Some Reservations', *The Economic History Review* 21(2), pp.296–306.

PNAC (2000) Project for the New American Century: 'Rebuilding America's Defenses', available at www.newamericancentury.org/RebuildingAmericas defenses.pdf (accessed 7 July 2008).

Pogge, T. (2004) 'The First UN Millennium Development Goal: A Cause for Celebration', available at www.socialanalysis.org (accessed 25 March 2006).

PPNS (2006) *Forging a World of Liberty and Law* (Princeton: Princeton University).

Pomeranz, K. (2000) *The Great Divergence: China, Europe and the Making of the Modern World Economy* (Princeton: Princeton University Press).

Pomeranz, K. (2002) 'Beyond the East-West binary: Resituating development paths in the eighteenth century', *Journal of Asian Studies* 61(2), pp.539–60.

Popper, K. (1957) *The Poverty of Historicism* (London: Routledge).

Post, K. (1978) *Arise Ye Starvelings!* (The Hague: Martinus Nijhoff).

Poulantzas, N. (1969) 'The Problems of the Capitalist State', *New Left Review* I/58, pp.67–78.

Poulantzas, N. (1974) *Political Power and Social Classes* (London: New Left Books).

Poulantzas, N. (1978) *State, Power, Socialism* (London: New Left Books).

Power, S. (2003) *A Problem from Hell: America and the Age of Genocide* (New York: Flamingo).

Prebisch, R. (1959) 'Commercial policy in the underdeveloped countries', *American Economic Review* 44, pp.251–73.

Ramo, J. (2004) *The Beijing Consensus: Notes on the New Physics of Chinese Power* (London: Foreign Policy Centre).

Rawls, J. (1993) *The Law of Peoples* (Boston: Harvard University Press).

Reddy, S. and T. Pogge (2003) *How Not to Count the Poor*, available at www.socialanaly-sis.org (accessed 3 March 2007).

Ree, J. (2006) 'Ethical correctness and the Decline of the Left', in T. Cushman (ed.) *A Matter of Principle* (Berkeley: University of California Press), pp.179–90.

Rees, J. (2000) 'Oil, Gas and NATO's New Frontier', *New Political Economy* 5(1), pp.100–4

Rees, J. (2001) 'Imperialism: Globalization, the state and war', *International Socialism* no. 93, pp.3–34.

Rees, J. (2005) 'Foreword: Nikolai Bukharin and modern imperialism', in N. Bukharin, *Imperialism and World Economy* (London: Routledge), pp.1–8.

Rees, J. (2006) *Imperialism and Resistance* (London: Routledge).

Reid, J. (2005) 'The Biopolitics of the War on Terror: a critique of the "return of imperialism" thesis', *Third World Quarterly* 26(2), pp.253–81.

Reinert, E. (2006) 'Increasing Poverty in a Globalized World: *Marshall Plans* and *Morgenthau Plans* as Mechanisms of Polarization of World Incomes', in H. J. Chang (ed.) *Rethinking Development Economics* (London: Anthem), pp.451–78.

Reinert, E. (2007) *How Rich Countries got Rich and Why Poor Countries Stay Poor* (London: Constable).

Reno, W. (1999) *Warlord Politics and African States* (Boulder: Lynne Rienner).

Retort (2005) *Afflicted Powers* (London: Verso).

Ricardo, D. (1973) *The Principles of Political Economy and Taxation* (London: J. M. Dent, first published 1819).

Ritzer, G. (1993) *The McDonaldization of Society* (London: Sage).

Ritzer, G. (2004) *The Globalization of Nothing* (London: Sage).

Robbins, P. (2003) *Stolen Fruit* (London: Zed).

Roberts, S., A. Secor and M. Sparke (2003) 'Neoliberal Geopolitics', *Antipode* 35(5), pp.886–97.

Robinson, B. (1996) *Promoting Polyarchy* (Cambridge: Cambridge University Press).

Robinson, B. (2002) 'Capitalist Globalization and the Transnationalization of the State', in M. Rupert and H. Smith (eds) *Historical Materialism and Globalization* (London: Routledge), pp.21–29.

Robinson, B. (2004) *A Theory of Global Capitalism* (Baltimore: Johns Hopkins University Press).

Robinson, B. (2007) 'The Pitfalls of Realist Analysis of Global Capitalism: A Critique of Ellen Meiksins Wood's *Empire of Capital*', *Historical Materialism* 15(3), pp.71–93.

Robinson, R. (1986) 'The Excentric idea of imperialism, with or without empire', in W.Mommsen and J. Osterhammel (eds), *Imperialism and After* (London: HarperCollins), pp. 267–89.

Robinson, R. and J. Gallagher (1961) *Africa and the Victorians* (London: St Martin's Press).

Roddick, J. (1988) *The Dance of the Millions* (London: Latin America Bureau).

Rodney, W. (1972) *How Europe Underdeveloped Africa* (London: Bogle L'Ouverture).

Rodrik, D. (2001) *The Global Governance of Trade as if Development Really Mattered* (Geneva: United Nations Development Programme).

Rodrik, D. (2003) 'Comments on "Trade, Growth and Poverty" by D. Dollar and A. Kraay', table 1, available at www.ksghome.harvard.edu (accessed 3 March 2007).

Rodrik, D. (2006) 'The Social Cost of Foreign Exchange Reserves', *International Economic Journal* 20(3), pp.253–66.

Rodrik, D. and A. Subramanian (2001) 'From "Hindu Growth" to Productivity Surge: The Mystery of the Indian Growth Transition', *IMF Working Papers* 04/77.

Roger Lewis, W. (ed.) (1976a) *Imperialism: the Robinson and Gallagher Controversy* (New York: New Viewpoints).

Roger Lewis, W. (1976b) 'Robinson and Gallagher and their Critics' in W. Roger Lewis (ed.) *Imperialism: the Robinson and Gallagher Controversy* (New York: New Viewpoints), pp.2–51.

Rogers, P. (2006) 'The United States vs. China: the war for oil', available at www.open-democracy.net (accessed 22 June 2006).

Rogers, P. (2007) 'The United States and Africa: eyes on the prize', available at www.open-democracy.net (accessed 15 March 2007).

Rosenberg, J. (1994) *The Empire of Civil Society* (London: Verso).

Rosenberg, J. (2000) *The Follies of Globalisation Theory* (London: Verso).

Rosenberg, J. (2005) 'Globalization Theory: A Postmortem', *International Politics* 42(1), pp.2–74.

Rosenberg, J. (2006) 'Why is there no Historical Sociology', *European Journal of International Relations* 12(3), pp.307–40.

Rosenberg, J. (2007) 'And the Definition of Globalization is..? A Reply to "In at the Death" by Barrie Axford', *Globalizations* 4(3), pp.417–21.

Rostow, W. (1960) *The Stages of Economic Growth* (Cambridge: Cambridge University Press).

Rowthorn, B. (1971) 'Imperialism in the Seventies – Unity or Rivalry', *New Left Review* I/69, pp.55–90.

Rowthorn, B. (2001) 'Replicating the Experience of the NIEs on a Large Scale', in Jomo K. S. and S. Nagaraj (eds) *Globalization versus Development* (Basingstoke: Palgrave Macmillan), pp.85–112.

Rubinstein, W. (1987) *Elites and the Wealthy in Modern British Gistory* (New York: St Martin's Press).

Rude, C. (2004) 'The Role of Financial Discipline in Imperial Strategy', in L. Panitch and C. Leys (eds) *The Socialist Register 2005* (London: Merlin), pp.82–107.

Rude, C. (2008) 'Hegemony Unfolding', *Relay* no.22, pp.20–5.

Ruggie, J. (1998) *Constructing the World Polity* (London: Routledge).

Rugraff, E., D. Sanchez-Anchocea and A.Sumner (2008) 'How have TNCs changed in the last 50 years'?, in their *Transnational Corporations and Development Policy* (Basingstoke: Palgrave Macmillan), pp.9–28.

Runciman, D. (2006) *The Politics of Good Intentions* (Princeton: Princeton University Press).

Runciman, D. (2008) *Political Hypocrisy* (Princeton: Princeton University Press).

Rutland, P. and G. Dubinsky (2008) 'US foreign policy in Russia' in M. Cox and D. Stokes (eds) *US Foreign Policy* (Oxford: Oxford University Press), pp.257–74.

Saad-Filho, A. (2005) 'The Political Economy of Neoliberalism in Latin America', in A. Saad-Filho and D. Johnston (eds), *Neoliberalism: A Critical Reader* (London: Pluto), pp.222–9.

Sachs, J. and A. Warner (1997) 'Sources of Slow Growth in African Economies', *Journal of African Economies,* 6(3), pp. 335–76.

Said, E. (1978) *Orientalism* (Harmondsworth: Penguin).

Sandbrook, R. (1985) *The Politics of Africa's Economic Stagnation* (Cambidge: Cambridge University Press).

Sanderson, G. (1974) 'The European partition of Africa: coincidence or conjuncture', *Journal of Imperial and Commonwealth History*, 3(1), pp. 1–34.

Santos-Paulino, A. and A. Thirlwall (2004) 'The Impact of Trade Liberalisation on Exports, Imports and the Balance of Payments of Developing Countries', *The Economic Journal* 114, ff.50–72.

Sardar, Z. and M. Wyn-Davies (2003) *Why do People Hate America?* (London: Icon).

Sarkar, P. and H. Singer (1991), 'Manufactured Exports of Developing countries and their Terms of Trade', *World Development* 19(4), pp.333–40.

Sartori, A. (2006) 'The British Empire and its Liberal Mission', *Journal of Modern History* 78, pp.623–42.

Saull, R. (2001) *Rethinking Theory and History in the Cold War* (London: Frank Cass).

Saull, R. (2005) 'Locating the Global South in the Theorisation of the Cold War: capitalist development, social revolution and geopolitical conflict', *Third World Quarterly* 26(2), pp.253–81.

Saull, R. (2007) *The Cold War and After* (London: Pluto).

Say. J.-B. (1997) *An Economist in Troubled Times: Writings*, ed. R. Palmer (Princeton: Princeton University Press).

Schiffer, J. (1981) 'The changing post-war pattern of development', *World Development* 9(5), pp.715–28.

Schmitt, C. (1996) *The Concept of the Political* (Chicago: University of Chicago Press).

Schmitt, C. (2003) 'The New Nomos of the Earth', in C. Schmitt, *The Nomos of the Earth in the International Law of the Jus Publicum Europaeum* (New York: Telos Press, first published 1955).

Schmitt, G. (2002) 'Our Ambivalent China Policy', *Weekly Standard*, July 15.

Schmitt, G. (2003) 'The Real Empire', *Weekly Standard*, August 27.

Schmitt, G. and D. Blumenthal (2005) 'Wishful Thinking in our Time', *Weekly Standard*, August 8.

Scholte, J. A. (2005) *Globalization: A Critical Introduction* (Basingstoke: Palgrave Macmillan).

Schumpeter, J. (1951) *Imperialism and Social Classes* (Oxford: Blackwell).

Schumpeter, J. (1954) *Capitalism, Socialism and Democracy* (London: Allen & Unwin).

Schwartz, H. (2000) *States Against Markets* (Basingstoke: Palgrave Macmillan).

Schwartz, H. (2008) 'Housing, Global Finance and American Hegemony: Building Conservative Politics One Brick at a Time', *Comparative European Politics* 6(2), pp.262–84.

Schwarzmantel, J. (2008) *Ideology and Politics* (London: Sage).

Seabrooke, L. (2001) *US Power in International Finance* (Basingstoke: Palgrave Macmillan).

Seager, A. (2009) 'World Bank calls on west to help relieve trillion dollar drain on world's poor', *The Guardian*, 22 June.

Semmel, B. (1965) 'On the Economics of "Imperialism"', in B. Hoselitz (ed.), *Economics and the Idea of Mankind* (New York: Columbia University Press), pp.192–232.

Semmel, B. (1970) *The Rise of Free Trade Imperialism* (Cambridge: Cambridge University Press).

Sen, A. (1981) *Poverty and Famines* (Oxford: Clarendon).

Sender, J. (1999) 'Africa's Economic Performance: limitations of the current consensus', *Journal of Economic Perspectives* 13(3), pp.89–114.

Sender, J. and S. Smith (1985) 'What's right with the Berg Report and what's left of its critics', *Capital and Class* 24, pp.125–46.

Sender, J. and S. Smith (1986) *The Development of Capitalism in Africa* (London: Methuen).

Seymour, R. (2008) *The Liberal Defence of Murder* (London: Verso).

Shafaeddin, S. M. (2005a) 'Trade liberalization and economic reform in developing countries', UNCTAD Discussion Papers no.179, pp.1–25.

Shafaeddin, S. M. (2005b) *Trade Policy at the Crossroads* (Basingstoke: Palgrave Macmillan).

Shaikh, A. (1979/80) 'Foreign Trade and the Law of Value – Part Two', *Science and Society*, 44, pp.27–57.

Shaikh, A. (ed.) (2005) *Globalization and the Myth of Free Trade* (London: Routledge).

Shaw, M. (2002) '10 Challenges to Anti-War Politics', *Radical Philosophy* 111, pp.11–19.

Shaw, M. (2005) *The New Western Way of War* (Cambridge: Polity).

Simmons, M. (2005) *Twilight in the Desert* (London: Wiley).

Singer, H. (1950) 'The Distribution of Gains from Trade between Investing and Borrowing Countries', *American Economic Review* 40, pp.473–85.

Singer, P. (2004) *The President of Good and Evil* (London: Granta).

Sklair, L. (2002) *Globalization: Capitalism and its Alternatives* (Oxford: Oxford University Press).

Smith, A. (1981) *An Inquiry into the Nature and Causes of the Wealth of Nations vol.2* (Indianapolis: Liberty Fund, first published 1776).

Smith, S. (1980) 'The ideas of Samir Amin: theory or tautology?', *Journal of Development Studies* 17(1), pp.5–20.

Smith, T. (2007) *A Pact with the Devil* (London: Routledge).

Solow, B. and S. Engerman (1987a) 'British Capitalism and Caribbean Slavery: the Legacy of Eric Williams: An Introduction' in B. Solow and S. Engerman (eds) *British Capitalism and Caribbean Slavery* (Cambridge: Cambridge University Press, pp.1–23.

Solow, B. and S. Engerman (eds) (1987b) *British Capitalism and Caribbean Slavery*, Cambridge: Cambridge University Press.

Stam, R. and E. Shohat (2007) *Flagging Patriotism* (London: Routledge).

Starr, H. (1997) 'Democracy and Integration: Why Democracies Don't Fight Each Other', *Journal of Peace Research* 32(2), pp.153–62.

Stedman Jones, G. (1970) 'The Specificity of US Imperialism', *New Left Review* I/60, pp.59–86.

Stedman Jones, G. (2008) 'Radicalism and the Extra-European World: the Case of Marx', in D. Bell (ed.), *Victorian Visions of Global Order* (Cambridge: Cambridge University Press), pp.186–214.

Steinfeld, E. (2004) 'China's Shallow Integration: Networked Production and the New Challenges for Late Industrialisation' *World Development* 32(11), pp.1971–87.

Stephanson, A. (1995) *Manifest Destiny: American Expansionism and the Empire of Right* (New York: Hill & Wang).

Stewart, H. (2008) 'Same old medicine for the new Europe', *The Observer*, November 2.

Stewart, H. (2009) 'G20 summit recovery package: "A global plan on an unprecedented scale"', *The Guardian*, April 3.

Stewart, H. and L. Elliot (2009) 'Hopes fading for salvation at the summit', *The Observer*, March 22.

Stiglitz, J. (1998) 'More Instruments and Broader Goals: Towards the Post-Washington Consensus', Helsinki: WIDER Annual Lecture, 7 January 1998.

Stokes, D. (2007) 'Blood for Oil? Global capital, counter-insurgency and the dual logic of American energy security', *Review of International Studies* 33(2), pp.245–64.

Stokes, E. (1960) *The English Utilitarians and India* (Oxford: Oxford University Press).

Stokes, E. (1969) 'Late Nineteenth Century Colonial Expansion and the Attack on the Theory of Economic Imperialism: A Case of Mistaken Identity?', *Historical Journal* 12(2), pp.285–301.

Strachey, J. (1959) *The End of Empire* (London: Gollancz).

Strange, S. (1989) 'Towards a Theory of Transnational Empire', in E. Czempiel and J. Rosenau (eds) *Global Changes and Theoretical Challenges* (Lexington: Lexington Books), pp.45–65.

Strange, S. (1989) 'Towards a Theory of Transnational Empire', in Eric Czempiel and James Rosenau (eds) 1989 *Global Changes and Theoretical Challenges* (Lexington: Lexington Books), pp.45–65.

Strauss, L. (1968) *Liberalism Ancient and Modern* (Chicago: University of Chicago Press).

Sullivan, E. (1983) 'Liberalism and Imperialism: JS Mill's Defense of the British Empire', *Journal of the History of Ideas* 44(4), pp.599–617.

Sumner, A. (2005) 'Epistemology and "Evidence" in Development Studies: a Review of Dollar and Kraay', *Third World Quarterly* 25(6), pp.1167–77.

Sutcliffe, B. (1999) 'The Place of Development in Theories of Imperialism and Globalization', in R. Munck and D. O'Hearn (eds) *Critical Development Theory* (London: Zed), pp.135–54.

Tarbuck, K. (1972) Editorial introduction', in K. Tarbuck (ed.) *Imperialism and the Accumulation of Capital* (London: Allen Lane), pp.5–44.

Teschke, B. (2003) *The Myth of 1648* (London: Verso).

Teschke, B. and H. Lacher (2007) 'The Changing "Logics" of Capitalist Competition', *Cambridge Review of International Affairs* 20(4), pp.565–80.

Thomassen, L. (2007) 'Beyond Representation?', *Parliamentary Affairs* 60(1), pp.111–26.

Thompson, E. P. (1965) 'The Peculiarities of the English', in R. Miliband and J. Savile (eds) *The Socialist Register 1965* (London: Merlin), pp.311–62.

Ticktin, H. (1992) *Origins of the Crisis in the USSR* (New York: M. E. Sharpe).

Tocqueville, A. (1988) *Democracy in America* (Chicago: University of Chicago Press, first published 1835).

Tomlinson, J. (1991) *Cultural Imperialism* (London: Pinter).

Tomlinson, J. (1999) *Globalization and Culture* (Cambridge: Polity).

Tormey, S. (2006) '"Not in my Name": Deleuze, Zapatismo and the critique of Representation', *Parliamentary Affairs* 59(1), pp.138–54.

Trotsky, L (1969) *The Permanent Revolution and Results and Prospects* (New York: Pathfinder, first published 1931).

Trotsky, L (1970) *The Third International after Lenin* (New York: Pathfinder, first published 1936).

Trotsky, L. (1977) *The History of the Russian Revolution* (London: Pluto, first published 1918).

Trotsky, L. (1980) *The Revolution Betrayed* (New York: Pathfinder, first published 1936).

Tucker, R. (1971) *The Radical Left and American Policy* (Baltimore: Johns Hopkins University Press).

UNCTAD (1998) *World Investment Report 1998* (Geneva: UNCTAD).

UNCTAD (2002a) *The Least Developed Countries Report 2002* (Geneva: UNCTAD).

UNCTAD (2002b) *Trade and Development Report 2002* (Geneva: UNCTAD).

UNCTAD (2004) *The Least Developed Countries Report 2004* (Geneva: UNCTAD).

UNCTAD (2006) *Trade and Development Report 2006* (Geneva: UNCTAD).

UNCTAD (2007) *World Investment Report* (Geneva: UNCTAD).

UNCTAD (2008) *Trade and Development Report 2008* (Geneva: UNCTAD).

van der Pijl, K. (1984) *The Making of an Atlantic Ruling Class* (London: Verso).

van der Pijl, K. (1998) *Transnational Classes and International Relations* (London: Routledge).

van der Pijl, K. (2006) *Global Rivalries from the Cold War to Iraq* (London: Pluto).

Vernon, R. (1966) 'International Investment and International Trade in the Product Cycle', *Quarterly Journal of Economics* 80(2), pp.190–207.

Wada, H. (1984) 'Marx and revolutionary Russia', in T. Shanin (ed.) *Late Marx and the Russian Road* (London: Routledge), pp.40–75.

Wade, R. (1990) *Governing the Market* (Princeton: Princeton University Press)

Wade, R. (2004) 'Is globalization reducing poverty and inequality?', *World Development* 32(4), pp.567–8988.

Wade, R. (2007) 'Should we worry about income inequality?', in D. Held and A. Kaya (eds) *Global Inequality* (Oxford: Blackwell), pp.104–31.

Wade, R. (2008) 'The First World Debt Crisis of 2007-1010 in Global Perspective', *Challenge* 51(4), pp.23–54.

Wallerstein, I. (1974a) *The Modern World System* (New York: Academic Press, vol. 1).

Wallerstein, I. (1974b) *The Modern World System* (New York: Academic Press, vol. 2).

Wallerstein, I. (1979) *The Capitalist World Economy* (Cambridge: Cambridge University Press).

Wallerstein, I. (2003) *The Decline of American Power* (New York: New Press).

Walton, J. and D. Seddon (1994) *Free Markets and Food Riots* (Oxford: Blackwell).

Waltz, K. (1979) *Theory of International Politics* (New York: Random House).

Waltz, K. (2001) *Man, the State and War* (Columbia University Press, first published 1954).

Walzer, M. (1992) *Just and Unjust Wars* (New York: Basic Books, 2nd edition).

Warren, B. (1973) 'Imperialism and Capitalist Industrialization', *New Left Review* I/81, pp.9–44.

Warren, B. (1980) *Imperialism: Pioneer of Capitalism* (London: Verso).

Weaver, R. (1984) *Ideas Have Consequences* (Chicago: Chicago University Press, first published 1948).

Webster, P. (2007) 'Tony Blair: "I wanted war – it was the right thing to do"', *The Times* (London), November 17.

Weeks, J. (2001) 'The expansion of capital and uneven development on a world scale', *Capital and Class* no.74, pp.9–30.

Weisbrot, M., D. Baker and D. Rosnick (2005) 'The Scorecard on Development: 25 Years of Diminished Progress' (available at www.cepr.net, accessed 24 July.2007).

Westad, O. (2007) *The Global Cold War: Third World Interventions and the Making of Our Times* (Cambridge: Cambridge University Press).

Whitford, J. (2005) *The New Old Economy* (Oxford: Oxford University Press).

Wickham, C. (2005) *Framing the Early Middle Ages* (Oxford: Oxford University Press).

Wilkinson, R. (2006) *The WTO* (London: Routledge).

Williams, D. (2008) *The World Bank and Social Transformation in International Politics* (London: Routledge).

Williams, E. (1987) *Capitalism and Slavery* (London: André Deutsch, first published 1944).

Williams, M. (2004) 'What is the National Interest? The Neoconservative Challenge to IR Theory', *European Journal of International Relations* 11(3), pp.307–37.

Williams, M. (2005) *The Realist Tradition and the Limits of International Relations* (Cambridge: Cambridge University Press).

Williams, M. (2007) *Culture and Security* (London: Routledge).

Williams, W. A. (1959) *The Tragedy of American Diplomacy* (New York: Norton).

Williams, W. A. (1972) *The Tragedy of American Diplomacy* (New York: W. W. Norton, first published 1959).

Williams, W. A. (1980) *Empire as a Way of Life* (Oxford: Oxford University Press).

Williams, W. A. (ed.) (1972) *From Colony to Empire: Essays in the History of American Foreign Policy* (New York: John Wiley).

Williamson, J. (1985) *Did British Capitalism Breed Inequality?* (London: Allen & Unwin).

Williamson, J. (2002) 'Land, labor and globalization in the Third World, 1870–1940', *Journal of Economic History* 62(1), pp.55–85.

Winch, D. (1965) *Classical Political Economy and Colonies* (Cambridge: Harvard University Press).

Wolf, M. (2003) *Why Globalization Works* (New Haven: Yale University Press)

Wolfowitz, P. (2000) 'Remembering the Future', *National Interest* 59, pp.35–45.

Wolpe, H. (ed.) (1980) *The Articulation of Modes of Production* (London: Routledge).

Wood, E. M. (1991) *The Pristine Culture of Capitalism* (London: Verso).

Wood, E. M. (1995) *Democracy against Capitalism* (Cambridge: Cambridge University Press).

Wood, E. M. (2002) *The Origins of Capitalism* (London: Verso).

Wood, E. M. (2003) *Empire of Capital* (London: Verso).

World Bank (1987) *World Development Report 1987* (Washington: World Bank).

World Bank (1989) *World Development Report 1989* (Washington: World Bank).

World Bank (1990) *World Development Report 1990* (Washington: World Bank).

World Bank (1992) *Governance and Development* (Washington: World Bank).

World Bank (1993) *The East Asian Miracle* (Oxford: Oxford University Press).

World Bank (1994) *Adjustment in Africa* (Oxford: Oxford University Press).

World Bank (1997) *World Development Report 1997* (Oxford: Oxford University Press).

World Bank (1999a) *World Development Report* 1999/2000 (Oxford: Oxford University Press).

World Bank (1999b) 'A Proposal for a Comprehensive Development Framework', at http://siteresources.worldbank.org/CDF/Resources/cdf.pdf.

World Bank (2001) *World Development Report 2000/01* (Oxford: Oxford University Press).

World Bank (2002) *Globalization, Growth and Poverty* (Oxford: Oxford University Press).

World Bank (2006) *World Development Report 2006* (Oxford: Oxford University Press)

Wrigley, E. (1988) *Population and Resources in Western Intellectual Traditions* (Cambridge: Cambridge University Press).

Wrigley, E. (1994) 'The Classical Economists, the Stationary State and the Industrial Revolution', in G. Snooks (ed.) *Was the Industrial Revolution Necessary?* (London: Routledge), pp.27–42.

Young, M. (1968) *The Rhetoric of Empire, 1895–1901* (Boston: Harvard University Press).

Young, R. (2001) *Postcolonialism* (Oxford: Blackwell).

Zakaria, F. (2008) *The Post American World* (London: Allen Lane).

Zheng, Z. (2002) 'China's terms of trade in world manufactures, 1993–2000', UNCTAD Discussion Paper no.161, pp.1–61.

Zizek, S. (2008) *Violence* (London: Profile).

Index

301